Shipmates

Shipmates

The Men of LCS 52 in World War II

Gary Burns

McFarland & Company, Inc., Publishers
Jefferson, North Carolina

LIBRARY OF CONGRESS CATALOGUING-IN-PUBLICATION DATA

Names: Burns, Gary, 1956– author.
Title: Shipmates : the men of LCS 52 in World War II / Gary Burns.
Description: Jefferson, North Carolina : McFarland & Company, Inc., Publishers, 2016. | Includes bibliographical references and index.
Identifiers: LCCN 2016035609 | ISBN 9781476666877 (softcover : alkaline paper) ∞
Subjects: LCSH: LCS 52 (Ship) | World War, 1939–1945—Naval operations, American. | World War, 1939–1945—Amphibious operations. | Landing craft—United States—History—20th century. | World War, 1939–1945—Campaigns—Pacific Area. | United States. Navy—Boats—History—20th century. | Sailors—United States—Biography. | United States. Navy—Biography. | World War, 1939–1945—Biography.
Classification: LCC D769.45 .B87 2016 | DDC 940.54/5973—dc23
LC record available at https://lccn.loc.gov/2016035609

BRITISH LIBRARY CATALOGUING DATA ARE AVAILABLE

ISBN (print) 978-1-4766-6687-7
ISBN (ebook) 978-1-4766-2646-8

© 2016 Gary Burns. All rights reserved

No part of this book may be reproduced or transmitted in any form or by any means, electronic or mechanical, including photocopying or recording, or by any information storage and retrieval system, without permission in writing from the publisher.

Front cover: Crew of the *LCS-52* surrounding one of her 40 mm guns; (background) the ship known as Landing Craft Support 52

Printed in the United States of America

*McFarland & Company, Inc., Publishers
Box 611, Jefferson, North Carolina 28640*
www.mcfarlandpub.com

Dedicated to all the World War II sailors
who rest eternally in the sea

Those who go down to the sea in ships,
who do business on great waters;
they have seen the works of the Lord,
and His wonders in the deep.
For He spoke and raised up a stormy wind,
which lifted up the waves of the sea.
They rose up to the heavens, they went down to the depths;
their soul melted away in their misery.
They reeled and staggered like a drunken man,
and were at their wits' end.
Then they cried to the Lord in their trouble,
and He brought them out of their distresses.

—Psalm 107:23–28

Table of Contents

Acknowledgments	viii
Introduction	1
1. The Maiden Voyage	9
2. How Did We Get Ourselves into This?	28
3. Practicing the Trade	44
4. Life at Sea	66
5. Black Sand and Suffering	82
6. By Land and Sea: The Battle for Okinawa	100
7. Birds of Prey	116
8. Downfall to Fallout	136
9. Ex-Kamikazes and Mysteries of the Orient	156
10. Rebuilding Lives	179
11. Death of 52	197
12. Roll Call *LCS 52*	199
Chapter Notes	239
Bibliography	249
Index	253

Acknowledgments

Special thanks to the following for their contributions:

Lois and Virgil Thill
Helen and Nick Stoia
Clifford L. Stewart
Anita Stewart—Daughter of Clifford L. Stewart
Beverly Johnson—Wife of Dewane Johnson
Bonnie Tastad Kupchik—Family of Dewane L. Johnson
Carol Harper Marsh—Daughter of John O. Harper
Cara Curtis, Cumberland County Historical Society, Pennsylvania—Benjamin L. Beittel
Diane Burns Brads—Daughter of Laton Burns
Elizabeth Beittel Hilliard—Daughter of Benjamin Leonard Beittel
Evonne Broten, Marshall County Historical Society, Minnesota—Adler W. Strandquist
Geoffrey Burroughs—Brother of Spencer Burroughs
Janet Hodges—National Archives and Records Administration, College Park, Maryland
Katherine King—Family of Larry Cullen
Mike Kaloz—Grandson of Claude H. Cook
Mildred Sandlin—Sister of Lloyd Clements Keith
Mordecai G. Sheftall—Japanese translations and kamikaze research
Norma Vines—Daughter of Larry Cullen
Patricia M. Burns—General editing
Pat Wood, Shirley Historical Society, Massachusetts—Abraham A. Scurrah
Reagan Grau—National Museum of the Pacific War
Robin L. Rielly—Former historian for National Association of LCS (L) 1–130
Saundra Syrian Goss—Daughter of John Syrian
Thomas H. Appleton—General editing
Violet Hensley—Niece of Albert Moschner
William J. Mason—Life aboard a LCS

I must acknowledge and reiterate my most heartfelt thanks to the following individuals who made this history possible. First and foremost, a special thanks to the person who provided the cornerstone of this work, Diane Burns Brads, daughter of Laton Burns. My special thanks to Carol Harper Marsh, daughter of Lieutenant John Harper, commander of *Landing Craft Support 52*. As well, thanks to David Weaver, business partner and lifelong friend of

John Harper in the postwar years. Had it not been for Mr. Weaver I would not have gained access to Mrs. Marsh's collection of her father's memoirs. I would like to thank Norma Vines, daughter of Larry Cullen, for her assistance and her friendship. Mrs. Vines was instrumental in my making contact with Lois and Virgil Thill. Virgil is one of but a handful of surviving *LCS 52* crewmembers. There are no words equal to the gratitude I have for Virgil Thill and his wife, Lois, who took so much of their time to talk to me and answer my questions. The same goes for the help that Nick Stoia provided. Also, thanks to his wife, Helen, for putting up with the bother. His assistance was priceless in providing firsthand knowledge of the ship and crew. I thank all former LCSers and their spouses for their sacrifice during the war and for their efforts in postwar America in making the country a better place. There were many more I owe thanks to, spouses, daughters, sons, nephews, nieces, grandchildren and friends of crewmembers who were extremely helpful and who participated in the completion of this work. I would also like to thank Rob Rielly, the LCS Association Historian, for sharing the Association's files. I had the opportunity to explore the bulk of his work on World War II in the Pacific at its new depository in Fredericksburg, Texas, the National Pacific War Museum. His years of research were invaluable in writing *Shipmates*. Many others contributed to this work and without each it would have been impossible to accumulate the research and complete a semi-comprehensive history of the ship and crew.

Introduction

As men become brothers on the battlefield so too sailors become one with their ship and their shipmates. I have an enduring admiration for men who trust their fragile flesh and bone to the confines of a bobbing metal shell in an infinite sea. Who would not become attached to or love such a steel-skinned guardian angel separating one's existence from trillions of gallons of saltwater? Men have trusted such flimsy craft to defeat and tame the rivers and seas, probably since he learned that some objects float. No vehicle has been with man longer except his own feet. Ships have carried mankind to new beginnings, safer shores, treasures, adventures, and, of course, a multitude of wars. It is in the latter that men truly find themselves an extension of their ships and their ships an extension of themselves. The following pages are a brief account of a few men who went down to the sea in ships, and the business of war they did there during the years of 1944 and 1945.

During my career as a U.S. Marine I had the honor of serving aboard many naval vessels of varying styles and functions. Being able to observe the daily life of sailors from the vantage point of a hitchhiker had certain advantages for a later historian. The connection they have with their ship is, as I stated, to be respected. Not the slightest disrespect of their ship is tolerated, nor should it be. The captain of the ship and his senior enlisted counterpart, the "Master Chief," demand, and with few exceptions through history, receive, unflinching obedience and respect.

The sailor, by necessity, is a meticulous and compulsive soul. When not preparing for battle his days are spent catering to the maintenance and routine of his ship. Many times a month that routine turns attention to the most important event known to a sailor, that of saving his ship in distress. These drills mimic the real-life scenario as closely as safely possible. I can testify by personal experience there is no greater anxiety than that created when locked into a watertight compartment and having no knowledge as to when it might reopen. The foreknowledge that the incarceration is merely a drill to test the efficiency of ship and crew is no consolation. The sound of the latches being dogged-down (locked) on a watertight hatch echoes through the captive's head until the moment the door reopens.

Second only in fear to being locked into a small, dim, closet-like compartment is preparing to go overboard. A man who goes overboard for any reason, into the depth and width of the ocean, has slight chance of surviving more than a few hours. His thirst is unquenchable, his fear unbearable. He is the most vulnerable creature in the water. It is a habitat in which he has no business and one in which he will find no prolonged joy.

Many of the drills and practices aboard ship revolve around the outbreak of fire. In spite of the steel bulkheads and solid metal frame, fire is still, even in modern times, the worst enemy of ship and sailor. All these apocalyptic scenarios must weigh heavily on a sailor's mind when he is out to sea. It is a fragile balance.

Aside from possible disaster, a ship is a cramped and uncomfortable place. Even aircraft carriers and battleships seem to grow smaller and tighter the longer the journey. Sailors and marines sleep in racks that are built as bookshelves are built. When occupied for sleep, much of the time a thin sheet of strained canvas is all that stands between privacy and intimacy with fellow shipmates. The lower decks are stifling and reek of oil. Bulkheads are low and hatchways curses upon the shin and forehead. In the midst of a storm a ship is a ride on a seemingly never-ending rollercoaster. No sailor remains a virgin to seasickness forever. When all the miseries of ship life are summed, it is hard to imagine that men volunteer for, and sing praise of, such a life, but they have always done so and will likely continue to do so.

Aboard this dot floating in what appears to be an endless ocean also exists centuries of naval tradition. Some traditions are the most juvenile of the juvenile. No sailor or marine aboard ship has ever been denied the privilege of viewing the elusive sea bat. Seldom is one quick enough to see the bat but they never fail to feel it. I once observed a young marine repeatedly scold the chief for walloping him across the butt with a mop handle and preventing him from seeing the sea bat captive under the bucket. A revered ceremony dating back to at least the early 1800s, if not earlier, is the rite of Pollywogs (one who has never crossed over the Equator) in becoming a Shellback. The initiation to shellback has over the centuries involved some very physically demanding requirements; sailors from all nations have had deaths occur, even in the last few decades. In the era of World War II which is addressed in this writing, reports of beatings with wet fire hoses were common. Many of the men also reported having the "devil's tongue" introduced to their midsections. The devil's tongue was generally a metal rod enhanced to conduct pinpoint electricity through it.

Some traditions are more solemn than the captive sea bat or pollywog to shellback ceremonies. When a modern ship enters Pearl Harbor, Hawaii, another naval tradition presents itself and has done so since 7 December 1941. The tradition involves sailors manning the rails. Manning the rails dates back many centuries to the method whereby sailors paid respect to a distinguished person by manning the yards. Men stood evenly spaced on the yards and gave three cheers to the honored person. It is still used by the United States Navy on the occasions when dignitaries are honored and when leaving a port and entering homeport. Nowhere on earth or sea is there a more humbling spot to man the rails than upon entering Pearl Harbor. While standing tall along the rails of the ship one ultimately passes by the sunken remains of the USS *Arizona*. It presents the illusion that you are literally passing over the top of her hull. At the right point along the rail you are at an angle which allows you to peer down into the darkness of her stacks. Any man who does not feel the chill along his spine at that moment is an emotionless stone. Knowing that this shadowy object lying on the bottom of the harbor is the gravesite of 1,177 Americans who were victims of the surprise attack on that Sunday morning in 1941 is nothing short of emotionally overwhelming.

It is looking upon the tomb of the men of the USS *Arizona* that the story of another ship and her crew really begins. Unlike the USS *Arizona* she bore no christened name. Her title, as with all one hundred thirty of her sisters, was nothing more than a number in that series. She was distinguished from all others molded like her simply as *Landing Craft Support (L) (3) 52*. Had that gloomy silhouette not rested on the bottom of Pearl Harbor, *LCS 52* and her sisters would have never been born.

It was because of all the men who lay entombed in the USS *Arizona* that the sleeping giant had awoken. When it did awake, every man, woman, and child in the United States rose with fury and purpose. By the end of December 1941 the military recruiting stations were lined with men waiting in throngs on the street to enlist and fight the Japanese. For every man choosing military service, twice as many women and men filled the factories and shops, hastily converting bread makers and car assembly lines into war-making machines.

While the Japanese presented the United States with a new enemy, many Americans still saw the old one as the greater threat. The United States refrained for almost three years from going to war with Germany, in spite of her brutality to every country in Europe. Since the disillusionment with the Great War had not lost its fervor in 1941, American citizens found no reason worthy to cause them to mix in European affairs again. In fact, since the time World War II in Europe had begun in 1939, the people of the United States had slept easy knowing that 3000 miles of ocean separated them from danger. Pacifism reigned supreme in the United States. Pearl Harbor forced them to look around the world at the desperate global situation they were a part of and could no longer hide from.

Within days of Congress's declaration of war on Japan, Germany and Italy backed the Three-Power Pact of 27 September 1940 with a declaration of war against the United States. The long and bitter debates for and against going to war with Germany were over for Americans. This was, however, another devastating blow to the people of China, Australia, and those across the Pacific suffering under the heavy hand of Japanese invaders. It meant that 85 percent of America's war machine would be directed at the European Theater. Allied operations in the Pacific Theater would begin the counterattack with barely 15 percent of America's military might. The American operations in the Pacific would be fought and won almost entirely by America's sailors and marines.

Sailors are unique among the armed services, even more so the navy men of World War II. They learned, or by nature were content, to live long periods in a tin can surrounded by a barren ocean.[1] The men who made up the crew of *LCS 52* were exceptional individuals. The homes they grew up in were different in many aspects but also quite similar. Most of the men were older than what might be expected by today's norms and by 1944 standards as well. Nick Stoia, one of the youngest onboard the 52, said, "We had guys on there that had grandchildren."[2] That was a unique occurrence in the 1940s. Before the war skewed the average life expectancy statistics, in 1940, a man was only expected to live to see sixty years. Men who were in their thirties and forties were considered quite old to be taking up the burden of combat.

Because of the generation they were born within, their American ethos of honor and courage on the battlefield was shaped by witnesses and participants of World War I, the Spanish-American War and even the Civil War who still wandered about within their communities. Literature such as Stephen Crane's *Red Badge of Courage* or Arthur Wesley Wheen's translation of *All Quiet on the Western Front* taught young men of the 1910s and 1920s that courage overcame adversity amidst the carnage of battle. So they naively believed in youth.

On the battlefield or in a cornfield, men of their day were God fearing. Whether parents were churchgoers or not was irrelevant; few denied the existence of a supreme being. There was an assumption of an ever-present spiritual over-watch and a struggle between good and evil which extended to the four corners of earth and included them.

Neighbors watched each other's children and were often as quick to administer corporal punishment *in loco parentis* as they were to report the misconduct. In turn, neighbors were a type of extended family. When harvest time came, it was a community effort as was hog slaughtering and other labor intensive chores. When children played outdoors, neighbors kept a watchful eye, and if someone was sick, neighbors visited and helped care for them.

Technology was limited and sparsely distributed, regardless of the area where *LCS 52* sailors grew up. Some neighborhoods had only one telephone and it was just downright rude not to share freely. Radios broadcast limited programming in the early years, both in air time and content. The first broadcast was the Harding-Cox presidential race on 2 November 1920. From there, opera music occasionally floated out to a handful of receivers. Just in time to give people an escape from their financial woes, in 1929–30 regularly scheduled programs included comedies such as *Amos 'n' Andy*, music by *Moonshine Kate* or crime shows *True Detective Mysteries* and *Sherlock Holmes*. Religious programs maintained their popularity along with news and sports. Radio grew with such a pace that by 1938 it was estimated that forty million people around the world gathered to hear the furlong-by-furlong report of the Seabiscuit and War Admiral match. One of the questions the census takers recorded during the 1930 interview was whether the family possessed a radio or not.

Motion pictures were the next most popular technology in the twenties and thirties, providing yet another method which reinforced an internal commitment to Americanism and the philosophy that good always triumphs over evil. Boys particularly enjoyed the westerns. Except for the very youngest, 52's crew had lived through the progression from silent to talking movies. The first full-length "talkie" came out in 1928. The 1920s saw almost every town big or small open at least one movie theater. On average Americans went to the movies once a week. Thanks to Henry Ford's mass production of affordable automobiles, by the 1930s almost every family could load up and drive to the nearest show.

Indoor plumbing was far in the future for the children of the 1920s. Some families were able to pump water into the kitchen but the outdoor toilet was likely a standard experience. They were resilient people who made the best of time, money and opportunity, even in the outhouse. Claude Cook, veteran of *LCS 52*, explained "one sometimes lingered longer than necessary," just to look over the goodies once more in the Sears and Roebuck Catalogue.[3] In their youth few attended anything more than a one-room schoolhouse, often with mixed grades from first through eighth. John Harper, the captain of the ship, was no different in his beginnings than any of the other boys. His first school day in 1923 was spent at the one-room schoolhouse called Kansas School a mile from his home. He remembered years later how "[he] had been looking forward to going to school for a long time."[4] A high school diploma placed one far ahead of the pack when entering the job market. Everyone worked at something other than school even if that was a family farm, downtown business or local store.

As diverse as their upbringings were, the boys of *LCS 52* shared one great equalizer regardless of their age, race, religion or origin—the Great Depression. It all began with the stock market crash of 29 October 1929 known as Black Tuesday. There were many reasons for the dearth that spread forth across America and the world in the decade that followed and everyone blamed something. Some blamed Wall Street, for rampant abuse of margin purchases. A few blamed the rape of vast portions of the land which led to the Dust Bowl. Erosion caused by over-farming was a reason less obvious to the public at the time, but just as life shattering. Many of the depression-era boys found hope in Franklin D. Roosevelt's (FDR) Civilian Conservation Corps (CCC). During the 1930s the camps repaired the erosion damage done to the land, building parks, trails, bridges and roads to name only a minute number of projects. It gave the unemployed a paycheck and hope. Over 90 percent of the CCC boys' pay went home to help support the family as well. It was hard work but afforded many a respect for others quite different from themselves. There was, in many camps, the opportunity to attend classes both academic and vocational, which would have been a pipedream in any other setting.

There was another aspect to the CCCs which went unnoticed until 7 December 1941. The camps were all run by military personnel and operated under a peacetime military model. The boys learned how to work together. They learned how to march in formation, drill and work as a cohesive unit. Some units drilled with wooden rifles. They learned the rudimentary things that would have normally taken up hours of drill-instructor time in boot-camp: how to make a bed, wash clothes, brush teeth, wear a uniform and lead small groups. They ate from surplus army mess kits, carried army canteens and wore surplus army uniforms. When Pearl Harbor was attacked, it was no great surprise to most CCC boys that they were given a choice, enlist or leave the CCCs. Most, as was true of their non–CCC counterparts, saw it as their moral obligation to enlist in service to their country. Having already been introduced to peacetime military life in the CCCs, instruction in surviving combat was pretty much all that remained for the regular military cadre to teach.

The men of *LCS 52* were shaped in their youth by extreme hardships that have never been repeated. They were also shaped by communities of tight-knit people who saw themselves as more than a collection of individuals. They looked out for one another. The community influenced them and helped raise them. Aboard ship they would become a small community, bringing hometown norms to share and developing a new set of customs among their shipmates. The war would change them, traumatize and haunt them, but it was a testament to their era and their upbringing that they survived it. Without the moral and economic challenges of the 1920s and 30s on every man, woman and child it is doubtful the Second World War would have resulted in the same outcome. They were in essence built tough enough for the responsibilities of their time. The story within *Shipmates* is about the journey through life from childhood to men at war. After the war they were left to pick up the pieces of lives put on hold. How they accomplished their lessons in elementary school to how they trained their gun sights on enemy planes focused their lifelong experiences and prepared them in rebuilding a postwar America.

Another story of World War II and its veterans might seem redundant to some. With almost 700,000 veterans still surviving—and about 430 passing away daily—by a 2016 estimate from the National World War II Museum, it would seem that all the stories of the battlefront and the home front have been told and retold. In a never before possible endeavor, efforts such as the Veterans History Project established and housed by the Library of Congress have succeeded in saving many thousands of those histories. Oral history projects have thus reconstructed almost every story of the surviving veterans' lives, recording for posterity their images and voices in the telling of those stories. Better treatment for post-traumatic stress has also increased the ability of veterans to record their own histories, regardless of how traumatic retelling certain aspects of their battlefield encounters might be. Immersion therapy, in which the veteran orally retells wartime experiences, has become a major tool in coping with posttraumatic stress. Advancements in computer technology have also made the ease of documenting veterans' accounts simplified and thereby saved thousands of histories that would have been lost only twenty years ago. A surge in genealogy and family histories studies has contributed greatly to the saving of veterans' wartime accounts. Family members hungry to save their ancestor's connection to world events provide one of the most comprehensive sources of on-hand material. However, even with all these available methods of saving their stories, there are still many veterans whose histories have not been recorded. As good historians and proud family members we owe it to those veterans to make sure that all their stories are told from the perspective that each veteran experienced them.

While the number of people, both military and civilian, who lived through World War II and survive today may seem large, that number is dwindling rapidly. Within twenty years from the writing of this book it is probable that there will not be a single World War II veteran surviving. Due to the failure in our record-keeping technology at the time, and sheer apathy on the part of the public, only a fraction of the histories of World War I veterans were compiled before they were all gone. We mourn the loss of those valuable historical accounts today but the fact remains they are gone forever and cannot be recovered.

There is another consideration when attempting to write yet one more account of World War II veterans and their experiences in the two theaters of operation. That is, millions of veterans are already gone and we have failed them and ourselves. As with the veterans of the Great War, we are left to piece together a puzzle with many of the pieces missing. Many family members, friends, and fellow veterans heard the stories told firsthand but never had the forethought to write them down as they were presented. We have always assumed in the moment that we had an infinite amount of time in which to jot down those tales of bravery and resilience. For those who have gone on, there are only their letters, photographs, diaries and other personal writings available to be used in the process of completing as much of that puzzle as humanly possible.

It was the personal writings of one veteran of the Pacific War which led to this story, which I called *Shipmates*. Having a deep personal interest in the histories of veterans, I was fortunate to be approached by the daughter of Laton Burns, veteran of the Pacific. She had located a journal, photo album and letters created during his war years. In spite of their age, all were well-maintained and easily authenticated. My original intention was to write a short story based on those primary sources. In the process of digging for collateral information to further that end, I discovered a deeper theme within the worn pages of those keepsakes. Shakespeare referred to the bond formed among fighting men as a "Band of Brothers." Since his time, no better words to describe the fraternal bond and love for the men who fight shoulder to shoulder with one another have been spoken. Their stories become so intertwined that there is no right way to pen one history without the other. This was as true in this case as it has been true for thousands of years.

The lives of soldiers and sailors are so bound together in a cohesive web that each time I investigated a single event, it tied directly to the perspectives and accounts of brother sailors who fought alongside that particular individual. Those links perpetuated one another and seemed to always lead to another source and additional story. The connections wove and extended ever further until at times they seemed to have no end. In the process I encountered family members, friends, and many others whose lives had been touched by those veterans, and who hungered, as I did, to have the story told, not as an individual account, but rather within the web that made up a small band of brothers.

The genesis of this specific work began with the viewing of the World War II journal and photo album of an Eastern Kentucky farm boy. His journal, while devoid of many daily events during his time aboard ship, told volumes about crew members who served alongside him. His entries were sufficient enough to make tracking his fellow crewmembers, or in the majority of cases relatives and friends of deceased crewmembers, reasonably accomplishable. I was also fortunate enough to have the assistance of veterans, ships' associations, and historians who had compiled comprehensive records, logs, and other documents, and were gracious enough to share information with me. In the end, as much as Laton and his buddies worked together to keep each other alive and win the war, hundreds of hands went into the writing of *Shipmates*. I suspect that Laton and his shipmates would have preferred their story told in the way it was lived, as a group of men brought together by a small ship, who lived, laughed, cried, and sometimes died in the presence of their brothers. We who wrote *Shipmates* were brought together in our own unique band and in the process formed our own web of brotherhood, with a common mission and a common pride in its accomplishment.

This story is as much about the ship as it is the men aboard her. The Landing Craft Support ship which Laton and his crewmembers served aboard was specifically created for the amphibious landings of the Pacific Theater and therefore short-lived. The LCS ships were developed relatively late in the war but their presence undoubtedly saved countless allied lives. Of the vessels by this design, created for this specific purpose, only one survives in its original state as an example of wartime ingenuity. It is *LCS 102*, located at Mare Island, California, and serves as a living museum in honor of the small fleet of these indispensable little ships that did their duty during World War II.

I have endeavored to make the text interesting to a broad audience, all the while maintaining as much historical integrity as was possible. The most important consideration in writing *Shipmates* was to ensure that the history of the men who served on *LCS 52* was not lost and will be obtainable for future generations to seek, find, and learn from. I have relied on primary sources whenever possible. Interviews with surviving veterans are used with the same trust as written documents pertaining to incidents and occurrences of the war years. It should be considered with any history that secondary sources such as interviews with family members will by nature include some embellishment or omission. However, these valuable sources cannot be excluded and can be considered bearing enough fact to forgive harmless discrepancies in the retelling from memory.

1

The Maiden Voyage

President Roosevelt's decision to fight "Germany first" was not the matter of personal choice most Americans of the 1940s and beyond believed. The War Plans Division, a subgroup of the Joint Board, was formed after World War I and tasked with developing possible strategies to meet future war threats.[1] Even in 1919 the board believed that the major threat of war lay with Japan. In each of the possible scenarios of war with major world powers, the potential opponents were issued code colors. Japan was deemed Orange. Great Britain, ironically as it turned out, was considered by the American planners to be the second largest threat. Red was the color assigned the Anglo cousins. Although the planners were blatantly off mark in their estimation of friends and foes, the initial plans to face a simultaneous Atlantic and Pacific enemy would be priceless in a few years.

The U.S did not realistically believe they could face off with the two largest navies in the world at the same time. Since Britain was by geography, the nearest threat, planners settled on an option of offensive operations in the Atlantic. In the Pacific, forces would defend along a strategic triangle formed by Alaska, Hawaii and Panama. Once the Red (Atlantic) threat was subdued, then resources could be turned on Orange (Pacific).

Germany's participation in a war against the Americas was considered a low priority in 1919. By the summer of 1939 the world situation had changed and planners began to focus on creating an action plan to deal with the possibility of a German, Italian and Japanese coalition. The new plans turned attention to coalitions of enemy states and was called Rainbow One through Rainbow Five. Rainbow Five envisioned an alliance among the United States, Great Britain and France. In the scenario which would come closest to world events in the winter of 1941, the plan still called for the defeat of Germany first while holding a defensive posture in the Pacific. The military preparation was left to the Army and Navy, the burden of forming political alliances fell to FDR.

Rainbow Five lost some of its standing by the summer of 1940. Rainbow Four then took center stage. When France fell to the Nazis in June, the president met with his military board. The top military men began to lobby for mobilization of American military resources. Roosevelt and his military advisors stuck by their belief that the Atlantic was the buffer between them and Germany-Italy. That buffer was held together by the presence of the British Navy. If Great Britain capitulated to Germany, the protective barrier of water would turn into a freeway for German blitzkrieg. In the end, America could not allow Britain to fall—it was Germany first. The United States was left to deploy the military asset which the Brits lacked, manpower. While the Brits had held their own on sea and in the air, their ground forces were small and spread around the globe. Rainbow Five returned to the most pragmatic plan. Planning underscored the ability of the Brits to defeat Germany alone. American forces had to be the braces which shored up the British foundation and assured victory in Europe. The die had been cast. By its roll, in the event of war with Japan, all American assets beyond Hawaii would be untenable and sacrificed. The strategic plan, renamed, but bearing almost the same provisions as Rainbow Five, went into effect. It was October 1941.

A rift between the two ranking commanders in the Pacific Theater quickly materialized over what direction offensive operations should take. Douglas MacArthur at times was obsessed with recovering the Philippines and seemed to only look in that direction.[2] Chester Nimitz at times seemed to begrudge putting any naval assets under the control of the Army regardless of the hindrance it might bring to the war effort.[3] The debate raged on through most of 1943. MacArthur favored an advance up the southwest side of the Pacific via the Solomon Islands and ultimately retaking the Philippines. After he had successfully returned to the Philippines, he was open to an attack on Japan. Nimitz proposed what he saw as a faster route to an invasion of the Japanese mainland. He wanted his navy and marines to advance up the central Pacific, through the Gilbert, Marshall and Marianas Islands, to Taiwan and invade Japan from China. No real compromise was ever really reached by the two headstrong commanders, but the decision was made by those above to allow each to prosecute his strategy. Nimitz went straight up the middle and MacArthur went up the west axis. The American public understood it as a grand military scheme, carefully planned and agreed upon and labeled as a two-pronged attack.

Almost eight months to the day after the surprise attack on Pearl Harbor, American naval and marine forces launched the first counter strike to Japanese occupation of the Pacific, west of Hawaii and north of Australia.[4] The attack was codenamed Operation Watchtower. It was the amphibious landings on the Solomon Islands, beginning with Guadalcanal. With the majority of manpower and resources committed to defeating Germany, Guadalcanal was the inevitable steppingstone toward recovering territory. The Canal was the manifestation of an offensive campaign Americans had been hoping, praying and clamoring for since the last holdouts on Bataan and Corregidor surrendered. The Americans were not the only people looking for a push against the Japanese; China, Australia, and a thousand islands suffering under Japanese occupation desperately needed the morale boost and the respite.

Beyond the two-pronged advance by MacArthur and his army units and Nimitz and his navy, American forces employed an "island hopping" campaign. Islands not hopped over, or skirted around, were assaulted by marines and soldiers in generally costly beach landings. Placing massive numbers of men and tons of equipment on beaches was a new and arduous process for the U.S. Navy. In such places as Tarawa and Iwo Jima, beach assaults became slaughterhouses. During the war years many new seagoing vessels were invented and adapted to support amphibious landings. To prevent the vessels from being stranded on coral reefs and sandbars, causing their human cargo to be systematically mowed down before reaching the beaches, a number of amphibious trucks and trackers were developed. Those new vehicles had the ability to traverse water from ship to shore, and possessed multiple wheels or tracks to continue to move across natural obstacles. The amtracs, an abbreviation for amphibious tractors, made it possible for marines and soldiers to ride onto the beach and then exit the vehicle on solid ground. Track-propelled vehicles prevented troops from becoming stranded on coral reefs, forced out into unknown depths of water, sometimes hundreds of yards from the beach under enemy fire. Problems with the troop carrying amtracs, though, included limited weaponry such as small machineguns and light armor on the hull.

Other problems existed with the troop landings themselves. The naval shelling and aerial bombardment of targets onshore had to cease as troops came ashore. Otherwise the danger of naval guns hitting landing troops was greater than the protection they provided. The larger support and transport ships could not move closer to shore to deliver accurate covering fire for fear of being beached themselves and becoming a sitting duck to enemy fire. This left infantry landings facing a gap in time at a critical moment in the assault in which they were left without close-support fire. Americans back on the home front collaborated with military planners to correct the problem and fill the gap with low-draft gunboats that could offer continuous covering fire.

Throughout the year of 1944 a solution to better close-in fire support for troops assaulting a beach sailed out of American ports and headed toward the Pacific islands. Lessons learned from earlier tragedies on Pacific island beaches brought about the development of the Landing Craft Support (LCS). American LCS's nomenclature included two designators: "L" for large and "3" for Mark 3 (3rd modification). A LCS (L) (3) was a gunboat approximately one-hundred-fifty feet long by twenty-three feet wide. The LCS sailed into battle with an arsenal of weapons designed to protect the troops on the beach and annihilate the enemy in front of them. The LCS had a series of guns including 20mm; 40mm twin radar controlled guns both fore and aft, .50 caliber machineguns, and a battery of 4.5-inch rockets. They could also lay down smoke screens and carried firefighting capabilities which assisted wounded ships battling fires and explosions. In the latter capacity, the LCS could pump 1500 gallons per minute at two-hundred pounds per inch onto a fire. Admiral Richmond Kelly Turner, attributed as being the first to nickname them, called them "Mighty Midgets."[5] Unlike destroyers and larger vessels, the LCS had a four to six foot draft which meant she could move to within 500 feet of the shoreline. They were also perfect by design and function in pinpointing fire on enemy guns aimed at landing troops. One-hundred-thirty LCS (L) (3)s were built during 1944 in two ports, Portland, Oregon, and Neponset, Massachusetts.

Portland, specifically, and the West Coast generally, produced the bulk of new ships headed for the Pacific. The manufacturers of wartime seagoing vessels employed 200,000 west-coasters. The employer of 30,000 of those shipyard workers was the Kaiser Shipbuilding Company, located on seven separate sites.[6] Kaiser Portland produced and launched one ship in ten days. It was a new record for ship building, only to be broken by Kaiser Richmond, California, workers who built one in five days.

The Albina Engine Works in Portland would be responsible for production of thirty-one of the one-hundred-thirty World War II LCSs. The first LCS the company launched was *LCS 48* on 26 August 1944. The last, produced by Albina was, *LCS 78*, launched 26 March 1945. Along with several longtime shipbuilders located on Swan Island before World War II, Albina shared space with the two behemoth newcomers, Kaiser and Oregon Shipbuilding Yards. An article in the 27 September 1943 edition of *Time*, observed that the little company of 4,500 employees worked "in the shadow of the giant." Albina sat adjacent to the Irving Dock and the Willamette River. Albina was not new to the business of war production; the company produced steel ships to help prosecute the Great War throughout 1918–19. The shipbuilder was contracted by the government to build minesweepers in the early part of 1941. These were presumably to go overseas to support future European allies.

Albina built a gamut of wartime vessels for the Army and Navy, ranging from sub-chasers to tugs.

Another version of the gunboat was introduced around the same time as the LCS. The LCI (L)s (Landing Craft Infantry Large) were the same hull design as the LCSs. Like the LCSs, many Landing Craft Infantry were modified by arming them to the teeth. These converts became designated as LCI (G) or "Gunboat." And like their sister LCSs they were designed to provide fire support for soldiers and marines storming Japanese-held islands from the tip of Australia to Japan proper. The LCI (L), the original design, remained a troop carrier, also with a lot of punch going to the beach. The Albina yard built twenty-one LCIs during the spring and summer of 1944. All of those were standard troop landing crafts at the time of their launch. A total of 923 LCIs were built during the war but only a small fraction of those were converted to gunboats or rocket boats.

In Washington, D.C., the new crew of *LCS 52* met each other for the first time as a whole. Most came up from the nearby Naval Amphibious Training Base at Solomons, Maryland, located ninety miles south of Baltimore. They boarded a passenger train refitted and refashioned to serve as a troop train and prepared for an uncomfortable trip cross-country.

The train was far short of the luxurious Pullman sleeper cars where train-riding civilians often reposed. Radar man Nick Stoia called them semi-open "cattle cars."[7] The men slept stacked three deep on wire-frame bunks. Little did they know, their quarters onboard a LCS would be in many ways worse. From D.C. to Portland took four days by rail. The train was old and still propelled by a steam locomotive. The black residue of the power source bellowed steadily backwards throughout the journey, assaulting the lungs and skin. The soot covered the men and their uniforms; there was not a crease it did not find and fill. Claude Cook agreed with Stoia, but in his customary tolerant manner "it was a long and dirty ride."[8] The train pulled into the Portland depot at 18:00 hours on 22 August 1944. Once they got to Portland, the enlisted men went to the base and the officers searched for lodging at a local hotel or at the athletic club.

The men were exhausted after being on the train for four days and four nights. When they got to base, they were fed chow and then ordered to unpack, square-away and stow their gear. They finally finished their tasks around 21:00. Because the men had completed all orders of the day the officers granted liberty call for all not too tired to enjoy a few hours off base. Suddenly the men, almost to the last, found themselves revived and feeling the need for some fun in the new town.[9]

Conditions seemed to indicate that they had arrived in a northwestern paradise. Stoia thought it was the best place he had ever been. The people were nicer than any he had met before. Everybody picked up walking sailors and gave them rides into town or wherever, Cook told his longtime girlfriend Caroline "Lynn" Artman back in Michigan, in a letter.[10] Even the navy accommodated the men more than usual. The crew had base liberty from 16:30 to 19:30 every day except for the days they were individually on guard duty.

There was talk about leaves being granted as well. The scuttlebutt was that some men would be granted as many as fifteen days, probably going to the married guys first. Other men would receive only ten days and the last poor souls would get none. The question remained who would draw what and when, and the officers were not divulging their method of selection. On the 25th they announced which twenty men would get ten days of leave. That was the magic number and that, as it turned out, was it.

For guys like Cook, who had to travel three days one-way to Michigan, ten days seemed simply too short to make it worth the trip. He had found a friend among the crew, Gerald Bilton, who was from nearby Melvindale, Michigan. Bilton's wife, Ardyth, was from Mt. Clemens and so was Lynn. It was always good to find a buddy from so close to home but it was also nice for the girls to have that connection in common. The toughest job may have been that of a spouse or girlfriend, separated by thousands of miles and having no one to commiserate with about the fear and loneliness.

By 2 September the tempo changed. The crew received reports from the captain that supplies had come in for the ship. That could only mean their time in Portland was drawing down. It was probably for the best. Some of the men had overspent in the hospitable city and could not afford to even venture out into town any longer without borrowing money. Worse, they had no money to go home if their leave did come through. Cook still had money but even his thriftiness was diminishing. He confided to Lynn in a letter that the night before, he had enjoyed the walk back to base at 02:00 under a beautiful moon after getting "tight" in town. He had not, as he admitted, enjoyed the Bosun Mate's reveille call or the hangover he had nursed that day. Shortly after that his leave came through.[11]

He rushed home, ignoring his original concerns of distance. He saw his girl first and then his family up north. Then back to Portland. All done in a fit of speed that would have made a racecar driver jealous. He penned a letter to Lynn on 17 September letting her know he was back safe in Portland. The trip he had hesitated in taking, as it turned out, was well worth the expense in time and money. It would, in fact, under the looming departure date for the Pacific, have been regrettable had he not gone.

The night of the 22nd was the last the crew spent in the barracks. The next day they moved permanently onto the ship. Some of the men packed their bags on the 22nd and stayed in town. It was the last big hurrah in Portland. The navy was no longer allowing them to wander off and get drunk or waste the day milling around base. The next week was daylight to dark, grueling work loading ammo and supplies for their trip into war. Cook told Lynn in a letter dated the 25th that they were not getting any "sack time," a term he described as meaning lying around in bed and "taking life easy." The days of preparation ended each night around 23:00 hours, long after taps had sounded for everyone else on base. The crew found little energy to go on liberty and drink as they had done regularly for the month before. Except for the diehard drinkers, everyone stayed on ship at night, wrote letters and sang along with a duo of shipmates playing a harmonica and spoons. Someone threw on the Bob Willis and his Texas Playboys' more up-beat western swing rerecording of "Red Wing."[12] It was their last night in Portland and the joint was swinging aboard *LCS 52*.

She launched from her birthplace at Albina Engine and Machine Works in Portland on 14 August 1944. After the usual shakedown runs to test her sea worthiness, she was prepared for open sea. Refitted and fueled, a brand new *Landing Craft Support (L) 52* made her way down the Columbia River from Portland on the morning of 4 October. She was built to negotiate shallow waters and capable of coming in danger-close to a shoreline, for instance that of a Pacific island. The journey down the fourth largest river in the United States seemed like a Sunday fishing trip for a stubby, low-draft ship like her. Following the Columbia north from Portland, she turned west near Longview and then pushed out to sea just west of Astoria, Oregon. At Astoria and the mouth of the Pacific Ocean she met her first challenge and the first test of her and her crew's mettle. At the river's mouth lay the Columbia Bar, a constantly shifting sandbar known to the maritime community as one of the most treacherous stretches of water in the world. Because the bar had caused the demise of so many ships in the past it had acquired the ominous nickname of the Graveyard of Ships. To negotiate such a feature took captains who were especially knowledgeable in navigational calculations and practices. That special kind of man stood at the conn of *LCS 52* as she glided down the Columbia with the states of Washington and Oregon drifting by to her left and right.

Lieutenant John Oral Harper, captain of *LCS 52*, while lacking experience, was nothing short of a navigational whiz. He was born 5 September 1917, to John Henry and Lyda Louise Davis Harper at Rocky Hill, Ohio. A schoolteacher before the war, Lt. Harper delighted in learning and especially enjoyed mathematics and the sciences. During the five years prior to the United States' involvement in World War II, Harper taught in the Milton Township school system in his home state. He was never idle when it came to his own education. He committed himself to continuing education and practiced what he preached. While he was teaching he took classes at Rio Grande College and at Ohio University during his summer breaks. When school was in session and time did not allow travel to college classrooms, he fed his insatiable educational hunger by taking extension courses. The courses that stood out most to him were those in geometry, integral calculus and differential calculus.[13] The subjects he found enjoyable, fun even, were the subjects others avoided at all cost. He frequently spent many long hours in the evenings solving mathematical problems and preferred working problems to their solution without assistance from his instructors. He seldom settled for anything less than an "A" in mathematics and graduated with honors from Ohio University in the summer of 1941.

Although teaching positions were abundant, Harper felt the best thing for him to do after graduation, at least for the short term, was go to Dayton, find a job, and work there until he himself entered service.[14] Like most young men of the day, he wanted to enter service but had no desire to be drafted and thrown into the infantry. It was Harper's nature to want something more interesting than the monotony of an infantry officer's life.

There in the factory mecca of wartime America, he looked for work, gathered information, and considered the possibility of becoming a Marine Corps or Navy officer. While he was evaluating those choices, he was hired at the Sheffield Gauge Company. He started out in the inspection division, which seemed like a perfect fit for someone who enjoyed and excelled at mathematics. Harper was also fortunate enough at Sheffield to be doing a job that he liked and to have his future wife working in the same factory.

He advanced quickly in the firm but so did his draft number. When his number came up the company immediately requested a deferment to keep him at his station. Because the gauges made at Sheffield were used in artillery pieces, his job was one considered essential to the war effort and he received a six-month deferment with no problem. When that deferment expired he was automatically renewed for another six months. However, at the end of one year at Sheffield, Harper began to look around the streets of Dayton and felt he might well be the only single male in town who was not already in service. When his third deferment came due, he refused to accept it, and instead volunteered for military service.

The Navy won out over the Marines and in October 1942 Harper headed off to the Navy's enlisted boot-camp at Camp Green Bay, Great Lakes Naval Training Center (USNTC).[15] Great Lakes Naval Training Center was established in 1905. Construction continued through 1911, ending that year with the completion of the original thirty-nine buildings including the famous 300 foot plus, red brick clock-tower building designated Building One. The base was located near both North Chicago in Lake County and the western shore of Lake Michigan. More than one-million new blue jackets marched across the parade ground at Ross Field during the war years. Most of those were sent to combat duty in the Pacific. For those sailors lucky enough to survive the war, Great Lakes also served as a main separation center for returning sailors formerly from the east coast and the central United States.

Openly admitting that one enjoyed boot-camp was never a popular opinion among sailors but Harper confessed that he enjoyed his time at Great Lakes.[16] He relished leading the battalion in morning exercises and graduated as Honor Man for his recruit company. Because of that distinguished honor he earned the right to choose any one of the Navy's occupational schools that he wanted to attend. Military occupational schools trained sailors for specific jobs they would perform throughout their career, be that a couple of years or more than twenty. There was no ambiguity on Harper's part; he knew exactly what school he would choose. For enlisted men, like himself at the time, the Navy quartermaster assisted officers in the calculations and process of navigating the ship. It was the kind of work that appealed to someone like Harper in search of an interesting job or at least an interesting job for the Navy. Therefore, quartermaster school was at the top of the list and one Harper believed would challenge his innate curiosity. The Navy keeping a promise to an ordinary sailor was low priority, and Harper found himself en-route to the Aviation Ordnance Command Training Station in Norman, Oklahoma, instead of his chosen course. In spite of the fact that it was not quartermaster school, Harper nevertheless found it interesting. As with every endeavor that he had undertaken thus far in life, he excelled in the courses. The Navy gave him another surprise, but a pleasant one this time. Just as he was on the verge of receiving his third class rating he was given orders to report to the V-7 training program at the University of Notre Dame in South Bend, Indiana. The wartime V-7 programs were designed to take college graduates and induct them into Midshipman courses for four months. With successful completion of the program the cadets were awarded an ensign's commission. For Harper it was a roundabout way to get back to the path he had originally started on when he left teaching and went to Dayton. He knew the training was going to be intense but he was capable and confident he would succeed. It was just who he was.

Harper's midshipman class was scheduled to begin in February 1942. He felt compelled to scout the campus before his fellow midshipmen arrived. His would be the second class to train at Notre Dame and he wanted to meet expectations. His early arrival permitted him to attend the graduation ceremony for the first Naval Reserve Midshipman's School to be produced at the University. Watching them march across and receive their commissions gave Harper extra motivation and insight as to what men who had succeeded in the program looked like. He also realized that in four short months that would be his class standing proud in new ensign's uniforms.

Harper's own class was made up of approximately 1100 midshipmen. The battalions were formed by alphabetical order. Second Battalion was made up of 369 midshipmen beginning with John Haig through John Ryan. Harper billeted in the campus' Morrissey Hall. Although they were on a university campus there was no doubt in anyone's mind that they still belonged to the Navy and were subject to its regulations. For the midshipmen a bugle sounded reveille each morning, and no matter where they went they marched in formation. The men went everywhere in groups of thirty-two, and it was a given for Harper to call cadence for his group as they marched. He took a certain pleasure barking out cadence, he admitted. He felt he was a natural for the task because he had a low-pitched voice but was able to produce the volume which allowed his commands to reverberate across campus.

The campus was not ideal for practical education of future seafarers. There was no large body of water close enough to practice the lessons the midshipmen needed to learn. And due to the large number of midshipmen, Harper considered his four months at Notre Dame "theoretical." The class only ventured out to Lake Michigan a couple of times. It was never long enough to consider the effort anything close to mastery of seamanship. Another problem was that the men did not know what type of vessel and what kind of environment they would be sent to after school. The training all became very general, damage control, navigation, fire drills, steering, use of semaphore flags, and dozens of other subjects that an officer aboard any ship was supposed to know and order without hesitation.

Harper looked upon the mathematical refreshers as curriculum he had to breeze through in order to get to the things that he really loved learning about, particularly navigation. "We were taught how to use the [sextant], the compass and the other instruments used for either coastal navigation or on ocean navigation using the heavenly bodies as guidelines," Harper said.[17] He delighted in those ancient mariner's techniques and seemed a bit repelled by the fact that most modern ships were guided by mechanical compasses, machines with no awareness of the prodigious feats they performed.

As it grew closer to graduation he requested assignment to one of the larger ships that had dedicated navigators, a position he deeply desired to fill. In spite of there being more than 1100 midshipmen who graduated with his class, Harper once more proved to be head and shoulders above all others. He graduated third in his class, which unbeknownst to him at the time sealed his fate for the near future. When assignments were passed out, it was then he first learned he would remain at Notre Dame to teach future classes of midshipmen mathematics and navigation. The second Midshipman's class conducted at Notre Dame graduated at 11:00 on 27 May 1943. For the new officers of that class, most would go directly to combat zones. Some would never return to the campus to walk its grounds again. One would wake up the following day and go back to class.

Teaching subjects that John Harper

John O. Harper impressed the cadre at Notre Dame with his love and talent for mathematics. John was also very proud of his military accomplishments. Years later, his partner and friend in the law firm, David Weaver, recalled John's delight when sharing his many sea stories (Carol Harper Marsh collection).

loved was a lofty assignment, but it posed problems, the most apparent one in his personal life. While he was still in Oklahoma his hometown girlfriend, Marjorie Halley, had made a trip out to visit him. During that visit, in January 1943, he presented her with an engagement ring. After his graduation he expected to receive a week of leave before reporting to his next duty station. The two were to be married back in Ohio during that week. Plans for the wedding had to be canceled in spite of the fact that Marjorie had already taken her blood test for the license. Fortunately, new plans quickly developed and most of the family traveled from Ohio to South Bend, where the two were married in a ceremony at the Methodist Church on 27 May 1943—following graduation ceremonies. As luck would have it, the new couple had less than twelve hours to call a honeymoon before Harper had to stand twenty-four-hour duty as Officer of the Day (OOD).

The two found a little apartment on Lincoln Way West. Life was good for the newlyweds at Notre Dame. The young couple enjoyed dancing to the big band sounds popular in the 1940s, playing golf and attending Notre Dame football games. Other than the daily regimens, the occasional Officer of the Day duties, the uniform, and the war news, life had become routine for the Harpers. But the Navy had not forgotten them and Harper's time in Notre Dame would come to a close. He received his orders, not to sea duty as a navigational officer assisting the captain as he had hoped, but to the amphibious training base Solomon's Island, Maryland. Marjorie and he barely had time to lease their apartment, move their furnishings back to Ohio, and head out to Maryland.

The base was located less than two miles north of Solomon's Island, a town so small the Harpers could not find a motel or hotel to stay in overnight. They seemed to always have uncanny good luck, though, and this time was no different. While driving around and exploring what little town there was, they noticed a family moving out of what appeared to be an apartment or farmhouse. On a hunch they stopped to ask if the place was going to be for rent soon. The families happened to be moving out, military orders to report to a new duty station. They took one of the apartments sight unseen, and it became their new Solomon's Island home.

Harper was soon made acquainted with a landing craft infantry ship (LCI). The LCIs were ships capable of taking up to two-hundred marines ashore on any sandy beach and had already been tested in combat in the Pacific islands. He did not know at the time but the gunship that would be his first command was built on the same hull as the LCIs. The major difference was, that LCIs were built as transports and his, the LCS, bristled with armament. The time spent learning to steer and maneuver the LCI was valuable experience that he would soon need to ensure the survivability of his own ship and crew. The lessons that he had learned, and many of the ones he taught in a classroom at Notre Dame, were now ready to be put into practice.

Training while at Solomon's Island was becoming closer to what life onboard their warbound vessels would be like for the new officers. They were given an LCI, a crew of about twenty-five enlisted, and sent on maneuvers. The three or four day exercises tested the officers' skills at handling the ship, docking with other ships, navigating day and night, and, of course, getting on and off shore with the ship. Harper figured out quickly that the magnetic compass was never a sure bet. The iron beams in the ship's hull played havoc with the needle, even with the best adjustments on his part. He preferred to rely on the truer method of guiding off Polaris, better known as the North Star. Then again he was personally confident in his navigational abilities. At least in theory he knew how to operate but there was always the lacking experience. That was in essence what these trips meant, a chance to take his skills off the Notre Dame blackboard and put them into practice. In that aspect he was no better or worse off than any of his fellow ensigns.

He and his fellow officers learned how to stack, pack and store ammunition, food, water and guns aboard the ships. The fitting of a ship for travel across a body of water the size of the Pacific was an art in itself. He would have to be good at it all. No one would be aboard he could turn to and ask what to do, he just had to know. Sailors did not like to run out of things, especially food or bullets. He also found out he would be doing another packing of a different kind. He received his overseas assignment with a departure date from Maryland for mid–August. He called on his family and packed Marge and their household goods up for a return to her mother's house back in Ohio. They came to the train station to wave goodbye, and he left with his new crew for Washington, D.C.

When they arrived in Portland, the *LCS (L) (3) 52* was still in the making. Each day after arrival Harper walked down to the docks and monitored her progress. He was anxious. The routine dragged on until weeks turned into months. Harper worked around the builders, fitting the ship with all the essentials he had been taught his ship and crew would need to fight a war. By September Harper was in the process of finishing out his ship when he received his promotion to Lieutenant Junior Grade.

Suddenly and surprisingly he was called with information that the commissioning ceremony was at hand. Everyone rushed to the dock, stood proudly while "a few patriotic words" were said and they ran up the commissioning pennant.[18] Thanks to his and the crew's diligence, *LCS 52* was ready to sail. Harper had not had time to get his half stripe added to his full stripe, sewed on to show himself as a Lt. JG. But with the raising of the skinny long pennant over his ship, he was automatically promoted to Lieutenant Senior Grade. It had all worked out in the long run.

The following day he took the ship and crew out for a short shakedown run up the Willamette River. Surviving that, the next test was a run down the Columbia. The only thing left after a good trial run down the Columbia was to pull her away from the Portland dock and head toward the open sea. The 52 sailed out of the Columbia River on 4 October 1944, reaching Astoria the same day, and then set her sights on San Diego.

The first sign of trouble aboard was not the rough sea and high roller-coaster waves that Harper had been warned of when entering the Columbia Bar by his experienced pilot. Rather the trouble was the semi-noxious odor of cooking liver emanating from the galley. He was not the only one who had taken in the smell and not the only one who found it a poor mix with the tossing seas. The well-meaning cook soon figured it out with limited subtle suggestion. He stowed the meat and substituted a lunch choice of soup or stew—something that went down a little more appealing than liver and came up a little easier later.

The journal was really nothing more than a pocket-size ledger book, a hardcover to protect its pages stacked with blue lines Laton Burns could fill with all the adventures he deemed important. Laton made his first entry on the morning *LCS 52* pulled away from the dock in Portland: "Got ship Sept. 23, 1944 At Portland, Oregon."[19] It was not much in the way of an exciting editorial but it served its purpose as a way to remember the relatively uneventful shakedown. In some ways Laton had grown up like Lt. Harper. Both had been raised on farms and had started their education in one-room school houses. Like Harper, Laton had taken

The LCSs were so small that they never rode on top of a wave. They were notorious for bringing on debilitating seasickness. The crew of *LCS 52* did not make it into open sea before the menace that every old salt knew had them all, except Thill, hanging over the rail (Virgil Thill collection).

his boot-camp at Great Lakes but beyond that there was little that the two men had in common. And now, aboard ship, there was naval protocol which dictated that they live in the same space but different worlds.

Laton Burns was born 7 January 1926, the third child of Ambrose and Florida Roberts Burns in Oneida, Clay County, Kentucky. His birth was ordinary for a child of the mountains in the 1920s. The morning was cold and frosty, the home heated by wood, or coal when available. Laton was delivered, as was everyone else, by a midwife, or granny lady, as they were called in the Eastern Kentucky Mountains.[20] The family moved several times during his childhood. One of those moves took Laton north of the Ohio River, where the family frequented the popular attractions at Coney Island outside Cincinnati. That did not last, though, and by school age, the family was back in the small community of Oneida, Kentucky.

In Clay County the people were typically very isolated from the rest of the world. They had been that way for generations but, in spite of that, few mountain men had ever missed their chance at going off to war. Every family in the county could recite a long list of family names who had served, some back to the Revolution. Laton Burns could trace his military heritage through his father's service in World War I, his grandfather during the Civil War and his great-great-grandfather in the Revolutionary War.

Southern Kentuckians honored their country by serving when called. It was simply thought of as part of their culture. Aside from neighbors and friends close to Laton, he had an older brother, Milton, already serving in the Army Air Corps when he joined the Navy. His first cousin Ambrose was in the Army's 32nd Infantry Regiment. Three of his future brothers-in-law served: Paul, 323rd Army Field Artillery, Neil P., 5th Air Force, and Glenn M. Dezarn, 3rd Army. There were hundreds of others from the little mountain communities, Laton knew them all as classmates, distant relatives and sports rivals.

The county seat of Clay was Manchester, which by the 1940 census claimed a population of 1509 people living within the city limits. It was to Manchester that Laton, like so many others from the hills and hollows traveled to enlist. As isolated as Clay County was from the world, the outside world knew even less about Clay County.

The only time news seemed to leak out was when two or more feuding families killed enough of the county's meager population to make headlines in a Chicago or New York newspaper. The state militia was once called to Manchester in 1899 to set a perimeter around feud leader "Bad" Tom Baker. He was secured in a tent surrounded by militia in the courthouse square. The opposition killed him as the militia diligently stood guard. Laton had not been around to see the murder of Bad Tom but like every other Clay County kid, he had heard the story told many times.

Laton and many other mountain youths attended the Oneida Baptist Institute (OBI), a school built by a relative of Laton's by the name of James Anderson Burns for the sole purpose of educating the feud mentality out of the children. The first building was being completed as someone from the other faction sniped Bad Tom. The school opened its doors in January of 1899, and Tom was killed the prior June. By the time Laton started at OBI, though, people said the feuds were over; that was what people said, mostly outsiders.

Laton's father seemed to always be moving around. The grass was always greener for him, and his children had to suffer under the pressure of finding new friends and new activities throughout their lives. Laton relished sports and played basketball and baseball at OBI. He was also a part of the school's 1942 undefeated softball team. He and his sister, Polly, arrived at OBI in July of 1941 from the Berea Academy. Berea Academy was a school for poor mountain youths of any color. The Burns children's record cards indicated that their father was a farmer but the year prior he was working road construction. They lived without a phone and were fifteen miles from a railroad station and four miles from a telegraph office.[21] Laton and Polly were both enrolled at the Academy, run by Berea College, for only one semester, from January to March 1941. It was just another example of the nomadic lifestyle Ambrose forced upon them.

Laton's father was witness to the Baker/Howard feud and a few more. It was probably the violence of the mountains and the poor chance of surviving economically there that drove Ambrose to join the Army in the years prior to World War I. Ambrose was a hard shadow for any son to move out from under. He had participated in his unit's move to Texas to chase Pancho Villa. Then, shortly after their return from the Punitive Expedition, they headed off to war in Europe. Serving as an infantry sergeant, Ambrose, more often than not volunteered to lead small teams of men across no-man's-land and into the German trenches. The team would attempt to make contact with the enemy and capture whoever they encountered. Once the prisoners were silenced, without killing them, they were returned to friendly lines in the hopes of extracting intelligence information from them. On one such mission an American was left behind. Ambrose returned alone to the enemy trenches and attempted to recover the man. On another occasion, Ambrose was shot in the butt, which only enraged him to a senseless state. He single-handedly assaulted, and took a machinegun nest with only his .45 Automatic pistol. Ambrose made his name known in the trenches of France, to put it mildly.

The Burns families lived on farms along a stretch of creek that joined the Redbird River called Big and Little Bull Skin Creek. They, as a group, had done so for a hundred and fifty years. Bull Skin was only a brisk walk to Oneida Baptist Institute. OBI was a boarding school and therefore students resided in dorms on campus. Early in their arrival at OBI, Polly Burns met and befriended another student named Kathleen Dezarn. Polly liked Kathleen and soon felt compelled to introduce her to her brother, Laton. The two found an immediate attraction.

Both Laton and Kathleen took on jobs at the campus to pay their own ways through the school sessions. It was a common practice to do such jobs and no student simply sat on their duff. The jobs involved upkeep of the campus and care of fellow students. Students did community laundry, carried fuel for the stoves, cooked, cleaned and performed basically any other communal chores needing done.

The budding love affair was doing quite well by the time 7 December 1941 rolled around. That cool morning, Laton happened to be in the town of Oneida, which stretched out below the big hill on which the OBI campus sat. The town was small; a general store run by the Hensley family was the main mercantile in town. Laton was related to the Hensley family through his paternal grandmother. There was a post office and a couple of hotels where loggers and other sorts spent an occasional night in Oneida, but that was as close to a town center as it got. On the far side of the town was the confluence of the Redbird and Kentucky Rivers. Before the Civil War there were prosperous salt works producing along the stretch of river bottom near the town's edge. The works had unfortunately belonged to two rival families—each on the opposite side of the war. The war became an excuse to burn out the opposition. Logging rafts still moved down the river to Frankfort and other sawmill towns, in Laton's youth. The hundred-foot-long rafts were made up of cut logs, tied together and floated to markets. They were a marvel to see.

News of the attack on the U.S. Navy in the territory of Hawaii was all that people were talking about and all they heard about on the radio.[22] Laton was overcome with emotion, angry that he could not then go and defend his homeland. He returned to the OBI campus and sought out his sister and girlfriend. He shared the news of the attack with both. He was only fifteen years old but made his vow that as soon as he was of age, he was going to fight. He kept his promise.

Laton was eighteen years old and one day when he joined the Navy. His education was set aside in his junior year of high school. He left school to do what so many young men felt was their duty, join the service and help win the war. On 8 January 1944 he made his way to the nearest draft board.

Laton loved farming too; he always had.[23] Being a sailor was just temporary duty, a rite that he had to pass through so that he could get on with life. His home in Clay County was primarily populated by farmers. Seldom did even the steepest hill escape the plowing and planting of corn. Some men worked in the burgeoning coal industry but they too did their best to own and tend some acreage for the sake of their families. He was not going to be any different from his belligerent ancestors or shy from his duty, but he knew well, that he would return and live out his dreams on a Kentucky farm.

Laton did not therefore enter the Navy with any illusion that he was going to make a career out of it. But there were few boys his age in Clay County, Kentucky who were not in uniform or at the very minimum working in a factory building war material. He himself had also worked a short time at Kings Powder Mill making ammunition and bombs but that was only temporary too. It was a complicated thing for a young man, reluctantly leaving home, plans, and aspirations while looking forward to paying the greater debt to his country.[24] His time came, and he and his best friend, Lloyd Keith, shipped out for basic training in April of 1944.

After his basic training at Great Lakes, Laton was sent to Fort Pierce, Florida, for further training. He arrived in the summer months of 1944 to find that the sunshine came with hordes of mosquitoes and sand fleas. Boot-camp taught men how to walk and talk like sailors but Fort Pierce taught them how to survive in battle. The new contingent of trainees arrived before the Fourth of July. Laton and Lloyd "Clements" Keith shared a tent with guys who Laton labeled fellow "hill billy's."[25] On the fourth they competed in watermelon eating and one-leg races, things that most of them might have been doing back home on that day. As always, Laton and Clements never missed an opportunity to play baseball. They were both excellent athletes.

The boys lived in tents. With all of the fellows in Laton's tent being from the South, they shared interests and traditions which connected them. They got along well and that helped dull the homesickness. The nights usually ended with singing. The last song was left to Clements, who closed with some "lonesome blues," Laton wrote to his sweetheart, Kathleen Dezarn, back in Oneida. At least three times a week the mornings began with a breakfast including beans, Laton complained to Kathleen. Aside from beans for breakfast, he did not like the chow in general. He felt it was because they had to cook so much at once, it was not good. The boys worked outside in their swim trunks and had become so tan from the Florida sun, Laton did not think she would recognize him. He still closed his letters to her with a noncommittal, "always a friend."

Laton told Kathleen that some of the boys dreaded exercises such as abandon ship drills. He shared that he did not. "I will take that as fun," he wrote.[26] The drill, as Laton described it, consisted of the men going overboard about a mile and a half out to sea and having to swim back to shore. He told Kathleen they were required to go into the water in life vests, but he did not like to swim in a vest. It was obvious he did not fully understand the difference between swimming in the rivers back home and being cast into the perilous Pacific.

He also described other training that he found fun or at least interesting. The new sailors viewed images of enemy planes flashed on a screen and were expected to identify the aircraft in that split second. There were as many as forty different planes they were tested on. He did understand the consequences of misidentifying a plane in combat. He did not know at the time how important to his survival in the future those cards would be.

He and Clements Keith were assigned to a gun crew together. They fired the largest gun on the ship, and he delighted in the accomplishment. Both practiced at firing the gun but Laton deferred to Keith as being the better at aiming. Laton really enjoyed the weapons training he received in Florida. It was a basic skill he had perfected as a youth and as familiar to him as farming.

As Laton sailed out to sea, the fun he had experienced at Fort Pierce was a distant memory, dulled by the misery of seasickness. He was not as twisted by nausea as most aboard were, but he had his moments. His friend from back home, Clements Keith, was still there by his side, fair or rough seas. They had somehow managed to hide their close ties from the Navy's eyes, which would have surely separated them otherwise.

The rough seas entering the Pacific affected everyone aboard *LCS 52* in some unwelcome way. Some of the sixty-five enlisted and six officers that Harper reported present on her maiden voyage were old salts. That, however, did not exempt them from the agonies of seasickness. As often as not, it was not the tossing and churning of the violent sea that brought stomach contents to the surface again but rather the sight and smell of other men puking. There were no shots or pills to prevent the terrible debilitation. While some old salts swore by sea remedies, there were no guarantees. Perhaps the worst part of seasickness was that there was no way of knowing if, or when, it would end. There was no relief, not a single place on ship where the effects were not felt. That was the summation of the crew's first day and night aboard their new ship at sea. On day two they sailed through a storm which compounded the misery of the already sick and weak. Some of the men were so sick they could not rise from their beds.[27] It was rough going but it would be the stuff many a future sea tale was made of.

Larry Cullen grew up accustomed to both the country and the city but not to the sea. He was born in the small community of Rowland, Alabama, on 13 November 1906. Rowland was the former McDonald's Station, established in 1878, a stop-over for the Louisville and Nashville Railroad. In 1913 Rowland once more decided it needed a facelift and retitled itself Tanner, oddly after the first mayor of nearby Athens, Alabama. Whatever name it happened to be going by at the time, Tanner was in Limestone County on the Tennessee River and a humid, hot place during the

Laton Burns kept his journal hidden away while aboard *LCS 52*. Thanks to all those who ignored and violated navy policy, we have thousands of contemporary accounts of the war. The journal is now in his daughter's possession (photograph by the author).

summer. The winters were nothing compared to Wisconsin where Larry's father, Harold Dempster Cullen, had been raised. Harold Cullen moved to Alabama and attended the agricultural college there in Limestone County. He worked his way through the ranks of the local school system from teacher to principal of Marengo County High School. While Rowland pondered another name change, the Cullen family moved to Birmingham in 1912.[28] Larry's dad started in the advertising department of the *Birmingham News* but then took off on his own and started a business called Direct Advertising Service. He and Larry's mom, Bessie French Cullen, successfully ran that firm for twenty-five years.

Larry found that life was just plain easier with a bit of humor thrown in.[29] He knew first hand that fun meant different things in the social settings between urban and rural life. One of his proudest pranks as a city boy had been to grease the tracks for the scheduled arrival of the uphill bound Birmingham streetcar. It was a masterpiece of ingenuity, and he had found no need to flee the scene before seeing the struggle of his iron victim slipping awkwardly toward his perch. Larry also had a poetic strike beyond his natural talent for making public transportation late. He loved poetry, the reading of, reciting of and even the creating of. He loved books in general, and that was a good hobby to have aboard ship. He joined the Navy on 17 March 1944. He was the second of four sons and as he sailed down the Columbia with the 52, he would be one of two sons serving during the war. Frank, his much younger brother, born in 1921, was then serving with the Army's 62nd Signal Battalion. Frank entered service in 1942. The 62nd Signal was part of IV Corps who had been operational since late May 1944 in the Mediterranean Theater.[30] Frank served in Italy, and unbeknown to the two brothers at the time, would be sent with the 62nd Signal to Japan after the surrender. Unlike

Larry Cullen was pushing forty years old when he joined the Navy. He was married to Alma, and their young children remained in her care while he went off to war (Norma Cullen Vines collection).

older brother Larry, Frank had a droll wit and loved opera music. Maybe it was the years that had made them so different; they were almost a generation apart. With Larry now in the Navy, headed for the Pacific Theater, the Cullen boys had land and sea covered.

After attending Phillips High School in Birmingham, Larry went to the University of Alabama for a year, but hard times still lingered and he was forced to leave school. Larry had also attended a business college. It was there that he one day happened to catch one of his female classmates conveniently placing her hand on a doorknob—which so happened to be the one he was reaching for at the time. He placed his hand over hers—a perfect introduction, and a story that Alma Llewellyn Millholland Cullen shared for the rest of her life. Becoming close and falling in love after that initial meeting, the two figured it was time to commit to a life together. They borrowed his father's car and drove to a nearby town, where they were secretly married within sight of two friends they had brought as witnesses on 20 November 1927. They left the ceremony and returned to their respective homes. It was almost a flawless mission, until father Harold noticed that the gas tank on his car was suspiciously lower than it should have been. Their wedding did not remain a secret for very long after.[31] Once they admitted their marital status they moved in with Harold and Bessie. It was as good a spot as any with the Great Depression looming around the corner. In spite of the financial hardships during the depression, Alma and Larry had their first child, Lewis, in 1932 and their second, Norma, three years later. Before the war he took the kids with him to work on many occasions. Norma liked playing with the letters of the typeset and rummaging through the office to see what she could find.[32]

It was his wife and children that Larry worried most about as he went off toward his first battle. Alma had taken over his position at work as head of the supply department. It was double duty, and he fretted over its toll on his wife. He worried about all the ordinary things that the younger, single boys did not have to concern themselves with: would the car start, were there enough ration coupons, how was Alma holding up under the strain?[33] And Toby, their old dog, a man had to worry about his dog too. It all seemed such a faraway place and time as the 52 bounced along the California coastline headed for San Diego.

Larry's ability to see the humor in any disgusting situation made its first appearance to the crew as a poem called the *Maiden Voyage*. Dedicated to and inspired by the greater majority of sailors who hung over the rails in puking convulsions brought on by rough seas between the sand bar and their Southern California port:

The Maiden Voyage of the 52

I'm telling you of the 52,
That went to sea with her hapless crew.
Not two hours out the waves got rough,
Half the crew had had enough.
    They were piled knee-deep in the crowded "head,"
And bodies strewed the deck like dead.
And everywhere the vomit's stench,
From bowsprit back to the anchor winch.
Quite a mess was the 52,
And quite a mess her groaning crew.
All day long the 52,
Ploughed the seas with her seasick crew.
And into the night when the waves got high,
Most of the crew now wanted to die.

The ship would hit in the trough with a smack,
And shudder and roll and grunt and crack.
And shiver and rumble from stem to stern.
The seasick crew for land would yearn.
But undaunted still the 52,
Butted the seas the long night through.
   The night somehow passed, and some of the men,
Felt just a little like living again.
A few still moaned and lay in their sacks,
   Or stretched on the fantail flat on their backs.
The seas had calmed to a steady roll,
But a day and a night had taken their toll.
And most of the crew was prepared to say

Frank Cullen, right, Larry's younger brother, served in the Army Signal Corps. The two met in Washington, D.C., before they each went overseas. They are posed in front of the Washington Monument, sometime in 1944. Larry was a prankster throughout his youth. His pranks were elaborate but always just short of criminal. He was also well-read and was comfortable talking about philosophy, history, poetry or the classics. His love of learning led him to a close friendship with Ensign Spencer Burroughs (Norma Cullen Vines collection).

> They didn't know sailors lived this way.
> They still felt like they'd always be sick,
> > And would like to be out of the Navy, but quick.
> With unslackened speed the 52,
> Southward carries her seasick crew.
> This must go on for three days more,
> Before the 52 heads for the shore.
> Sail on, sail on, O 52,
> For I am one of that seasick crew![34]

The seasickness was the first reminder that there are few pleasures and even fewer comforts aboard a ship at sea. Sailors enjoy the scenery and the freedom of the sea, but the thing that makes life on a ship tolerable is the camaraderie of shipmates. Men grow close to one another; they become as brothers. That bond is compounded once they have faced death together. The men who were aboard the 52 when she sailed from Portland would soon face all the terror and tragedy of combat. They would become as close as any family could possibly be, and that connection would last throughout their lives. The story of one sailor would blend so with his shipmates that, by telling one, it was the telling of all.

2

How Did We Get Ourselves into This?

In 1931 when Americans spoke of war they were typically referring to the Great War. Still struggling in the third year of the Great Depression, few Americans had time to concern themselves with Japan's invasion of Manchuria on 19 September of that year. However, marines, soldiers and sailors, who had been first stationed in China in 1900, were suddenly caught between Japanese and Chinese clashes. The *China Marines* watched, for the decade prior to the bombing of Pearl Harbor, the ruthless aggression of the Japanese military on the Chinese citizenry. If anyone could have predicted the atrocities to come, it was the American military then stationed in China. As the war escalated, in June 1939 Japanese forces built barbwire containments around French and English concessions in Tientsin.

Back in America there were few tangible signs that a war was being waged abroad. On 28 March 1935, Americans went about their daily chores and gave no more thought to the invasion of Ethiopia by the Fascist Italian army, or the consequences of that far-off crisis, than they had China. Even as Nazi forces invaded Poland on 1 September 1939, Americans remained mentally and militarily detached from conflicts occurring on the other side of the world. America's former allies in World War I, however, were not in a position to simply ignore what was happening on the continent. Less than a month before the invasion of Poland by Germany, the British signed a mutual assistance treaty with the Polish government. Britain, France, Australia and New Zealand all declared war on Germany on 3 September following the Nazi invasion. On the 5th, the United States reaffirmed its commitment to neutrality. As the Germans entered Paris on 14 June 1940, Denmark, Norway, Belgium, Luxembourg, the Netherlands and Holland had already surrendered under pressure of the German blitzkrieg.

The 4th Marines, stationed in Shanghai, the largest contingent of U.S. forces left in China by November 1941, were removed to the Philippines in an effort to exclude them from the deteriorating situation. The morning after Pearl Harbor was bombed Japanese forces surrounded the remaining American marines at Peiping, Chinwangtao and Tientsin. The marines were forced to surrender, and were all temporally imprisoned at Tientsin. The 202 captured marines were then sent to a camp fifteen miles north of Shanghai called Woosung. Woosung POW camp sat on ten acres which contained former Chinese army barracks. The marines arrived to find seven barracks still standing and the camp surrounded by an electric fence. They joined the approximately 1200 military and civilian prisoners captured at Wake Island already there.

The closest vantage point to war the average American citizen had was to see the devastation and death frequented upon their world neighbors in a Movietone News broadcast in the comfort of their hometown theater. For those who wanted to reflect on 1941, for instance, they got to the cinema early for the showing of "In the Navy" starring Abbott and Costello."[1] Castle Films produced a recap of the year which aired under the title "News Parade of 1941" shown before the featured Hollywood production. Included within the 9:36 minute newsreel was the brief account of the USS *Kearny*'s, ill-fated encounter with the German submarine, *U-568*. The Castle Films account ignored or failed to mention the initial report from the Navy, claiming no casualties were reported and the ship was under its own power. That was only half fact and Castle Films aired President Roosevelt admitting instead that eleven sailors had perished from the attack. FDR also aired his response to the attack on radio. In that particular broadcast he cited the attack on the *Kearny* as an attack on America herself. He added that, "The *U. S. S. Kearny* [was] not just a Navy ship. She belongs to every man, woman, and child in this Nation."[2] FDR also used the attack as an opportunity to claim that he had a secret map which contained evidence of Hitler's planned domination of the Americas as well as Europe. That bit of information was left out of the Castle Films piece. The official Action Report pertaining to the attack on the *Kearny* would not be declassified by the Navy until 1964.

For the public's education on war, the story of the USS *Kearny* was preceded by an overview of marines and soldiers in Iceland, put there to ensure a secure ocean route between Britain and the continent. The footage of the *Kearny* followed under the title head of "Nazi Torpedo Cripples USS Kearny." To the American viewer, it had little more impact on the consciousness than did the Walt Disney Productions' of *Dumbo*, which hit the big screen days after the attack on the *Kearny*. Americans had other things on their minds. It was the first time in the preceding decade Americans had jobs and money to go to movies. They flocked to factories making war material, not for their boys, but for British boys to use. They were content in their isolation and what they believed was steadfast neutrality. The first hint of future casualties of a world war came with the torpedoing of the USS *Kearny*. It was clear, even before Pearl, from FDR's rhetoric following the *Kearny* incident that he wanted more than pacifism from the people of the United States.

The USS *Kearny* was a destroyer commissioned on 13 September 1940. She was built at the Brooklyn Navy Yard. The ship was first assigned to convoy protection duties. German U-boats were wreaking havoc on British shipping. Keeping the lifeline open for suppliers in America to move their goods to the few remaining free countries in Europe was critical for their survival. She began her mission of escorting North Atlantic convoys on 23 September. She made her first successful run from Reykjavik, Iceland with an American convoy on 11 October and then returned safely with a British convoy. Late in the night on the 15th she was reassigned to convoy SC-48, British shipping headed east. At ten minutes past midnight three torpedoes were fired from an unseen sub at the *Kearny*. One missed the bow and another swam past, missing the stern. The ship was not so lucky with the third; it struck her center of the starboard side. The explosion tore through the main deck and deckhouse. There was initial major damage to the superstructure deck, bridge and director but collateral damage affected almost every part of the ship. As electrical fires spread throughout the ship, the generators that were operational had to be shut down. Once power was restored, the steering was shifted to hand steering from below and voice commands from the deck. As the *Kearny* fought for her life, she was directed by the commander of the destroyer squadron to head for the nearest port. *Kearny* turned toward Iceland, escorted by the USS *Greer* and USS *Monssen*. She was so disabled that her captain was forced by necessity to navigate by the North Star.

Below decks QMC McDougal manned the aft conning station. He began steering the ship by hand when he determined that no other method existed. QM John Booth stationed in and now locked behind the watertight hatch, in the after steering engine room managed to convert the ship to hand steering so McDougal could maneuver the ship. QM Muscoe C. Holland discovered Booth, still at his battle station, alone and trapped in the compartment if the ship were to sink. Holland opened the hatch from the outside, thus freeing Booth if they had to abandon ship. He brought Booth a life vest and then manned the station with Booth.[3] All three later received Letters of Commendation from the Secretary of the Navy and were advanced to the next highest rank.

Muscoe Coleman Holland, Jr., was born in Axton, Virginia on 9 November 1921 to Muscoe and Theresa Bondurant Holland. Axton was a tiny community located in Henry County. His father had worked in Norfolk as a laborer in 1911, but as a muscular farmer in Axton he registered for the draft on 5 June 1917. He went into the Army later in 1917 and stayed until 1918. Before Holland Jr.'s tenth birthday the family picked up roots and moved to Fort Lee, New Jersey. Muscoe Sr. worked

Muscoe Holland joined the crew of *LCS 52* as the most senior enlisted man aboard. He served aboard the first American war ship to be sunk in the Atlantic before official U.S. involvement in the war against Germany. His heroic actions that day earned him formal recognition (Virgil Thill collection).

as a carpenter and farmed during the late 1920s. The family rented their home for $30 a month and were among one of the few families in the neighborhood to have their own radio. At forty-seven years of age in 1942, Holland Sr. once more was required to register for the draft. By then married, with adult children, and working at Ford Motor Company in Bergen County, New Jersey, he was never called.[4]

Muscoe Jr. enlisted in the Navy on 13 June 1940, at New York City, two years before his father received his second draft registration notice. He was received aboard the *Kearny* on 13 September 1940, for her maiden voyage. He remained aboard after the attack and was promoted to coxswain in January of 1942. He parted company with the *Kearny* on 9 May and was assigned to the receiving station at New Orleans. Muscoe was reassigned from the 8th Naval District at New Orleans to the USS *George Clymer* on 21 June 1942. He continued to excel at navy life and was promoted to Boatswain's Mate Second Class in August. In navy speak, he was officially assigned to "Commander Landing Craft Flotilla, South Pacific" on 24 April 1943; it was his turn to fight in the Pacific now. He left the USS *George Clymer* and reported to *LCI (L) 23* on 29 April 1943. Working aboard an infantry landing craft, Muscoe got his first close-up taste of the Pacific War.

In June, Holland's ship brought marines and supplies to New Georgia in the Solomon Islands chain. First to go ashore was the 4th Marine Raider Battalion on 20 June 1943. Then on the 4th of July LCIs raced to the beach and dropped Army and Marine Infantry. They continued to support Army and Marine units, dropping off replacements and supplies through 7 July. On the 7th, LCIs 23, 24, 63 and 65 were anchored off Rendova Island when an enemy bomb fell between 24 and 65 during a raid. The explosion rocked both ships and caused them to list and come to rest on the bottom. *LCI 24* suffered two men killed and three others wounded. The crews were subsequently stranded on the beach and forced into foxholes for the night while the sea battle in nearby Kula Gulf played out.

The LCIs, including 23, departed Guadalcanal for Vella Lavella with the landing force on 14 August 1943. Four fast destroyer transports carried the first wave of infantry ashore at 06:45 on the 15th. They were followed by twelve LCIs. The beach was too short to accommodate all twelve of the vessels beaching at the same time. Eight LCIs unloaded their troops, while four nervously waited their turn. At 09:15 the LCIs cleared the beachhead so the third wave could be brought in by LSTs. The three waves placed approximately 4600 men ashore. The landings were relatively unopposed other than sporadic bombing runs made by Japanese aircraft. The battle for the island ended on 3 October when the allied forces were unable to prevent the last Japanese defenders from slipping away by sea.

Holland's ship next took part in the Battle for Treasury Islands, part of the Solomon Islands. The landings began on 27 October with elements of the 3rd Division, New Zealand troops, followed by American marines. The landings by the Kiwis were their first amphibious assault since the 1915 World War I battle of Gallipoli.[5] The 23 remained in the area until late October when she was refitted and prepped for the assault on Cape Torokina, Bougainville.

At dawn on 1 November 1943 the fleet arrived off Empress Augusta Bay. The American marines began landing at 06.45. Taking part in the marine landings that morning was Holland's old ship and mates, the *George Clymer*. Bougainville was not secured until late November but *LCI 23* moved on to her next mission in mid–September.

In September the LCIs supported the landing of the 32nd Army Infantry Division on Morotai, Western New Guinea. The only excitement on the final leg of the journey to Morotai was that a soldier accidently went overboard from a LCI during the night. He was later located and recovered unharmed by another LCI. The fleet arrived off Morotai on 15 September 1943. The troop landings began at 08:30. LVTs and LCVPs transported troops to their respective beaches while LCIs laid-down a heavy covering fire with rockets. The LCIs also disembarked soldiers and equipment on Red Beach. The ship remained in the area of the Solomon Islands through June 1944, supporting mopping-up operations. Holland was promoted to Chief Boatswain's Mate on 1 April 1944. He left the ship at the end of April, transferred back to the United States. Morotai was Holland's last combat operation aboard *LCI 23*.

Chief Holland, already a veteran of the European and Pacific Theaters, joined the crew of *LCS 52* on her maiden voyage as the senior enlisted man aboard in September 1944. He would be the most combat experienced man aboard when the 52 embarked for war. His presence would be a godsend to the young crew.

On the very day *LCS 52* cast off for her maiden voyage the front page headlines of the *Chicago Defender* read "50 Sailors Face Trial for Mutiny." As with every judicial case there were two distinctly differing notions of how Americans looked at the origins of those headlines. Without more than a cursory examination, it might be explained that the story began on the evening of 17 July 1944. On that day the *SS Quinault Victory* and *SS E.A. Bryan* were being loaded with munitions at the Mare Island Naval Ammunition Depot, located at Port Chicago, California. Port Chicago was located approximately thirty miles north of San Francisco. The facilities there ran twenty-four hours a day.

As the two merchant ships were being loaded with over 4600 tons of explosive material, there were 400 additional tons of explosives nearby on rail cars. In the close proximity of the ships, either loading ammunition or working along the docks, were over 300 Navy ordnance men. Except for their officers, the majority of the sailors were African American. Things might have been different that night if the sailors had been afforded any training on how to do the high-risk loading jobs, but they were not. It was also rumored that their white officers routinely pushed them to rush beyond common sense safety.

At 22:18 hours a chain of explosions reverberated up and down the docks for several seconds. No one would ever be able to fully determine what had set it off. The explosions were so powerful they shook the ground in far-off Nevada. A plume of flames rose into the sky, some as high as two miles. A pilot, flying above that height, reported he saw shrapnel shoot past his plane. The explosions left 320 sailors dead and undetermined numbers injured. More than 200 of the sailors lost that day were black. Survivors stood their ground against the three-mile-wide inferno, fought fires and gave aid to the injured. Some other time they would have been regarded as heroes.

What happened on 9 August was almost as devastating for the surviving sailors as the explosions. They were ordered to Mare Island to once again continue loading ships without training or reevaluation of operating procedures. The battalion ordered back to duty under the same circumstances which had led to the 17 July disaster was comprised of 258 black sailors, of the total 328 in the unit. They soon drafted a rebuttal to the order to load ammunitions and told their officers they would do anything else, but would not load explosives. Their answer came swiftly; they were arrested and locked in a barge. Just as quickly came the Navy's indictment: fifty of the men determined to have been the plotters and leaders were charged with mutiny. The charge of mutiny during wartime was an offense which could result in execution if found guilty. The majority of mutineer followers were given bad conduct discharges and booted to the street with forfeiture of pay. In less than eighty minutes, counting lunch, the court found the fifty alleged leaders guilty.[6] They were sentenced, some might have been led to believe, to a mere fifteen years in prison instead of the death sentence.

What happened at Mare Island was only a fleeting glimpse at the real problem. Anglo Americans saw the explosion as another tragedy in a long string of misfortunes over the past four years. The trial for most Anglo Americans was verification of what they had been told by their parents and grandparents for eighty years. Blacks were troublemakers and instigators. African Americans, however, could easily see that the explosion was the result of non-whites being subjugated to menial dirty jobs that were often too dangerous for untrained sailors. The trial was just another atrocity that many blacks saw as ironically similar to those being perpetrated against races in Europe Hitler claimed were inferior. In America the official social policy was separate but equal. America was definitely separate, but it had a long ways to go to be equal, especially in 1944.

The United States military was the first to recognize that they needed every able-bodied man to fill the Spartan ranks depleted after World War I. After Pearl Harbor was bombed, men of every color turned up at recruiting stations in hordes to volunteer for service, with few exceptions. All services reluctantly accepted blacks, with conditions. The Navy and Marine Corps were the most unwilling to integrate blacks into their ranks. For those blacks wishing to sail the seas, as many of their forefathers had done, they were encouraged to resign themselves to status quo positions as cooks and stewards.

The recruiters had the knack for enlisting African-American men to positions which included shining officers' shoes and brass uniform accouterments. When a black man arrived to enlist, always close at hand was a poster displaying the proud figure of Doris "Dorie" Miller. Miller was, as a recruiter was quick to highlight, a mess attendant by Navy job title.[7] Miller served aboard the USS *West Virginia* when the Japanese bombed Pearl Harbor. In spite of Miller's normal role as a noncombatant, he manned a 50. Cal. machinegun and defended his ship. He had never received training with any of the ship's weapons but had watched numerous times as the gun crews ran drills. He fired the gun at attacking planes until running out of ammunition. For his actions on 7 December, Miller earned the Navy Cross, the nation's second highest military decoration for valor under fire.

The down side of using Miller as a role model was that he was living testimony to what blacks had been saying since World War I: they were just as good as the next man in frontline positions. They might even be better if someone would train them to use a weapon. It was an epiphany whites did not want to hear. Like their non-black counterparts, the main reason they wanted to join-up was to fight for their country like all good Americans were expected to do. Miller was trained to help move the wounded during a battle as a secondary job. It seemed to make more sense to man a gun and prevent more wounded sailors from piling up on the deck. All stewards and black sailors typically polishing brass were assigned such secondary duties but it never involved actually firing a gun as Miller had done.

The up side to using Miller's reputation as a recruiting aide was that he ordinarily accepted his lowly post and served chow. Being as Miller was born and raised in Waco, Texas, it could be assumed he understood and went along with the "Plantation Mentality."[8] It was a learned response from childhood but one not confined to the Southern states. However, the Old South enforced its Jim Crow laws with a passion. It was difficult for blacks in the South to see any other way. They were kept from good-paying jobs. Their housing, infrastructure, school facilities and medical care were abysmal. Life was spent almost completely segregated from any better quality-of-life. With good reason, blacks feared drinking from the wrong cooler, or entering the wrong bathroom, restaurant or train car. A simple indiscretion could result in physical harm or death.

By 1944 the United States was hurting for men to wear the uniform. Things had in many ways improved, and black men and women were putting on the uniform in growing numbers. Many of them saw an opportunity to shake off the Jim Crow South, if but for only a little while.

Ulysses Johnson, a resident of 1280 Lion Street, Memphis, Tennessee, at the time of his enlistment, was one of them. Ulysses joined the Navy on 27 April 1944. Before that, he grew up in the very segregated and very corrupt town that everyone knew belonged to Edward Hull "Boss" Crump.

Ulysses' parents were Johnny W. and Florence Henderson Johnson. Johnny Johnson supported his large family by farming, as did the majority of the community. Born on 29 September 1914 in Lucy, Tennessee, Ulysses was thirty years old when he entered the Navy. Ulysses married Dorothy Faye Shannon, also of Lucy.

When the Depression struck hard in the early 1930s, the mostly black township of Lucy followed others of their color to the nearby cities to attempt to secure factory work. As Ulysses grew into adolescence, the little community of Lucy, on the outskirts of Memphis, was the home of poor blacks who worked the cotton fields. Before the Depression, Lucy thrived on the cotton industry. One of the well-to-do residents of that era was a man named Joe Meese. He founded a cotton gin, mercantile and coffin factory in Lucy. His name apparently became so entwined with the local economy that residents began to refer to Lucy unofficially as Meesetown.[9] When the cotton boom slowed to a halt, the migration began.

The residents of Lucy headed to Memphis and looked for jobs in the two largest factories of the day, Fisher Body and Murray. Those blacks that could not get work in either stayed with what they knew, picking cotton in Arkansas. Buses or trucks took day workers over the river and brought them back well after dark. The factories were segregated, though the small number of whites that worked there were supervisors. No blacks had any notion they would ever be supervisors; it was not done. One former black resident of Lucy echoed the familiar saying, "Mr. Crump don't allow."[10] Blacks did the most dangerous and hardest work, for the least pay, and there was nothing to be done to change the fact.

Ulysses grew up performing the menial jobs that Boss Crump made sure blacks in Memphis felt they had to accept. Memphis swelled with defense factories after the war started, but Boss Crump's political machine made certain that blacks seldom filled those new jobs, just as he had done in the early years of the Depression. Ulysses lived within three miles of the center of community life for blacks in the 1930s and 40s, Beale Street. Aside from being the origin of W.C. Handy's "Blues of Beale Street," Ida B. Wells once ran her paper *Free Speech* out of a storefront on Beale Street. By the late 1930s Blues clubs dotted the length of Beale Street, along with restaurants, billiard halls and shops where blacks could actually frequent without fear of insult or threat. To go east, though, was to enter a foreign and dangerous land.

Ulysses understood the Plantation Mentality, and life in the Navy starting out was little different from what he was used to. Basic training was conducted for African Americans at Great Lakes but training remained segregated. As could have been expected he was assigned as a steward. His first ship would be *LCS 52* and as could be expected, he was the only black sailor aboard. Unlike the *West Virginia*, where Dorie Miller had served, the 52 was small and segregation was not a feasible concept. Also, during battle stations, he went where needed, even if that meant carrying ammunition and loading the guns. He discovered something else too, living in close quarters with a bunch of white sailors: they treated him well and even liked him. Laton Burns took down Ulysses' permanent address in Memphis in his cherished journal with the same promise of post-war contact as his other mates. Ulysses may have had the same old job set aside for black sailors, but he would discover that things were different among enlisted men on such a small ship.

As the 52 got underway on her maiden voyage, the second youngest crewmember, Virgil E. Thill, went about performing his duties, maintenance, painting and general care of the ship. During general quarters he manned the portside 20mm antiaircraft gun.

At seventeen years old, Virgil's life was filled with the experiences most people did not accumulate in an entire lifetime. One of his shipmates, Russell S. Copeland, often sat quietly on the upper deck and listened to Virgil's stories. Russell always left the session by exclaiming that he would one day write a book about Virgil's life.[11]

Virgil grew up on a 200-acre dairy farm in the township of Fayette [Fairbanks] on Big Bay de Noc, Michigan. He was born at home in the farmhouse in March of 1927. Virgil's grandmother, Myrtle Lang, was a midwife. She was taught her skills of midwifery by her own grandmother. Within her lifespan she delivered around eighty-five of the babies in the Fayette area, including Virgil. The farm was about a mile and a half from Lake Michigan, close enough that during the warmer parts of the year he enjoyed swimming there. His mother, Ida, married David Thill, who in turn raised Virgil and his siblings on the farm.

The history of Fayette was as boring as life on the farm. The community was nothing more than a fishing town in the mid-eighteen-hundreds. When the Jackson Iron Company discovered the area had three features readily available to turn a profit, hardwood, limestone and ease of access, they moved in and brought a following of workers. Fayette became an iron ore boomtown through the 1880s. However, the hardwood needed to make the charcoal for the smelters ran out and in September 1889 so did the Jackson Iron Company. Fayette reverted to its former ghost-town like atmosphere. With the peninsula stripped of timber nothing was left for the remaining residents except farming and fishing. Those who remained in the area were, as the Thill family, isolated and resigned to only seeing family members for the greater part of the year.

Virgil, like most of his shipmates, attended a one-room schoolhouse with no electricity or indoor plumbing. Going to school in such conditions was not abnormal for Virgil; his home also lacked any modern conveniences. The farm would in fact be absent of a phone long after he had left there for good.

His home was an old two-story farm house. The windows and planks never sealed well enough to keep out the winter winds. The kids slept together to stay warm during those cold months. When they awoke it was typical to find the floor and their blankets covered with a layer of snow.[12]

He and his brother Lyle attended school together at Mud Lake School in Fayette. The teacher was Miss Leda Gierke, who taught grades one through eight. Virgil enjoyed school. It provided the social contact and friendships he was denied on the remote farm. His attendance record reflected school was a welcome distraction, showing him in perfect attendance 1933–36 and again in 1938. Each year the school put on Christmas programs at the Fairbanks

Town Hall. Virgil sang with the student body and occasionally, such as in 1933, at age six, sang solo. The local newspaper, *Escanaba Daily Press*, listed his song that year as "I'm Very Glad." He excelled in the school spelling bees and often won competitions. He made the Honor Roll in first and third grades. The subject he favored least was math. However, every minute at school was a minute away from the farm no matter how bad it got.

The school sat on a hill which in winter was always covered with a blanket of snow. When recess or lunch break sounded, the boys rushed to the crest of the hill to race down it on their sleds. One winter day, Virgil mounted his sled and roared down the hill. He somehow failed to spot a stick protruding from the snow. His sled hit it at full speed, driving the top of the stick into his mouth. The accident knocked out all of his front teeth. The teacher, being the only one available to attend to all the children, would not leave to take him home. Virgil sat in the classroom, enduring the pain, until class was dismissed. Virgil made it through the eighth grade and then dropped out of school.

The closest movie theater to Virgil's home was in town nine miles away. The first movie he recalled ever seeing was *Snow White and the Seven Dwarfs*. The kids were loaded onto the school bus and taken into town to watch it. Another time he got to go see the *Black Stallion*. Once, the community set up a big tent and brought in a projector. Everyone gathered to watch a movie about gangsters—it did not impress Virgil and he never remembered who the featured criminal was. Other than those few outside entertainments, life on the Upper Peninsula was hunting, fishing and swimming.

Farm life never suited Virgil regardless of his age. He did not enjoy the seven days a week, never being able to leave the farm for anything, lifestyle. The days started too early and ended too late to please him. He was not lazy by any means, it was just the farming. At fourteen he ran away from home, lied about his age and joined the Civilian Conservation Corps. That too was short-lived. The camp, in the Upper Peninsula, had no electricity and the stoves burned hardwoods. The *buzzing crew* that Virgil worked on supplied the wood. They were rousted from bed at five in the morning. They then went out to cut trees with their bow saws and returned for breakfast around six-thirty or seven. Then they returned to cut wood until dinner. He soon left camp, finding the chore of cutting wood for the fires as much drudgery as farming.

He managed to get back to the farm but left there to live with his Uncle Fred Lang, his mother's brother. He and Fred always got along well. Fred taught him how to play poker and the two played enough that Virgil never seemed to earn a paycheck he did not lose. In spite of always losing to Fred, he enjoyed his time working for him. After that, he worked some as a logger, cutting timber and as a commercial fisherman and then off-and-on as a carpenter. The thing he was always chained to though was the farm.

There was one more thing that he was chained to and it was ruining his life; Virgil was already having problems with alcohol. The family routinely made homebrew and Virgil had ready access to it at an early age. He took liberal advantage. Everyone had a job in the process; he was the bottle-capper in the brewing scheme. On rainy days, when farm work could not go on, the family outings entailed going to a bar. Virgil shimmied up on the stool and was served a drink like everyone else. His parents paid for his drinks. He recalled being drunk at age nine or ten. Even during Prohibition, the family would go to "blind pigs."[13] One of their favorites was a blind pig that belonged to an elderly widow woman. It was set up in her home and she served beer, wine and liquor; it was cheap. His drinking landed him in jail on several occasions during his early teenage years. He was often away from home on a bender for days at a time, which did not mix well with the demanding farm schedule. His father was a "pusher" as well and never allowed him and his brothers a moment's rest, unless the family drinking assemblages were taken into account.[14]

By the time he turned seventeen his mother had had enough. She told Virgil that he would have to go into the service. Because of his drinking problem, it was the only answer she had. It seemed a bit hypocritical to Virgil. She had never denied herself poor judgment and she had never denied Virgil access to the demon she scorned him for accepting. However, when Virgil voiced his wish to join the Marines, his mother vehemently objected. She instead picked the Navy as a mandatory sentence to ostracize him. In keeping with her demands, Virgil enlisted in the Navy on 26 April 1944.

Lyle, Virgil's older half-brother, joined the Navy, also at their parents' profound suggestion. He joined on 12 August 1942. Lyle served aboard the patrol boat *PC-1079* on antisubmarine duty along the northwest coast of the United States during the ship's first year after commissioning. His ship, like *LCS 52*, was also manufactured by Albina Engine and Machine Works. Lyle's ship participated in the invasion of Saipan and security around the Marianas. She roamed the Pacific during the war acting as a submarine screen for allied shipping. *PC-1079* remained in the waters off Korea and China after peace was declared and assisted with occupation duties in those areas.[15] While both brothers served aboard ships in the Pacific and despite being in close proximity to one another, they never met while in the Navy. Their older brother was deemed necessary to the running of the farm and exempted from military service by their parents.

Before Virgil left for service he joined a group going hunting on Big Summer Island, part of Delta County, on Lake Michigan. Big Summer was an uninhabited island covered in hardwoods and a dense layer of cedar. Boat was the easiest way to access it. Virgil was dropped off along an expanse of gravel beach on Wednesday, 17 November 1943. He killed a deer that morning with his small caliber rifle and decided to return to where the boat had left him. Realizing that he was disoriented, he began to walk one direction up the beach, stop and then go back the other direction, hoping to see a familiar marker. He repeated this cycle until he was exhausted, going a bit further on each attempt. At one point he slipped off a small cliff and landed in the lake up to his waist. As daylight faded away he settled down in his soaked clothes for a cold night.[16] According to the Friday edition of the *Daily Telegram* from Adrian, Michigan, Virgil was found by a search party the following evening. It was Virgil's first time hunting.

For Virgil, the Navy turned into a compulsory abstention program. When Virgil was on ship and training there was no alcohol to be had. His program started with basic training and seemed to be marching in lockstep with his assignments to the ship. The availability of alcohol actually decreased and so did the number of times he was able to get intoxicated. He became a functioning member of naval society, except when ashore and alcohol was to be found.

Virgil was assigned as one of the maintenance guys aboard the 52 but he soon found he had a knack for steering. What boy his age did not want to drive a ship? He became one of the regular helmsmen and soon felt he could steer better than any of the others.[17] He had an uncanny ability and took pride in being able to maintain a true course right behind the lead ship. Here he was, seventeen years old, steering a U.S. Navy gunship across the Pacific.

Life aboard ship had unveiled another natural ability in Virgil, one the other boys would have given their right arms to have. He was immune to seasickness. There was only one time when he threw up a tiny bit, and that was more commiserating with a fellow shipmate who was puking, than being sick himself. The downside was he was usually the only completely healthy person onboard. That fact made him available for all the work details that nobody else was able to perform. He promised himself that if he decided to stay more than one tour in the navy, he was going to learn how to be seasick next go-around.[18]

Pharmacist Mate John A. Syrian was the closest thing to a doctor aboard *LCS 52*. Syrian was the assigned medical person aboard *52* and had been with her since her shakedown. Whether rolling plaster bandages in preparation for burn victims or injecting a shot of penicillin, being the only medical person on ship was routine and typically unexciting.[19] Regardless of how mundane any job aboard was in peacetime, all training was dedicated to what might happen in battle and Syrian's was no different. Pharmacist Mates attended one of three schools after 1942, once they had completed basic training. The most common school for attendance as a medic was at Great Lakes. Other schools were started in 1943 at Farragut, Idaho, on 4 January and Bainbridge, Maryland, to keep up with wartime demands.

Syrian was raised in Mount Clare in the Grant District of Harrison County, West Virginia. John was first-generation American and one of fourteen children. He was born on 9 November 1914 to Italian-born Sam and Rose Fratto Syrianni. Rose arrived in America in 1910 and Sam in 1904. In those years coal companies recruited Italian laborers and brought them into the Clarksburg, Harrison County, area, many times to take the place of less cooperative union workers. The area where John grew up was populated almost exclusively by Italian immigrants working in the coal mines. Italians were in fact the majority of the twenty nationalities brought from abroad to work.[20]

John's father Salvatore [Sam] worked as a loader in the coal mines for most of his life. By 1908 the Fairmont coal field in Harrison and Marion Counties produced 7,185,036 short tons of coal.[21] Hutchinson Coal Company and another smaller company mined near Mount Clare, Hutchinson Hollow and Florence Hollow respectively. The coal was dug by hand with pick, loaded onto cars and dragged to the railroad in Mount Clare by teams of mules.[22]

During the depression years of the 1930s the miners tended to do better than average economically but were by no means close to middleclass. In 1939 Sam earned $1000 and owned his home valued at $700. Only one of his neighbors earned more as a foreman on a Works Progress Administration (WPA) program. Sam only worked forty weeks that year but just ten years prior he was renting a house at $10 a month.[23] The average loader in the area made around $6.37 a day, which was much better than being on government relief.[24]

His children too were doing well for their age. All of his children of school age went to school and like Sam and Rose, they knew how to read and write except for the oldest. Lizzy was born in Italy and came to America the same year as Rose, six years after Sam arrived.

Sam expected his children to go to work and support the family. All the children typically went to eighth grade and then the boys went to work in the coal mines. Sam was none too pleased when John reported he wished to go through high school.[25] It caused such a rift between him and his father that he moved in with his two older sisters and continued on in high school. He went to Victory High for about a year and then transferred to Roosevelt-Wilson High School. It was there that he discovered his athletic potential. He played baseball, which he was superb at, football and a little basketball. He worked part time at the country club as a caddy to earn money. One day he happened to meet a doctor's wife who made an offer: if he would teach her how to drive, she would teach him to play golf.[26] Golf became a lifelong passion with John. He grew into an exceptional golfer.

John held a position as First Sergeant in the Civilian Conservation Corps (CCC) and earned $540 working in camp in 1939. John's brother Pete, two years younger, earned $396 working in the camp dispensary that same year. The greater percentages of the CCC boy's paychecks were allotted to the families. The closest CCC was Camp Parsons. The camp was established approximately a half-mile outside the city limits of the town of Parsons.

Being one of the junior officers in camp, one of John's tasks was to drop off clothes at the laundry. Nepha Gordon, from nearby Bretz, took in the laundry for the officers. Nepha's son, Blair Gordon, was a truck driver in camp in 1940 also. While turning in the laundry for the officers one day, John happened to notice a young lady helping her mother, Napha.[27] Her name was Kathleen, a Parsons High School student. The two would fall in love and marry while she was still in school.

The Great Depression did have dire effects on the isolated immigrant mining towns. At one time there were thirty mines operating in the general area around Mount Clare, all competing with mines run by those with deep pockets such as Rockefeller. Sam had been around mining long enough to see the tensions and violence ebb and rise between union men and mine companies. Company stores controlled the economies of those towns built and owned by the companies and prices were often bordering on criminal. There was no guarantee that anyone on the labor force of a mine would be so employed the next day or the following year. There was also the physical devastation of working inside or above a mine caused to a body; longevity was something miners never hoped to have. When there was a way out, it was best to take it.

John became the first in his family to complete high school. He graduated from Roosevelt-Wilson. In April of 1942 Pete Syrian took the Army as the way out of the coal mines. John soon followed and enlisted in the Navy Reserve on 12 October. The two brothers, in spite of Pete being a twin, were very close. They had both changed their surname from Srianni to Syrian, the only siblings in the family to do so. The closest newspaper in the area reporting the happenings in Mount Clare was the *Cumberland Evening Times* of Maryland. On 9 October the paper reported

The ship's Pharmacist's Mate, John Syrian, took care of every wound from mosquito bites to shrapnel. He grew up in the coal region of West Virginia and was a member of FDR's Civilian Conservation Corps before joining the Navy. World War II would not be his last war (Virgil Thill collection).

that John Syrian of Parsons would leave Sunday for Charleston where he would be inducted into the Naval Reserves. In May, prior to John leaving, his wife, Kathleen Louise Gordon, raised in nearby Bretz, graduated from Parsons High School. She followed John to Newport News while he was stationed there.

Few of the men aboard had excelled to the heights that Claude H. Cook had before the war, and this despite the adversity he had faced throughout his life. Claude was born to Annie Cook on 14 January 1913 in the small township of Cheboygan, Michigan. The following year Annie suffered a severe infection and died. Soon after her death, Claude's father, Earl, for reasons known only to him, decided he could no longer care for a child. Still with young children of their own at home, Benjamin and Anna, Annie's parents, took Claude into their home in Munising, Michigan. Earl disappeared from the child's life. Anna and Ben raised Claude as their own.

Claude recalled his life as a child in "Ma" and "Pa's" house as happy and carefree. Anna, "Ma," was born in Canada to parents who had emigrated there from the Highlands of Scotland. She often worked as a cook in Michigan logging camps and ran boarding houses. She went where Ben, "Pa," went and she shared in whatever burden or progress. While Anna was a short, five-foot woman, her husband was over six-feet and broad shouldered. Ben had a quick temper but in general liked people. Ben ran logging operations and hunted to supplement provisions. The Upper Peninsula of Michigan was booming with timber and milling operations throughout the first decades of the twentieth century. The last camp that Claude knew Pa worked in was called "Cold Wood" but it had long since turned into a ghost town. Like Claude, Ben knew little about his own mother and father. He had a brother somewhere but they remained estranged his whole life. He met Anna in Canada and the two married in 1883 in Nottawasaga, Canada. They moved to Witmore, Michigan after their daughter, Mary A. Cook, was born in 1891. Anna's mom, who only spoke Gaelic, immigrated with them. She passed away while they still lived in Witmore and was buried there. Ben found work as a stone mason after they moved to Munising.

The memories that Claude took with him to the navy were of Pa's Sunday ritual of stretching out under a large mountain ash in the front yard of their home at the bottom of Ski Hill.[28] The house had a wide verandah running around the front and one side, and from it Claude could look down at Munising Bay of Lake Superior. The town of Munising sat on the southern end of the bay. Since 1908 the lighthouse on Hemlock Street in Munising guided ships on Lake Superior with its steady beacon. Next to the Munising Cafe on Superior Street, a boy could have a soda and enjoy some candy after leaving the Delft Theater next door. Claude was like every other boy of the day and especially enjoyed the cowboy stars, Tom Mix, Harry Carey, and Hoot Gibson.[29] A boy his age could while away an hour in the old west and if lucky have some ice cream while there.

Lured by the urgings of their oldest son, Charles, Ben and Anna moved back to Canada. The post-war demand for wheat caused a boom and Charles had left the States to take advantage of it. He was working with Anna's brothers and they too were praising the profits to be made. It was enough to draw the rest of the family north. The family left Michigan by train in 1921 bound for Saskatchewan.

Claude, as was his nature, loved the flat lay of the land when it was covered in crops. It seemed the whole family was back together. Ben worked his brother-in-law's farm and Charles lived about a mile down the road. Claude had a trusty pony named Barney and a faithful dog named Dick. His uncles were for all intents and purposes his brothers. It was good to be back with them and have them to talk with.

Claude loved harvest time too. Farmers and workers came from miles around to help harvest the wheat. The women gathered and fixed feasts to fill the bellies of the hungry labor force. Claude and the other boys got to ride to the granaries on the wagons filled to the brim with wheat. In spite of the bitter winters and frequent blizzards during, Claude loved his life in Canada. There was, however, trouble in the making for the adults and by default the kids. Charles was the first to give up and go back to Munising and Ben was soon obligated by financial necessity to follow—the wheat boom had died out.

The attempt at prosperity had failed. The effort had also taken its toll on Pa physically. He purchased some property and began construction of their new home. The house was only partially finished but the family moved in anyway. Life was still pleasant for Claude for the time being, though Ben had to sell Barney and Dick had to remain in Canada with Uncle Jack.

The family relied on their own ingenuity to make their life tolerable. Pa hunted and stored venison. Fish were stored in brine and berries picked in summer were turned into jams. Claude went with Ma to the railroad station in autumn, where they bought bushel baskets of fruit from vendors who marketed goods as soon as they came off the train. The fruit was then prepared, canned and stored for the next winter. Summers spent storing away food meant not going hungry in winter. Pa seldom had masonry work during winter and in turn no money to buy groceries. Groceries came from the stocks of canned goods, whatever there was.

One day Claude saw Pa coming down the road to the house. Something was obviously wrong. His gait was off and he was staggering as he fought each step. Claude helped him to the house and into the bed. For the next two years, Ben remained bedridden, unable to work.

In spite of the thriftiness of Anna and the family, the venture in Canada had caused financial difficulties. The family had run up an unmanageable debt at the local grocery, Walter's Grocery Store. Claude did his share by taking two routes delivering the *Munising Journal* to half of the town. When school was out during the summer, at fourteen years old, Claude lied about his age and began working on the pulpwood and coal boats to make more money. He worked the timber stacked in the hold and on the deck of the freighters. He often had nightmares, "dreaming of hauling and tugging at the logs with [his] picaroon and peavey, getting up as tired as when [he] went to bed."[30] Claude still went to school when it was in session. The first year that he worked he returned to school with only two weeks left in the first semester. He was determined not to fail, though. He made up all of his school work and passed all of his courses, except gym. The course load included Latin, which caused some initial doubt from his teacher that he could have passed without cheating. Claude straightened the matter out to the teacher's chagrin. Being large enough to fake seventeen in order to work the boats also made him a potential candidate for sports. He played guard on the junior varsity basketball team and organized softball for many years, even after high school.

Benjamin never recovered from the stroke he had suffered. Benjamin F. Cook, Pa, died on 27 May 1928 and was buried in the Maple Grove Cemetery in Munising. Without a life insurance policy, the family went into further debt to pay for his funeral.

Claude finished his sophomore year in 1929. The Great Depression was only in its beginning stages. There were only Claude and Ma left at home now. He made up his mind then that she would not do without in her later years.³¹ The first thing be wanted for her was to have a nice home. The only way he could earn more money was to work more and that meant he would have to leave school.

Claude was hired on at the paper mill, at sixteen years old. He did not know it at the time but he would spend the entire Depression decade working at that mill. During the Depression, there were times when he only got one day of work a week. In spite of being a young boy in an adult workforce in the middle of the worst depression in world history, Claude paid off the debts, including the grocer and the funeral home. With the assistance of Ben Jr., Claude put in a basement and fixed the house. When done, Ma had a new kitchen, basement, living room and two bedrooms. It was the home Ma deserved and he was delighted to give it to her.

Things seemed then as if life had turned around and Claude was finally going to be set for good. However, Ma was old and simply worn out. She, like Pa, became bedridden. In order to keep working, Claude had to hire a nurse to stay with Anna. Anna was so frail that Claude had to carry her from her bed to the table. Then something he could not have foreseen happened. Between caring for Anna at night and working all day he was also exhausted. One morning he came home from work and collapsed. The doctor called it nervous exhaustion.³² For two weeks Claude could not leave the house to work. It was the setback he could have never anticipated.

One day in 1937, Ma finished her lunch. Claude picked her up and started to take her back to her bed. Ma never made it to her bedroom; she died in Claude's arms as he carried her. She was buried next to Pa, in the Munising cemetery. Everyone else in the family was married and off on their own. Claude was once more alone.

Claude stayed on the job at the paper mill. The German-American foreman still called him "keed" in his thick accent, what he had called him when he had first begun there years before. One day out of the blue, Fred, the foreman, sauntered over to where keed was working. Why don't you apply to be a State Trooper? He asked Claude. Claude did not think he was right for the job but it left him thinking about the possibility. He thought about it so much that he finally sent for an application.³³

Claude showed up for his initial interview for trooper in his work clothes from the mill. He had left there after working from midnight right up until it was time for the interview. He made an impression but it was not the one he wanted to make. The corporal conducting the interview recorded his opinion, "a slow thinking, honest, small town boy, of average intelligence."³⁴ The corporal had no way of knowing from Claude's over-taxed state that this was a guy who had learned a semester of Latin in two weeks. The second interview went much better. The same corporal did not recognize the clean-shaven, well-dressed and rested Claude Cook in the hallway. Claude reported to recruit training in Lansing for initial preparation to become a Michigan State Policeman on 18 September 1939. The class began with seventy-two recruits but that number would dwindle considerably before graduation. Some of the men were physically unable to keep up, others simply not willing to accept the arduous curriculum. Except for time off to attend church services on Sunday, training began at 06:00 and ended late at night, seven days a week. On 7 November 1939 thirty-three fresh troopers graduated from the academy, including, of course, Claude Cook, who proudly pinned on badge number 209.

He was assigned to West Branch, Michigan, a small town in the Lower Peninsula. Claude pulled up to the post building in his faded 1934 maroon Chevrolet and reported for duty. He spent his six-month probation period at West Branch and was then transferred to Detroit. The buildup for war brought a population of factory workers to the area. With them came every type of illegal activity known to law enforcement. Claude investigated burglaries, prostitution, illegal gambling and murders. There was nothing ordinary or mundane about any of Claude's time in Detroit. What made his first real post special was law enforcement itself. He quickly understood what it was to be part of a different kind of family than that which he had loved and lost. Police work was Esprit de Corps and knowing that a brother officer protected you even at the risk of losing his own life produced a special kind of brotherly love.[35] Police work was long with tough days that took a toll on the mind as well as the body. It was also the most rewarding job anyone could have. Stopping crime and being able to save the lives of those unable to save themselves was a paycheck all in itself. The hours were long and the pay poor, but Claude had found a career he loved.

He worked in Detroit until 15 July 1942 when he was transferred to a newly established post in Center Line. The post there was housed in a former bank. It was there that he happened to take notice of a court reporter by the name of Caroline Artman. The two became steady friends, and it was evident by 1944 they were deeply in love.[36]

Claude had spent his life helping other people. He had sacrificed his education, his own ambitions and sometimes his health to put the well-being of others first. As a trooper he had placed himself between evil and those they attempted to commit violence against. It was a self-imposed obligation to protect and serve all Americans. It was that obligation to protecting the greater society that caused him to take administrative leave from the MSP and enlist in the military. On 26 April 1944, Claude said goodbye to the life he loved most and joined the U.S. Navy. A new chapter in his life had begun and, like his shipmates, it would change him forever.

Everyone aboard the 52 had differing reasons behind their enlistments in the Navy. They had all endured the hardscrabble existence forced upon them and their families by the Great Depression. The country had just begun to recover and folks were back to work building material to support the Brits and Russians' war needs, when the economy turned downward again due to the Japanese attacks. Rationing took over denying the common necessities of life where the depression had left off. Then there was the obligation that young men and women of all nationalities, races, religions and colors felt they owed to America. The country had been hurt and its soldiers and sailors killed or imprisoned. People, especially young men who knew of their father's and grandfather's sacrifice for their country in previous wars, could not cower from their own time and duty. Each and every man also had personal reasons to go to war. Some ran from trouble, others from boredom and still others from a dead-end future in with they saw no chance of improving their lot in life. They went regardless of the danger and the knowledge that some would not return.

3

Practicing the Trade

There was seldom rhyme or rhythm as to the why the Navy did things the way they did. San Pedro, California was designated as home port for *LCS 52*, though after this stop she would have rare occasion to visit there. The Navy's battle fleet was stationed there until 1940, after which it was moved to the Hawaiian Islands as a deterrent to Japan's continued advance across Manchuria. There were still schools for small craft, firefighters, merchant marines, and so on functioning there but it was far from a going concern in 1944. San Pedro was in reality a tiny port city which had been swallowed up by Los Angeles as early as 1909. It was perhaps out of habit and nostalgia that people still called the port by its former independent name. After a very short stop there, *LCS 52* pushed off down the coast for San Diego.

The men who were supposed to make sense out of the Navy inconsistencies, and then translate something half intelligible to the enlisted men, were the officers aboard ship. Aside from Harper, the ship left Portland with the crew of five officers. The executive officer and man who typically took charge in the absence of the captain was Ensign Jerry Paul Duvendeck.

Jerry was born 11 December 1921 to Ray Howard and Marguriete Duvendeck in Michigan. Jerry's grandfather, William Duvendeck, came to Ohio from Germany and married a local girl Emma. There in Ohio, Ray was born. Jerry was the Duvendecks' first child, born about a year after they married when his parents were living in Michigan.

During the beginning of, and throughout the worst years of, the Depression, Ray was employed at the Portsmouth Savings and Loan in Ohio. He continued to hold jobs at various savings and loan companies and worked his way to secretary and treasurer. By the time he was forced to register for the World War II draft, he was working at the Royal Savings and Loan Company on Gallia Street in Portsmouth, Ohio.[1]

Portsmouth sat in the confluence of the Ohio, Scioto, and Little Scioto Rivers. The town, as would be assumed, was prone to flooding. Jerry lived through a particularly noteworthy flood in the year 1937. City officials, fearing the flood walls would be breeched after the river valley experienced up to twelve inches of rain in January, decided to deliberately release water into the business district. In the end, little stopped the water from pouring over the ten-foot flood walls. The water covered the streets and homes of the more than 42,500 citizens. Men in small boats could stand up and easily touch the traffic lights hanging in the center of Portsmouth streets. Townspeople tied their boats off to their front porch roofs and gingerly stepped into second story windows to their temporary living quarters. At the theater, water obscured the letters on the marquee of Sonja Henie's name, her debut film *One in a Million*.

Floods or not, the Duvendeck family thrived in Portsmouth. No one was more up-and-coming among the family than Jerry Paul. He made his first appearance in the *Portsmouth Daily Times* in 1928 when he made the spelling honor roll. The following year the eight-year-old made the school's math honor roll. As he grew to adolescence, he was a frequent attendee at the Portsmouth Country Club dances, or one of the specialty dancers in the school's production of Charles Ross Chaney's "Belle from Barcelona." He did the ads for the Portsmouth High School yearbook *The Trojan* and helped with devotions at church. He was a town socialite at an early age. Jerry was attracted to the curiosities which lay outside the city limits as well. He joined Boy Scout Troop 26, run by Mr. J. W. Montgomery, as soon as old enough. Jerry attended every camp and outing possible. He earned merit badges at a remarkable rate. At age fifteen he earned his Eagle Scout, the zenith of scouting. Jerry's father also played a part in the troop, often sitting on the court of honor for the potential badge earners. Jerry's love of the outdoors would remain with him throughout his life.

Jerry and his sister were accustomed to trips back and forth to Michigan. Aside from their mother's family there, the older Duvendecks retained many friends. Their ties certainly must have played a part in Jerry choosing Alma College in Alma, Michigan after high school. Alma was founded as a private Presbyterian college which focused on degrees in liberal arts. At college he quickly picked up his normally energetic pace. He was on the debate squad and joined the Kiltie band. Jerry was also accepted in Delta Gamma Tau and lettered in track as a freshman. A corps of waiters served students and faculty in the dining hall at Alma; by the 1938 school year Jerry had worked his way to assistant head waiter. He was also the first Alma student to be accepted to the V-7 program.[2] Regardless of the area of interest or requisite, Jerry Paul found his way to the top of that particular arena.

Jerry graduated in 1943 from Alma College. He married another Alma student before leaving Portland. Isabelle Frances Purdy was a bright and beautiful young lady from the city of Alma. She was seen in the Alma *Scotsman* yearbook in such settings as one of the court of the homecoming queen. The two were married, with many of the officers from the ship in attendance, in the First Presbyterian Church in Portland. When *LCS 52* left for overseas, Isabelle remained at their quaint bungalow on Irvington Street in Detroit.

Jerry made the trip to Portland with the rest of the crew. He stood the many tedious Officer of the Day watches while the ship was fitted and shared the same rumbling seas to San Diego. The captain and the crew expected much of the officers. They stood seemingly endless daily watches and yet were expected to be alert at all times. Most important, they were expected to look out for those under them, even when it meant putting themselves in harm's way.

Friday, 6 October 1944—Ensign Clifford L. Stewart, twenty minutes after his watch began, noted the Ano Nuevo lighthouse "abeam to port" at a distance of two and a half miles. The lighthouse was nineteen miles north of the city of Santa Cruz. The island upon which the lighthouse rested was inhabited by four Coast Guardsmen, sometimes their families, and always an obnoxious number of noisy seals.[3]

The lighthouse was barely out of sight before the pilot vessel, the T-8031, experienced engine trouble and went dead in the water. The convoy came to a halt. Clifford made the log reflect the vessel went dead at 16:35 hours. At 16:37 he took the 52 out of formation and stopped her engines to await repairs on the pilot vessel. He reformed at 17:15 and they continued down the California coast. With a little less than an hour left on his watch, he spotted

Point Pinos lighthouse. The lighthouse was forty-six miles south of Santa Cruz hugging the crescent-shaped coastline. Clifford had no intention of sightseeing and maintained a true course toward San Diego. At 19:45 Clifford turned the conn over to Ensign Burroughs.

Clifford Stewart and Albert Parker were the two single officers aboard the 52 on her commissioning. Stewart was born 30 June 1916 in Clarence, Missouri, to Lola M. and Jeptha Lee Stewart. The family lived in the Warren Township of Marion County through the 1900-teens and in Yellow Creek Township through the 20s and 30s. His father worked as a telephone and telegraph operator for the Chicago Burlington & Quincy Railroad. Jeptha suffered with lung problems from an injury which kept him out of World War I. He died in 1940.[4]

That year Clifford was working in Butte County, California, for the Civilian Conservation Corps. He pulled duties as a forest fire lookout and as a bus driver. Clifford enjoyed the act of learning; he attended San Jose State and Chico State while he was living in Northern California. He recalled, even as a boy, Saturday was the day he took the horse and buggy, rode into town and exchanged that week's books for six more unread ones at the local library.[5] In 1937 Clifford tried his hand at being an apprentice seaman and the seafarer's life had its perks. That would be the spark which lit the flame on a long career.

The decision to take up that life came quickly and easily on that "day of infamy" at Pearl Harbor. By January 1942 Clifford was signed up for the Navy and off to San Diego for bootcamp. With his basic successfully completed, he was sent to communications school. He graduated and the Navy found a use for Clifford at the Brooklyn Navy Yard, New York, working in the communications pool. That job only lasted until mid-1942.

Around July 1 a detachment of soldiers and sailors reported to the harbor to board one of the nine ships anchored there. Clifford was among that group. Clifford was assigned to the *MS Tarn*. It would turn out to be a strange marriage. The *Tarn* was a Norwegian merchant ship built nine-years prior. The crew was all Norwegian sailors, who at best spoke little English. That included the freshly trained radioman, Christian S. Christensen. The ship had limited space for human cargo and aside from the regular crew there were quarters for twelve passengers. Clifford shared that space with a detail of soldiers, all sent to instruct the British 8th Army in the use of the weapons and equipment in the ship's hold.

In command of the dozen Americans was an Army captain by the name of James G. Paterson. The equipment carried on the *Tarn* amounted to more than 300 M4 Sherman tanks and 100, 105mm howitzers.[6] Codenamed Convoy AS.4 departed New York harbor on 13 July. Headed for Recife, Brazil the convoy seemed to be proceeding in relative safety. Five destroyers accompanied the transports, the USS *Kearny*, USS *Livermore*, USS *Mayo*, USS *Gleaves*, and USS *Wilkes*. Muscoe Holland had transferred from the *Kearny* less than three months prior to her mission to guard Convoy AS.4.

Early morning on the 16th, the soldiers on *Tarn* were out on the top deck using what open space they could find to finish up a session of calisthenics. Churning along behind the *Tarn* was SS *Fairport*, second ship in the port column, and SS *Exhibitor*.[7] The master of the *Fairport* was Captain George Starling Hancock; it was the *Fairport*'s maiden voyage. At 08:43 Albrecht Achilles, captain of the German U-boat *U-161*, launched two torpedoes at *Fairport*. Both torpedoes struck the *Fairport* but it was the second which hit in the number-one tank that caused her to list to starboard and ultimately sink. The destroyers immediately began to circle the area where they believed the U-boat might be. They rained depth charges down on the unseen sub, but *U-161* was long gone, having left after hearing a second explosion.

The USS *Kearny* returned to the vacant site of the *Fairport* and pulled the lifeboats from the sea, miraculously containing all one-hundred-twenty-three of the crew and passengers alive. She broke from the convoy and took the *Fairport* survivors back to New York. The rest of the transports went full speed to their first port of safety in Brazil.

The *Tarn* made Cape Town, South Africa, on 5 August. Convoy AS.4 was joined that day by a larger convoy, WS 21P, carrying 100,000 British troops to replace and strengthen the 8th Army. The Americans were allowed a couple of twelve-hour liberty parties. The British boys remained cooped up on their ships. The South Africans were hospitable and very kind to the Americans.[8]

The convoy remained at Cape Town for three days and then moved on to Aden, a seaport city of Yemen. They departed Aden on 29 August. Before entering the Red Sea, each ship deployed a barrage balloon both fore and aft. Barrage balloons were tethered to the ship by heavy metal cables. In theory, their purpose was to deny attacking planes low-altitude approach. The antiaircraft balloons were used with success in World War I and carried-over to the Second World War. The balloons were also used extensively to supplement insufficient ground based anti-aircraft weaponry throughout North Africa.[9]

The convoy arrived in the Suez area the same day. The convoy anchored at Port Tewfik, Egypt, at the mouth of the Suez Canal. Tewfik was the drop-off port for all the equipment the convoy had brought across the Atlantic. The *SS Seatrain Texas*, the replacement ship for the sunken *Fairport*, arrived from the States shortly after the main convoy began to offload. She brought with her replacement Sherman tanks lost with the *Fairport*. The *Seatrain Texas* was commanded by Captain Kenneth G. Towne and made the eighteen-day trip across the Atlantic alone and loaded with 250–300 newly-designed M-4 Sherman tanks.

The British situation when the convoy arrived at the end of August was stable but precarious. During the Battle of El Alamein (later known as the 1st Battle), July 1942, the combined forces of the British Empire halted *Generalfeldmarschall* Erwin Rommel's *Panzerarmee Afrika* approximately sixty-six miles north of Alexandria. Rommel understood that the British could not allow him to stay in such close proximity to the Canal and major ports. Rather than throw his troops against a strong defense, Rommel's forces dug in and waited for the Brits to attack them.

With Lieutenant-General Bernard Montgomery as their new commander, the attack on Rommel's lines began on 23 October. With the help of tons of American ammunition, equipment and a little instruction, British tenacity prevailed. The second Battle of El Alamein was a turning point in the war. It ended the threat to Egypt, kept the Suez Canal open and allowed much needed oil to flow through to prosecute the war in Europe.

The *Tarn* performed some further duties which took them up and down the coast of Africa through 16 October. They departed Cape Town and arrived in Philadelphia on 6 November. They sailed back to New York on 15 November. Compared to Clifford's next adventure, Egypt was like a day in Central Park.

Clifford spent his holidays in the States. Just after New Year's he received orders to report to the USS *City of Omaha*, before midnight on 3 January 1943. The ship was scheduled to sail the following morning.[10] A steam powered transport ship built in 1920, *City of Omaha* could haul 6124 tons of cargo. She joined five more ships leaving New York and ultimately bound for Molotovsk, Russia. The "Murmansk Run" made by more than a dozen convoys during the war would later be described by Winston Churchill as "the worst journey in the world."

The *City of Omaha* had made the Murmansk Run before. On this occasion, heavy headwinds and rough seas slowed the convoy to a crawl. The group arrived at the Firth of Clyde on 28 January only to find that they had missed their rendezvous with the rest of the original convoy headed to Murmansk. The six ships were joined by eighteen more on the 13 February and all headed for Loch Ewe, Scotland.[11]

The convoy now known as JW-53 arrived Loch Ewe on 15 February. Also gathered were some thirty Allied destroyers and other armed ships making up the convoy's "Armed Guard" escort. In the total were eight U.S. transports, *City of Omaha, Artigas, Beaconhill, Israel Putnam, Francis Scott Key, Mobile City and Thomas Hartley*. From the start, the weather was treacherous. The waves were at times exceeding thirty feet. Nearby ships were unable to signal one another with lights, routinely only capable of seeing more than the top of a mast behind a wave. Clifford, assigned as a signalman, had little to no success communicating with other ships in the convoy.

If the weather cleared, the German planes came. The convoy was first spotted by an enemy plane on the 23rd. More planes returned the following day and dropped bombs with little effect. The next day, the 25th, brought the most determined attack by a sortie of a dozen planes. No damage to ships was reported but the *Bering* sustained a too close for comfort miss. They retaliated by shooting down the attacker.

The convoy separated into two groups on 26 February with one sailing for Molotovsk, the other anchoring at the Kola Inlet the following day. German planes continued to make high altitude bombing runs at the moving ships. There were near misses, but the fact was, dropping bombs from those heights relied on sheer luck not accuracy. On 2 March the *Beacon Hill*, the *Bearing*, the *City of Omaha*, and the *Israel Putnam*, arrived at Molotovsk.

The bombing raids became more determined and accurate once the ships docked. Daily raids went on if weather permitted through May. The eight U.S. ships that were anchored at Molotovsk endured the attacks while they awaited orders for a return convoy to form. However, the armed escorts had left to fight bigger sea battles going on in the Atlantic.

The months became one long day, filled with boredom and perpetual sunlight. At times the temperature dropped to eight below. In town the people were poor, poorer than what most Americans had experienced during the Great Depression. The eight ships stranded at Molotovsk were already being called the "forgotten convoy."[12]

The boys began to adapt to their confinement. They learned of a dance which was held twice a week in town. The Russian Intourist agency provided an interpreter who negotiated dances, dates and entertainment.[13] Little did they know at the time, they would be there so long, his services would become obsolete. The sailors formed small groups and hitchhiked their way through sightseeing expeditions; some ventured as far as 200 miles from port. Ship's crews produced theatrical productions when they could not attend the occasional movies in town. The Russians helped as much as they could with rations of vodka.

Clifford and the boys from *City of Omaha* had an idea as pure as mom's apple pie. They took work gloves and gloves used on the barrels of 20mm guns and designated them baseball gloves. A sailor who mended uniforms stitched leather boot heels over a rubber core wrapped in string to make a pretty fair replica of a baseball. The machinists used the lathe to turn tree branches into bats. Even the Russians, perhaps out of nothing more than curiosity, helped to level a baseball diamond. The finishing touch was using gunny sacks for bases. Each ship formed a team and from that a league developed.[14]

In spite of ingenious methods devised to cut the boredom, after months of dipping into food supplies that were meant to last weeks, things began to get sparse. When those were used up they had to depend on the Russians for food. That was a problem; one only had to look at the starving stick-figure prisoners offloading the ships to know the people had no food to spare. Nonetheless, somewhere they came up with meager amounts of rice, beans, tea, fish, and cheese for the Americans and Brits.

In October, a ship carrying mail for Clifford and the men of the forgotten convoy arrived. It was the first communication with the outside world they had had since they were left behind. Clifford received a letter from Columbia University.[15] To his surprise, it was his acceptance for the officer training program held on the campus of Columbia. It was wonderful news which would have made him ecstatic had it not been for one small detail. His reporting date was 30 May 1943. Had he not been marooned at the top of the world his life would have been quite different.

Around 3 November the forgotten ships finally picked up an escort. They fought their way back to Gourock, Scotland, arriving on 8 November. The worst damage to any of the ships on the return was caused when the *Mobile City* and *Francis Scott Key* collided. The forgotten ships returned to New York in the early part of December, just in time for Christmas. Clifford later pulled one more relatively uneventful trip to North Africa. After that, he headed off to Norte Dame for a second chance to attend the officers' training course. He brought a lot of memories back from his time in Russia, and a White Sea League baseball and bat. The bat bore the autographs of his teammates from *City of Omaha*.

Clifford graduated from the Midshipman's School in May 1944. His first ship as an officer was *LCS 52*. He was assigned, as would be expected, as the Communications Officer. He would be the only officer aboard who would walk on deck with two years of combat experience.

Saturday, 7 October 1944—Ensign Stewart began his OOD watch at 08:00. At 08:38 he looked out to port and then noted in the log, Point Pedernales, just north of Santa Barbara, at "094° T." At 09:41, Clifford recorded in the log, Point Conception, less than forty-miles south of his last mark, "bearing 092° T." At 11:45 hours, Ensign Clifford Stewart was properly relieved from duty by Ensign Burroughs. To some, the monotony of life at sea might have seemed unappealing. Clifford knew it to be something quite different, something he loved. Six decades after the war ended, he would still say, "I never had a bad day in the Navy."[16]

Coronado went by on the starboard side as the ship headed into dock in San Diego. They were met by their mail and all were thrilled that it had caught them before they moved on to Hawaii. With the happiness of news from home also came the bad from overseas. That evening Claude Cook sat down to write Lynn Artman. He had received more bad news from home and he needed an understanding ear, even if it were two-thousand miles away. His cousin Bud had been killed while fighting in Europe. Buddy was special to Claude. They had grown up within a block of each other. They had played soldier, Claude recalled, and he confided to Lynn he had carried a gut feeling that Buddy would never make it home. He let his anger and hurt flow onto the paper and vowed that they would pay for Buddy's death. "I'll never be satisfied now until I get over there and get back at them," he told Lynn.[17] He found some solace in reading Lynn's five letters he had received, with the bad news from home, over and over.

The men were anxious to find some time off but before that would happen they had some special work to do explicit to them and their ship. They spent the next few days learning how to deploy and extract marine frogmen. The frogmen were specially trained to swim undetected to shore and perform reconnaissance to locate obstacles such as mines hindering beach landings. Those same frogmen also mapped out locations of coral reefs, sand bars and other natural obstacles. Without them, landings could easily turn into disasters. The 52 had to perfect her skills at sneaking in and dropping the frogmen off and had to be in the right spot to retrieve them with their priceless information.

Around 10 October the crew got the days off they had hoped for. San Diego was a navy town and she had all the trappings to entice young sailors on liberty. Like most cities, San Diego felt the squeeze of gas rationing and shortages brought on by the war. Public transportation replaced private vehicles. Complementing their security badges from their defense industry jobs, women sporting victory rolls, curled bangs, pageboys and other hairstyles crowded the streetcars and buses twenty-four hours a day. Along with the seemingly exclusive population of Rosie the riveters were lines of sailors and marines waiting for tables at restaurants, on street corners, bar stools, or public benches. Everywhere one looked the familiar white Dixie cup caps the men of *LCS 52* were themselves wearing bobbed and comingled in the nondescript crowd. There was no escaping the sea of sailors; lines even formed for a twenty-cent street-corner shoeshine. It was hard for the eyes to find a wall or window that was not still draped and plastered with the wartime warnings, "Loose Lips Might Sink Ships" or the image of the victorious sailor explaining he "Couldn't have done it without you!"

While in San Diego, Laton Burns purchased and mailed a "sweetheart pillowcase cover," Navy theme of course, to his own hometown sweetheart, Kathleen. Kathleen and Laton married shortly after his return home from service, but he had no guarantee of that when he bought the pillowcase. These trinkets were also known as mother's pillowcases. The sweetheart pillows and cases became popular during World War I and carried on their novelty through the Second World War. The cases were typically about twelve inches square, made of silk and often had some type of fringes all around the edge. If the cases did not display a romantic poem for the wife or girl they had an equally sappy poem for mom. The other theme was gung-ho for the military branch of service or the location premise, such as "Hawaii" or "San Diego." Most families ended up with a pillowcase stored away in a chest somewhere after the war. They were the refrigerator magnets of the 1940s.

While on liberty, a group from 52 could not help but to venture across the border. It was an exciting international expedition for boys like Thill and Burns who had barely been outside their home states before joining the Navy. Virgil Thill and William Eldon Gardner posed for pictures behind the bars of a fake "Tijuana jail" cell. There were plenty of bars serving copious amounts of cerveza to put them behind the real jail doors. Laton went just for the novelty of saying he had been to Mexico. He figured he would have enjoyed it more had he been able to speak the language.[18]

The training in San Diego was more gunnery practice and chemical warfare drills. Laton dreaded the idea of a gas attack. It was hard for him to understand how people could use such a terrible weapon. He was getting more proficient with the guns, though. He seldom missed his target.

The second day of October, Laton was on duty in the pilot house of the ship. He took time out to write Kathleen. It was 24:20 in San Diego. He explained that was military time for 12:20 a.m. Every hour on the hour he was required to check the temperature, record how high the clouds were and which direction the wind was coming from. Their time in California was drawing short, he mentioned. He liked Oregon better than California but no state suited him more than Kentucky, he told Kathleen. He hoped he never had to pass through Florida ever again.

Whether to impress her or simply to muster his own courage Laton began to include in his letters to Kathleen boisterous bravado. "I will come back with a string of stars or there will be a star up in the window one." He added in an earlier letter…"boy! Will I be glad when we go over[.] [Really] I'm wanting a crack at the Japs."[19] It was the boyish idea of glory an eighteen-year-old who had never seen combat believed and spouted. On the other hand, his letters were going to Kathleen at Melrose Hall, the women's dorm on Oneida Baptist Institute, where he confided that he would rather be that year.

As soon as he could get to one, Harper went straight to the nearest phone and called home. It was 2 a.m. back in Ohio. When his sister-in-law told him that Marge had left for the hospital a few hours before he became a bit alarmed. That meant that their first child was well on the way to being born. Their daughter Carol was in fact on her way at that moment and by the time he made a couple more calls he learned of her arrival. He was relieved to be told that both mother and daughter were doing well. He made up his mind he had to get there. Flying was the only answer with such a constrained time limit. But there were no direct flights in those days and certainly none to the small town of Dayton. He grabbed some much needed shut-eye and then began a series of hopping flights. The flights he could get were short, on average around three to four-hundred miles a hop. It was up and down all the way until he finally landed in Dayton.

He spent the next twenty-four hours meeting his new daughter. She was not what he expected. He had been led to believe that newborns were small and wrinkled. Carol was none of that. She was almost nine pounds when she arrived, full of energy and smooth as could be. When the two left the hospital they would go back to Marge's mother's where she had been living since Maryland. Harper liked his mother-in-law and her generosity made him feel somewhat better about leaving them. His sister-in-law was also living there. Her husband was also a Navy officer who had just recently been sent to Hawaii. Time soon ran out for Harper. There was little choice and he had to get back to his own ship, so he jumped on whatever quick up and down he could find and made his way back to San Diego the same way he had come.[20]

Larry Cullen had discovered something about himself and the ship. The 52 was too small to be on top of two waves at the same time, therefore it was always meeting another wave at the same time it was dropping over the first. That was the cause; the effect was that he was unusually prone to seasickness, even when others seemed okay with the ride. That did not matter at the moment; the ship was docked and so was he. Larry did not mind the San Diego crowds either. He strolled by the lines and gaggles of sailors and offered them a hearty "Hi, Mac." He had also discovered that every sailor in the Navy went by Mac.[21] He knew that in a navy town like Diego there would be the two things he enjoyed, real Lucky Strike cigarettes and beer. He understood that the beer would not be his favorite brand but it would have to suffice till he could do better. In a pinch he had made homebrew and then stored it in his basement at home to ferment. That was before he joined the Navy and surely a sailor could stir up a store-bought beer somewhere in town.

Virgil Thill was also being called by the local bars. He found San Diego to be too congested with other sailors to suit him, though. But all in all, San Diego was still nice and he made the most of it. For someone seventeen who had never been too far from the Upper Peninsula of Michigan it was different and exciting. He had befriended Radioman Harvey W. Schroeder also from the 52 and the two toured the town together.

Harvey Schroeder grew up in Beaver Dam, Wisconsin, just northwest of Milwaukee. The town was west of Lake Michigan and less than three-hundred miles south of Virgil's home in Fairbanks. Although Beaver Dam was one of the largest towns in Wisconsin, it was a quiet, small community even by 1940s standards. The biggest news from Beaver Dam in 1944 was that the government opened a German POW camp there around 1 June. They put little thought into names and simply called it Camp Beaver Dam. The camp was nothing more than a tent city behind a fence and housed around 300 prisoners. As was true of most POW camps in the States, prisoners often worked on local farms rather than wallow in the boredom of captivity.

Harvey was not like Virgil in one aspect: he had been deathly seasick the entire trip down from Portland. In fact, he was constantly sick whenever the ship was moving. When the ship was not in motion, Harvey dedicated himself to a good time. Ship's records showed Harper issued Deck Courts to Harvey on 2 and 5 November before they sailed for Hawaii.

The time off flew by, more so for some than others. As the 52 pulled away and headed out to open sea it could be described as a good start; they were leaving with everyone they had landed with. Harper recorded in his log that the 52 departed San Diego for Hawaii on 6 November 1944. They sailed up the coast in convoy with four other LCSs. Accompanying the 52 in that convoy were LCSs *31, 32, 33* and *51*. Protocol took over and they had to go back to San Pedro before they could sail west. Laton made a few matter-of-fact journal entries for those days at sea, "Left San Diego Nov. 6, 1944. Arrived in San Pedro Nov. 7th 1944. Left San Pedro, Calif. Nov. 8, 1944 for [overseas] duty." He later became more precise about leaving and added in the time of departure, "Nov. 6th left San Diego at 5:30 pm."

As *LCS 52* left San Diego, Engineering Officer Spencer Burroughs, at the conn, set course to 245 True for Hawaii. In spite of the Navy's fraternization policies, men who share similar personalities are drawn to friendships, especially when working in such close quarters aboard a small ship. One such close, officer and enlisted, friendship formed between Larry Cullen and Ensign Burroughs. While all the men admired Burroughs, he and Larry spent many hours together arguing books and philosophy.[22] Both shared an appetite for reading, and rank structure was not going to prevent them from partaking of lengthy discussions on their extensive knowledge of various subjects.

Spencer Burroughs was born in Susanville, California, on 15 August 1920. His father was attorney Ephraim Spencer and his mother, Olga Adela Wemple Burroughs. Susanville was a small mining and logging town in northeastern California, located on the Susan River. The town had humble beginnings as a trading post built by Isaac Roop along the Nobles Emigrant Trail in 1854. In 1913 the railroad came to Susanville and transformed it into a major lumber milling center.

The Burroughs family had extensive ties with Susanville. Spencer's grandfather, H. D. Burroughs, was Superior Court Judge of Lassen County of which Susanville was the county seat. After his grandfather died, Spencer's grandmother took his position on the bench and later became a Deputy Attorney General for the state of California. She was also the first mayor of Susanville and thereby the first in California. Ephraim Spencer tried his hand at private practice, living in San Francisco, but that was short-lived. Shortly after Spencer was born the family moved to Sacramento where his father took the position as Principal Attorney for the Division of Water Rights. Spencer's father had also served as an ensign in the Navy during World War I. It seemed fitting that his son would follow in those same footprints.

The home that Spencer grew up in during the depression years was better off financially than the large majority of the nation. The family kept a houseboy throughout the depression decade.[23] One young fellow of Asian ancestry, Sadow, boarded in the home, did his chores, and worked on a public education. Spencer and a close friend also provided a private education to Sadow. They instructed him in fluent profanity. Another, Robert Fox, an orphan who was taken in to work for room and board, committed to becoming a marine after Pearl Harbor. A physician advised Robert to whistle in order to increase his lung capacity. The Burroughs house of 1942 was thus filled with unremitting tunes from Robert. He made it into the Marines, whistling or not. Through 1940, Mildred Sasaki, a California-born Japanese-American, also lived and worked in the home. She was, as were so many, ordered to the Tule Lake internment camp after the attack. She had never been to Japan and was detained because she had taken Japanese language classes.

The Burroughs home sat at 2748 Curtis Way, an affluent section of town occupied by professional, white-collar types. Spencer was athletic and kind to others beyond normal. He always had time for his little brother, sixteen years his junior. Geoffrey recalled how that Spencer stopped in the middle of dressing for his wedding to participate in an epic toy soldier battle. It was an unusual but effective confirmation that his big brother was not forsaking him for a woman.[24]

Spencer's mother was a brilliant painter who studied under Otis Oldfield in the early thirties. She belonged to the Kingsley Art Club but curtailed her passion around the time her last child, Geoffrey, was demanding more attention. She never tired of political and social activism, though. The local colonel over the Corps of Engineers once caught the brunt of her determination in keeping trees along the flood levees. His military training (whatever it may have been) was insufficient to handle Olga's attack. He resorted to calling on E.S. Burroughs to get the hounds off his back. That accomplished little more than a delay of his inevitable defeat—the trees stayed where they stood.

The love story which was Elaine Baker and Spencer's was the stuff of movies and sometimes romantic comedy. In 1939 the Baker family moved in on Curtis Way next to Spencer's grandmother, Gladys Burroughs. Spencer suddenly found a new zest for cutting and trimming every leaf and blade in grandma's yard to excess. He was not fooling anyone with his purported new-found enthusiasm for lawn care. The Bakers' one month shy of sixteen-years-old daughter was the draw. Elaine found the eighteen and a half year-old quite appealing to look at and talk to, running the gamut of lame excuses to be outside while he overworked the yard.[25]

He finally mustered the courage to ask her to a movie. The age difference between the two was of much concern for her parents. He was, after all, a freshman at Sacramento Junior College and she was a sophomore at nearby C.K. McClatchy High School. The date was reluctantly approved and the two journeyed forth. When Mr. Baker in a post-date interview inquired of the play-by-play events he grew even more disturbed than before. Spencer Burroughs, it seemed, was a Nazi sympathizer! He could only conclude such based on the testimony of Elaine, who stated Spencer talked nonstop about Adolf Hitler, Nazism, and current affairs as it pertained to Nazism. It was not that farfetched for Mr. Baker to assume such in

1939. Just the year before, the famous Charles Lindbergh was planning on moving to Berlin and had received the Service Cross of the German Eagle on behalf of the Fuehrer. Of course, Spencer had no desire to move to Berlin and no love of Nazism; he was simply too intelligent and involved in world affairs for his own good. Mix a gregarious nature with that kind of intellect on a teenage date and false assumptions were bound to arise.

After the erroneous status of Spencer's Nazi affiliation was expunged from his record, Mr. Baker allowed further contact with his daughter to proceed. Spencer ferreted out more time with Elaine by picking her up in the mornings on his way to drop off little sister Brooke to California Junior High School. Elaine was courted on the way to school in the family four-door 1935 Studebaker. The car was a status symbol for both the high school-bound Elaine and Spencer. His use of it signified his standing in the family, and meant his father relegated himself to the 1926 Studebaker, known affectionately as the Blunderbus or Belch-fire Twelve.[26]

Spencer finished his associate's degree at Sacramento Junior College, followed by a year off to contemplate his choices. Elaine graduated from high school in February of 1941. For all intents and purposes it looked in 1941 that Spencer would start law school at Hastings when his life planning concluded. His deep interest in politics seemed to be pulling him another direction, though. He sought out information on a career in the Foreign Service branch of the State Department. To his utter disappointment, Spencer soon discovered that young men who acquired positions in the State Department were groomed from youth by their influential, insider, eastern parents. He had none of those attributes. He happily resigned his destiny to be that of studying law as his family had done for three generations. He did manage to pull himself from Elaine and Curtis Way for a six-week separation to work a temporary job in Beatty, Nevada, laying telephone line.

He returned in 1941 and entered Hastings Law School as planned. The curriculum at Hastings was easily mastered by someone of Spencer's intelligence. He found the majority of his peers who complained incessantly about how difficult the study was to be annoying and irrational.[27] Spencer enjoyed learning for the sake of learning. It was hard for him to see learning as work.

Elaine was completing her first year at Sacramento Junior College when the news came of the attack on Pearl. To that point, she saw her and Spencer's relationship and future as a spinoff of a Noël Peirce Coward play. She thought, "We were anglophiles and saw ourselves as leading a beautiful, intellectual, smart life."[28]

Within six months of the attack, Spencer joined the V7 program at University of California at Berkeley. Being in the V7 program and preparing for the Navy was not enough for Spencer. He also got a job working at Kaiser's shipyards in Oakland building Liberty Ships while at Berkeley. He graduated in 1943 with a major in political science and then went on to Notre Dame for Midshipman's school in October. One of his instructors there was in fact Lieutenant Harper. Harper recalled him as a leader in his midshipman's class and trusted him unconditionally.

The *Reno Evening Gazette* of 14 February 1944 reported, "Miss Elaine Baker and Ensign Spencer Burroughs were married in Sacramento 23 January." The wedding was actually staged at Elaine's home on Curtis Way. The paper went on to say, "the bride chose a blue afternoon dress and a corsage of orchids for the civil ceremony which was read by Judge Annette Adams." Elaine was also a student at the University of California. The paper added Elaine and Spencer would be headed for his next duty station, at the time, Raleigh, North Carolina.

3. Practicing the Trade

The military was ill prepared during the war. They lacked training facilities in particular. The Navy contracted facilities at colleges and universities across the United States in which to conduct specialized schools. The local college in Raleigh hosted the Engineering School. Raleigh was different for two people such as Elaine and Spencer, who had been born and raised in the west coast social and cultural climate.

They located a woman who had a room available for rent. The apartment was one of four constructed out of a former single family house built sometime before the Civil War. Cultures soon clashed after the newlyweds moved in when the landlady accused them of bringing in bedbugs. Spencer, in a less than diplomatic rebuttal, engaged his knowledge of judicial proceedings to establish that the bedbug problem was preexisting. He went on to explain that another issue, broken pipes, was not his responsibility either. Finding no worthy counter argument for the former law student, the landlady went on her way without financial gain, outside the rent.

There were other culture shocks beyond scheming landlords. Elaine never got used to the Jim Crow South. Segregation was very much a part of the community; blacks never dared venture across the imaginary line which separated them from white drinking fountains, stools at diners, or the front of a bus. There was also the issue of buying alcoholic beverages. Elaine said:

> It was a liquor control state, service men could not buy at the state store and I was not 21 yet and so we had to drink black Jamaican rum which was plentiful and not rationed. I learned to make hot buttered rums which was the only thing that would make it palatable. Beer and wine were sold at bars.[29]

Elaine turned twenty-one while they lived in Raleigh. When Spencer finished school he was sent to D.C., where he awaited his next assignment.

In the fall of 1944 Elaine left Spencer in D.C. and returned to Berkeley for school. However, after Spencer arrived in Portland, she took leave from school, delaying her midterms, and raced to her husband's side. She arrived to find that Spencer had rented a two-bedroom apartment with one of the other ensigns from the ship and his wife. The couples having shared interests, thanks to the Navy, became good friends. Oregon was another liquor control state, but the Navy men handled that with ease. They had become members of private clubs that kept lockers for their patrons. Within the locker, members could store bottles for personal use.

Those who could afford to bring their wives out to Portland were treated to a kind of family day aboard *LCS 52* upon her commissioning. "I could envision how he lived," Elaine said. Elaine in her inquisitive manner wanted to know from the captain's lips why the LCSs earned such a hazardous role in island landings. His reply somewhat shocked her. Because they were "expendable," Harper answered.[30] What he meant was that the little ships were cheaper, easier and quicker to replace if one was lost than, say, a destroyer. For Elaine, his response was more like that of a doctor answering the question, "Am I going to die?" with a "Yes," instead of expounding by adding that "everyone does eventually." Elaine stayed in Portland for six weeks before she had to go back to school.[31]

The ship pulled into San Diego and Elaine was already plotting her next visit with Spencer. She jumped on a south-bound train to San Diego. The couple procured a room at the U.S. Grant Hotel. The hotel was founded in 1910 by Ulysses Grant, Jr., and named in honor of his father. The man who had caused a lot of the phobia surrounding clandestine

American Nazis, Charles Lindbergh, had stayed there in 1927. Spencer and Elaine enjoyed the legal unencumbered flow of booze at the hotel's Little Club. The Little Club hosted a string of 1940s big bands, something they both enjoyed.

San Diego was "wet" and the booze may have been consumed by any adult, but that did not mean it was approved by Grandmother Gladys Burroughs. Olga had arrived in San Diego to assist Brooke, a student at UCLA, at the time presenting at sorority houses. Gladys had showed up as well. She inquired of Elaine where her absent grandson was. Elaine, not having the code of abstinence Gladys did, blurted out that he was in the Little Club, having an adult beverage. Apparently, Gladys' lifelong temperance was overridden by the idea of a sailor going off to war needing a drink. Nevertheless, she filed no criticism with the new bride.

The Burroughs women, less Elaine, left for other parts. Elaine remained for a couple more days but when scuttlebutt spread the ship was pulling out, she grudgingly retreated back to classes. As would happen more than not, the rumor mill could not be depended on; Spencer did not leave for two more days. When they did leave, they headed back to San Pedro. There, they took on fresh water and refitted.

Wednesday, 8 November 1944, Ensign Spencer Burroughs on duty as OOD since 04:00 hours prepared to take the ship out of San Pedro harbor. At 07:05, Spencer relieved Captain Harper at the conn.[32] Spencer was sailing further from his bride and family just like the rest of his shipmates. No one knew what lay in store for them in the future but all shared equally in the fear of the not knowing.

The trip over to the Hawaiian Islands was uneventful, Harper thought.[33] No one else argued otherwise. The convoy arrived off the Hawaiian coast on 17 November; it was just past dawn when they saw the island. The sun was shining bright. Harper thought the water was actually getting bluer as they neared.[34] The island could only be described as beautiful that morning. Then there was a bitter reminder of their maiden voyage. The seas became rough as they started into the harbor and many had to revisit the rail once more. Breakfast that morning had included canned pineapple, which seemed to have the same taste coming up as it did going down.

They entered Pearl Harbor at 11:09 and headed for the shallower part of the harbor Tare 13, West Loch. They would moor there for three days before beginning practices. Most of the men were seeing the aftermath of the Japanese attack for the first time. Harper took note of his crew's reaction. It was startling how much evidence of the attack three years earlier still remained. Perhaps more alarming, for those aboard who had not been kept in the dark with the general public, was the 52's assigned anchorage.

In May 1944 West Loch had been the site of what people referred to as the second Pearl Harbor disaster. On the 21st of that month the bulk of the Saipan invasion force was anchored at West Loch, including 29 Landing Ships Tank (LSTs) all loaded to max with ammunition and other explosives to support the 2nd and 4th Marine Divisions.[35] That afternoon an accidental explosion on *LST 353* set off a chain of explosions which resulted in 136 killed and 396 injured. Six LSTs, three LCT's and 17 LVTs were destroyed by the ensuing explosions and fires. Along with the wreckage of 1941 visible in Pearl Harbor, the charred bow of *LST 480* protruding from the water at West Loch was a morbid reminder of the extreme death and destruction the harbor had seen in the last three years. The crew did not have long to think about past carnage. Their minds had to turn to practicing the prevention of further such attacks.

The 52 moved on the 21st to Kewalo Basin, Honolulu, and moored at Tuna Wharf until 29 November. The ships and crews spent both the Christmas and New Year holidays anchored off some of the smaller Hawaiian Islands. For Christmas Eve, and Thill thought it an odd place to be parked on such a festive day, the ship anchored off Molokai Island.[36] It was strange, only because the small island was better known as Leper Island.

Beginning in 1866, Kalaupapa, a small community on the northern peninsula, had been the drop off point for Hawaiians infected with the disease. It was still an active settlement when the 52 bobbed off its coastline. A cure had been developed in 1941. A sulfone drug called Promin administered through painful injections put the disease in remission. That did not make the boys onboard want to go see for themselves.

The days leading up to Christmas made thoughts turn to home. Laton Burns religiously gathered with a close little clique each Sunday on the upper deck. He played a little guitar and the boys sang along. Everyone had a good time and it was a good substitute for church services. It brought back memories for Burns of former times, more peaceful times, when the church bells would reverberate across the campus of Oneida Baptist Institute, calling the students to the chapel. The thought prompted him to pen a letter to the school that December 1944, so they would know he was grateful for their influence in his life. The paper, the *Oneida Mountaineer*, printed his letter in their January 1945 issue. In it, they referred to Burns as a "star athlete, a perfect physical specimen." Burns closed his missive with a prayer that next year all the boys would be home for Christmas. They would not.

For New Year's the ship took anchorage at Maui. There was not much for excitement but a few cans of beer for the enlisted men. The officers located the local officer's club, a shack converted to dispense soft drinks, beer and canned peanuts. There were New Year's sardine sandwiches for everyone regardless of rank. The men raided the pyrotechnics locker and set off a homemade fireworks show, on Uncle Sam's dime, much to Harper's chagrin.[37] Just because Maui was not San Diego or Honolulu with readymade thrills for sailors on liberty did not mean the crew could not have fun on the holidays. The end of December report reflected the aftermath. Harper issued five deck courts. There were three men who stayed past their leave time by more than a day and one other who stayed less than twenty-four hours past.

Sometimes, a good time is hard to turn loose of. Five more men were charged with absent without leave under twenty-four hours and one more over. The ship lost forty-one days' worth of man-hours to confinement from Court Martials, according to the report. While the officers were not tardy, they too discovered the best of places to frolic. Ensign Parker and companions found La Hula Rhumba at 744 Lunalilo Street in Honolulu to be topnotch. The restaurant was, as advertised, "The better dine and dance spot."[38] La Hula Rhumba was a two-story stucco building that had the look of a sixteenth-century cathedral, tall arched entrances, a balcony overlooking the street, and a broad staircase leading into the pleasures of the islands. The club was touted in radio ads in 1940 as "sophisticated and elegant." By 1945 it was also known as a "clip joint" for servicemen.

When the enlisted men went into town, they went as a crew. Seldom did anyone on the street see a group of sailors or marines who were not from the same unit or ship. In that aspect the groups were segregated from one another but, within, they were clannish and tightknit. When it came to the crew, that was the family and they went everywhere together. Wartime pictures of every serviceman reflected that pack behavior. The Hawaii pack of *LCS*

52 located a photo shop where they could have their pictures made with a couple of pretty local girls. The girls were smart enough to know that provocative dresses and friendly smiles increased business. They threw out the red carpet for the LCSers. The same two girls appeared with just about every sailor from the 52 pack. Eugene De Maio and Ulysses Johnson wanted to be remembered with the girls sitting on their laps.[39] Donald Hedger and Harvey Schroder framed themselves with the girls standing in front with their heads romantically touching together and arms joined in front. Ulysses Johnson and Jordon Brantley went for the same pose in another session. William Gardner wanted to be remembered with just him and his girl—which happened to be everyone else's girl too. It looked for all intents and purposes that the boys had met the loves of their life. The only thing that revealed the truth was the comparison of pictures with a variety of LCSers cuddled with the same two women. Brantley, Anthony Jawor and De Maio wanted a photo together but with De Maio appearing as the only one having a girlfriend. However the combinations lined up, it was the boys of 52 together and on the town. Their togetherness also pointed to the fact that they were becoming a unit, a team and a brotherhood.

On the 12th the LCSs moved back offshore of Maui and practiced firing at targets towed by aircraft. That particular day was only six hours work consisting of four practice runs at the beach. On each of those runs *LCS 52* practiced moving close to the beach and firing her rockets at targets on the beach, as she would be doing in an actual battle. These types of maneuvers were the LCSs' bread and butter; what they were designed to do. Laton later amplified in his journal: "Jan. 12th, 13th, 14th and 15th practiced invasions off the island of Maui."

The days of the 17th and 18th were spent in joint operations with the destroyers and LCM (M)s. The ships practiced a simulated landing (as it would look on Iwo) off the shores of Kahoolawe Island, smallest of the Hawaiian Islands. Those scenarios were staged to look as close to the actual landings as possible, with concentration devoted to live-fire exercises over the heads of landing troops. Once the fire missions were run, the marine Shore Fire Control Parties from the 4th and 5th Marine Divisions landed and established battalion spotter parties and observation posts, just as they would do on Iwo a month later. In total, four rehearsals were completed while in the Hawaiian Islands and two more would be run later off Saipan before the actual invasion of Iwo Jima.

While in Hawaii the LCSs and LCIs were provided another opportunity to work with the frogmen, officially known as Underwater Demolition Teams (UDT). The Naval Combat Demolition Training and Experimental Base, Maui, gave advanced demolition training to the teams after they left their initial training at Fort Pierce, Florida. Like the LCS, the frogmen were relative newcomers to the Pacific Theater.

In November 1943, when landing craft failed to make the Tarawa beach because of the uncharted shallow reef, marines were stranded in the water and slaughtered as they struggled the more than three-hundred yards to shore. Admiral Kelly Turner believed the time had long passed for beach reconnaissance prior to infantry landings. Turner approached Lieutenant Commander Draper Kauffman, head of the Navy's Mine Disposal School, with a proposal to create units capable of performing such operations.[40]

Kauffman requested volunteers from the Navy and Marine Corps who considered themselves in superb physical condition and especially comfortable in the water for long periods. Scouts and Raiders supplied raw material from the Corps to fill many of the team billets Kauffman was seeking. After intense training and rehearsal through the beginning of February

Ulysses Johnson (right) and Eugene De Maio (left), unidentified women. Photo taken in Hawaii. The boys of *LCS 52* stuck together as a group. That brotherhood was stronger than the norms of the day or color of skin (Virgil Thill collection).

1945, it would fall on teams 12, 13, 14 and 15 to go on to Iwo Jima and be the first Americans ashore.

The missions and tactics of the frogmen were highly classified and highly dangerous to perform. Their mission, August 1944, to reconnoiter Yap Island had resulted in three marines of a four-man team being captured, tortured and executed.[41] *LCS 52*'s training with the frogmen operating with 3rd and 5th Marine Divisions was not taken lightly. They could very easily be the ship designated to drop and recover one of the teams sent ashore on Iwo Jima prior to the infantry landings.

Radioman Harvey Schroeder had been debilitated by seasickness throughout the trip over to Hawaii and during the training. Harper could no longer allow Harvey's propensity to hang over the rail to go on. It placed the crew and the ship in danger and combat was no place for someone too sick to protect himself.

Harvey was transferred to Base Hospital Number 8 at Pearl Harbor on 19 January. He would remain a land-bound sailor for the rest of the war. In exchange for Harvey the ship picked up Harry E. Tucker as the new radioman, transferred from *LCS 32*.

Harry Tucker was the son of Robert L. and Rosie Lee Tucker of Fairmont, West Virginia. He was born in 1915 and raised in Fairmont, the county seat of Marion County. The town grew around the Monongahela River and coal mines. Surrounding the town, in the West Virginia coal heydays, were the underground mines of thirty-six companies. The coal boom in Fairmont began with James E. Watson, himself born in Fairmont in 1859. By the 1890s there were few businesses from the Bank of Fairmont to the Fairmont Gas and Light Company that Watson did not own or have controlling stock in. He was also instrumental in bringing the railroad through Fairmont.[42] It was rumored that at one time the little town of Fairmont had one-hundred millionaires living within its city limits.

The Tucker family was not one of the coal tycoons. However, Harry and his father, Robert, were never forced into the mines by economic factors even during the depression years. Robert Tucker farmed and was self-employed as a barber.[43] Twenty-four year old Harry married Jessie Ann Silver on 4 July 1939. The two crossed over to Monterey, Virginia, to get married. Harry worked as a truck driver before enlisting in the Navy on 11 April 1944 in Huntington. The couple lived in Fork Lick, West Virginia, at the time of his enlistment and Jessie worked part-time as a saleswoman.

Tucker was not the only new addition to the communications gang. After boot-camp Nick Stoia was sent to gunnery school. On the way to Hawaii the word spread that an opening in the radio section was forthcoming. It may have been the one the seasick Schroeder was about to relinquish. The word carried down to Stoia and he applied for the position of radioman striker through the communications officer, Clifford Stewart.[44] Ensign Stewart saw the possibility and took Stoia on as radioman, untrained, of course. When the ship arrived in Hawaii, Stoia had the opportunity to attend a basic radioman course at Pearl Harbor.[45] After he completed what time he could in the classroom, before the ship sailed west, he took the test and became a full-fledged radioman striker.

On the 22nd the ship also received Lt. Philip Jacobson aboard. He would remain on the ship through the Iwo Jima campaign. Some of the crew believed that Jacobson was present aboard to learn from Harper but his real purpose was unknown, at least to them. He was never attached officially as a member of the crew but rather listed on musters as a passenger. When he departed, Jacobson was placed in LCS Group Seven's Executive Officer's spot. He remained as next in command after Lt Commander Frank P. Stone until the end of the war.

Philip "Phil" Jacobson was the son of Maurice, sometimes spelled "Manria" and later "Morris," and Dora Jacobson. Morris was born in Romania and Dora in Poland. Morris worked his own wood turning business in the 1920s, which later became Ohio Turning and Planing Company.

Philip was raised in Cincinnati, Ohio. His family lived at 835 Blair Avenue through the early part of the 1930s. In 1930, Philip's older brother Edward was a stage actor. His older brother Jack worked at the newspaper as a checker. Phil's older sister Saralee was married to Benjamin Horn and they had six-month-old Gerald with them on Burton Avenue in Dayton, according to that year's census. The family moved to 907 Lexington Avenue by 1940. The two-story, plank home on Lexington was built in 1910 and was only slightly over a mile from their old home on Blair. The home cost them $55.00 a month in rent. Saralee was divorced by that time and living with her parents, along with her son. Also living with the family was William Isaac Hart, Dora's unmarried brother. In his earlier years, Isaac had made his living selling cars but was then working as a deputy sheriff for the county. Isaac continuously gave the location of his birth as England; apparently after leaving Poland the family had resided in Great Britain for a time.

The old house on Blair sat in front of the Evanston Jewish cemetery. The entire community was in fact another one of the immigrant enclaves but, in this case, a predominantly Jewish one. The American Jews, much like blacks in the 1940s, often received the brunt of prejudice and preferred to remain residentially segregated. Such American icons as Henry Ford bore a candid and boisterous anti–Semitism. Beginning in 1918, Ford published a series of ninety-one articles on the alleged evils of Jews and Jewish capitalists in a self-owned newspaper, *The Dearborn Independent*. He was not alone in his bigotry in those prewar years.

Jews were often viewed as weak, pacifists to a degree, but more so downright cowardly. They were seen as draft-dodgers and if they did enlist, they were rumored to seek out specialties which kept them to the rear of the fighting.[46] This ideology was rampant in the military ranks among non–Jews as well. Sometime in the 1930s a New York college professor shared what he considered an appropriate joke for the time, to the effect, "The battle Hymn of the Jews is 'Onward Christian Soldiers,' we'll make the uniforms."[47] None of the stereotypes concerning Jewish martial abilities ever proved any more true than they did for other religious sects. One problem was that Americans and Europeans somehow associated being a Jew with nationality. That was as far from the truth as any idea could possibly be in the war years. Jews had no one homeland and resided in, and emigrated from, hundreds of countries. While their religion may have drawn them together in U.S. cities, many spoke mother tongues foreign to their neighbors. Still, Yiddish was the most common language of communication for American Jews. Both of Philip's parents spoke Yiddish and considered it their first language.[48]

Whatever anti–Semitism stirred among the men or women on American streets usually remained confined to harsh stares and racist jokes. It was easier on the body to take insult versus injury. Morris was born in the northeastern town of Iasi (Jassy in English), Romania in 1882. Iasi was the former capital of Moldavia. The town sat along the trade route between Poland and Bessarabia. Its location was not only convenient for commerce but afforded persecuted Jews a safe haven for most of the sixteen century. Romanian Jews also fell victim to massacres and prejudice but managed to thrive in Iasi in spite of the sporadic attacks. In the year Morris was born, and then again in 1884, economic congresses met with the intent of boycotting Jewish owned and operated businesses within Isai. To a great extent, the boycott worked. Almost two-hundred Jewish businessmen were forced to close their shops and more Jews were forced out of town. Jewish children were expelled from public schools and the university at Isai grew into a hotbed of anti–Semitic activities. It seemed Morris either saw the dark clouds on the horizon or someone close to him pointed his eyes in that direction.

He left Romania in 1899 and made his way to the Ohio Valley. He showed up in the

1909 Cincinnati directory living in the rear apartment of 714 W. 6th Street and working as a wood turner. By 1911 he had moved to 939 W. 7th Street, and then, listed as a "woodworker," he appeared in the 1915 directory at 832 W. 8th Street.

Only a year after Morris arrived in America, the family of Harris and Fannie Hart also arrived and settled along the Ohio River near Cincinnati. The Harts were Polish Jews. Harris made a living in clothing sales and specifically in "gents clothing." Of the daughters the Harts produced, none went by the name of Dora in her early years. It was likely not her name at birth or a variant of a middle name. Somehow, "Dora Hart" and Morris Jacobson found themselves together in the early years of the 1900s, married and started their own family in Cincinnati.

Life for the Jews in both Romania and Poland had deteriorated in the year since the Harts and Morris Jacobson emigrated westward. In fact, for Jews throughout Europe, life had become abysmal. When Germany and Russia invaded Poland in 1939, Poland boasted the highest population of Jews in Europe, somewhere close to three and a half million.[49] When boundary lines were set by the two invaders, two million Jews were stranded in German-occupied territory. When the invasion began on the 1st of September, German forces purposely targeted Jewish business districts, homes, synagogues and individuals. Both invaders immediately continued or initiated their mass policies of imprisonment, execution or enslavement of Polish citizens, mainly Jews. Romanian Jews in the early 1940s suffered brutalities under the anti–Jew reign of the fascist Mareşal Ion Antonescu dictatorship which took power via a 1940 coup. By the time the war ended in 1945, fourteen-million people, the majority of whom were Jews, would perish in the area historian Timothy Snyder labeled the "Bloodlands." The areas encompassing Poland and Romania sat in the middle of the Bloodlands during those years of slaughter.

In Morris Jacobson's birthplace of Isai, a June 1941 Russian air raid became the excuse by German-Romanian intelligence officers (believing the Jews were signaling the aircraft) to execute thousands of Jews on the spot. Those who somehow managed to avoid the Isai pogrom were captured and put on two deportation trains, filled beyond capacity. Along the way to their incarceration points, the trains stopped occasionally to dump suffocated Jews along the tracks. There were no accurate figures, but it was estimated that close to 10,000 Jews may have been murdered between the pogrom and death trains.[50]

Contrary to what non–Jews believed about Jews lacking martial abilities, throughout the war Jews fought back, rebelled and joined or led partisan groups. The most famous and perhaps successful of the groups was the camp organized and led by Alexander, Tuvia, Asael, and Aron Bielsk of Belarus. The Polish resistance group Żydowska Organizacja Bojowa or ŻOB was instrumental in the 1943 Warsaw Ghetto Uprising. A second Polish resistance group operated throughout the war under the name of Żydowski Związek Wojskowy or ŻZW. There were hundreds of internees in Nazi work camps and ghettos who organized uprisings. In the conventional forces, 550,000 Jewish men and women served in the United States armed forces. Another million served in Allied armies during World War II. Three Jewish servicemen earned the Medal of Honor and sixty-six others earned the nation's second highest award. Sixty percent of American Jewish doctors served, many of those on the frontlines or in hospitals directly behind the front.[51] The Jacobson family also did their part during the war to defy the stereotypical image of Jews as noncombatants.

Philip Jacobson was the fifth of the five sons born to Morris and Dora. He attended the prestigious Walnut Hills High School, which reorganized as a classical high school for grades seven through twelve in 1919. Students were selected from schools within the city and prepared at Walnut Hills to attend and master college. Philip began his education there in 1932 as a seventh grader. He graduated in the 1937 class. From there, Philip attended the University of Cincinnati. Philip became a member of Phi Lambda Upsilon (The National Chemistry Honor Society). He graduated with a B.A. in the 1941 class.

Lt. Jacobson was a veteran of the Solomon Islands Campaign. Between August 1942 and November 1943 the waters surrounding the Solomon Islands were the scene of ten separate sea battles in which both U.S. and Japanese naval forces suffered extensive losses in ships and men. His presence onboard the 52 prior to their first battle helped to shore up the confidence of the other officers. Lt. Jacobson was greatly admired by the men. He possessed a unique blend of intelligence, common sense, and empathy which endeared him to the officer corps and made him popular with the enlisted men. After his stint with the 52, he moved on to become the Group X.O. aboard the *Landing Craft (Flotilla Flagship) LC (FF)-484*. One of the signalmen who had served with Jacobson since training at Little Creek, Louis Plant, said that Mr. Jacobson was "a regular guy." Plant went on to describe Jacobson as a person who was not past bending the rules if it benefited the sailor at no cost to the mission.[52] He was also without doubt greatly admired by Lt. Commander Stone.

The convoy to the central Pacific departed the Hawaiian Islands on 22 January 1945. Twelve LCSs made up the larger group. Moving at ten knots, they crossed the International Date Line on the 29th and arrived off Eniwetok Island in the Marshalls on 3 February. The convoy had traversed 3000 miles of sea.

The date of 17 February marked the one-year anniversary since the Americans had taken Eniwetok Atoll back from the Japanese. In comparison to the ones that followed, the battles for Eniwetok Atoll were trifling; nevertheless, thirty-seven soldiers and marines were killed there. A garrison of 800 Japanese soldiers gave their lives defending three of the thirty islands in the atoll.

Harper described the atoll as a circular coral reef with coral cropping dotting the waters around that formation. The highest spot on any of the islands is only fifteen-feet above sea level. The atoll had three entrance points where ships could enter the lagoon for anchorage. The water was clear and had a pretty tint of blue that Harper admired. He said that the white coral, "when the sun shone on it and the waves broke over it ... made all kinds of pretty colors for us to watch."[53]

Perhaps feeling it unbecoming for the senior officer aboard to do, he allowed himself to live vicariously through his boys. While anchored in the lagoon, he gave them time to take a swim. Some donned swim shorts, while others stripped down to what they came into the world in, and quickly took advantage of the captain's generosity. They took their turn diving off the deck into the water, swimming out a short distance and quickly returning to the ship. That became the norm after word spread that there might be sharks in the lagoon. No one wanted to venture too far from quick access to the safety of the ship.

A swim was about the extent of fun to be had on tiny Eniwetok. Aside from that, they came there for replenishing chow, water and fuel. With that accomplished, they set sail for Saipan on 5 February, via the Philippines. They cleared Eniwetok Harbor at 07:45 hours. The ship made a short stop on Samar Island, and took on fuel and fresh supplies. They left the following day for the 1200-mile journey to Saipan. From the 6th through the 9th, the ship went to General Quarters each morning and evening. Each day they went through emergency drills at least once. The procedures were another indication of how close they were coming to dangerous waters.

They arrived at 10:10 hours on 10 February, after another uneventful leg of the journey. Anchorage off Saipan was usually in Tanapeg Harbor north of the city of Garapan. Some of the men were allowed to go ashore. Virgil Thill was one of them. The beach was nice, very pretty, so Virgil decided to walk down it. The other boys went toward town. As was typical with Virgil, he wandered toward the first thing that caught his eye. Virgil spotted a cave near the beach and decided to explore it at closer look. It seemed like it should be harmless by this time. However, he was also aware that there were many Japanese holdouts roaming around. There was the established possibility that there were hundreds living in the caves and the jungle-covered mountains of Saipan. The passive holdouts, it was reported, mostly came down to steal food and to occasionally use the Americans' showers.[54]

They were not always so benign. Japanese soldiers lived by a code which absolutely loathed surrender. Whenever it was attempted in the presence of another holdout, allowing such a shameful act disgraced all, could not be tolerated and the offender was quickly dispatched. It was the duty of the strong to show respect for the weakling's family and kill him before he carried through with such an unthinkable deed.

Almost as soon as Virgil cautiously entered the cave, he spotted the body of a Japanese soldier lying near the entrance. He recognized the mustard colored uniform of the Japanese soldier. It appeared he had made the fatal mistake of wanting to give up to the Americans. Virgil surmised that from not only where and how he had fallen, but from the condition of the body. It was a fairly fresh kill, no decay, too fresh. Virgil realized that he had stumbled into a place where he had no business being. He exited the cave and put as much distance between it and himself as his young legs could muster.[55]

During the Japanese defense of Saipan, all the caves were used as bunkers; it was improbable that Virgil would not have found some evidence of the horror experienced only a few months before his arrival. Nevertheless, he was shaken by the experience. He quickly sought a way back to the ship, where he was safe.[56]

For *LCS 52* and her sister ships the mooring at Saipan was fairly routine. Ten miles south of Saipan was the island of Tinian. The task force commanders considered Tinian beaches to be similar to Iwo, and training for the actual assault began soon after arrival near Saipan. On the morning of the 12th at 05:36 the convoy got under way for the western coast of Tinian. At 07:30 the ships lined up for their practice runs in such numbers that Harper believed they stretched for somewhere between two to two and a half miles long when they formed up abreast. They were all headed for the northern beach of Tinian, one of the few capable of handling infantry landing crafts. The crew of *LCS 52* watched helplessly as *LCI (L) 627* somehow got caught between the line of advancing ships and the beach line. The LCI's captain tried to turn into the advancing ships and maneuver between them. The attempt failed and as luck would have it, she collided with *LCS 52*. Seven minutes after they had started their run for the beaches, the bow of the LCI collided with "starboard bulwark at frame 12" of *LCS 52*. The accident caused no relevant damage, at least none below the waterline.[57] All one-hundred-fifty-six rounds of 40mm ammunition, stored near where the rail was torn apart, became suspect and had to be discarded overboard. The collision spread black powder from the damaged ammunition across the deck. That was an easy fix; the men broke out the fire hoses and washed it into the ocean. Everyone was just content that the accident had not resulted in fire or explosions—there was always more ammo. *LCS 52* carried on with the practices. She picked up with the second practice run on the beach at 08:22 and then sailed for Tanapeg Harbor for repairs.

She moored next to the USS *Phaon* (ARB-3). The *Phaon* was formally *LST-15*, built in Tampa, Florida, in September. She was reclassified as a battle damage repair ship in January 1943, Lieutenant George Fay Watson commanding. The *Phaon* had been part of the retaking of Saipan and had remained there to repair ships headed for Iwo Jima.

After-action briefings dissected problems with the practice operations that day on Tinian. Problems resulted from the same difficulties marines had encountered while fighting to take Saipan and Tinian: there were few beaches suitable for landings. Shore parties had to be landed out of sequence which caused some confusion with the support ships designated to provide fire on future operations at Iwo.

The repairs to *LCS 52* were completed by the *Phaon* on the 14th. Laton Burns made a sterile note in his journal, "Feb. 14th left Saipan at 1600 for (Iwo Jimo) [Jima]." No one was officially allowed to keep a journal diary, so if that rule was to be violated then the indiscretion had to be kept to a minimum. Burns, it seemed, had lost track of days and perhaps had not allowed for the time difference. The captain's log confirmed that the ship got underway at 15:41 hours on 15 February not the 14th. *LCS 52* became part of task unit 52.5.4, assigned to take and hold the island of Iwo Jima. Between them and their destination lay roughly 724 miles of open sea.

4

Life at Sea

There was no privacy aboard a LCS and the 52 was no exception. The living quarters for the enlisted men were stifling. The paltry air ventilation system seldom circulated enough fresh air to rid the berthing compartments of the stench of men soaked in sweat from work in a tropical climate. There were two showers for the entire crew of sixty-five men. Those showers, more often than not, used seawater rather than waste the precious fresh water used in cooking and drinking. Saltwater showers were better than no showering at all but the men seldom felt much cleaner afterward.

It was fortunate that the crew worked around the clock. Shifts and watches made daily hygiene activities seem a little easier. However, it took little to throw the schedule off and cause a logjam at showers or sinks. The head, a navy term for latrine, consisted of three small round sinks in a tight row affixed to a bulkhead. Mirrors were added above each sink, and this was where shaving, brushing teeth and combing hair went on. Next to the last sink was the single washing machine for cleaning clothes. There was a wringer affixed on the top of the machine for ridding them of excess water. However, clothes were dried on lines, typically hung on the top deck when non-combat conditions permitted. Much like the sinks, the row of three toilets guaranteed elbow rubbing with the man in the next spot. Toilets were purged by a stream of seawater running underneath. There were no curtains or partitions to offer the least amount of privacy. Therefore, there were no secrets among the crew; everyone knew everyone else's every blemish and idiosyncrasy, eventually.

Every space onboard, except for a sailor's assigned bunk and his locker, was public domain. The sea-bag, another navy term synonymous for duffle-bag, containing a sailor's worldly possessions, was typically hung from pipes on the ceiling of his sleeping quarters. The lockers issued to each crewman were too small to store more than a few prized keepsakes and valuables. At one point during the war, Larry Cullen's locker became overfilled with letters from his wife. He was forced to go through and pick out his favorites. The letters which did not make the final cut were inserted into an empty shell casing and buried at sea. The navy pea coats, a double-breasted wool coat for inclement weather, would not fit in the lockers either. The coats were often found hanging from pipes or off the fronts of lockers.

The sea-bag held every possession an enlisted sailor was issued and therefore expected to have on hand at all times. Enlisted wore a white visor-less canvas cap with the brim turned up. The cap, called affectionately a Dixie cup, was worn with all uniforms, day or night. For pictures they could be tilted to the extremes of the back of the head. On the other end, all uniforms could be finished off with black leather oxford shoes. The second type of footwear issued was roughouts, brown half-length boots used for work. In one picture taken on liberty, Lloyd Keith was up to bat while wearing his roughouts during a baseball game. Roughouts were not commonly issued to garrison sailors. The Dress Blues uniform was worn for ceremony and while on liberty call. Also worn on liberty were the Dress Whites, not to be confused with the solid white cook's uniform. The most distinguishable work uniform during the war was the denim pants and, both long and short-sleeve, chambray shirt.

Other items in the sea-bag were the ditty bag, towel, leggings, socks, underwear and hygiene gear. If they chose to hang on to it, for reference, each sailor received a *Bluejacket's Manual*, in boot. After boot camp the basic skills manual frequently retained the name the training cadre called it by, the bible. The sea-bag could be filled with tightly rolled clothing and other gear in a matter of minutes. The sea-bag, once packed, was slung across the shoulder by a web strap and all eighty to one-hundred pounds went as far and as fast as the sailor carrying it.

Only the captain, Lt. Harper, and the executive officer, Lt. (jg) Duvendeck, had a two-man room. The other four officers shared a single living compartment, midship. For the enlisted men, their quarters were subdivided by a stack of four folding bunks, floor to ceiling. Their personal lockers sat adjacent to the bunks. The bunks, attached to the bulkhead by a hinge device, could be folded against the wall when not occupied, so that men could have a reasonable walking aisle through the compartment. The forward enlisted living compartment slept twenty-two men. The bow quarters were mostly seamen like Virgil Thill. Thill slept second from the top. In mid-ship, the men shared a sixteen-man compartment. They had the luxury, due to rank, of sleeping in bunks stacked three high. A stairwell led from topside to the middle enlisted and officers' quarters. The enlisted quarters were on the starboard side and across the passageway

Lloyd Keith enjoying one of the many sports in which he was proficient. He was among the majority of crewmembers who had been high school all-stars before the war (Diane Burns Brads collection).

were the officers on the port side. Nick Stoia and the rest of the radar gang slept in the mid-compartment. Stoia's bunk was third row—a hefty climb just to sleep. Storekeeper Larry Cullen also bunked there.

The remainder of the men, twenty-eight, shared a compartment to the rear of the ship. There, bunks were once again stacked four high in a space totaling only twelve by twenty-two-feet. The engine room guys, "Motor Macks" or "black gang," stayed in the aft quarters. The only advantage to life in the aft enlisted berthing was it was located on the starboard side of the ship, which conveniently placed it directly off the mess hall. The disadvantage to aft living was the almost twenty-four-hour-a-day clanking and clattering from the mess hall.

The mess hall and galley, or kitchen, consisted of a vegetable locker, a meat locker, stoves and three tables that seated between six and eight men at once. When the men pushed up to the table for a meal they shared a three-man bench, four with a bit of squeezing. The tables, like bunks, folded up against the bulkhead when not in use. The tables served a more morbid purpose as well. The ship's Pharmacist's Mate, John Syrian, kept a locker next to the last table, where he stored all his medical supplies and instruments. When casualties occurred, or routine sick-call was held, the tables acted as operating and exam tables.

Officers ate in a separate area and had a table which could, under the best circumstances, seat all six at once on individual chairs. When the officers turned up for chow, Steward's Mate Ulysses Johnson brought it to the wardroom. Because the officers lived separate from the enlisted men, the steward's mate carried their meals from the galley, through a passageway, climbed a ladder way, went down another passageway and served it in the officers' wardroom. Along with the table, the wardroom had a desk where logs and other administrative duties could be completed by the officers. On the *LCS 52*, the wardroom was also the storage place for entertainment items, such as games, books, and a phonograph.

For those who worked in the engine room, their conditions were probably the most grueling on the ship. They worked in a compartment that was always hot and extremely noisy. The exasperating heat was created by eight GM engines propelling the ship. Those engines could produce a maximum of 1800hp when needed, creating about sixteen knots maximum, or flank, speed. Members of the black gang, like John Keilty, made sure the engines and generators stayed up and running regardless of hour of day or what might be happening topside. Unlike the other officers who habitually remained pristine no matter what, Ensign Spencer Burroughs seemed to always be in a uniform covered in grease. He seemed to like it that way. Virgil Thill thought he must have been doing a lot of work himself to stay so greasy.[1] It endeared him to the enlisted men, as they felt he did not think of himself as their better. Keilty also perpetually wore a uniform covered in grease.

Electricity was generated by two GM generators. Both provided 450-volt current and ran off diesel fuel. Typically, one generator was enough to supply sufficient power for the ship. The second generator remained in standby or shut down for maintenance. It was possible to run both at once if necessity dictated. Fresh water could be produced by a distilling unit below deck. The unit could produce up to 1000 gallons of fresh water a day. It may have seemed like a large amount of fresh water but, in reality, fresh water was scarce.

If there was such a thing as a routine day it was one filled with well-designed unpredictable activities. There was the constant necessity to practice not only the art of war, but emergency procedures. A typical day might look like Friday, the 13th of October 1944. That afternoon began when the crew participated in a flag hoist drill. Flag hoist drill was an exercise in displaying and identifying signal flags which represented alphabetic or numeric characters used in nautical messaging. Ship-to-ship messaging with flags was the signalmen's, such as Gerald E Bledsoe, area of expertise. That event was secured at 13:30 hours. Lt. (jg) Duvendeck sounded the fire drill at 14:19 hours. The crew secured from fire drill at 14:28. At 14:29 an abandon ship drill was called. Two minutes later, the ship secured from the abandon ship drill. At 15:10, Duvendeck sounded a collision drill. The men secured from the collision drill at 15:20.

The honing of messaging and emergency drills under the pressure of a clock taught the men to operate on automatic under the stress of combat. When fear acted as an obstacle to thinking, the training and repetition kicked in, and they simply did what had to be done. The sailor, in the end, was as much a well-oiled machine as the engine or the generator.

That evening, after 20:00, the officers mustered a couple of the boys who had failed to find their way back to the ship at the proper times. One was found guilty of absence without leave—he had stayed three days in San Diego past what was allowed. He was sentenced to "six days of solitary confinement on bread and water, a full ration every third day." The next sailor carried a lesser offense and therefore a lesser sentence. He received ten days restriction. The officers involved secured from Deck Court and Captain's Mast at 20:20.

Deck Courts and Captain's Masts maintained a discipline aboard a seagoing vessel which had evolved over centuries. Only a hundred years before, the two sailors extending their liberty beyond what was authorized could have easily been sentenced to any number of lashes across their bare backs.

Reveille for all hands typically went at 05:30. Fifteen minutes later, every man was to be engaged cleaning every compartment in the ship. Breakfast was then served at 06:15. Colors went at 08:00. The time liberty parties left the ship depended on varying factors. Before they left ship the men were inspected and given the dos and don'ts for the particular area and limits. When they were docked at a stateside port, there were the odd duties such as telephone watch on the dock. Pulling extra duties and watches took up the lion's share of time for both officers and men.

Everyone had a primary job and sometimes several secondary jobs. Nick Stoia, for example, was a 3rd Class radar man. When the ship went to general quarters he became a loader on one of the twin 40mm guns. Even on the guns themselves, the positions rotated so that men did not become overtaxed in one job. Loaders became gunners; gunners carried ammo and back again. Many of the men were qualified for secondary specialty jobs; at least the crew considered them so. Joe Floyd Chavez was the ship's barber and cut the crew's hair throughout the war.[2] Chavez was born in Colorado on 23 September 1925. He was living in Weston, Colorado, when he went into the Navy.

Others vied for the position of cook. Cook was a much sought after assignment. John Di Priter and Jim Nelson both served a stint as cooks. John Di Priter enlisted on 15 May 1944. The nearest recruiting station was the town of McKeesport. Both he and Russell Copeland were from Allegheny County and both signed up at McKeesport. Di Priter was living at 500 George Street, Turtle Creek, Pennsylvania, when he enlisted. He was another first-generation American, born in Wilmerding, Pennsylvania, 22 September 1913. His father, Angelo, was born in Italy. Angelo came to the United States in 1906. John's mother, Mary, was born in Brazil but listed her native tongue as Italian. She arrived in the United States in 1902. Angelo provided for his family by doing general carpentry work.

Porter Barron was a cook during the Iwo Jima operation. Ralph J. Prendergast became one of the last cooks before the war ended. Virgil Thill took on the ship's laundry. It was supposed to net him a small stipend but he admitted he never saw it.[3] Larry Cullen became the storekeeper, as well as frequently steering the ship during combat. His extra job also included being mailman and handling what was probably the most effective manipulator of morale in any war.

Aside from the important battle stations, everyone had to maintain the ship. Saltwater was particularly hard on ships. It was a constant battle to quickly identify a festering bubble as rust under the paint, and then scrape, sand and repaint it before it became cancer to the ship. Cleaning compartments and storage of foodstuffs were also continuous chores. Ship's logs constantly reflected refueling, taking on water or other supplies. Resupply took greater priority the smaller the ship. The

Joe Chavez (left) had the important job of cutting the crew's hair while at sea. He poses while in Hawaii with De Maio (Virgil Thill collection).

largest percentage of open space went to the storage of ammunition. The loaded magazines for the 20mm guns, for example, hung like picture frames on bulkheads. With ammo taking up all the prime real estate, food, bags of flour, cans, and other dry goods came in second. Tropical areas, even when the ship harbored miles off land, invited all manner of critters to visit the unsealed spaces where food had to be stored. Virgil Thill recalled that bugs once contaminated the food supplies. The little pests subsequently ended up mixed with cooked grub. With the ship at sea and unable to simply drop in to dock and refit, the crew had the choice of, consuming the bug-infested food or going hungry for a very long time.[4] They picked the extra protein over hunger.

On laundry day, when not in a combat zone, the ship's deck was festooned with clean sheets and pillowcases. Here, the sea breeze dried the clothes and bed linen as *LCS 52* moves toward her next battle (Virgil Thill collection).

Something that at the time seemed unique to the 52's crew was the huge generation gap aboard ship. Nick Stoia, one of the younger group, said "I was just a kid and all these guys were older. We had guys on there that had grandchildren."[5] Nick's younger group often added the endearing title of "Pop" to the older guys' names. Thill recalled the crew calling Gerald Davis, born 18 May 1910 in West Virginia, "Pop Davis." He was a good candidate for the title; Gerald married his wife Iva Morgan on 30 March 1929. Most of the younger boys on ship were still in diapers when Davis started a family. Stoia recalled the boys called Richard F. Hile "Pop." Pop Hile was born 29 January 1915 in Sprague, Nebraska. Lawrence C. Cullen, born in 1906, was the most likely choice for the nickname but may have been exclusively called "Pop" by Ensign Burroughs.[6]

The youngest onboard may have been John T. Keilty, who enlisted in December of 1943. He told members of the crew that he was fifteen and had used his brother's birth certificate to get into the Navy.[7] He joined on 15 December 1943. John only had one older brother, Edward John Keilty, Jr., born 27 December 1926. Later records showed John's real date of birth as 12 June 1927. John's age would have been twelve days short of seventeen when he joined, using his brother's birth date, and would have still required a parent's signature. However he got in, he was fifteen when he joined. He enlisted in Bellingham, Washington, the city where he had attended high school.

The Keilty family lived in Spokane, Washington, during the 1930s and early 40s. Edward Sr. was a doctor of dentistry. Edward Jr. also enlisted in the Navy on 26 December 1944, the day before his eighteenth birthday. Edward served until 22 July 1946. The 1940 census showed Edward living outside his parents' home by that year. The census also indicated that Margaret, Edward and John's mother, was the only wage earner. She worked as a sales clerk in a local department store. Their father, Edward Sr., indicated he earned an income from sources other than wages and salary—probably pertaining to his dental profession.

Laton Burns maintained a small journal, though the content was limited to what he thought might one day jog his memory. The same kind of outline journal was kept by Nick Stoia and Ensign Albert Parker. The three read almost identically as if there was some collaboration. Under the best and loosest circumstances, these documents were frowned-upon. The billions of letters that came and went from and to servicemen in both theaters were closely censored. Nothing was to be written down for fear that it might by some faint chance fall into enemy hands and cause catastrophe. Journals filled with the comings and goings of naval task forces and ship makeup would have certainly been valuable intelligence sources for the enemy.

Included with the forbidden fruit of diary keeping was picture taking. If a sailor wanted to have his picture taken with an exotic local gal in Honolulu or Tijuana that was one thing, but possession of cameras in a combat zone was best left in the hands of newsmen. Nick Stoia never intended to have his camera or film fall into view of wandering Japanese eyes. Through-

Virgil Thill (left) and Nick Stoia are most likely the last two surviving enlisted men from the original crew. After the war, both became the Americans every American hopes to be (Nick Stoia collection).

out the war he produced an abundance of pictures. They were duplicated and ultimately ended up in almost every 52er's wartime photo album. He was not the only dissenter. Pictures of the 52 were taken by other sailors aboard other LCSs, while she rode the crests of waves and lay enveloped in a thick layer of cordite smoke off Iwo Jima. While anchored off Okinawa a series of pictures were taken, presumably by Stoia, of the forward 40mm gun and several of the crew. Chief Holland even made a guest appearance in some. In nary a photo was found an officer of any rank. The officers of 52 may have turned a blind eye to picture taking but hypocrisy only went so far. The last thing an officer's career needed was to show up in a photo that somehow bounced its way around the fleet till it reached the commodore.

Ensign Albert G. Parker was assigned as the ship's gunnery officer. It was Parker who controlled, directed and took ultimate responsibility for every round and rocket fired. The ship's contingent of rockets was controlled and fired by Parker or under his direction from an electronic control panel in the conning tower. It was his responsibility to ensure that the forward deck was clear of all personnel before launching the rockets.

The boys were always happy to take their pictures with the biggest guns on the ship, the 40mm. Stoia, who secreted a camera on board, took a series of photos with the Number Three 40mm. Over the years, memories of faces faded and it became harder for the surviving crew to identify those men in the pictures. The man holding the shells is believed to be Cullen. To his immediate right, a face that never changed through the years, is Burns. To his right is Jawor, in a black watch cap like Burns. On the far left, standing on the gun platform is Cazee. The man on the far left at the edge of the picture is believed to be Syrian. The man's helmet and left eye, barely visible, is probably Williams. The man to the immediate left of the shell holder may be Blough. The man whose head is visible above Syrian's left shoulder may be Nelson, the ship's baker. Because of his size and posture, the man in the light colored sweat shirt may be Parham. (Virgil Thill collection).

Behind the forward twin 40mm gun sat the launching rack for the 4.5 rockets. The rockets were fired from racks housing ten rows stacked twelve rockets deep. The 4.5 rocket was nicknamed "old faithful" by the sailors of World War II. The rocket, which looked more like an overgrown German potato masher grenade, was thirty inches long and weighed twenty-nine pounds. Each rocket had its own propeller motor and was effective up to 800 to 1,000 yards. With a press of a button by Ensign Parker, an electric charge triggered a single or all one-hundred-twenty old faithful rockets. They zipped from their rack in a stream which reminded sailors of a gigantic fireworks display and sounded like a hurricane. Within sixty-seconds, all one-hundred-twenty rockets could be launched and hit the beach or inland target. The LCS would then move back out to a safe distance from the beach and take about fifteen minutes to reload the rack. The first rocket fired was used to mark the range and accuracy. Once the range was determined to be correct, Parker could launch a salvo using the strike of the first rocket as a guidepost. The rocket launch racks were fixed at a forty-five-degree angle. The rise and fall of the ship's bow was used to provide better accuracy.

The 52 was equipped with two twin-40mm antiaircraft guns, one on the front of the ship, just forward of the pilot house and conning tower, and one on the rear. The bow 40mm was a single barrel, common to most LCSs. Their rate of fire per barrel was approximately one-hundred-twenty to one-hundred-fifty rounds per minute. The guns were fed manually by a sailor shoving clips consisting of four rounds, weighing twenty pounds per clip, into the gun magazine. The rounds had a maximum range of 11,000 yards but were seldom fired to that distance. Most of the rounds manufactured later in the war had a type of failsafe or self-destruct built in. A self-detonating tracer round was included which exploded the rounds at 4,000 to 5,000 yards. The reason for such construction was to prevent rounds that missed their intended targets from travelling into nearby friendly ships. The round traveled at 2,890 feet per second; without such a safety, ships had little chance of avoiding an overshot round.

Each 40mm gun was controlled by a Mark 51 Director. The Director was the instrument which served as the gun fire-control. The device enabled automatic targeting with or without radar or optical sights. Claude Cook was in charge and responsible for handling the function of the director on his gun. His good friend Johnny Pfahl ran the second twin-40 director. The 40s were highly accurate weapon systems, especially when coupled with radar. The 40mm guns were the most widely used antiaircraft weapons during World War II. Defeating the mass kamikaze attacks would have been almost impossible without them.

Galen Carl Libby was gun captain for the forward twin 40mm. Galen was the first son of Perley Leroy and Susie "Ella" Gildden Libby. His parents were married 29 July 1922 in Dexter, Maine, wasting no time to start a family; Galen was born 3 July 1923.

The Libby men of Maine had served honorably in the armed forces, dating back to the Civil War. Perley Libby enlisted in the Student Army Training Corps (SATC) at Colby College on 10 October 1918. The SATC allowed cadets to continue their regular education while they took classes in military subjects and completed army basic training. The war ended on 11 November, and Perley received an honorable discharge from the army on 12 December of that same year.

Galen's family moved in the 1930s from Jefferson Township to Garland, Maine. Garland was another small rural community, much like the ones most of his shipmates had arrived from. Local excitement was provided exclusively at the Garland Grange Hall, which also doubled through the years as a meeting house. Galen enlisted at the Penobscot County seat of Banger on 15 February 1943.

The 20mm antiaircraft guns were run by two men. They, too, alternated when possible. One man fired and the other loaded. Like their bigger brother, the 40mm, the 20s were equipped with a Mark-14 gyro sight. The man firing the gun rested his shoulders up to the armpits in two crescent-shaped yokes. He then strapped himself into the gun by means of a belt which went around his upper waist. By these means he could lean back to an incline position in order to better elevate the trajectory of the rounds. Spent shell casings were caught as they were ejected in a cartridge bag, which hung down below the gun in front of the firer. The 20s were bolted to the deck of the ship via a base stand and could be placed just about anywhere in any number. There were four 20mm guns on LCS 52.

Each magazine held sixty 20mm rounds. When the last round was fired from a magazine, the bolt on the gun locked open. The loader then removed the empty and replaced it by securing retaining lugs on the fore end and a magazine catch at the rear of the well. Under optimal conditions, the rounds were loaded in magazines before they might be needed. Each round was greased with mineral grease before being put into the magazine. The loading of magazines was another of those constant jobs which had to be done and done properly.

The 20mm AA guns were originally designed by the Swiss company Oerlikon. They were probably the most widely used AA gun during World War II, by all forces. The 20mm could fire up to 450 rounds per minute, per barrel. Their range depended on type of round fired and elevation of the gun barrel. For example, at ten degrees a high explosive (HE) round could travel up to 3,450 yards at an average of 2,725 feet-per-second (fps). At the barrel elevation of forty-five degrees the round could travel out 4,800 yards.

The 52 also had five .50 caliber machineguns. The 50 Cal, as it was commonly called, was brought into service at the end of World War I. The design was updated and modified in 1933, creating the M2 version used during World War II. The M2 was used on aircraft, sea craft and by infantry. The original design was by Browning and the gun was as often as not referred to as the Browning .50 Cal. During World War II there were nine different manufacturers of the M2, including Frigidaire, but Browning was not among them.

They were not the biggest guns aboard but they could fire from 700 to 850 rounds per minute. The gun weighed sixty-one and a half pounds. It had a maximum effective range of more than 4,900 feet and a velocity over 3,900 feet per second. The bullet was almost two and a half inches long. A standard belt of one-hundred rounds of ammo weighed close to thirty-five pounds. The M2 was a recoil-operated, belt-fed, air-cooled automatic machinegun fed by a metallic link disintegrating belt. They could, under the right circumstances, bring down enemy planes and under any condition cut a man in half.

Everyone had a job to do and it did not always involve firing a weapon. Signalmen seldom received awards for heroism, but they were the voice of the ship when within close quarters to other ships. It was they who stood perched on their stand during storm and enemy attack and communicated with sister ships. One of the signalmen who joined the first crew of LCS 52 was Gerald Eugene Bledsoe of Moline, Illinois. Moline is a town in Rock Island County. The actual island from which it took its name sits in the middle of the Mississippi River between Iowa and Illinois. There was a military post on the island which had served many purposes over the years. During the Civil War it housed a prison for Confederates so notorious for poor treatment that it turned out a considerable number of galvanized Yankees—those who changed sides for the reward of freedom, fighting Indians out west.

Gerald was born 5 September 1926 to Frank A. and Charlotte Bledsoe. Gerald was the second son and second child of the couple. His father was a salesman in a local department store. In the 1930 census the family rented a home for twenty-two dollars a month, a steep price in the early days of the depression. Just ten years later, Frank was working for the National Biscuit Company as a salesman, still, but was a homeowner at 2220 6th Street in Moline. The home was valued at $5,500. This was the home from which Gerald enlisted into the Navy for his first tour. He was seventeen when he enlisted on 5 January 1944 at Rock Island.

The ship was built small so that it could deliver the full effects of its many weapons in close fire support to marines and soldiers on the beach. The downside of the LCS's size was its constant battle with a rough and tumble ocean. Aside from the extreme difficulties the crew had endured at the Columbia sandbar and their first storm, seasickness was an ever-present woe.

Dewane L. Johnson worked in the radio room, deciphering coded messages. He recalled the days spent working on encoding and decoding, with a pail between his legs. He worked, puked, and returned to work again. It was a cycle he grew accustomed to but never content with. Dewane Johnson was born in Aurora County, South Dakota, on 17 September 1922. He was the only son of George O. and Ida Smith Johnson. George was a farmer and Dewane shared his father's love of tending the land and animals. Dewane's dream had always been, and would always be, to own a large farm.[8] He and his older sister were raised by their father; his mother died the same year he was born. Dewane enlisted in the Navy on 10 December 1943.

The radio and signal men had to be some of the most alert and careful workers aboard ship. A misunderstood message, or misread, could turn naval guns on their own ground troops. Those men selected for such decoding, for example, had to be able to write (decode) twenty words or more a minute. Each operation required a fresh booklet of radio call signs assigned to every unit and ship in the area of operations. The booklets, *Communication and Organizational Digest*, were distributed before operations began as classified "Secret" documents. Once the operation kicked off on D-day or L-day, the booklets were downgraded to "Confidential." Lengthy instructions were printed on the cover sheet explaining when and how they should be destroyed if the imminent possibility arose they might fall into enemy hands.

Included in the booklet were the call signs for each unit or vessel in both continuous wave (CW) transmissions and voice transmissions. Morse code was the most common vehicle used in CW transmissions. A CW call sign for transmissions to Headquarters 2nd Marine Division (Operation Iceberg) would be transmitted as "1DB." If a ship or unit was calling the same headquarters by common voice transmission they would have called out to "ALAMO." The voice call signs were generated as random as possible during pre-planning. The call sign did not reflect the prowess, history, mission or description of the ship or unit. Call sign PETTICOAT, the USS *Kittson*, had no more to do with their combat effectiveness than did BATTLEAXE, the call sign for the USS *Owen*, with theirs.

In the case of voice communications, a select group of transmissions, such as contact and amplifying reports, had to be authenticated using the then-common "Shackle" system. If a voice transmission in any way sounded suspicious to a radioman, he could challenge the call and force the other caller to authenticate as well. Coding and decoding was accomplished with a pencil and paper, not typewriters.

To increase the difficulty in unwanted ears decoding the messages, random nonsensical phrases were often entered before the message and after. These were to have no connection in any way to the message, but rather to confuse the enemy listeners into believing they were part of the coded message. During World War II the most ironically astute of such nonsense phrases appeared during the bleak hours of the Battle of the Philippine Sea from Admiral Thomas Cassin Kinkaid to Admiral William Frederick Halsey, Jr. Halsey had taken the decoy bait and pursued what he believed to be the entirety of Japan's carriers. Taking his Task Force 34 carrier group and obsessively chasing the Japanese carriers, he left the allied naval forces surrounding the Philippine Islands to be swarmed by a superior-sized Japanese attack force. Kinkaid, in the heat of battle, sent Halsey a desperate coded message, "Where is TF 34?" The message was encoded along with the required arbitrary beginning and ending phrases. What appeared on the other end was equivalent to waving a red flag in front of the "Bull." It read, "TURKEY TROTS TO WATER GG WHERE IS TASK FORCE THIRTY-FOUR RR THE WORLD WONDERS."[9] A well-read young radioman on Bull Halsey's flagship allegedly saw right through the thin veil and attributed the last inquiry, "the world wonders," to the same line in Tennyson's poem "The Charge of the Light Brigade." That battle, at Balaclava, was fought, again ironically, on 25 October 1854. As it so happened the battle of the Philippine Sea was then playing out on 25 October 1944. Like Kinkaid, the odds were against the brave six-hundred who rode into the mouth of the cannon ninety years before. "When can their glory fade? O the wild charge they made! All the world wondered."[10] Fate had a different outcome for the U.S. Navy in 1944, though the fuming Halsey did not turn his carriers around in time. The addition of the final nonsense phrase, which had more bearing on the situation than any other part sent, caused a stir for many years after.

The knowledge that censors, usually a designated officer, perused every piece of mail that exited the ship caused many sailors to develop their own personal codes. Those codes were not designed to give away any secret military strategy or even to hide such information. Sailors detested the idea of not being able to speak intimately with their sweethearts and wives without fear, say, of their executive officer passing them on the quarterdeck and shooting them a sly grin and a judging eye. The intimacy codes ranged from very sophisticated to very easily broken. A sailor might simply refer to a night to remember, a blanket and a tree. The rest was left to the censoring officer's own imagination. There were the more elaborate communications between families and sailors meant to relieve them of worry. Had the censor been able to decipher such codes there would have been hell to pay. Wives and husbands created code words to let the families back home know where they were, what their condition was and if they were headed into battle. A common word used in a sentence, such as Oklahoma or orange, might indicate he was off Okinawa.

Sailors wasted no time in letting their long-suppressed thoughts flow out over the paper as soon as the censors were called off after the surrender of Japan. On the day that the surrender was signed in Tokyo Bay, a LCSer fired a message off to his sweetheart detailing the "gown" he wanted to view her in, "instead of PJs." The gown, as he so loosely referred to the garment, was easier described by including a picture—after all, a picture was worth a thousand words. The "pinup" girl featured in the picture wearing the gown, he had apparently had for quite some time, left nothing to the imagination. She reposed with her ample buttock centered and well-aimed at the viewer, like twin-barreled 40mmers. The gown was a full-length black see-through item which lacked the density to double as a mosquito net. The pinup model contorted herself at the midsection so that her smiling face reflected how happy she was to be unencumbered by bulky sleepwear. How the whole suggestion was received would never be known—other than that the sweetheart stored the letter with all the others he had sent during the four years he was off with the navy.[11]

Operation slinky gown was by no means an exception to the ordinary libido of servicemen during wartime. If a man owned a small corner that was his and his alone, there were good odds a pinup girl might be found there. Like the pinup picture shared by the gown requester, many of the pinups of the day were well-drawn artist's renderings. Artists of the era climbed to the top of their profession with drawings of well-endowed girls clad only in garter belts, silk stockings and other lingerie items. Gil Elvgren was perhaps the most famous and productive of these artists during the war years. His pinups became known as Elvgren girls.

There were, however, many photographs taken during the war to be used exclusively as motivational aids—giving the boys something to fight for. Like future Playboy models, each pinup girl had her own following. Betty Grable, Jane Russell and Rita Hayworth all made their appearance in movies, magazines and footlockers as morale builders. Movie star Rita Hayworth's photo of her kneeling on a bed in a low-cut silk gown was one of the top 1940s masterpieces found in lockers across Europe and the Pacific. Pinup doll Hayworth even appeared on the cover of *Life* magazine in August of 1941 wearing a two-piece swimsuit. To believe such pictures, both drawn and photographed, did not exist on *LCS 52* would be at the pinnacle of naivety.

Ray Hunt was not a LCSer during the war, but he certainly knew what it was like to be absent of things that kept a man going. Before becoming a guerrilla operating on Japanese-occupied Luzon, Ray escaped his captors while on the Death March, lived in the jungles and mountains and evaded recapture for the better part of two years. Ray discovered a lot during that time about himself and the nature of men in general. He maintained that when "one was sick and starved thoughts of romance [were] remote." As soon as those vital needs for survival were met, the company of women took over as the number-one requirement.[12] He discovered that he would even take risks of recapture to spend some quality time with a friendly gal. Judging merely by the trail of pictures with friendly locals, the boys of *LCS 52* had their pictures taken with during and right after the war, Ray must have known what he was talking about. The ship had only recently docked in San Francisco from occupation duty when a photo of Laton Burns and a friendly local girl appeared in his photo album. He was sitting with an unidentified buddy and sandwiched between them was a girl who could have passed for a pinup model herself. Through the years following the war he never revealed, if he could recall, her identity. She was important enough at the time to have a picture taken with her. The encounter did not have to lead to sex, marriage or a long-term relationship, just the presence of a woman satisfied the hunger—even if that woman happened to be a black and white illustration, when nothing else was available.

In the same picture in which Laton Burns had the California beauty cornered, he held between his fingers an object that most World War II vets held as dear as food or women. Pinched between his fingers was a smoldering cigarette. Like most of the men, Laton had never been a dedicated smoker before the war. Most of the boys picked up a cigarette for their first time to calm their nerves and quiet the shakes before, during and after battle. That did not leave a lot of time when they did not have a smoke dangling from their lip or clinched in a free hand. The man who suffered every kind of dearth, Ray Hunt, said that he had once

Laton Burns (left) enjoys two of the most sought-after commodities during and after the war: female company and cigarettes. It was purported by some, who had done without either for long periods, the craving of both often came before the want of food. The other sailor is unidentified (Diane Burns Brads collection).

chosen a cigarette over the offer of food, even though he had missed several meals at the time.[13] Burns kicked the habit shortly after his return home but there was no argument from veterans that a smoke had gotten them through some pretty hard times. Not to mention, cigarettes were much more readily available to a sailor than was booze or the company of women.

When the ship was at sea, free time was confined to the four corners of the ship. Activities turned to small instruments of joy that required no baseball diamonds, basketball courts or golf courses. The officers had the wardroom stocked with such games. Ensign Parker's pastime, or one of them, was to go to the wardroom and play cribbage on the worn leather board placed there by who knows who. Lt. Harper was another officer who played cribbage and routinely enjoyed it. He liked card games as well, Rook and Bridge. He was not quite sure where his wife, Marge, had learned to play cribbage, but she made too much of a habit of trouncing him at the game back in Notre Dame.[14] At least with the other officers he stood a chance.

When the enlisted men were not battling incoming kamikazes or pulling maintenance on the ship, they enjoyed their fair share of cards. Aside from writing letters it was the universal activity that everyone, at one time or another, spent time doing. A deck of cards was small, easy to carry anywhere and easily taught to newcomers. Most card games aboard ship continued, with intermissions to fight the war, for days, weeks and sometimes months at a time.

Even in ground combat units someone could always produce a deck of cards from their rucksack when the shooting ceased.

Every sailor had an often unexplainable pride and confidence in their ship. Those attributes could not be traced directly back to the size or firepower of the ship itself. Motor Torpedo Boats (PT) were the smallest boats deployed during the war, both in size and number of crew. They were so small they could not traverse the ocean alone. They were picked up and taken to operational areas by larger vessels. Each PT boat was served by a crew of fifteen. The primary function of PTs was fast hit-and-run torpedo attacks on enemy ships. A PT boat ferried MacArthur off the doomed Corregidor to live to fight another day. PT boats fought valiantly at Guadalcanal and Leyte. Their most famous skipper was future president John F. Kennedy, captain of *PT 109*, sunk in combat.

Stuck between PT boats and destroyer escorts were the one-hundred and thirty landing craft support (L) (3) s, the smallest transoceanic ship the Navy had. Destroyer Escorts (DE) were only 306 feet long. They were manned by 228 officers and men. They were smaller and more lightly armed than their big sisters, destroyers (DD). Like LCSs, DEs could be manufactured faster and cheaper, outpacing the enemy's ability to reciprocate. The big boys, bat-

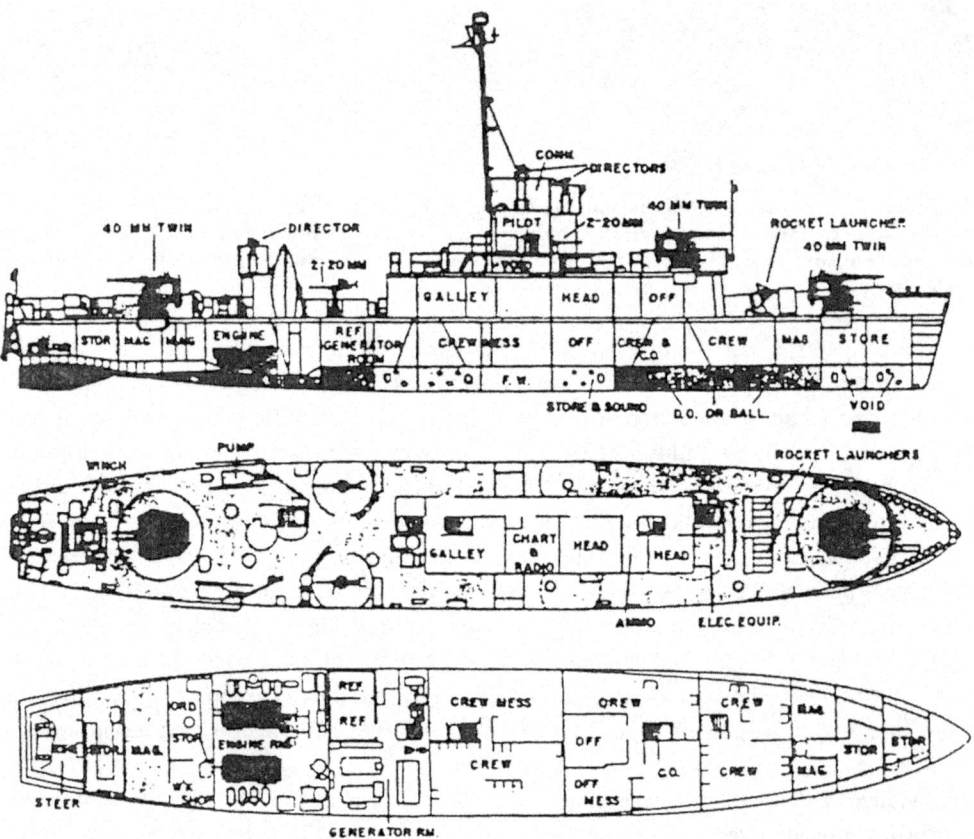

Among Lt. Harper's keepsakes from the war was a page from a manual showing a cross-section of a LCS. From the diagram, it is easy to see how tight the living arrangements were. It is no wonder that the crew became a family (Carol Harper Marsh collection).

tleships, were crewed by close to 2000 sailors. They were almost three times the size of a DE and, in turn, a DE was well over twice as big as a LCS. A LCSer was quick to tell anyone that would listen, size did not matter; they were the best armed vessels in the Navy, pound-for-pound. Claude Cook called them a "walking arsenal."[15]

In their short tenure in the U.S. Navy, LCSs evolved well beyond their original mission of providing close-in fire support. Before the war's end, their duty included salvage operations, laying smoke screens for capital ships, rescue operations, towing, observation platforms for Marine and Army fire-control teams, pinpointing enemy positions for larger ships, radar picket and, finally, occupation duties.

5

Black Sand and Suffering

Iwo Jima, as was true of most of the Pacific Islands where Allied forces were fighting and dying, was another almost unpronounceable name to the folks back home. For all those with loved-ones heading there to do battle with the Japanese defenders, Iwo was just one more opportunity where their husbands, fathers, brothers and sons might lose the good grace which had thus far kept them alive.

The pork-chop-shaped island was a logical next stop in the military strategy which had thus far brought the Allies within bombing range of Japan proper. Iwo Jima was 750 miles from southern Japan. After the Allies seized and occupied the Mariana Islands, the big B-29 bombers could strike Japan at will. However, with airfields on Iwo Jima remaining in Japanese hands, Japanese fighter planes could take a heavy toll on the American bombers en-route.[1] If the bombers were crippled during their sortie, having no friendly airstrip between Japan and Saipan, approximately 3000 miles, the possibility of surviving a crash and rescue at sea was minute. Anyone with a map could see that Iwo Jima lay directly between Saipan and Tokyo, and American ownership might in future air missions save lives as a midway stopping point.

The war had to some extent made every mother and father, wife and girlfriend, an amateur tactician. Mothers marked troop movements on maps hung in dining rooms or anywhere near a radio.[2] By 1945 they knew the Pacific as well as anyone could who was fighting there. In spite of the hush-hush nature of military planning, word leaked out and spread. War correspondents traveling with troops had more liberties and early access to landing sites, objective locations and ground actions than ever before. Aerial photos of landing craft headed toward the beaches of Iwo Jima appeared in newspapers across the United States within twenty-four hours of their occurrence. With daily dispatches going out by wire service, information on operational situations spread quicker to the public, in some ways making the not-knowing less stressful and in others only compounding the worry.

Laton Burns recorded in his journal that *LCS 52* pulled away from Saipan and headed for Iwo Jima at 16:00 hours on 14 February 1945. With the exception of Ensign Stewart and Chief Holland, the crew was primarily made up of untested warriors. On Saipan and even Pearl Harbor they had seen the aftermath of other men's battles. They had certainly pondered the hour they would face the carnage of their own battles. As they grew ever closer to that volcanic island their worries of how well they would perform under fire also grew heavier. Men always feared that they might be overcome with paralyzing panic at the critical moment and fail their mates.

The men of the 52 had grown close to one another and friendships had formed which were nothing short of those of brothers. Larry Cullen and Spencer Burroughs, sharing the same intellectual interests, had quickly become best friends. However, when liberty was sounded or at times when his and Spencer's rank prohibited contact, Cullen palled around with Ralph J. Prendergast and Chief Holland.

Ralph Prendergast was the trustworthy type. He had first appeared in his Hammond, Indiana, hometown newspaper at the age of thirteen. Ralph was one of the Boy Scouts of Troop Ten then being honored with merit badges in the 17 February 1939 issue of the *Hammond Times*.[3] While in Hammond High School he shared the position as vice president and secretary for the Press Club. He was just another of 52's all-American boys, whose steady nerve would mean the world to the crew in the coming days.

Ralph Jr. was born to Ralph Joseph and Mary B. Prendergast on 14 May 1926, in Hammond. He grew up at 5422 Wood Avenue in Hammond. At fifty, Ralph Sr. was obligated to register for the draft, even before his son enlisted in the Navy. Ralph Sr. was born in Illinois but had been a resident of Hammond for many years. He worked for the Northern Indiana Public Services Company supplying gas and electric to households and electric trollies.[4]

Hammond was one of many immigrant enclaves spread around and within large cities like Chicago. The town was founded by German farmers along the confluence of the Grand and Little Calumet Rivers and incorporated in 1883. George Hammond started a meat-packing plant in town in the late 1800s. The town became infamous for its part in the Pullman railway strike of 1894. Federal troops had to be sent to quiet the situation. However, troops only made matters worse and escalated the violence. A Hammond man was shot and killed by the troops before it was over.

Things had settled down considerably by the time Ralph was born. The town in the 1920s -30s was known for its quant main street stores and movie theaters. When Ralph was not earning merit badges he could venture down to Hohman, the Paramount or the Parthenon Theaters. In 1915 Hammond High School changed its name to Hammond Industrial High School but even the school yearbook still called it H.H.S. Ralph's older brother, Robert, was the athlete, frequently taking trophies in events such as the 220-meter swim.

In April 1944 the Press Club, which Ralph was a member of, took a trip over to Chicago. They visited the R.R. Donnelly Printing Company and saw *Time* and *Life* magazines in the printing. The group went over to the *Chicago Tribune*'s headquarters as well.[5] There, the boys watched as the latest news of the warfront shot from the presses. Less than a half-month later, Ralph enlisted in the Navy.

One friendship aboard ship stood out above all others. On the day Laton Burns enlisted in the Navy, he went into the recruiting station with another Clay County resident, Lloyd Clements Keith. Keith was barely a month younger than Burns but was much larger in stature. Keith had always been exceptionally big for his age. He had started on the Manchester High School basketball team as a freshman. In fact, he and Laton first met as rivals on the basketball court. Burns played on the 1942 Oneida Baptist Institute team and Keith for Clay County. Keith was a member of the Clay County High School 1940–41 baseball and basketball teams as well.

Keith was born and raised less than ten miles from the hollow the Burns family called their old homestead. He grew up in Greenbriar, Clay County, Kentucky, on the outskirts of Manchester. Lloyd, or Clements as he preferred to be called, was the son of Taylor and Perlina Mitchell Keith. Taylor, like Laton's father, served in World War I. He served twenty-two months in the 305th Infantry, 77th Infantry Division, a unit his son, Clements, would provide protective fire for in the next war. Taylor was severely wounded during a gas attack and hospitalized for a long period.[6] After the war, Taylor Keith returned to Manchester and did what work he could as a butcher for Taylor Baker in his grocery store. Clements had an older stepbrother, J.C., and a younger sister, Mildred. The family lived pretty much as all the families in Clay did, raised a small garden and enjoyed watching Clements' feats of athletic prowess.

Clements was a popular kid. His sports abilities were sought after by coaches and he loved to please. He was very personable. Everyone liked him and he was easy to get along with. He was most liked by Evelyn Sparks, a schoolmate he had been sweet on for years.

Clements and Laton were very close even during their school years' rivalry. It seemed, to those who knew them, impossible that one would join the Navy without the other. They would not; Clements and Laton shipped out together on 29 April 1944.

After basic training, they were transferred to Little Creek, Virginia, to learn the skills that would keep them, their brother sailors, and their ship alive. There, new sailors were assigned to the USS *Wyoming*, then serving as a gunnery training ship. The USS *Wyoming* was a World War I era battleship brought to Norfolk in 1942 as a training vessel for the Operational Training Command. From January to 10 April 1944 she was refitted with the newest fire-control radar and twin 130mm guns. During the months following graduation from basic training until 11 August 1944, the two Kentuckians trained aboard the *Wyoming*—nicknamed the *Chesapeake Raider* because of her familiar appearance off the coastline. The USS *Wyoming* was placed back in actual naval service in June of 1945. (She remained in service until August of 1947.[7]) After gunnery training, Clements and Laton were transferred back to ATB Little Creek and awaited assignment to their first ship, the *LCS 52*. The two would serve on the same forward 40mm gun crew during the forthcoming battle for Iwo, and never shirk their responsibility to protect one another.

On the morning of 19 February 1945, an incredibly tranquil sea greeted sunrise. A gentle seven-knot wind massaged nervous faces. Onboard the 52 the men who had been on the midnight to 04:00 watch (Ensign Stewart, O.O.D.) witnessed the hail of huge shells from the big guns arching overhead, the preparatory bombardment before the landings. The island was still too far off, though, invisible in the darkness, for the sounds of shells impacting on Iwo Jima to be heard. Still, in spite of the distance the men knew that every churn of their screws brought them closer to battle. The fear began to mount inside and gather in their stomachs. Seaman 2nd Class Cullen described what he felt:

> But we are getting close enough now for our bellies to tighten up and cramp in the anticipation of what is, for most of us, our first action. We grin at each other in the pre-sunrise darkness; we are being bold and nonchalant, but we picture the hell of shells bursting on our deck, and the screams of injured men. We are scared.[8]

Lt. Harper sighted Iwo Jima at 06:45 at a distance of seven miles. The Captain took the conn from Lt. Philip Jacobson at 05:05 and would not stand down until 21:30 that night. Ensign Albert G. Parker would remember he celebrated his twenty-third birthday on D–Day at Iwo Jima. In the daily narrative section of his journal Laton wrote a brief highlight of the morning: "Zero hour was at 07:30. Invasion of Iwo Jima (sp) was the 19th of Feb." The many hours he had spent loading and firing thousands of rounds of ammunition from the guns of the 52 were about to be the difference between life and death for thousands of marines. Burns would not himself be required to step foot on Iwo Jima, although, except for the vessels which carried the marines onto the beaches, no other ships ventured as close to the island as LCSs. Realistically the knowledge that whatever could hit a marine on the beach could also hit the 52 and her crew, did not ease the nerves.

While the sea was calm, the island, becoming more and more visible in the break of dawn, was far from peaceful. The pre-landing naval and air bombardment caused the island to literally shudder and tremble under a mass of explosions. Some observers compared it to a volcano on the verge of erupting.[9] Prior to the marines' landing, the island was given three days' naval and air bombardment. Men who looked over the rails of ships at that massive devastation could not have fathomed, at that moment, how anything or anyone on the island could be alive to meet the Leathernecks.

Stretched beyond eyesight around the island were 485 ships of all sizes and purposes. Although it would not hold that title for long, the fleet surrounding Iwo was the largest armada ever assembled in the Pacific Theater. From the first landings at Guadalcanal to Iwo Jima the higher command had learned some hard and costly lessons. With Iwo Jima many new innovations and techniques had taken their place among some tried and true. Iwo Jima would be the first landing of the war where an Amphibious Group Commander coordinated all pre-landing operations.

The radio traffic to control the rolling barrage, the operation and maneuvering of vessels, and the landing was inconceivable at the lower echelon of naval personnel. To coordinate all that in as safe a manner as possible, a frequency was designated as strictly a Naval Gunfire Control Net (NGCN). A backup frequency known as Naval Gunfire Overload Circuit was designed to be open for emergencies, calling and halting fire, should the NGCN be overloaded at that instant when someone needed to have priority. The LCSs and LCIs also had a new method for communication which centered on their own frequency called the Gunboat Control Net.

The master plan also allotted for four hours of rolling barrage, walked just ahead of the anticipated pace of ground forces.[10] As the reality of the Japanese defense later set in and troops became further and further delayed and bogged down, the barrage had to be continually modified to achieve any results at all. Once the landing force lined up, the LCSs took up assault positions between the landing force crafts. Their flanks would also be protected by a contingent of Fire Support Ships. The LCSs, twelve in total, preceded the leading landing craft, also known as the first wave. The mission of the LCSs was to clear the beaches for the landing force. They were to accomplish that by firing two salvoes of 4.5 rockets, one preliminary to landing and another just prior to the first wave of marines disembarking on Iwo.

The LCSs were perfect for the job of moving in close and firing salvos of rockets. One of the bitterest lessons of D–Day at Normandy was the waste of 9,000 rockets fired by Landing Craft Tank (Rocket) ships. The LCT(R)s were too far out to see that their rockets were falling short of the beach. The LCSs, on the other hand, moved in close to the shore and were able to see the impact of their 4.5 rockets, thus preventing them from wasting their stockpile.

At 06:30, from his flagship, Admiral Kelly Turner commanding the amphibious forces issued the now common command, "Land the landing force." Marines swung their feet over the sides of their transport ship and began the precarious climb down the nets to their Higgins boats. Others took interior ladders down into the bellies of their Landing Ship Tanks (LST) and mounted-up on their amtracs. The amtrac marines would be the first wave of Americans

LCS 52 lined up off the shores of Iwo Jima to give close fire support to the marines trying desperately to get a foothold on the black sand beaches. The little ships were finally doing the job they had been designed and built for. For most of the young crew of *LCS 52*, it was their first fight. They were close enough to the beaches to see the slaughter, a sight that would haunt them for the rest of their lives (Virgil Thill collection).

to set foot on Iwo Jima's beaches. Once loaded and in the water, the landing craft went into a circling mode. The drivers waited impatiently, as did the marines, for the final word to proceed.

The twelve LCSs began their first run toward the beach designated by codename "Green One" at 07:39. The visibility was average; there was intermittent rain but not hard enough to hinder the accuracy of the ships' weaponry. From 3,500 yards out they sped in; at 1800 yards the 40mm guns began to seek out and pound targets on the beach. Burns and Keith were on the forward 40mm, Burns as a loader. It was their first time firing at something they knew contained human beings—the enemy—but still humans.

At 1,400 yards from the shore the 20mm guns opened up. Lt. Harper directed fire on any enemy pillboxes that were spotted inland from the beach. He reported that gasoline drums were not discovered as was originally thought. The barrage of rockets that were to be used against the drums was redirected against pillboxes. In the after-action report the Commander Amphibious Group Two explained that prior intelligence had shown a possibility of containers of gasoline being ignited by the Japanese as further obstacles to halt landing American marines. The original plan required the LCSs to fire rockets into these, thus setting them off long before the marines arrived.

Harper spotted the strike of his first salvo of rockets at a distance between 100 and 300-yards inland from the beachhead. He had hoped that the impact of rockets would be no further inland than 500-yards from the beach. The 52's rockets were therefore right on the target. Ensign Parker's keen eyes had not failed him in accurately launching. Once the rockets were fired the 52 turned to port and commenced firing her guns on the left flank of Green One for five minutes. Harper observed no return fire from the island on the first run.

The second run was made at 08:27 and included the first wave of the marine landing force in their sixty-eight Landing Vehicle Tracked (LVTs), moving toward shore in the wakes of the LCSs. As the landing force turned toward the beaches B-24 Liberators made their last bombing runs. At 08:57 the rumble of the last salvos of naval bombardment on the beaches ceased to echo. Radio operators across the fleet listened intently to their only source of news. At 09:05 the radios hissed and a voice followed with, "Assault troops on the Beach." Lt. Harper's log reflected, "0900 First Wave hit beach. LCS(L)s Firing on Left Flank of beach area."

Three minutes later, the LVT launched, the first wave of marine-laden amtracs touched the beach. The LVTs were already halted by a fifteen-foot terrace at the far edge of the beach. Most were unable to elevate their barrels above that wall and could not provide covering fire for the marines as planned. The marines jumped off and discovered immediately that there was no hurrying on Iwo Jima beaches. Their feet sank into the black sand-like grains up to their ankles.[11]

Clad in their olive green fatigues and helmets covered in a tan camouflage cloth, the first marines were greeted by sporadic and light small weapons fire. All of their uniforms had been freshly laundered and coated with a disinfectant. Navy medical personnel encouraged these practices in hopes of preventing infection if the marine was wounded. Each marine also painted his face with a zinc-based anti-flash cream to prevent flash burns from the rumored gasoline drum booby-traps. Some marines wore jackets which bore his name stenciled across his upper back. Even from the deck of an LCS, the living could put a name to a dead boy's face down on the beach. There would be many to see before the day was done.

Six of the LCSs were designated to lead the landing assault ships (the LCIs) into the beach. The LCSs maintained a loose formation so that the LCIs and troop carriers could shoot past them to the beach. There were fewer LCIs to accompany the LCSs due to several losses two days prior to D-day while they were protecting UDT operations. Twelve of the LCIs engaged in earlier UDT operations suffered severe casualties and damage to their ships. The LCSs were ordered to spread out, with wider gaps between them and their sister vessels, to cover for those missing LCIs. In turn, they were required to cover a wider beach and inland area with their bombardment than originally intended. LCSs led the assault ships by 600 yards. They began firing in the same sequence as they had on the first run; 40 then 20mm guns. At 08:49 *LCS 52* fired another 120 rockets into the center of Green One. According to Harper this rocket salvo landed inland at 200 to 400 yards at a range exactly predetermined. It was a perfect run. Once the assault force neared the beach the LCSs turned to port in *line-astern formation*, shifting their fire to the left flank. The after-action report further explained that this maneuver put the LCSs in a bow-to-stern line with their guns on the starboard side firing on the left flank beach, around Mount Suribachi.

Once the LVTs dropped the first wave of marines, the LCSs moved to the flanks to support designated marine battalions. It became difficult to accurately pinpoint where rounds were landing as smoke and dust covered the area just inland. Many of the threats in front of the first waves were reduced by the guns of *LCS 52*. At one point, before 09:10, they observed enemy troops laying down small-arms fire on marines on the beach. *LCS 52* opened up with her 40mm guns and quickly neutralized their fire. Harper reported that after this the small-arms fire was greatly reduced toward the marines on Green One.[12]

At 10:10 *LCS 52* delivered a call for fire on Mount Suribachi, codenamed "Hot Rocks." Just below and to the right corner of the volcano was Green Beach One. The men who were mired in the black grain on that beach were Colonel Harry Liversedge's 28th Marines. Liversedge was a career marine, born ironically in Volcano, California. He had commanded the 1st and 3rd Marine Raider Battalions in combat before being transferred to the 5th Marine Division. He graduated from the University of California, where he had been a star athlete in track, football and rugby. In the 1920 Olympics he represented the U.S. in the shot-put and brought home a Bronze Medal. On Iwo Jima his regiment took up positions as the extreme left flank of the Corps' units. That placed them in the closest proximity to the forthcoming withering fire from the hundreds of hidden gun placements in and on Suribachi.

General Tadamichi Kuribayashi, the architect of the Iwo Jima defense, was born in the Hanishina District, Nagano Prefecture on 7 July 1891. It was believed that his family had lived in that same region for more than five centuries. He was a soldier's general who believed in sharing the daily hardships of his troops. He was adamantly against the use of unorthodox

LCSs line up to deliver fire on Mount Suribachi, Iwo Jima, 19 February 1945 (U.S. Navy photograph, National Archives).

and wasteful tactics such as banzai charges. He was a graduate of the Imperial Japanese Army Academy, class of 1914, and the Army's Cavalry School in 1918. He followed up his military education by graduating from the Army War College with honors in 1924. In 1928 he was appointed as deputy military attaché to Washington, D.C. He remained in the United States for three years. During that time, he travelled throughout the country taking in military facilities and methods of training unencumbered by any suspicions of future reprisals by his mother country. He studied at Harvard for a time during his tour. Kuribayashi also made close examination of the industrial capabilities of the United States. He was witness to the first three years of the Great Depression but still understood how quickly the United States could mobilize its mighty peacetime industrial machine to that of an unrelenting war engine; "By one button push,"[13] Kuribayashi explained. After his tour in the United States, Kuribayashi was sent to Canada as Japan's military attaché to that country. Kuribayashi was a lifelong poet and writer who had aspirations of being a journalist before his path led to the military.

United Press correspondent William F. Tyree hitched a ride over the battlefield in a Navy plane. From that vantage point he shared with the world the devastation taking place on the ground. He observed that smoke and fire covered the entire island. The marines were taking fire from fortified pillboxes he could see dotting the island. Through his headphones, Tyree listened as Marine units called to the ships for fire-support. He watched the response, the flames from the impact of the huge shells rising upwards into the sky. He labeled it "systematic murder and destruction." In its original context, he intended the statement to describe what the Japanese defenders were receiving. In the days ahead it could be applied more accurately to the American forces. He ended his dispatch with an estimate that it might take as long as a week to secure the island. His most precise prediction was "an awful lot of blood would be spilled."[14] At least he would be correct in the latter assumption.

Ensign Parker, along with others, used binoculars to watch the events unfolding on the beach. They were glued to those tools, unable to comprehend the chaos. When the ship moved onto the beach, they no longer needed optical assistance to witness the hell the marines were experiencing. "It was terrible watching the slaughter on the beach," Parker later said, but there was no avoiding it. "It's murder," Larry Cullen thought. He watched as, "Several amphibious tanks [got] direct hits by mortar fire. There [went] three within ten seconds."[15] Cullen looked-on as an Avenger on a strafing run was shot down almost on top of the beach. Virgil Thill also watched as a reconnaissance plane cut across the beach and turned inland. Japanese guns riddled the low-flying plane. It crashed without any sign of the pilot having a chance to eject. A few moments later another plane followed almost in the path of the first. He met the same fate at the same spot. It was all very surreal, to be so close and watch as the beachhead filled with wounded.[16] The ship was close enough that with a little optical assistance, the crew could see the Japanese guns chewing up the marines huddled in the black volcanic sand. The men on *LCS 52* tensed in fear. It seemed as if no one would survive the day.

Things got progressively worse on the ground. By 10:00 the marines were crowded onto the narrow beachhead. Machinegun and mortar fire was slowing advances beyond the seawall. Equipment, which could not negotiate the volcanic mush, sank to their axles. More troops and equipment poured onto the beach, even though the bogged-down marines already ashore wished them away. Dangerous congestion was everywhere, blocking evacuation of wounded as well as causing men to be stranded out in the open.

Then, as per Kuribayashi's plan, the Japanese defenders opened up with a hailstorm of lead from more than four-fifths of their original positions, relatively untouched by pre-landing bombardment. It was at that point, as Tyree had said, methodical slaughter. Japanese anti-aircraft guns were mounted and depressed to sweep the beaches. Somewhere between 700 and 800 large guns let loose on pre-ranged coordinates along the beach. From caves, ravines and pillboxes, barely protruding above the surface of the ground, machineguns and mortars opened fire, intent on butchery until no marines were left to advance and take the island. The fire was accurate and extremely concentrated. It sank landing crafts and amtracs, further blocking the sea supply route from the marines who needed their wounded extracted. It was all shaping up as Kuribayashi envisioned it, or so it seemed. In spite of the carnage, the marines would not back down. By twos and threes they assaulted pillboxes, one by one. As one fell, a squad or platoon moved forward, like opening a can one turn at a time they advanced.

The 52 engaged call-for-fire targets from 09:10 until 14:00 hours on D–Day. Heavy cruisers resupplied the LCSs with ammunition. The 52 fired on anything, including underbrush that looked as if it could cover or conceal enemy positions. If nothing else, perhaps it kept the enemy's heads down. The 52 answered a request from a Marine unit at 13:55 hours to reduce a mortar position. Their reply was a ten-minute barrage of 40mm, 20mm and rockets. At 14:42 they fired a full salvo of rockets on the beach near the "volcano." Twenty-one minutes later they returned to fire at a cave in the volcano. The LCSs made a huge dent in enemy mortars falling on the marines struggling for a foothold on the beach. Led by *LCS 31*, 52 and others, LCSs formed up in line and made smoke to cover the transports, which went on from 19:15 to 20:00 hours. When nightfall came, four LCSs remained to support Marine battalions ashore. Throughout the day, without the LCS's unique ability to move in close to the beach and their arsenal of weapons aboard, the marines could have been held on the beach even longer, lost more men and possibly been pushed back into the sea. At 23:00 *LCS 52* secured from G.Q. and, for the first time since dawn, Lt. Harper left the conning tower. He turned the ship over to the care of the combat veteran Ensign Stewart. Somehow, but by the grace of God and a few hundred navy ships, the marines were still holding out on the island. It was a miracle in some respects and a credit to combined arms in support of ground forces.

The Amphibious Force Commander had heavy accolades to cast upon the performance of the LCSs at Iwo Jima. He stated that they were indispensable at firing into ravines which ran down to the sea. On Iwo Jima the LCS could spot where the American lines were with greater accuracy than the forward observers on the beach could discern.[17] This also helped to prevent the feared and demoralizing friendly fire episodes from the bigger ships miscalculating distant and unobserved targets. It was on Iwo Jima that another use was found for the little gunboats. When a target was spotted by the LCSs, they would fire a steady stream of tracer rounds into the center of the bunker or stronghold. The destroyers and big boys would then align their 5-inch and larger guns on the spot being *marked* by the LCSers.[18]

The troops on the ground used the LCSs to both spot enemy positions and engage those targets more and more as they saw and began to trust their superior effectiveness. In the after-action report for the Naval Gunfire Support operations, the brass had this to say about the Mighty Midgets' success during the first day's landings:

> Until their departure from the area, these units delivered fire on all types of targets, both in deep support and with Shore Fire Control Parties attached to units moving through coastal areas. They were

resourceful and unstinting in meeting all the harassing problems connected with the support of amphibious attack. Their work created both confidence and respect among the troop units.[19]

Illumination was used copiously throughout the first night. A severe weather front approaching forced the Navy to restrict the ships' fire the following day. Fear that the weather might limit or halt ammunition transfer and in turn cause a disaster for a Marine unit who had an emergency when the naval guns ran dry prompted some rationing. That turned out to be a short-term concern and soon after the Navy was able to return to its regular transfer of ammunition to the gunboats. No weather damage occurred or was reported.

Marines learned quickly to appreciate the effectiveness of the Mighty Midgets and understood that their unique position close to shore gave them a valuable vantage point. By the 20th, ground forces were keeping the LCSs busy with call for fire missions. The 52 began her second morning in combat at 08:20 with G.Q.s sounding. She received a Marine liaison request for fire support at 08:55 that morning. That fire mission continued until 09:19 hours. The same stubborn area was bombarded again between 09:50 and 10:15 hours. For the remainder of the day, they moved, shot, moved again and shot again. They fired everything onboard at enemy troops, bunkers and gun emplacements. At 14:00 observers spotted a buildup of enemy troops and *LCS 52* unleashed fifty rockets on the gathering Japanese. The 52's guns did not fall silent until 22:00 that night, ending her day with a ten-minute barrage of 40 and 20mm rounds. She was recognized as responsible for knocking out one machine gun nest in front of a Marine unit and spotting and marking two larger gun emplacements for destroyers. Harper stated that their fire was reported as "very good" by the boys on the ground. When the guys fighting it out in the dirt were happy, that was the best thank-you any ship's crew could ask for. General Quarters was secured at 22:06 and the ship went to condition two watches with Lt. (jg) Duvendeck in charge of the ship.

Many of the fire missions the Marine infantry requested were on enemy pillboxes. Although reconnaissance of island defenses was accumulated in a later "special staff study," it stated that these pillboxes were used mainly for light machineguns. The walls of these defenses were built of one to two feet of reinforced

Lt. John Harper, Captain of *LCS 52* throughout the war, spotting the fall of his ship's rockets off Iwo Jima (U.S. Navy photograph, National Archives).

concrete, as was the overhead cover. They were small and this made them almost impossible to spot from the seaward side. They were built to provide mutually supporting fire as well. They were "cunningly" camouflaged, the report said, with planted grass, sand, brush and natural material, making them even harder to target.[20]

Sailors, like their marine counterparts on the ground, stayed in constant motion. There were always call for fire missions to be answered or a Marine unit that found themselves in need of a few heavier guns. *LCS 52* received a call for fire at 02:15 hours and answered with one full hour of gunfire. No rest for the weary. As daylight broke on the 21st, the 52 took command of three of her sister ships and the group conducted firing runs on pillboxes and other inland targets until noon. Ground units reported back that at least one pillbox had been demolished. The LCSs worked hard on the third day, thanks to a low cloud cover which reduced the big ships' visibility and significantly hindered their fire missions. After leaving the morning's fire support detail, the 52 was sent to Green Beach One for a salvage mission. Once the demolition team arrived, the 52 began trying to drag small boats off the beach. With any luck they might clear off some of the obstacles causing congestion to and from the beach. While performing salvage operations, the 52 became a target for enemy shells and small-arms fire. Lt. Harper stated that the number three 40mm was peppered by small-arms fire. They incurred no damage and none of the crew was hit. Lacking the proper equipment to perform the salvage work, "including a bow anchor," Harper reported that the mission was less than successful. Having lost three heaving lines, four fenders and parted three lines, they no longer had enough line to continue salvage. At 19:10 they gave up for the day. They anchored off Red Two until they were sent to rendezvous with their sister LCSs.

The following day was just as busy. *LCS 52* began her day by taking on 8000 more 40mm rounds, ferried over to them from the USS *Nevada* (radio call sign, PUPPYDOG).[21] The seas were so rough that the 52 banged into the side of the *Nevada* while she came alongside. There was no apparent damage. Coming alongside another ship, especially in high seas, was one of the most dangerous maneuvers a ship could perform. Following the transfer they moved to a new area to await orders. At 08:00 the following day they moved within sight of Mount Suribachi.

When all the battles of World War II were over, Iwo Jima would not be most remembered for its carnage or tactical or political value. Rather, what would make Iwo Jima a battlefield recognized throughout history were two acts carried out by six men who barely knew one another. On the morning of the 23rd a detail of men led by First Lt. Harold Schrier, Echo Company, 28th Marines, climbed Mount Suribachi. Their purpose was to raise a small American flag on the summit. The flag was raised without too much fanfare and almost no opposition at approximately 10:20 that morning. A photographer from *Leatherneck,* the Marines' magazine, Staff Sergeant Louis R. Lowery, snapped excellent pictures of the flag going up.

The Marine Corps brass were not happy—the flag was simply too small to be seen from a distance. A larger flag, ninety-six by fifty-six inches, was located on an LST. Another group of marines trudged to the top. The larger flag would be raised as the small flag was brought down. Joseph John Rosenthal, a civilian photographer, was in the process of adjusting the settings on his Graflex Speed Graphic camera when out of the corner of his eye he saw movement. He turned and instinctively pointed and snapped. Unaware of the quality of the first picture, he posed the participants and shot a few more.

The significance of the larger flag to those who witnessed it, and even those who raised it, was minor in the moment. Seaman Second Class Virgil Thill, from the deck of the *52*, recalled he "vividly" saw the flag on top of the mountain but could not recall whether he saw it raising or not. He put it in perspective when he added that there was a lot of action going on, on the island and onboard ship—the flag being raised at that moment seemed "insignificant."[22] Laton Burns too, made a, by now typical, entry in his journal, "Feb. 23rd at 10:34 AM Old Glory was raised on Hot Rock." General Quarters were sounded at 09:17 and Lt. Harper had just secured from G.Q. at 10:17; most of the men would have still been milling around on deck. Harper also wrote in the ship's log, "American Flag raised on Suribachi (sp)." That event occurred at 10:34 according to him as well. By those two entries it was evident the men of *LCS 52* watched the second flag raising. When G.Q. was sounded that morning the ship was "Standing off Hot Rocks," close to the base of Mount Suribachi. Ensign Albert Parker said, "We were close enough to shore to watch with binoculars the famous raising of the flag atop Mt. Suribachi!" At 11:18 the ship left the area.[23]

It did the men on shore and at sea good to see their flag flying atop the highest point on the island after four bloody days of fighting. Beyond that, there was little thought given to the presence or process of the flag being there. By the early morning issues of newspapers across America and the world, on the 24th, there was only one picture dominating the front pages, the single haphazard shot that Rosenthal had come within a split-second of missing. Before the end of the year it would be a three-cent stamp and be the foundation icon of several war bond drives. Unknown to the six men in the picture and the photographer, it would become one of the most recognized photographs in history.

It was the perfect marriage of moments and actions. Had Rosenthal not turned and snapped the picture at that moment, the flag raising would have likely been forgotten in the wake of larger events. However, without the passion and effort displayed in that instant he snapped the shot, the photo would have been brushed into the forgotten pile like the series of pictures which followed. There was no way it could have been reproduced, but it did not have to be. For the men who watched it, like the rest of the world, it was insignificant, as Thill put it, at the moment. By the time the war was over, they would forever recall with great pride the day they saw the flag rise over Iwo Jima.

Oren Clifford Tweet watched the flag go up through binoculars. He was the pointer of a 40mm crew and was looking toward the hillsides at the moment the flag went up. Oren was born 26 October 1923 to John and Olive Hayes Tweet in Reeder, North Dakota. He grew up on a farm in Adams County, the oldest of eight children. The Tweet family shared a two-room sod house on their farm in North Dakota.

Tweet joined the Navy on 28 April 1944. Oren did his training at Fort Pierce through the end of July and reported to the USS *Wyoming* on the 29th for gunnery instruction. Reeder was the former township of Leff, North Dakota. In 1908 the township became Reeder, named after an assistant chief engineer for the Chicago, Milwaukee, St. Paul and Pacific Railroad, which cut through the town. In the early 1940s, the town claimed no fewer than 270 residents.

Oren's father was a farmer by all accounts; there was little else to do around Reeder. However, in his early forties, in 1930 he was working as a North Dakota Highway Patrolman. By 1940 John was back working on the farm. Both John and Olive were born in Iowa and married there. Both of Oren's grandparents were from Norway and still spoke their mother tongue. Oren's sister, Alice, moved to Washington State during the war and worked in the shipyards as her contribution to winning the war. All the Tweet children graduated from Reeder High School.

Another task that represented their diverse capabilities came on the evening of the 23rd when the LCSs were called on to lay down a smoke-screen. Enemy planes were expected to make an appearance so the 52 spent most of the evening blanketing the area with covering smoke—19:15 to 21:15 hours.

Laton noted in his journal that he spotted two of the hospital ships, "Hospital ships *Solace*, and the *Samaritan* were here." He was probably aware of their grim mission and perhaps was thinking of how busy they were. The hospital ships would have been to the rear of the armed ships for their own protection. *Solace*'s radio call sign was NIGHTINGALE. *Samaritan* drew the more provocative call sign of LIPSTICK.

On the 24th, *LCS 52* was ordered to move north on the east side of the island to the Boat Basin, located about midways of the island. Once there, they laid down fire on targets inland that were giving some marines trouble. Good reports from observers on the ground came back to Lt. Harper. The best of those compliments was probably that the marines were advancing under the covering fire the 52 was unleashing. Throughout the remainder of February, *LCS 52* stayed on a hectic schedule, knocking out gun emplacements, targeting caves, buildings and any enemy position the marines could coordinate fire on.

LCS 52 provided a call for fire on the 25th at 09:25 and secured from G.Q. At five minutes past noon a Marine spotting party joined them aboard to direct fire. The Marine Lieutenant in charge of establishing communications with the shore fire control was J.J. Sweeny. John J. Sweeny was a twenty-one-year-old Second Lieutenant. He was born in Denver but raised in Utah. His father, Michael, was a timber man. His mother was the former Grace Akolt. John joined the Marines in 1942. He completed advanced officers training at Quantico in July and artillery school in November of 1944.

Lt. Sweeney, as young as he was, became one of the first, if not the first, artillery officers to recognize the benefit of coordinating fire from LCSs. The first day of the invasion, Sweeney boarded *LCS 51*; sitting 650 yards off the shore at the boat basin, he directed her guns on spots that were giving the marines hell. Once he brought the *51*'s tracer rounds on target, the 6-inch guns of the USS *Vicksburg* zeroed in and terminated the targets. That afternoon, assisted by four more LCSs, they eliminated a forming enemy counterattack before it could advance.

Before he left the 52 that day, Sweeney had directed three fire missions. He disembarked at 19:05 by small boat to return to his unit. The 52 ceased for the night at 21:15 hours with "excellent" reports from the marines' shore spotters.

Sweeney would later be wounded by a hand grenade blast in late February but remained on the line. On 1 March, after several days of heavy fighting, he was wounded again, when his leg was broken. He was taken out of action and returned to the States. Lt. Sweeney would earn two Purple Hearts and a Bronze Star for Valor for his actions on Iwo Jima.

On the 27th the 52 scored direct hits on a building and caves that were halting marine movements. They secured for a much-needed rest at 17:07 hours that day. On the following day, 28 February, *LCS 52* knocked out an enemy gun emplacement according to the reports sent back from an observation plane.

The sea around the island of Iwo Jima was so crowded with ships that frequent collisions occurred while attempting to maneuver. The *LCI (L) 627* which had struck the *LCS 52* back in Saipan was damaged again when she collided with the USS *Finnegan* (DE 307) (call sign,

LCS 52's guns bellow smoke as they suppress enemy positions on the island of Iwo Jima. The LCSs could move into the shallow waters off the beach and lay down a hail of precision fire. The LCSs often hosted marine and army spotters aboard, whose help only added to the accuracy of the barrage (U.S. Navy photograph, National Archives).

FISHERBODY). Ships drew fire from enemy guns on shore as well. Men also drew fire. Virgil Thill stopped to chat with Porter Barron, Jr., one of the cooks. Porter was standing on deck in the solid white cook's uniform. A Japanese sniper managed to lob a shot at the figure standing out so plainly against the backdrop. The bullet had lost much of its power and, luckily for Porter, struck his belt buckle causing only "a little red mark on his belly."[24] The buckle was a standard slide web belt made of double plates of brass making up the front and back. The web belt slid through the opening and locked in place by the tension of a piston which ran the length of the buckle vertically. The bullet penetrated the outer brass plate, the web belt and stopped in the back plate. Had it not hit the belt, but rather flesh, Porter would have been headed to the hospital ship.

Porter Barron, Jr., was born in Nelsonville, Ohio. His father, Porter Sr., was a coal miner. Porter's dad and his younger brother, Robert, were working in the nearby coal mines by the time they were sixteen. Mining was the major employment for Nelsonville and the surrounding southern Ohio area. Porter "Jr.'s" mother was Margaret Birtcher Barron. She later remarried and became Margaret Whitmore.

In 1940 the population of the town of Nelsonville was just over 5,360 residents. There was little for entertainment. The Hocking River ran through town and so did the electric railroad after 1920. Stuart's Opera House closed the year Porter Jr. was born. It was around that time that the coal boom slowed to a halt. In the same square with the boarded-up opera house was the Dew Hotel. The Hotel had pampered guests since the early nineteenth-century. In 1912 Theodore Roosevelt arrived in Nelsonville on the campaign trail. He used a balcony on the Dew to give a rousing speech to Athens County voters.

When Porter enlisted on 21 October 1942, he lived at 179 Grosvenor Street, the home of his grandparents. He was raised there from the time he turned five years old. His father, born in 1902, was serving time in 1930 and would not see forty-seven-years old. Porter's grandparents were Lydia Margaret Six and John Barron. His grandmother would die two months before Porter was discharged from the Navy. Porter Junior's Uncle James, who he had grown up with, was serving in the Army in the Pacific. His uncle by marriage to his Aunt Vivian, Arthur Lee McQuaid was also serving in the Army.

D–Day plus seven, 26 February, began in earnest at 08:20 with naval gunfire and land-based artillery laying down preparatory fire to cover an impending attack by the 25th Marines. The guns of *LCS 52* were happy to contribute. Gunners Mate 2nd Class Charles John Kochanowicz was acting Chief Gunner on *LCS 52* at the moment. He was pleased with the smooth operation of 52's guns and their crews. When the guns were operating at their best, his job was an easy one.

Charley, by naval custom, was an old salt. He enlisted in the Navy on 19 November 1942 from Philadelphia, Pennsylvania. Before joining *LCS 52* he served on the USS *Sloat* (DE 245), a destroyer escort. Charley joined her crew on her commissioning date of 16 August 1943 from the Navy Training Station at Norfolk. He travelled with the *Sloat* on escort duty up and down the eastern seaboard, New York to Norfolk and back, throughout the later part of the year. On 11 November, *Sloat* joined convoy UGS-24 headed for Casablanca. They stopped briefly at Hampton Roads, Virginia, and then headed out to sea. Arriving at Casablanca, they made a quick turnaround and returned to New York on Christmas Day. It was on that trip that Charley made his 3rd Class. Leaving on 10 January, the ship completed another uneventful escort trip to Casablanca. In March, the *Sloat* joined a large convoy going to Bizerte, Tunisia. Convoy USG-36 started across the Atlantic with 150 transport ships and twelve escorts. The *Sloat* took up a front position on the starboard corner of the huge formation. To her right was the USS *Rhodes* and to her left, USS *Decatur*.

The armada of ships, even in the Atlantic Ocean, stuck out like a sore thumb to the Germans. The first attacks came in the late evening of 31 March, via U-boat. The sub was detected on sonar at 22:13 hours, before it could launch torpedoes. Destroyers dropped depth charges and deterred any further attempts.

The moon had barely disappeared from the sky. It was 04:00 on the morning of 1 April when twenty enemy planes came into sight.[25] The night sky lit up with parachute flares, dropped by the Germans. The Allied ships retaliated with copious amounts of antiaircraft fire. Streams of tracers, announcing their accompanying solid-jacketed brother rounds, sprayed lines across the sky. For their twenty minutes of efforts, the Germans were believed to have paid with the loss of up to five of their planes. The Allies' cost was damage to one ship. That was the *Jared Ingersoll*. She was hit by a torpedo bomb at 04:12. The crew of the *Jared Ingersoll* was ordered into the water and the ship temporarily abandoned. When the flames began to subside, the crew went back aboard and fought the fires to a close. She was towed to Algiers for repairs. No Allied service members lost their life during the attack.

Charles remained with the *Sloat* until 5 May 1944, when he was transferred to the Amphibious Training Base, Fort Pierce, Florida. He, like Chief Holland, carried the unique credentials of having served in both the Atlantic and Pacific as enlisted men. Charles was also another one of the older guys aboard ship. He was born 27 January 1915 to immigrant parents from Poland. By all accounts, he was hard to get to know.[26]

Most of the boys thought of him as a loner. He did his job but never socialized with anyone. At Iwo Jima, as Charles was rushing to carry a drum of 20mm to one of the guns on D plus seven, he dropped it. As luck would have it, it fell directly on his foot. The physical damage was tolerable. The accident went relatively unnoticed until some would-be war reporter caught wind of the misfortune while doing a story about the ship. The story of the injured foot ended up in the June 1945 issue of *Our Navy* magazine.

The 1st of March was another one of those unfortunate days for shipping off the beaches of Iwo. *LCT 1029* ran into an unseen obstacle at 03:10 on the 2nd near the beach. In efforts to salvage the vessel, she overturned. There was no choice but to drag her out to sea and sink her. The USS *Hercules* ran aground on a shoal just after noon on the 2nd. Her fate was much better, and she was cleared with minor damage. A hole was found in the bow of the USS *Bennett*, just below the waterline. It was believed that it was caused by a dud which had struck the ship when dropped by an enemy plane during the day. The hospital ships that Burns had noted both departed for Guam, filled with wounded, at 17:00 that evening.

While coming alongside *LST 224* to pick up a Marine observation party led by Lieutenant Colonel Dillon on 2 March, *52* rammed *224*, causing a large amount of damage to her. The *52* was spared serious damage and went on with her mission. Harper made no reference in his log about the accident but it was recorded on the ComPhibsPac Action report.

Thill added that the *52* used her anchor to act as an ad hoc winch to keep her in tight on the beach while the observation party communicated with ground units. The marines acted as the middlemen to direct fire. Their observation capacity was improved by being aboard the gunboat a-case-of adapt-and-overcome the enemy with good American ingenuity. The remainder of the day, *LCS 52* and her shore party patrolled the northern half of Iwo, spotting mortar and other enemy guns. Close-fire missions off Iwo Jima ran day-in and day-out in a kind of frantic routine. It was no wonder that the little gunboats in their urgency rammed other ships in the overcrowded waters.

No other Marine officers named "Lt. Col. Dillon" were present on Iwo at the time, and it could be assumed this was Edward James Dillon, a career Marine officer who had already fought the Japanese when he was stationed in China in the 1930s. Dillon moved from the position of executive officer to commander of 2nd Battalion, 23rd Marine Regiment shortly after his day with *LCS 52*, when most of the officers in his unit became casualties. He continued to serve throughout the war and into the 1950s. He was known as a strict and by-the-book Marine who believed in unrelenting discipline, sometimes at the expense of his image with the men under him. Lt. Colonel Dillon received the Navy Cross for gallantry on behalf of his actions during operations on Iwo Jima.[27]

Letters home were being heavily censored prior to the invasion and during the battle for Iwo. In the heat of their first battle the tempo was also too hectic to sit down with pen and paper. Claude Cook's usually regular volley of letters to Lynn had been reduced to one in late January and one on the 4th of March. The mail coming to *LCS 52* had also been delayed considerably by the battle. Their first mail delivery in three weeks caught them on the 3rd of March. Cook attempted to gently refute Lynn's scolding for going three weeks without a letter. The crew, as he explained, was a letter-writing bunch but everyone had ceased due to the long days and nights in support of the marines. The prior days included only fight and then sleep when there was time.

By the 5th, the crew was dreaming of far off home. Galen Libby from Garland, Maine, was showing his pictures of snow back home around when he interrupted Cook, writing a letter. The two northerners engaged in building an imaginary wintery paradise where they could run in snow up to their necks. Libby left to go write home and Cook returned to his own letter to Lynn. Minutes later Libby burst into a cursing fit, his letter spoiled by the heaving, rolling ship in rough seas.

In the early days of March the 52 received credit for blowing up two separate ammo dumps. Secondary fires and explosions were observed by ground forces, confirming those actions. The 52 was also credited with silencing a Japanese machinegun nest that was using a cliff for protection and concealment. In his journal Laton Burns made an entry that on "March 6th Army P-51's and P-61's landed on Iwo." He is the only one of the crew that seems to have taken note of these landings. Early on the morning of 8 March the 52 took on another observation party. This time they transferred them directly from the *LCS 31* with no incidents. They patrolled the area along the shore, firing on targets called out by the observation party, until 10:30. Lt. Harper received orders to fall back to the rear and prepare to depart Iwo Jima.[28] Laton Burns recorded in his journal: "March 8th left Iwo for Saipan." Their first fight was over, and by the grace of God they had saved many lives, including their own.

William Gardner (left) was a camera-hungry cutup who got himself in more pictures than any other crewmember. Ralph Prendergast (center) was assigned as one of the last cooks to serve the original crew. Porter Barron (right) was assigned as a cook during the Iwo Jima operation. Porter was wearing his mess whites when he was struck by a sniper's bullet. His life was saved by a cheap Navy-issued brass belt buckle (Virgil Thill collection).

5. Black Sand and Suffering

At 16:28 hours on the 8th, seven ships formed two columns, leaving three-hundred-yards between each vessel as per standard procedure in hostile water. LCSs 52, 53, 56 formed the port column and *LST 783*, LCSs *31, 54* and *55* formed the starboard column. They turned toward Saipan at a speed of nine knots. After a two-day uneventful trip, they arrived and anchored in the outer harbor off Saipan.

Claude Cook finally found time and patience to sit down and write Lynn while the ship was moderately still. He described his settings as peaceful, the stars showing bright in the sky as a cool breeze drifted across the ship. The trip from Iwo Jima had placed them in a world without rocket explosions, gunfire and distant artillery. Life was absent of the seemingly constant back and forth of boats loaded with casualties speeding from the black sand beach to the hospital ships. War and killing was yesterday's memory.

The 52 moved into Tanapag Harbor on 13 March and began restocking food and water. The following day the USS *Fulton* pulled alongside and moored. The crew of the *Fulton* began the needed repair work on *LCS 52*. The crew of 52 got out of their way and went ashore to stir up a ball game and a couple of beers. When Cook wrote Lynn on the 15th, he apologized for being too tired to write. He had celebrated their first day on land in over two months by playing a little too hard. He had returned to ship early and gone straight to bed. He told her that in spite of the soreness he felt good. It was something, he said, which a year before would have just been a "pleasant day," but was now a real "luxury." Time off also meant time to think about what they had been through at Iwo. There were a lot of boys not "as fortunate" as the crew of 52 to have that "luxury" and they knew it.[29]

It was a peaceful time but short-lived; the ship was restocked with provisions, water and plenty of fresh ammunition. They would need them all more than anything they could then imagine. On 25 March at 06:07 hours *LCS 52* cleared the Outer Harbor nets of Saipan and headed north toward Okinawa. Harper's instructions were defined in the Top Secret Operation Plan No. A1–45. She fell in convoy with the Demonstration Group 51.2, commanded by Rear Admiral Jerauld Wright.

Because the waters north of Iwo Jima were still technically enemy waters, the convoys had to be on the lookout for enemy submarines. The 52 and her sister ships remained at condition two watches for the duration of the trip. Condition two required that half the crew and officers were awake twenty-four hours a day. The waters turned out to be pleasantly absent of enemy subs.

6

By Land and Sea
The Battle for Okinawa

In post-war histories the extreme hardships of the ground battles for Okinawa have often deemphasized the Navy's crucial part during that campaign. Most accounts, unless told by veteran sailors, are scant snapshots of ships' encounters with kamikazes. Books on the battle seldom devote more than one or maybe two chapters to the kamikaze attacks and much of those to the American pilots who flew against them. There was more to the Navy's participation in the fight, and their losses both in human life and vessels told the full story.

In an attempt to underscore their share in the battle for Okinawa it is most revealing to examine what the American Navy was confronting. The idea of kamikaze, meaning "Divine Wind," ran deep within the spirit and superstition of the Japanese people. In both 1274 and 1281 great typhoons wrought havoc on the fleets of Kublai Khan (1215–1294) and prevented his certain invasion and subjugation of Japan.[1] Various Japanese military leaders believed with adamant conviction that divine intervention could be called upon in the late stages of World War II to prevent a second attempt and almost certain invasion of the homeland. They, unlike their ancestors, believed the Divine Wind could be aided or summoned mechanically to appear. Although kamikaze has become synonymous with "suicide" since World War II, it should be viewed strongly in the years of 1944–45 as the keystone to a crusade and hopeful victory on the part of the Japanese. While that may not make the concept any easier to Western ideology it may promote an understanding of the dedication to mission success, not just an attempt by a large contingent of implacable zealots to go out in a blaze of glory.

The idea of producing a manmade divine wind was already in effect by the time Task Force 58 and her land forces sailed toward Okinawa in early 1945. In late October of 1944 the first formal kamikaze unit flew against ships engaged in the allied return to the Philippines. It was in the Philippines on the eve of the allied invasion that the concept of deliberate suicide attacks was discussed and sanctioned. During a meeting with Vice Admiral Ohnishi in the town of Mabalacat, Commander Rikihei Inoguchi proposed that manned planes be equipped as flying bombs and sent on one-way missions, crashing into American carriers. Commander Rikihei believed that on a conventional mission to attack carriers the pilot's odds were poor—it was, in fact, a suicide mission regardless. He believed that by making the mission "one-way" up front, the mission had greater hope of success. Inoguchi's proposal met with success and so did the first efforts of the kamikaze pilots. Over 1,200 Japanese planes took part in kamikaze attacks during the Philippine campaign and sank thirty-four ships, leaving around 288 more damaged.[2]

Modern movies have left an image of the pilot of these flying bombs as that of a lone madman in an explosive-laden plane circling an allied ship as a hawk stalks its prey. As he lines up, he nose-dives into the deck of a ship, happily taking his own life and that of hundreds of sailors if by sheer expert gunnery he is not blasted to pieces before his impact. There were hundreds of just such examples in the last days of World War II in the Pacific; however that was not the original expectation of action for the kamikaze. By the time the Battle for Okinawa kicked off the corps of kamikaze were made up of the poorest planes and pilots that the Japanese air force could muster. Some were ancient biplanes, and many pilots were at times less than the fanatic, implacable volunteers seen in the movies.

In order that they might have a minute chance at committing the sacrifice, they were escorted by experienced and valued pilots and planes. Much as the days of the bamboo spear charges had ceased on the ground, so too were the days when Japan could afford to throw their best craft and pilots at the sides of ships. The better craft were to distract and engage the allied fighters which would have made short work of the slow planes and almost-inept pilots of the later-day special attack squadrons. The better Japanese planes would do their fair share of damage, bombing and destroying allied aircraft as well, but crashing only as a last resort.

Proof that the strategy would work came on 19 March 1945, twelve days before the first infantryman stepped onto Okinawa. Early that morning a Japanese dive-bomber successfully connected with the carrier USS *Franklin*, dropping two bombs on the flight deck. The ship was by some miracle saved but at the cost of more than 2,000 casualties, 724 of those killed in action. While the captain of the *Franklin* was fighting to save his ship, Task Force 58 was experiencing attacks by close to 200 enemy planes and the first taste of kamikaze actions in the battle for Okinawa—sixty-nine suicide planes in the group.[3]

Japan's military hierarchy determined that the kamikaze might be the only answer to halting American and allied sea power. Sea power was, after all, the only source of, or threat to, the physical invasion of Japan proper. At the latter stage of the war Japan had been severed of its war-fighting raw resources—the very material they had begun the war to obtain and protect. However, she would never see herself as defeated until the last Japanese citizen had committed to and perished in the fray. If the kamikaze could destroy the bulk of America's navy at Okinawa, then there was a chance that the final battle on Japan might never come. Under those circumstances, and even in ultimate defeat, she might be able to negotiate an honorable peace.

While each and every sailor scanned the skies for the dreaded flying kamikaze, the threat did not solely limit itself to the above. The Japanese resorted to a small fleet of plywood motorboats as part of their suicidal arsenal as well. Little attention has been given this aspect of the larger kamikaze scheme because the majority of boats were spotted from an American aircraft before they were close to being deployed. Soon after observation, close to 300 of these "Q-boats" were destroyed by an infantry unit. In their reduced numbers, the remainder became ineffective against the allied naval vessels on station near Okinawa. Nevertheless, the Japanese did not discard the plan to use special attack boats. Suicide boats would cause damage, if only on a reduced scale.

Each Q-boat was armed with a 264-pound depth charge and operated by drivers with the same zeal to sink an allied ship as their airborne counterparts. Had they gotten loose in adequate numbers among the allied armada the toll on shipping could have been devastating. The realistic fear of suicide boats still existed for the sailors.

There was one more craft assigned to the Japanese list of kamikaze tactics, the behemoth battleship the *IJN Yamato*. It was the largest of the battleships and was outfitted with nine 18.1-inch guns capable of launching a 3,220-pound shell nearly thirty miles. As part of the overall combined air and sea suicide mission known as Operation Kikusui Number One, she was to sail with a scant armada of smaller vessels toward Okinawa. *Yamato* and her sister ships were to distract and draw allied aircraft from the main aerial attacks. Then, once she penetrated the outer perimeter of the allied fleets, *Yamato* was to wreak havoc on the transport and support ships anchored around the island. When her fuel was gone, loaded for a one-way voyage, she was to beach and expend her ammunition as a gargantuan artillery battery might in support of ground forces. The result was anticlimactic, in spite of being heavily armed with anti-aircraft guns, the *Yamato*'s suicide mission ended without a single shot being fired at another ship. She was sent to the bottom 200 miles from her target by American aircraft.

In the historical world of what might have been, there were only the devastating losses caused by the airborne suicide attacks available to contrive an estimate. Had the Q-boats or the *Yamato* managed to complete even half their goals, the loss to allied vessels could have, as the Japanese hoped, steered the war in another direction and cost even more lives on both sides. Nevertheless, the fear of this great unknown taskforce of suicide craft weighed on the hearts and minds of every allied sailor sailing toward Okinawa.

The Ryukyu Islands are a group of one-hundred-sixty islands including Okinawa Shima. Okinawa is approximately sixty-four miles long. Its width at its narrowest is two miles and at its broadest it is eighteen miles across. The civilian population was estimated around 430,000 in 1945. Shuri Castle, which would play a pivotal role in the ground fighting, was the ancient capital of Okinawa. The castle was built on a series of connected razorback ridges running the width of the island. In the 20th century, the seaport of Naha served as the capital city. The Japanese came and then conquered the island in 1867. By 1874 the Japanese Home Ministry ruled Okinawa as a prefecture. As the Allies moved closer to Japan proper, in 1943, Okinawa and seven other islands were formed into the Home Islands District of Kyushu. For all intents and purposes, Okinawa was Japan.

The 52 (radio call sign, IBEX-52) and the rest of Demonstration Group 51.2.9 arrived off the Japanese island of Okinawa on March 31, 1945. They were met there by ships carrying the 2nd Marine Division. Most of the 22,000 marines of the 2nd Marine Division were combat veterans of Guadalcanal, Tarawa and a few of China. Their fake landing ruse during the actual invasion of Okinawa would exclude any of them from placing a boot on the island. That did not settle the nerves of men who had seen their buddies blown apart in their landing crafts as they made their way to the beaches of Tarawa. The purpose of the feigned landings by the 2nd was to convince the Japanese they were the real deal and pull assets away from the actual landing sites. To draw fire was to have played the part well.

The crew of *LCS 52* had also learned other valuable lessons from their first fight. One beach landing under their belts and they knew from experience there would be no time the following morning to digest a huge meal. Easter Sunday dinner was therefore celebrated on Saturday night.

It was just before dawn when a single suicide plane appeared and targeted one of the big ships positioned among the hundreds of ships in the flotilla. The USS *Hinsdale* (APA-120) (call sign, SOFTSOAP) was about twelve miles off the southern tip of the island when the plane picked her out. The kamikaze seemed to come out of nowhere, low to the water;

there was little time to engage the attacker. The *Hinsdale* was a well-armed Haskell-class attack transport preparing to offload marines into the landing crafts when she was hit at 06:00 hours on 1 April. The suicide plane crashed into her port side setting off the three bombs it was carrying. The bombs penetrated into the engine room of the ship, barely above the waterline.

Harper and the above-deck crew watched the explosions. Secondary explosions from ammunition igniting sent streams of light rocketing into the pre-dawn sky like fireworks.[4] When dawn broke, the listing *Hinsdale* clearly showed three holes in her hull, one seven feet in diameter. Harper thought how frightening it was "to realize that one small plane and one pilot had caused that kind of damage."[5] It was also unsettling how close the 52 had been to the *Hinsdale*; it could have just as easily been Harper's ship.

As odd events cause strange reactions in combat, Harper attributed the witnessing of the crash on the *Hinsdale* to causing a sort of adrenalin purge which kept the men of the 52 cool during the demonstration landings.[6] The fact that no withering fire erupted from the enemy as the ground troops of the 2nd Division puttered toward the Minatoga Beaches probably did not dull that steadiness. Like their ground-pounding counterparts on the other side of the island, the sailors saw the mostly peaceful panorama before them as a Godsend. Lt. Harper noted that it was considerably different from the "fiery beaches at Iwo. We were rather pleased with the rural scene that confronted us—neat gardens, houses, barns, fishing villages, pastures, and one white horse," Harper said "he sauntered casually through our bombardment of the beaches that morning and was back for a repeat performance the next day."[7]

By 08:30 on the western Hagushi Beaches the troops of the actual landings established a broad and unopposed foothold. At the time the troops had no way of knowing that the Japanese army had moved into the interior and fortified caves, tunnels, and mountains on the southern end of the island. At least in part, the feint had drawn some defenders away from the landing beaches. Soldiers and marines quickly seized both the major airfields at Yontan and Kadena. They, too, were deserted. Americans faced little more than Okinawan conscripts known as the *Bimbo Butai* or Poor Detachment on their sprint across the island the first day. Few of the conscripts had any desire to die for the emperor and went home.

Meanwhile, the initial shore bombardment by *LCS 52* began at 08:15. As they had done off Iwo, they moved in, emptied their rocket launchers, moved back, reloaded and returned to fire again. The mission of making the Japanese believe their shelling was a prelude to an actual landing went well. The demonstration ended at 13:45 hours and *LCS 52* began patrol duties. She headed north to Nakagusuku Bay (later called Buckner Bay). The minesweepers had been working feverishly in the bay cutting the anchor lines to underwater mines all day. The loose mines bobbed on the surface, harmless unless one of the prongs made contact with a hull of a ship. The assigned LCS's followed close behind the sweepers and waited for notification that a mine had been cut loose. Waves were at four to five feet that day and the best opportunity to spot the floating mines was when they rode the top of the wave. When a clear shot presented itself, the boys on the guns opened up until they hit a prong and triggered the explosion. A geyser then shot out of the water throwing hot shrapnel into the air. The chunks of sea mine sometimes landed on the decks of the ships.[8] The operation continued throughout the day. When it became too dark to safely spot and destroy the mines, the operation was called to a halt. The operation had cleared a lane sufficient enough for allied ships to move in and out of the bay safely.

One of the useful capabilities of the LCS was her ability to lay down a heavy smokescreen. When her guns and rockets fired volley after volley of fire support for the infantry units, she could almost create a cloak of smoke equal to the efforts of her smoke generators. This photo was taken from the deck of another LCS and shows the 52 speeding toward the landing beach off Okinawa, guns blazing (Diane Burns Brads collection).

During the first night off Okinawa, the crew of the 52 listened to the blasts of bombs and antiaircraft fire coming from the fleet off the western shores. They had no way of seeing what was happening, but the din of explosions established that the kamikazes were giving the sailors hell. The *West Virginia* (call sign MARKSMAN), a survivor of the Pearl Harbor attack, was struck by a kamikaze at 19:03 on the first evening. The bomb carried by the plane detached and failed to detonate but the crash still cost four sailors' lives and wounded twenty-three others. At 19:08 a suicide plane hit the USS *Alpine* (call sign EPWORTH) killing sixteen sailors and wounding nineteen more. At 21:00 the USS *Vammen* (DE-644), (call sign ARGENTINA) hit a mine and was seriously damaged. USS *Achernar* (AKA-53) (call sign ADRIATIC) was struck by a plane at 00:43 hours on 2 April, with five killed and forty-one wounded. H.M.S. *Indefatigable* (R10) was also hit on 1 April. Although the bomb on the enemy plane did not detonate, the crash caused twenty-one men killed and twenty-seven wounded.

Day two began for the 52 by rejoining the Demonstration Group and making more bombardments and fake landings along the eastern beaches of Okinawa. The 52 was released from demonstrations at noon and ordered to the western beaches to lay down smoke cover. They remained off the western beaches for the next two days, laying down smoke screens when and where needed and performing antiaircraft screening. In the daylight the men watched the steady train of Japanese planes coming down from the north. Harper admired the tireless efforts of the Marine fighter pilots who labored to intercept those enemy sorties.

He noted that it seldom took more than two to three minutes for them to pick up the enemy planes and splash them. The Marine pilots "certainly lived up to their reputation as fine pilots and good gunners," he said.[9] Each time a kamikaze burst into flames in midair, it saved countless sailors' lives. The naval picket or screen was also created that day, a circle around the island made up of destroyers with radar controlled guns having the capacity to pinpoint and fire night or day. It would be known more familiarly as the Radar Picket (RP).

The rumors were spreading among the crew. One ship had been sunk when a kamikaze managed to elude the fighter planes, antiaircraft guns, and flew down the smokestack of the ship. They heard about the ships running into sea mines, and even the occasional suicide boat ramming into allied vessels and causing damage. For that reason the mission of *LCS 52* changed.

The crew switched their eyes from the sky to the surface from 5 through 8 April, screening for small boats. The hunt for, or screening for, small motorboat suiciders was called "Skunk Patrol" by the officers and men. The *52* moved to Kerama Retto and performed those small boat patrols. Harper described Kerama Retto as nothing more than mountaintops sticking out of the water. The mountains of Kerama Retto held many caves in which several suicide motorboats were discovered and also played host to Japanese gun emplacements. These were the same anchorages where units of the 77th Infantry Division had discovered hundreds of boats while securing the island in the last days of March.

Kerama Retto is one of thirty islands making up the Kerama islands, between twelve and fifteen miles off the southwestern shores of Okinawa. Most of the islands are surrounded by coral reefs but Kerama Retto had ideal anchorage spots. The first American landings occurred on 26 March. Unlike the marines who had fought on Saipan, the units of the Army's 77th whose presence triggered the 700-person mass suicide of indigenous islanders were stunned by the sight. Japanese propaganda had created the same level of fear of American atrocities on Kerama Retto as on Saipan. The islanders cut each other's throats and others were bludgeoned to death by their family and friends.[10]

For *LCS 52* her time at Kerama Retto was less morbid than what the Army had experienced. The island by April was used for safe anchorage where damaged ships could be repaired and refitted. Harper allowed some of his crew to go ashore and stir up a ball game to relieve a bit of tension. Some of the men even swam along the white sand beaches and enjoyed reasonable safety.

The day started very early. It was 04:00 and *LCS 52* was crossing the entrance out of Nwca Gus Uku Wan. They were ordered to act as a screen for UDTs operating off the beach at Tsu Gen Island. That mission would take them out of the action and exclude them from the largest suicide attack to date.

Overcast skies in southern Kyushu threatened to hinder or halt the air phase of Operation Kikusui Number One. Skies over Okinawa on Friday, 6 April, were clearer, clear enough for a divine wind to blow. At 08:00 Japanese fighter planes took off from Kanoya. Their mission took them skirting along the chain of small islands that led south to Okinawa. They were bait, thrown out to lure American fighter planes away. Once the American planes were drawn into action against them, three more sorties would slip past and make their way into the anchorages of Allied ships. Among the hundreds of Japanese planes dispatched to Okinawa that day were eighteen planes from the Thunder Gods Corps—kamikaze.

By 18:00 the *Yamato* was ordered to begin steaming toward Okinawa. She was a survivor of the last-ditch effort to stop the Americans in a decisive naval battle at Leyte Gulf the previous October. She was also the last surviving battleship in the Japanese fleet. The Japanese efforts at Samar had failed and *Yamato* would not survive her encounter with the Americans again.

As soon as the battleship lost her escort fighter planes, the Americans located her. It was now seven days since the first American infantry had landed on Okinawa. The rain was steady by noon. The carrier planes dove at the world's largest battleship, dropping bombs and torpedoes. By 14:00 the damage done by that swarm sent the *Yamato* to the bottom of the sea. Ironically, despite her frequent proximity to battle, the ship's enormous guns had never fired a shot in anger.

The air attack of the day before *Yamato*'s sinking had, in reality, been less successful than hoped. The attacks from land based Japanese planes, including kamikaze, continued through the 8th of April. The initial reports were encouraging and, though flagrantly erroneous, they cited two carriers, one battleship, a destroyer and approximately eleven lesser American ships sunk. The reports prompted the Japanese Military Headquarters to order the go-ahead with Operation Kikusui Number Two.

The *Charles J. Badger* was anchored off Brown Beach on the 9th of April. The ship learned the hard lesson that evening that suicide boats still had the capacity to strike in the middle of ship anchorages. A boat came in close enough to drop a depth charge which lifted the *Charles J. Barger* momentarily out of the water. While the crew was recovering from the blast effects, the boat fled, making good its escape. When suicide boat crews felt they might not be able to avoid detection in their crafts, they sometimes left their boats and attempted to swim close enough to ships to deploy hand-grenades.[11] It was also reported that Japanese crews turned to canoes and rafts in an effort to attack shipping.

Again on the 10th the 52 supported the UDTs operating in Nakagusuka Wan and Chimu Wan, Okinawa. That was a one-day mission, and they returned to Kerama Retto for logistical preparation. On the 12th the 52 moved off the western beaches of Okinawa. They were tasked with skunk patrol and generating smoke to cover the anchorage. There was no relaxing from the war; the harbor at Nago Wan remained under pressure from Japanese bombers. Just before midnight on the 21st, *LCS 31* (call sign DOLLY-31) shot down a Vel bomber with her 40mm fire. The clock ticked into the early hours of the 22nd when a Japanese float plane appeared and seemed to take an unhealthy interest in the 52, as she laid down a column of smoke which led back to her stern. A "Flash Red Control Green" was sounded by the duty officer Lt. (jg) Duvendeck at 01:02.[12] He woke the captain. The "Jake" flew along their trail of smoke straight to them. At 01:06 the ship went to "Control Yellow."[13] At 01:11 hours the plane dove in and dropped a single bomb which landed in the water about twenty-five yards behind the ship. Their guns fired on the plane but they could not confirm any hits. The anchorage was so obscured by smoke that *LCS 31*, anchored 500 yards off 52's starboard side, was unable to engage the plane as it passed over. It disappeared into the night. The 52's luck held once again and no damage to the boat or injuries to the crew occurred.

Nago Wan was a bay on the northwestern section of the main island of Okinawa. The ships routinely used it as anchorage during the nights, when not on some other assignment. It was for all intents and purposes considered safe, or safer than most, waters. Lt. Harper allowed what he called exploring on shore around the city of Nago. He and one party of explorers discovered a one-room schoolhouse, which he considered large. That descriptor was likely attached in comparison to the one-room he had attended as a youth. The school was "hastily deserted" and material was left asunder as if the explorers had just missed the class at their desks. He found it delightful that some of the notebooks contained mathematical problems he could decipher, though having no knowledge of the Okinawan language—proof that math was itself a universal language. Some of the men took abacuses as souvenirs. It was also fascinating that the children were learning to write English.[14]

It was almost peaceful. The ship rocked in rhythm with the small fleet of LCSs anchored nearby at Nago Wan. A boat came alongside after midnight to investigate small-arms fire in the vicinity. Other than the watch, no one much cared about the incident. As the sun rose on 19 April, Ensign Stewart relieved Ensign Burroughs. That afternoon the whaleboat from LCS 53 came alongside and picked up Lt. Harper and Group Commander Stone. The two returned to the 52 about an hour later. Other than the visit by the Group Commander the day meandered by. At 20:00 the ship took up its routine duty of making smoke to cover the larger vessels at anchor.[15]

The 19th was the one-year anniversary of Nick Stoia's entry into the Navy. During battles Nick and the other radio and radar gang were typically resigned to below deck, unless assigned to back up a gun crew. It was nerve-racking duty, never knowing the status of the fight, often anticipating the worst scenarios. They, nevertheless, went about their duties, staying busy and hoping the deck hands did their job to perfection.

Nicholas Stoia joined the Navy on 19 April 1944. Nick was born and raised in Alliance, Ohio. He was just short of completing his senior year of high school when he went in the Navy at seventeen. Nick was the oldest son of Solomon and Sofia Stoia. Both his parents had immigrated to America from Romania, and their native language was a familiar household sound. Solomon arrived in the port of New York with sixteen dollars in his possession in April 1907. He learned to weld and made a living for his family working with sheet metal, in spite of the fact that he could neither read nor write.

Being one of the youngest guys onboard, Nick Stoia hung around with Virgil Thill. His other pals were Robert Payne, also from Ohio, and Don Schultz. Donald H. Schultz was born in South Bend, Indiana. Donald was born 12 December 1926. He was the son of Harry E. Schultz, who at twenty-one was raising his three-year-old son in the home of his parents in Noble, Indiana. Donald lived in Herman and Amelia Schultz's, his grandparents' home until he joined the Navy in 1944.

In the mid–1930s the family moved to 1236 N. Eddy, in South Bend. Both Donald's father and grandfather worked as hired laborers on farms during the 1930s. By the 1940 census, Harry had left the home of his father but thirteen-year-old Don remained. Herman was working as a fireman at a school run by a prominent family and Amelia was working there as a maid. South Bend was the home of both Indiana University and Notre Dame's Mendoza College of Business.

Schultz, Stoia, Payne and Thill all shared a common background: small towns and farms. Payne was the oldest of the group but shared the same enlistment month as the others. They had been a tightknit little group since they had joined the Navy, partaking in liberty, and war.

The relative peacefulness came to an abrupt end. In one day the 52 went to battle stations for seventeen air raid alerts. However, she and her crew were about to meet the real onslaught of operation Ten-Go. Late evening on the 27th, the 52 moved to Radar Picket duty at Station 3. The RP (*Roger Peter*, the sailor's acronym) was designed to act as a screen to transport, hospital, and supply ships anchored off Okinawa supporting the men on the ground. They were to give an early warning to, or halt an attack on, those more vulnerable ships. The RP stations were, however, miles from the protection of the massed fleet and their many antiaircraft guns. Originally there were eight picket stations but they eventually increased to fifteen stations forming an outer perimeter around Okinawa. It was on RP duty that the allied navies met the brunt of the kamikaze attacks and where the greatest loss of allied shipping and men took place.

The *52* went on RP duty at Station 2 on 28 April along with LCSs *110, 18,* LSM *198* (call sign WOODPECKER-198) and the destroyers *Hudson* (call sign CULPRIT) and *Van Valkenburgh* (call sign ODDFELLOW). The 28th was a clear day, with excellent visibility, unlike the rainy, foggy day that had preceded it. The three stations, 1, 2, and 3, were in direct line between Japan to the north and Okinawa to the southeast. Throughout the campaign these three RPs would bear the greater weight of the Japanese kamikaze attacks.

On RP Station Two the Combat Air Patrol (CAP) was doing most of the work throughout the day, fighting off between thirty-five and fifty Japanese planes headed south. Around 17:00 the Corsairs were forced to break away and go back for fuel and ammo. That left the ships on station to contend with the next five planes headed their way. The subsequent attack resulted with the radar being knocked out on the *Daly* and two of her crew dead before all enemy planes were downed.

That same evening, the hospital ship *Comfort* was headed for Guam with a full load of wounded patients from Okinawa. Approximately fifty miles south of Okinawa the ship was picked up by a suicide plane. The hospital ship was fully lit and displaying the Red Cross on the sides. The pilot pointed the nose of his plane at the Red Cross and dove into the ship. The crash killed thirty patients and medical staff and wounded forty-eight more. Although Laton Burns was not privy to the information, his first cousin, Ambrose Burns, Jr., wounded during ground combat the day before, was aboard the *Comfort*.

General Quarters were sounded at 02:05 on the 30th. LCS *52* received warning that a Japanese plane was approaching. The Japanese Helen bomber came in at 500 feet, flying low, approaching from the front on the starboard side of the ship. She passed down the length of the ship from bow to stern, about 4000 yards away. Even at that, she was too far out for the gunners to lock on to her and they were forced to temporarily hold their fire. LCS *18* (call sign DUNGEON-18) was closer and opened up with her 40mm and 20mm guns. When one of the destroyers also fired on it, the plane reversed direction and came back down the column of ships. This time *52, 110* and *18* all engaged the plane. Gunners on the .50 Cal, the 40s and 20s all let loose as it passed. The 40s got off forty-six rounds, the 20s one-hundred-twenty and the .50s fifty-six rounds. Harper could see the plane taking hits. Flames began to engulf the plane and she lost altitude. The gunners kept hammering it with bullets, frozen on their sights and triggers. She crashed into the ocean about 3000 yards off the starboard bow. The plane hit the water at 03:11, less than three minutes from the time it had first been sighted. LCS *18* took credit for the kill with an assist from LCSs *52* and *110*. Harper still allowed his boys to paint a symbol indicating the demise of another Japanese plane on the side of their conning tower. He was almost certain it had been his guns which brought the bomber down and the other two ships had assisted him.[16]

Virgil Thill enjoyed the fight. He did not know exactly why but the sounds and actions of the guns excited him. Everything about the steady metallic clank of brass casings hitting the deck and the rumble of shells leaving the barrel was thrilling. Perhaps those others who were filled with profuse fear might have thought him crazy but he liked the adrenaline rush.[17]

The men had grown accustomed to seeing what seemed to be a ubiquitous following of sharks around the ships. It was as if they knew something or someone would eventually enter their water. Thill was on deck after one of the many bouts between shipping and kamikazes. Virgil's eyes were drawn to someone floating in the water. As he focused his full attention on the object, he realized it was clearly the pilot of the suicide plane most recently shot down. He was drawn to the floating mass, dressed in his flight suit and gently raising and falling with the waves. He stood for a while, his eyes locked on the man. His staring was interrupted only by the sight of something else in the water. It was the sharks; they had come for what they patiently awaited. They swam in an ever-decreasing circle, closing with their motionless quarry. Virgil about-faced and nonchalantly walked away. He felt no remorse for what was sure to happen.

A world away, on the 30th as the Russian forces fought for possession of Berlin, Adolf Hitler committed suicide. Reichspräsident Karl Dönitz was left at the helm of Germany and to negotiate peace. Instead, Dönitz vowed the German people would fight on. Papers across the world filled their 1 May front pages with headlines of Hitler's suicide and the stubborn stance of the new fuehrer. In spite of Dönitz's bold talk, Churchill predicted the war in Europe would be over in a week. He was the closest to correct. The only thing the boys in the Pacific wondered was what it all meant for them.

Their turn for RP duty rolled around again. *LCS 52* and *88* (call sign EGGHEAD-88) reported to PR Station 5 on 10 May at 17:00 hours. It was only *LCS 88's* second time on RP duty. *LCS 114* (call sign MORNING-114) was also present and in charge of the smaller gunboats on station. Also present on station were *Patrol Motor Gunboat 20* (PGM), *LCS 109*, USS *Douglas H. Fox* and USS *Harry F. Bauer*.

Kamikazes continued their mass attacks. There was, however, mounting evidence by this time that attitudes, even in the hardcore kamikaze ranks, were changing. Both on land and sea, though still small in numbers, more and more Japanese fighting men were willingly choosing surrender and life over a futile death. Even in the early part of April, *LCS 115* had picked up a surrendering survivor of an aircraft attack. He was happy to attempt in establishing a rapport with the Americans. His efforts were not well received.

The *Bauer* informed *LCS 114* that she had spotted a bogey closing on the RP at 07:58 on the morning of 11 May. Lt. G.W. Mefferd, commanding *LCS 114*, ordered his support LCSs into a *wide-V* formation. At 08:00 the two destroyers spotted a twin-engine plane, thought to be a Sally, within range of their guns (about 14,000 feet). The destroyers opened fire at the approaching plane. Two minutes later two more planes, Kates, were seen to the north of the LCS's formation. The planes were both hanging close to the surface and making ever-decreasing circles, as if to work their way in to the sterns of the LCSs. They were six miles out and closing.

The men of *52* rushed to General Quarters. Antiaircraft fire coming from the destroyers alerted the *52* to two planes headed for the formation. Five minutes later, the planes were observed approaching from the stern, still some four miles out. Harper ordered his ship hard rudder to starboard, which allowed every gun aboard to have a clear field of fire at the oncoming enemy planes. All three 40mm guns opened up, along with two 20mm guns and one of the .50 calibers at approximately 3500 yards. *LCS 88*, closest to *52*, opened up with her guns.

The lead plane was being riddled by bullets from every American ship, but held fast to its course. Lt. Mefferd could see bullets striking the plane. It turned westward and headed for the two destroyers. It flew about a 1000 yards in front of the 52, crossing from starboard to port. It burst into flame and for a moment seemed to gain altitude. It appeared to rise up over the *Bauer* and then plummet. The plane crashed into the water as if hitting a concrete wall. It sank rapidly into the water about 1000 yards to 52's port, just after it passed the bow of 52, and 1200 yards off the *Bauer's* starboard side.[18]

There was no time to cheer the victory. The second plane headed for the rear of the 52, closer out than the first at 600 yards. The gunners shifted fire to engage it. The second plane zoomed across 52's stern and up her port side. Harper believed, and later reported, that fire from the 52's guns exploded the gas tank. Even in the machine's death throes, its pilot was undaunted by shell and flame. As it passed over *LCS 88*, it dropped a 200-pound bomb which impacted directly on the aft 40mm gun. The 40mm gun kept a steady fire on the plane until the bomb detonated, subsequently causing the plane to crash. The bomb exploded with such force it blew the huge gun mount off the ship. Everyone manning the aft gun was killed, except for one man reported missing. It was later felt by the XO that the sailor had been at the center of the blast and most likely disintegrated from the explosion.[19]

Lt. Mefferd heard a second explosion he believed was her gas tank going up. In another misfortune of war, a piece of shrapnel sped through the air, striking an officer in the conning tower, Lt. Casimir Bigos, captain of the ship.[20] The doctor onboard *PGM 20* was quickly taken over to *LCS 88* to treat their wounded. Mefferd ordered the ships without wounded to circle 88 and *PGM 20* while they made the transfer. The attack caused the death of nine of *LCS 88's* crew and wounded seven more.

Harper turned the 52 toward her damaged sister landing craft support ship. Everyone turned to the task of saving the wounded ship and her surviving crew. As they approached the 88, Virgil Thill gazed at the charred naked bodies of the gunners aboard the 88, their clothes seared off their corpses. The dead, still draped over their guns, gave testimony to their last breaths drawn fighting for their ship and mates. It was a "terrible thing" for Virgil and the other teenage survivors to see.[21] In a letter home, Larry Cullen gave another candid account of that day to his family. He saw three men, members of the aft gun crew, all dead with their "clothes blown off; there were several burned and others killed by shrapnel." He recalled that the 88's "Captain bled to death of a neck wound while we were standing by."[22] The sight would stick with them for the rest of their lives.

At 08:25 Lt. Mefferd ordered the cluster of ships around the 88 to scatter. Another plane was approaching the formation. The Zeke came in low, hugging the water, and approaching the formation on a northeast heading. The fire from the ships hammered into the plane; he turned and went for the destroyers. The LCSs ceased fire as the plane took up a trajectory which placed the destroyers in line of friendly fire. The destroyers took up the fusillade.

During the second plane attack, and reported as occurring at 08:13, Seaman 1st Class Jack D. Gloor aboard *LCS 52* was struck by shrapnel from the plane. He had a severe laceration over his right eye. The plane had crashed about 500 yards off 52's port side and the metal which struck Gloor had travelled that far to find a target. At 08:22, the 52 started toward *PGM 20* for treatment of Gloor's injury. The 52 tied off with *LCS 88* at 08:42, transferred Gloor, and then cast off to fall back into formation. He was transferred later that day to the hospital ship *APA 21*. Gloor was barely dropped off when the Zeke dove at the formation of ships. The 52 engaged it along with the *Bauer*. The guns of the *Bauer* completely severed the tail section off the plane. Somehow, if only by sheer will, the plane kept coming. The plane cut cables and lines aboard the *Bauer* as it skidded across her deck and into the water on her port side. Once again a Navy ship had experienced a welcome lucky break.

An hour later the *114* observed the pilot's body from the *88* attack floating nearby. *LCS 109* requested to pick him up. The request was never approved and was not addressed in *LCS 109*'s action report.[23] The *114* moved on. She came alongside *LCS 88* to transfer plasma for her remaining wounded. At 11:30 *LCS 88* was taken under tow back to meet *ATF 76*, who towed her back to anchorage for repairs. Two of the pilots from the enemy planes were noted to wear life jackets. These devices led Lt. Mefferd, for one, to feel that they were not designated as kamikazes—at least initially.

Jack Denzil Gloor was born 19 June 1926 to Clarence H. and Eunice E. Gloor in Paulding County, Ohio. He was raised on a farm in Hicksville, Ohio. In the 1920s, the family worked a grain farm. They rented their home and were one of three families to own a radio. By the start of the 1940s, Rex, Jack's only older brother, was working as a laborer on Hicksville farms as well.

Jack attended Hicksville High School. Like most of the boys of *LCS 52*, he was athletic. In the 1943 school year, Jack played on the junior varsity team, called the "Little Aces," as a sophomore. The same year, Jack donned number "46" jersey and played on the Hicksville football team. Jack was a lanky teenager with a head of thick dark hair which helped to conceal his protruding ears. Off the court or field, he took classes in agriculture. The class president acknowledged Jack in the yearbook as being a leader among their class throughout the 1943 school year. Jack moved up to the "Big Aces" basketball team in 1944. Jack would have graduated in 1945 but he joined the Navy on 19 April 1944. His big brother, Rex, had enlisted in the Army in April of 1942.

When *LCS 88* was struck by a kamikaze, Jack Gloor was the one unlucky sailor aboard *52* hit in the face by shrapnel. Jack was quickly transferred to a nearby ship which had a doctor aboard. He would make a full recovery but would never return to his old ship for duty. Jack was another crewmember who was a superb athlete in high school and dreamed of being a farmer (Virgil Thill collection).

Across the island of Okinawa, northwest of RP 5, the USS *Hugh W. Hadley* (DD774), USS *Evans* (DD552) and three LCSs had arrived on 10 May to assume duty at RP 15. At approximately the same time on the 11th the ships at Station 5 were being mauled by the kamikaze force coming down the eastern side of the island, Station 15 was reporting a sortie of enemy aircraft coming their way. In his Action Report, the Skipper of the *Hadley* later described the initial radar contact as "hordes of enemy planes closing" with the American ships.[24]

Aboard the *Hadley* was a nineteen-year-old, former Sprague, Nebraska resident, named Donald Lee Hile. Donald was the youngest of the seven children born to George Edward and Minnie Vanderhook Hile. George worked as a blacksmith and carpenter. He was well-known and depended on for his woodworking skills in the small town. George's parents were born in Pennsylvania. Donald's maternal grandparents were both born in Holland.

Other than a branch of the Missouri Pacific Railroad running through its center, Sprague was a "Methodist Church, post office, hardware store, grocery store, garage (with the old glass-globe gas pumps), beer joint, and barbershop (maintained by the barber in her home)," according to Donald.[25] The town had only been incorporated since 1913 and was really nothing more than an offshoot of nearby Centerville. Sprague was about thirteen miles southwest of the city of Lincoln.

Donald enlisted on 14 June 1944. Before he enlisted he worked in dairy creameries in Lincoln as a milk bottler and as a bottle washer. Like his older brothers and sisters he had attended a one-room school with coal stove heating and no electric. Days as a youth in Sprague were filled with innocent fun, skinny-dipping and ice-skating, depending on the season. The town was populated by less than 100 people.

After basic training at Farragut, Idaho, Donald went to gunnery school for 20mm guns. Donald was assigned to the *Hadley* for her commissioning voyage in November 1944. The *Hadley* was manned by a crew three times the size of the town of Sprague. Donald's normal duty was Radar Striker but he was assigned to a 1.5-inch gun during General Quarters.

As the "horde" of Japanese planes approached RP 15 at 07:55, they were first met by the accompanying CAP at approximately fifty-five miles out. The *Hadley* and *Evans* were descended upon by a half-dozen aircraft or more each. The destroyers attempted to close on each other so that they could deploy mutually supporting fire but the attacks came with such ferocity, they could not pull in tight. The *Hadley* shot down more than a dozen planes but they kept coming. At 09:00 the *Evans* was knocked out of the fight; the *Hadley* stood as the only destroyer engaging the enemy. In the ensuing ninety-minute battle, the *Hadley* was hit by a bomb, a Baka and a suicide plane.

During the attacks on the *Hadley*, the concussion of a blast knocked Donald off his feet. The fall caused him to hit face-first against the projectile hoist of his gun turret. The impact broke his jaw. He still managed to abandon ship with the crew and was recovered from the water by another ship. He was ultimately sent to Guam for treatment.

Although the sailors' intricate scuttlebutt and seagoing grapevine was good at passing news, the 52 had her hands full surviving the kamikazes at RP 5. There was no time to contemplate what was happening across the island. Richard, "Pop" Hile, also born and raised in Sprague had no way of knowing the whereabouts or condition of the *Hadley* that morning in May. Therefore, Richard, being the oldest son of George and Minnie Hile, had no way of knowing whether his youngest brother, Donald, was alive or dead. Being the oldest child, after his sister Margaret, Richard was married to Helen Thiesen and had a daughter of his own long before Donald joined the Navy. Richard and his family lived with Helen's parents in rural Oak, Nebraska, in the early forties, a few miles from his parents' home where Donald was growing up. Richard was working at a diary in Lincoln and had his own milk route. Richard was almost twenty-years older than his brother Donald. He was a newborn when Pop Hile was a grown man. But they were still brothers and their parents knew better than they did how close to danger they both were aboard ships off Okinawa.

On the 8th day of May, the German army surrendered to the Allies. That day became forever known as Victory in Europe Day or simply VE Day. There was no fanfare aboard *LCS 52*, at least not about VE Day. The crew's lack of excitement over victory in Europe was reflected in Claude Cook's letter of the 9th, in which there was no mention at all of the war's close. "There is a great rejoicing aboard the L.C.S. 52–mail finally caught up to us." Claude personally rejoiced in his receipt of twenty-three letters. Furthermore it was obvious from the day's activities at RP 5 on the 11th the Japanese were far removed from any notion of surrender. Europe made no difference to the men on either side in the Pacific.

The remainder of RP duty at Station 5 was relatively quiet. The USS *Bennion* (DD-662) (call sign BOLERO) joined the LCSs and *T. H. Fraser* on station. The 14th was her twenty-ninth day on RP. They were relieved the following day by the *R.N. Smith*. *LCS 52* remained out on RP until relieved by *LCS 123* at noon on the 17th. Before they could get back to the anchorage, they spotted, or were spotted by, two bogies in the vicinity, close enough they were forced to go to G.Q. each time. It seemed the kamikazes were everywhere.

During the time *LCS 52* and *88* spent on RP in early May, a swarm of kamikaze rolled down from bases in Japan to attempt and turn back the Allied tide approaching the homeland. After the war, Japanese military records went up in a titanic conflagration. Many officials were afraid that what was contained in those records would bring revenge on the Japanese people. Included in the burned documents were histories of the kamikaze pilots. Little historical evidence survived of what type of plane they flew, the course they followed, and the ship they targeted.

The Special Attack Squadrons of 10–11 May flew under the code name Operation Kikusui Six. Kikusui Six was carried out by eighty Army planes and seventy Navy planes. The sorties were flown by various types of aircraft. One of the pilots known to have died on 11 May was Haruo Araki. Araki was a Second Lieutenant and the commander of the 51st Shinbu Special Attack Squadron out of Chiran Air Base at the time of his last flight. He was raised in the city of Tokyo and both his parents survived him. On the late evening of 9 April, twenty-one-year-old Araki arrived home for one night of leave. He married that same evening, spent a few hours with his new bride and returned to duty. Their wedding night was the last time his bride would see him; neither would the son she became pregnant with that night ever see his face. The plane reported to have dropped the bomb on *LCS 88*'s aft gun-tub was believed to have been an Oscar. It would be impossible to say if Araki was that pilot, but it would be almost impossible to prove he was not.

His widow, Shigek, was told later that he died in an attack on shipping in Kadena Bay, Okinawa. She admitted that they had no proof of that as fact. On 11 May, the 56th Shinmu Squadron did make it to, and attacked within, Kadena Bay, however no record showed pilots of the 51st made it that far. From Chiran Air Base, RP Five was almost directly south. RP 5 was, however, east of Okinawa, and Kadena Bay was across the island and to the west.

The same day that Haruo Araki died, twenty-two-year-old Ensign Kiyoshi Ogawa flew his plane into the USS *Bunker Hill*, killing 393 sailors and wounding over 250 more. He was a member of the 7th Showa Squadron, departing from Kanoya Air Base. He was positively identified by papers and a name tag found on his remains.

Claude Cook sat down late in the evening of 23 May to write Caroline "Lynn" Artman.

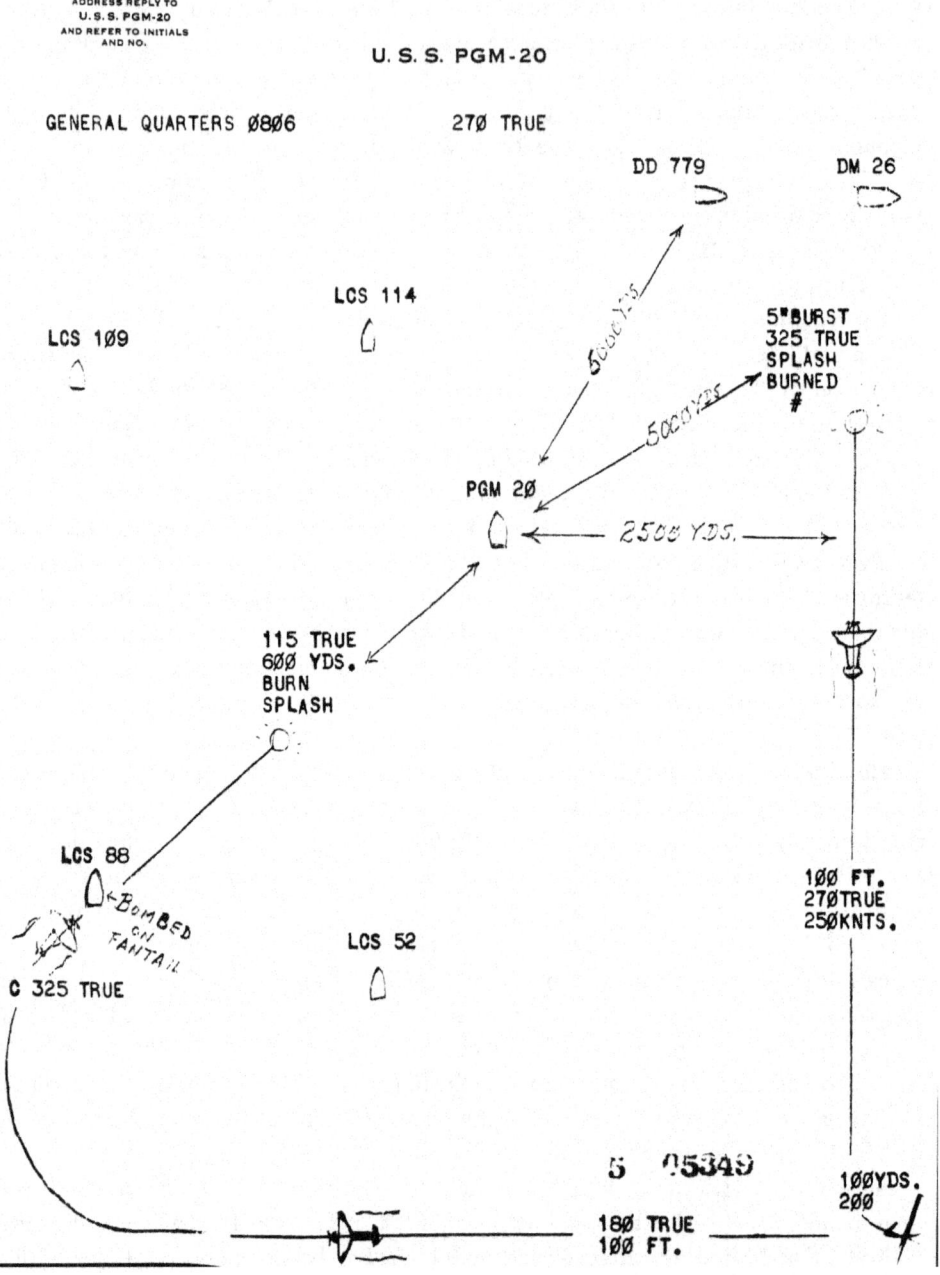

Each After Action Report contained a diagram drawn by the ship's captain or his designee. The above example was the pictorial account by PGM-20 of the action on May 11, 1945 (photograph by the author).

He had been given a battery of shots that day, something the boys had all grown tired of. The alternative was worse, of course. Aside from an overabundance of injections, the things they could talk about in their letters were pretty mundane. Life aboard ship may have seemed routine after the censors finished with the letters but that was one of the underlying purposes. Things had to seem upbeat for the folks back home. Claude closed his letter by sharing that he was going on watch at 03:00 and hoped nobody woke him before that time. The men were starved for mail; they went weeks without, as evidenced by the "jackpot" of delayed letters which arrived on 9 May. When it did arrive, as in Claude's case, they might get fifteen or more letters which had been held up and gathering dust on some tin can for months. The next opportunity for Claude to write home would not come until after they had finished their forthcoming RP duty.

7

Birds of Prey

The ship and her crew drew radar picket duty again. This time at Radar Picket Station 15-A, formally Station 1, considered the most dangerous position in the ring of early-warning pickets to make up the perimeter. Station 1 was located on the northern side of the circular chain of posts about fifty miles north of Okinawa. Pulling duty there placed the ships making up that group between the remaining Japanese airfields and Okinawa. The sailors now referred to RP 15 by its reputation as being "in the slot" or pulling duty at "coffin's corner."

Typically there were two destroyers and four gunboats assigned to a Radar Picket (RP). On 27 May 1945 one of those two was the USS *Lowry* (DD-770) (call sign OTHELLO). The other, one of the newest destroyers, USS *Drexler* (DD-741), carried an old friend of Harper's from Notre Dame, Lieutenant Junior Grade George W. Hood. George was a navigator's assistant on the *Drexler*, the job Harper had wanted out of midshipman's school. George graduated in the midshipman's class following Harper's. Like Harper, he had been selected to stay on and teach future midshipmen instead of going straight to a ship. The two men and their wives became close and spent many hours of leisure together back in Indiana. The war, which had separated the men, now brought them within a few hundred yards of each other.

When Harper realized George was nearby he employed the navy's unique and exclusive ship-to-ship communications devices to chat with his old friend. Using semaphore flags and signal lights, the two struck up a welcome but public conversation. No one aboard George's ship seemed to mind and even joined in the unusual reunion dialogue. The biggest news of the day was the transfer of Fifth Fleet command to Admiral William "Bull" Halsey. The officers, if not the lowliest seaman, knew Halsey's reputation for aggressive actions. He would not disappoint in that arena in the coming days.

Fifty special attack planes received their orders to mobilize and be ready to fly by dusk. It was 27 May and the orders ushered in the start of Operation Kikusui Number Eight. The date also had special significance for Japan and its military forces. It was Navy Day and the fortieth anniversary of the Japanese naval victory over Russia. Kikusui Number Eight targets were ships berthed in the anchorages off Okinawa.[1] Most of the kamikaze aircrafts for that mission were reconnaissance planes modified for explosive potential. Before a single Japanese pilot could reach his target he had to negotiate through the American CAP, the RP and then the AA fire from land and ships in those anchorages. Most pilots understood they stood a slim chance of success.

During the day of Sunday, 27 May, two fresh LCSs arrived on post to relieve two others.

One of the ships came in close to the 52 and transferred mail over. With as much moving around as the 52 had been doing since day one of the invasion, mail had been unable to catch up to them. It had been a long and depressing time without contact from family and friends. Few things renewed sailors' hopes and cheer more than mail from home. As part of his duties as ship's storekeeper, Larry Cullen separated and distributed mail to its rightful and impatient owner.

One of the added pleasures on this particular occasion was a package containing phonograph records sent from Ensign Burroughs's wife. There was a small record player maintained in the wardroom, and everyone was looking forward to catching up on the latest top hits. That evening the sounds from the records echoed through the steel bulkheads, carrying music through the ship for all those who had time to stop and listen. Burroughs had also received some books and was willing as always to share those as he was the records. Other men shared the news accompanying letters from home. News from one hometown was news for all.

Things began to pick up around dusk. Bogeys were spotted in the area by the Combat Air Patrol (CAP). The CAP went after them and Harper saw at least one kamikaze swirl into the sea. After darkness fell, destroyer radar began to pick up more planes, which, from their direction of approach, could only be Japanese. They were circling the ships, keeping a four to six mile distance but looking for a vulnerable target. General Quarters were sounded at 21:58 hours and reluctantly everyone bolted from the wardroom, their berthing areas and galley. Burroughs was the ship's engineering officer and he armed himself with a sidearm and made his way below to the engine room. Burns and Keith, dressed in their life vests and helmets, hurried to their twin 40mm gun. Thill also made his way to his battle station at the front starboard side 20mm.

The destroyers were the first to notice several enemy planes approaching. They were probably hunting the prized destroyers and appeared to be heading for them. It had become a too common practice. However, that did not mean that the LCSs were safe from attack. The suicide planes went for any target that seemed exposed or alone and offered the possibility of sinking her. The LCSs, their maneuvering controlled as a group by Harper, lined up one behind the other. They began maneuvering back and forth at slow speeds to prevent sending out white wakes which might guide a plane straight to them if followed.[2] Every gun was manned, and the tense waiting period for the planes to make their attack approach began.

Life of a ship and its crew in kamikaze-infested waters depended on the abilities of the radar men. They were considered by the Navy to be some of the smartest men aboard ship. To be selected for the training required college-level intelligence but not necessarily a college degree. Radio and radar operation was a job exclusive to enlisted men. The first radar operators were selected from those men who already operated the radio, either having been formally trained or having learned on the job. The men selected for further training had therefore already scored high on the Radio Technician Selection Test (RTST, Nav Pers 16578), more commonly referred to as the Eddy Test. The test, unlike other aptitude tests, was strictly a one-time, pass or fail endeavor. For those individuals who did pass, their rigors were only beginning.

In spite of the Eddy Test, many of the men found that they did not have the proper motivation for the primary training courses to become radar operators. Therefore, in 1943, the Navy established a Pre-Radio School to further exclude men incapable or unwilling to complete the extensive training. Selectees attended one of four preschools, operating out of facilities at Wilbur Wright or Theodore Herzl Junior Colleges, Hugh Manley High School, all in Chicago, or at the Naval Reserve Armory in Michigan City, Indiana. The students were issued their course books, including *Wartime Refresher in Fundamental Mathematics*, and were expected to have mastered high school level algebra, physics, chemistry and other upper-level subjects before moving on to one of the primary schools.[3] Those who passed the four-week course went on to one of the Primary Schools scattered across the country.

Radar was a relatively new invention that was improving throughout the war. In 1941, the development of radar was in its infancy and a well-kept secret by the Allies. For the students attending one of the schools, even as late as 1944, they were under strict orders to keep their knowledge of the instrument hush-hush. Use of, instruction in, and the technology surrounding radar instrumentation was still labeled "Top Secret." Their classes were conducted in facilities that could be secured to that end. Often the students were trained inside fenced-off buildings with armed guards walking the outside perimeter.[4] As numbers dwindled, successful students went on to one of three Secondary Schools devoted to seaborne radar systems. By this point, remaining sailors and marines were using the language of radar. They were proficient on alternating (AC) and direct current (DC) theory, electromagnetic propagation, vacuum tubes, modulation, transmitters, receivers, duplexers, sweep circuits, and megacycles, to name only a few. It was a vocabulary which sounded close to that of a foreign language to the average sailor.[5] There was one more aspect of their training at sea: they were the only repairmen present to fix damaged or malfunctioning circuits and instruments, sometimes in the heat of battle.

The radar and radio men of 52 called themselves the communication gang. The lead radar man was Benjamin Leonard Beittel from Carlisle, Pennsylvania. Also in the gang were Clarence A Bauer of Mankato, Minnesota, and Nick Stoia from Alliance, Ohio. Together, they were the voice and ears of *LCS 52*.

Ben Beittel was born in Columbia, Pennsylvania, and raised in Carlisle, Pennsylvania. He was born on 5 November 1914 to Cleon Benjamin and Gertrude S. Albright Beittel. Ben's father managed one of Jacob E. Trimmer's five-and-ten-cent stores. Trimmer owned a chain of twenty-three stores at one time.[6] Ben also worked at the Carlisle store as a clerk while still living at home. His older brother, Cleon, worked in the grocery as a clerk.

To grow up in Carlisle was to grow up surrounded by history; much of that was military history. The town was founded in 1751. Then in 1757 Carlisle became the site of a British supply depot, what would later become Carlisle Barracks. The British abandoned the barrack before the revolution began, which left the compound open for occupation by the Continentals. The Continentals renamed the post Washingtonburg.

After she showed off her artillery knowledge, Molly Pitcher settled in Carlisle and became a well-known cleaning woman. She was buried in Carlisle at the Old Graveyard. George Washington also came to town once and attended services at the Carlisle Presbyterian Church. During the Civil War the supply depot at the barracks was reopened by the Union. During their campaign into Pennsylvania, with only home guards to slow them, the Confederates occupied Carlisle almost unopposed. After bivouacking on the campus of Dickinson College and the Barracks, the Confederates left a few days later, leaving the campus pretty much as they had found it.

After the war ended and in the wake of Manifest Destiny, Anglos began to uproot Native-Americans once more with a passion. Attempting to continue with the work he began at Fort

Marion, Florida, in the late 1870s, Richard Pratt opened the Carlisle Indian Industrial School in the Carlisle Barracks buildings. The School opened its doors in early 1879, dedicated to Pratt's motto of "Kill the Indian but save the man." The legendary Jim Thorpe attended school there and played sports there. The more legendary Apache, Geronimo, stopped in to visit the school on his way to stand near Theodore Roosevelt on the inaugural platform.[7] The school became the example that all Indian boarding schools strove to copy. Carlisle Indian School operated until 1918 but was not the last of the boarding schools. As it turned out, the idea of boarding schools did more damage to Native-American culture and autonomy than pretty much any other wrong perpetrated by non–Indians.

In 1904 the trolley line came to Carlisle. By the time Ben was old enough to enjoy the amenities of Carlisle there were three movie theaters in operation. The Comerford opened in 1939 and boasted the only building in town with central air-conditioning. In 1936 Grover Hunt, a former maintenance man at Dickinson College, and his partner, Linwood Gagne, a former student, opened the Standard Piezo Company. They are commonly considered the fathers of the crystal-cutting business in Carlisle. The crystals were a critical component in radio sets. The industry grew exponentially as the military's demand expanded during the war. The war became more evident to the citizens of Carlisle when in 1943 they converted the former CCC camp into Camp Michaux POW integration facility. The Camp was classified secret but, as it was located approximately fifteen miles south of Carlisle, locals had to have heard rumors. The year before, the Navy built a supply depot at nearby Mechanicsburg, ten miles east of Carlisle. Many local residents of Cumberland County worked at the Navy Supply Depot through the 1940s.

As was the case with so many of the veterans, it was a combination of reasons that made them feel they

Ben Beittel, one of the only known pictures of him in uniform. Like Cullen, he had a wonderful sense of humor, a valuable commodity in a war zone (Betsy Beittel Hilliard collection).

were obligated to do their part. Brothers Cleon and Ben Beittel were close in age and in character, hard workers who had been brought up in the church. When Cleon enlisted in the Army on 6 March 1944, Ben would not be far behind. Ben enlisted in the Navy on 5 April of the same year.

Ben was married on 30 March 1934 to the former Grace Harbach. The two were married at one in the afternoon at the Otterbein United Brethren Church by the Reverend Charles R. Beittel, Ben's uncle and pastor of the church. Ben had a son, born in 1935, and two daughters, six and four, when he left to go overseas. Everyone liked Ben. He was easygoing and loved to tell jokes. He always had time for his kids regardless of what was going on in the work world. He often joined in games of hide-and-seek with the neighborhood kids. He played card games with his kids and never failed to give them his time. He was a "wonderful family man."[8]

Radio Technician 2nd Class Clarence A. Bauer was the man aboard *LCS 52* assigned to repair the intricate electronics of both radar and radio equipment. He grew up in Mankato, Minnesota. Clarence was the son of longtime Mankato residents Frank and Ida Bauer. His father, Frank, was a cigar maker. There were more than thirty local cigar manufactories in town at any given time. Competition was ever-present and brisk. Frank Bauer started in the business as a boy at the turn of the century and spent his life perfecting the craft.

Through his maternal grandmother, Clarence was familiar with the family's old-country roots, the pre–Hitler Germany. After Henrietta Tatge was widowed and unable to care for herself, she moved in with Clarence's family. Henrietta emigrated from Germany in 1870. She and her husband, Henry, farmed in Cass County, Illinois, and then moved to Mankato and raised their family there.

The Bauer family was steeped in German tradition but they gave their all for the United States. Frank lost his younger brother Joseph A. on 13 September 1918 while serving with Company L, 163rd Infantry in the Great War. The family's sacrifice was far from done. On 19 July 1943, Clarence's older brother Joseph G. was killed in an accidental plane crash. Joseph was serving as a cadet pilot in the Army Air Corps stationed at Bruce Field, Ballenger, Texas. His plane went down eighteen miles southwest of the town. Joseph was a full-time printer before the war. Frank would eventually have both his brother and his son shipped back to Mankato for reburial close to home.[9] Clarence enlisted less than two months before his brother's death. Both had been born and raised in Mankato.

Mankato, the county seat of Blue Earth, was settled in a bend of the Minneapolis River and the Blue Earth River. The town was settled in 1852 and became infamous the day after Christmas 1862 when it was the site of the largest public execution ever carried out in the United States. Following what was labeled the Santee Sioux uprising the previous August, 303 Dakota Sioux were convicted by a military court and sentenced to death by hanging. President Lincoln stepped in and pardoned all but thirty-eight, who were hanged on a large scaffold in the town square.

Ten years after the Great Minnesota Execution, the suffragist Julia Sears became the first principal of a public college in United States history, Mankato Normal School. In 1888 a construction company owner building bridges for the railroad began construction on the Saulpaugh Hotel. The four-story hotel, built from local stone Thomas Saulpaugh had originally been in search of for railroad bridges, was a gathering place for sophisticates and celebrities such as Sinclair Lewis. One of the many amenities the hotel offered was fine cigars locally made by F.A. Bauer, available for purchase for 10¢ at the lobby cigar shop. Bauer produced them as a specialty item under the brand name of *Saulpaugh Cigars*.

Clarence Bauer joined the Navy on 23 April 1943, from his hometown. Prior to enlisting, he attended SS. Peter and Paul grade school and then graduated from the Jesuit-run Loyola High School, also in Mankato. Clarence knew cigars, but he also knew surface radar and radio sets. He joined the 52 when she first sailed from Portland, and he knew the glitches and capacities of her radio and SO-2 radar equipment. He was highly respected among the crew, and when it came time to defer to his expertise, everyone stepped aside.[10]

Being on duty at the ship's radar set the evening of 27 May, and early morning the 28th, the task fell to the radar man to deliver the bad news to the officers in the conning tower. One of the kamikaze planes was bearing down on a course straight for their ship.

One of the radar men, and that usually meant Ben Beittel, would then sit at his radar panel and watch intensely the sweep circuit spin around the scope—identifiable to laymen as the white line moving around the circular screen. When Beittel saw the "pip" or blip appear he would know where the enemy plane was and could calculate how long before it would be in gun range. A conduit of vital information on the whereabouts of the enemy would begin from his station and end with the ship's guns. That communication was accomplished via a "voice tube" from the radar man's seat to the conning tower.[11]

The kamikazes came in hugging the water. They had learned two lessons in their month-long efforts to sink allied ships. If they attacked from high altitudes, first the radar would pick them up and track them. Second, if they came down on the ships, especially the destroyers, the big guns could come to bear on them. However, if they came in low along the water, then they could get under the guns and sometimes avoid the radar. Training manuals were created for the kamikaze pilots based on past successes. One such manual described to pilots how to improve their chances of mission success:

> An extreme low level horizontal attack is employed in a surprise raid, when the ceiling is low, at night, at dawn, at dusk. The collision point will vary with the type of plane, kind of target, its size and speed... . In case of an extreme low-altitude, the best point will generally be amidships, slightly above the waterline... . It is essential at this time not to miss the target because of shutting one's eyes.[12]

The theory of low-level attacks only worked sometimes. It did not work with the LCSs and their 40mm and 20mm guns which could drop their elevation and lock in on the plane. The effectiveness of the American radar systems was the major problem with Japanese kamikaze efforts. There was little surprise when radar was picking up approaching planes long before they were in range of the guns. These were some of the reasons why the LCSs and the destroyers made a good team on radar picket.

Because *LCS 52* was the lead vessel, speed and evasive maneuvers had to wait until the last moments. When Harper saw that the lone kamikaze was, in fact, headed for them, he increased to flank speed. Harper watched intently as the plane closed in from a couple miles out. He could see the propellers shining through the dark sky, strangely lit up by the reflection of the destroyers' 5-inch guns throwing up steady fire. Larry Cullen became hyper-aware of his surroundings. He was in the pilot house manning the wheel, steering the ship. The radar room called up the distance and direction of approach of the bogey, and the guns swung around as if tethered to their instructions. With the kamikaze approximately a half-mile out, every crew-served weapon opened up. Cullen knew from experience that the gunners were immediately blinded by the muzzle flashes of their own guns. They tried to offset that effect by firing in short bursts. The tracer rounds pouring out of the guns at intervals, along with standard rounds, created a solid strand of light which the suicide pilots routinely used to guide their planes back to the ship.

Harper could tell that his and the destroyers' guns were getting hits on the plane but it continued to speed toward his ship like a relentless hungry bird after its prey. When the pilot got within 1,000 yards of the 52, he pulled up, pointing the nose of his plane upward. He then turned and dove at full speed at the 52, aiming his nose at the midsection port side. The two American destroyers beamed light from their search lights onto the approaching plane. With their bigger guns unable to decline further, and therefore ineffective, light was the best assistance they could give at the moment. They had their own troubles; the other suicide planes had not forgotten their own missions and bore down on the destroyers.

At a mere one-hundred yards from the ship, Harper could tell by the maneuvering of the plane that the pilot still had enough life in him to steer. From the spotlights of the destroyers he also saw that his ship's guns were pouring a continuous stream of bullets pointblank into the attacking plane. Cullen saw the plane, almost on top of the ship bank toward the stern and dive, in a line which appeared to be toward the propellers of the ship. The aft 40mm gun fired to the last second, literally shooting into the propeller only feet away from their turret. Their efforts paid off. Somehow, as if by a miracle, the plane rose and went over the top of the stern. It passed so close to the deck that men working the stern gun claimed they ducked to avoid being hit by the wings as it passed. There was an unmistakable sound of an explosion of fuel and bomb load all going off simultaneously just off the starboard side. There the miracle ended.[13]

When Engineering Officer Spencer Burroughs felt the speed of the engines change, he could not understand why. It was his job to investigate the cause and see to the correction if one was needed. He moved toward the hatch which led from the engine room to the deck. Crawling up the ladder he opened the steel hatch and stepped onto the deck. It was at that instant the plane exploded. Spencer was struck by a large piece of shrapnel in the left temple and killed instantly.

Russell Copeland was on one of the 20mm guns. Just before the plane had made its final approach, he was sweating profusely so he took his helmet off to cool down. Lt. Duvendeck spotted his uncovered head and screamed at him to put his helmet back on. The lieutenant was not polite in his request. Copeland promptly stowed his helmet back on his head. The plane exploded a split-second later, peppering his helmet with shrapnel. Had Duvendeck not seen him, and had he not followed the lieutenant's order immediately, he would have surely been killed.[14]

Robert G. Payne was loading rounds into the 40mm gun when the plane exploded. A piece of shrapnel struck the primer on a live round causing a chain reaction explosion. The explosion severed his arm completely. Robert walked over to Copeland, almost nonchalantly. Copeland looked at his missing arm as Payne explained, "I lost my arm." Copeland picked him up and draped him over his back. He carried Payne to the lower deck enlisted mess where the medical staff was working on the wounded.[15] When Copeland got Payne there, Burroughs's body was lying on the deck. Copeland had to pass him as he made his way further into the room. A wounded seaman, James Hawks, was stretched out on the table. Hawks was alert enough to recognize Copeland. Hawks asked him if he would shake his hand. Of course,

Copeland obliged him and took his hand. He did not recall who, but one of the officers yelled at him to return to his gun. He headed back up on the top deck to do what he was ordered.[16]

Twenty-one-year-old Oren Clifford Tweet was working the same 40mm gun as Payne. The explosion from the ammunition hammered Tweet's helmet down into his head. He momentarily blacked out from the concussion. When his senses returned he went to check in at the makeshift hospital ward. The men there were worse off than he was. They were lacking in almost every comfort. He retrieved his blanket from his bunk so that one of his shipmates might be wrapped and covered properly. Bringing it back, he dropped it off and returned to duty.[17]

In the pilot house, the Quartermaster looked out the closed porthole as the plane exploded. The blackout lid came crashing down on his head. It was not serious but left him with a headache and a bump. Cullen, much like the rest of the crew, thought the plane had hit the aft. He worried about the men in the engine room, possibly his friend Spencer Burroughs, being trapped.[18] He quickly decided that he might give them a chance if the engines were stopped. He called down to the engine room and told them to stop the engines. He then tried to call the conn to let them know what action he had taken. No one there answered. The silence on the other end of the phone seemed to drag on for minutes, but was probably only several seconds. Cullen figured they had all hit the deck or had been knocked to the deck. They finally picked up. Cullen had no way of knowing that by the time he had stopped the engines his friend Spencer was already dead.

Shrapnel, chunks of plane, and various pieces of the pilot blew across the deck from stern to bow. Holes were torn into the deck and the search lights of the 52 were shattered. The night went strangely dark and eerily silent for moments after the crash. The guns went still and it was as if the ship itself had gone into shock. Those manning positions at the front of the ship thought the plane had crashed directly into the stern. In the aftermath the deck was littered with parts of the pilot. His belt buckle was found lying on the deck by Gerald Bilton. The buckle bore Japanese writing, which, someone was erroneously told, translated to "die for the Emperor."[19] What the buckle actually bore was a hand-engraved (probably by the owner) inscription "chuu kou"—"Filial Loyalty/Piety."[20] These were central Confucian values, followed closely by duty and honor. In its purest sense the pilot was reaffirming his loyalty to his parents and honoring them. In Japan prior to 7 December 1941 the country had also adopted a paternal duty to the Emperor and nation. The inscription certainly told a story of a man willing to sacrifice for what he believed in strongly.

Among the wounded were Fireman 2nd Class Wilford Carl Crowe, Seaman 1st Class Eugene Albert De Maio, Seaman 2nd Class Donald C. Hedger, Seaman 1st Class Anthony David Jawor, Seaman 2nd Class Robert R. Fields, Seaman 1st Class Richard F. Hile, Seaman Horace C. Burnette, Fireman 2nd Class Paul A. Hanning, and Seaman 1st Class Robert G. Payne, whose hand was severed by shrapnel.

Seaman 2nd Class James Lee Hawks was firing one of the 20mm guns during the attack. He was hit in the upper arm by shrapnel from the explosion. At first it seemed that the wound was not serious enough to be life-threatening. However, James was losing a lot of blood and the doctor, temporarily aboard for picket duty, was concerned more for him than any of the other wounded.

Also wounded was Ensign Adler Wilhelm "Swede" Strandquist, who held the position of First Lieutenant aboard the ship.[21] Strandquist was hit in the arm by shrapnel but his

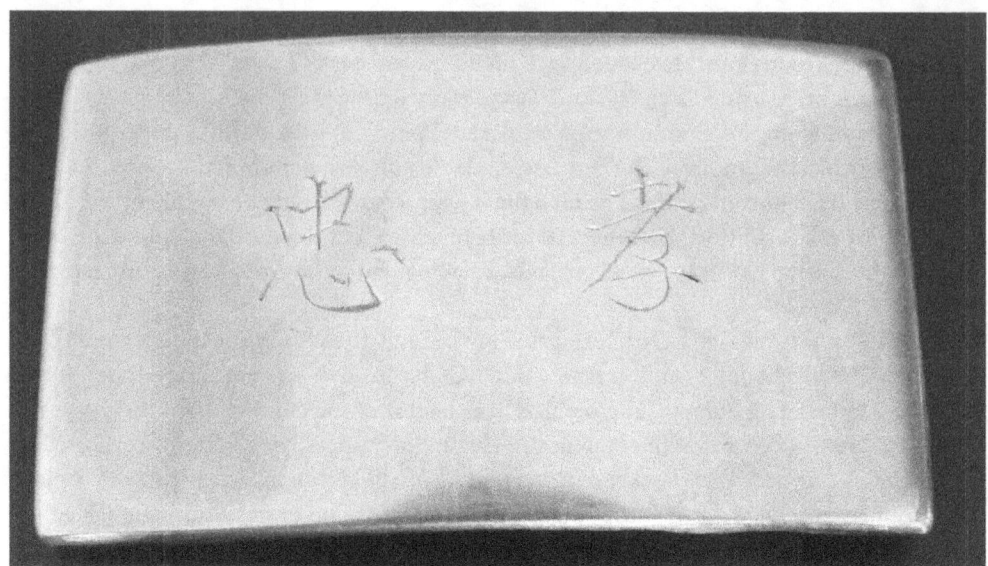

Little was left of the kamikaze pilot who singled out *LCS 52* for his final act of devotion to his Emperor— except for his belt buckle. What was found by the crew was unceremoniously thrown overboard. The buckle is now in possession of Virgil Thill (photograph by the author).

wounds did not appear to be as life-threatening as Hawks.' Adler Strandquist was originally from the rural township of Foldahl, Minnesota. Foldahl was a handful of farmhouses southeast of Warren, which contributed to the agricultural economy of Marshall County. Warren was the county seat of Marshall County. Foldahl was also as close to the community of Strandquist, to the north, as to Warren. Both the towns of Strandquist and Warren were known as little more than railroad stops for the Great Northern Railway. The country communities, generally founded by Swedish immigrants in the late 1870s, tended to their crops of wheat, soybeans, potatoes, and sugar beets.[22]

Adler was born to Andrew Emmanuel and Lilly T. Strandquist on 12 June 1921. While Andrew was born in Minnesota, his wife Lilly was born in Sweden, as were both of Andrew's parents. Andrew, who had either voluntarily or via bureaucracy Americanized his name from Andreus in his youth, lived and worked for his father in the township of Stranquist. In 1918 he registered for the World War I draft from there. Adler's Swedish-American family and neighbors were devout, hardworking and ambitious, and he spent his youth following their example and exceling at everything he tried.

Adler graduated from Warren High School but not before winning the 1940 decathlon, the inaugural year of the award.[23] It was rumored that Adler was coaxed from Argyle schools to play basketball for Warren. The 1939–40 Warren team took the district runner-up trophy, under the leadership of team captain, number 48, Strandquist. He left his mark at Warren High. The motto he chose for the 1940 annual was "Good character is priceless." He ran track in his sophomore, junior and senior years. He played on the football team in his junior and senior year. He was on the class staff and was Vice President of his class in his junior and senior years. He played basketball from his sophomore through his senior year and was captain of the team in his last season. Adler played baseball as a sophomore and was a member of Future Farmers of America as a senior. Adler was a large teenager with a broad nose, a strong protruding chin and deep-set eyes. He helped his father on the farm and worked as a janitor part-time.

In 1941 he began college at Concordia in Moorhead, Minnesota. Adler was involved in diverse and popular extracurricular activities at Concordia. In his freshman year he pledged the Delta Rho literary society and took a spot on the basketball team.[24] The following year as a sophomore, Adler played on both the undefeated conference champs football team and again on the basketball team. In February 1942, Adler, who was enrolled under the Civil Aeronautics Act's Civilian Pilot Training Program (CPTP), completed his first test flight.[25] Adler moved to the starting lineup on the basketball team the following year, as well as acting as one of the music representatives for the student forum. The 22 January 1944 edition of the *Moorhead Daily News* reported that Adler was among the sportsmen to win athletic "letters" that season. He graduated from Concordia the following month. It seemed that few local newspapers went a week without covering some feat of athletic or academic prowess by Adler. One week he was running-in a touchdown as a converted fullback, another he was making arrangements for the Faculty Women's Club annual outing.

Hailing from the same county as Adler was a girl attending the Moorhead State Teacher's College named Bernice A. Olson. Adler and Bernice had known each other since high school and had both graduated from Warren High. The two announced their engagement to be wed in the *Moorhead Daily News* on 22 January 1944.

CAPTAIN STRANDQUIST AND RUNNERS-UP TROPHY

Adler Strandquist, Warren County High School 1939–40 yearbook (Marshall County Historical Society, Minnesota).

There was one more endeavor that Adler had worked on while attending Concordia, he enlisted in the Naval Reserve Officer Training Program. The program he enlisted under was known as the V-7 program. It differed from the V-12 programs that Harper and Burroughs entered under in that it was a strictly academic program. Adler never ventured off campus and practiced nautical skills or set foot on a boat during his time at Concordia. Nevertheless, with his graduation came the commitment he had made to the U.S. Navy. That contract had brought him to *LCS 52* and placed him in harm's way on that Sunday, 27 May 1945, north of Okinawa.

Copeland returned to his gun to find the gun pit filled with "broken up parts of the bomber and hunks of Japs bodies as large as hams." Someone shoved a large coal shovel at him. They did not have to explain what to do with it. He commenced shoveling up body parts and tossing them over the side of the ship.[26]

Russell S. Copeland was born in Boston, Pennsylvania, on 8 October 1918 to Joseph W. and Verna B. Copeland. Russell's parents were first-generation Americans. In 1920 his father worked as a clerk at the tube works and the family lived in the small township of Elizabeth. Joseph worked as a clerk in the steel mills through the 1930s. Most of the population around Allegany County worked for one of the steel producers.

Russell attended McKeesport High School. He was noted as training in "Vocational Industrial" in the 1938–39 yearbook. In his senior year, Russell joined the invitations committee. In high school, Russell had a handsome, intelligent look to him. He did not seem to take to sports as many of his fellow sailors did. Russell graduated from McKeesport High and soon married. He and Betty rented a house in McKeesport for twenty-three dollars a month. Russell worked as a truck driver for a local bakery as his first job after marriage.

McKeesport by 1940 was a booming steel mill town of 55,355 people. The town sits at the confluence of the Monongahela and Youghiogheny Rivers near Pittsburgh. National Tube Works was the largest employer during the peak years of steel production. National Tube Works, where Russell's father worked, made iron pipes and provided jobs for as many as 10,000 men during the war years.

Russell joined the Navy on 15 May 1944. He and Betty were living at 94 Scott Drive, Dravosburg at the time. He attended boot-camp at Great Lakes and was assigned to *LCS 52* as his first ship. One of Russell's closest friends aboard ship was Larry Cullen.

Virgil Thill was at his 20mm gun during the attack and explosion. The gun was portside, next to the conning tower. He manned his gun during the attack and stayed on it until daybreak. Someone finally came to relieve him for breakfast at daylight. The body parts of the Japanese pilot were everywhere. Thill too had a gun turret filled with blood and intestines. "I had to step on them or around them" to get out, he said.[27] However, he could not see the extent of damage to the ship itself from his gun. He never knew why someone did not relieve him that whole night. With the casualties spread out in the mess hall, the most likely reason was the cooks had no way to prepare and serve meals. With everyone drawn to the makeshift operating room to try and help, keeping men at their post got them out of the way of medical persons and diverted their minds from the carnage. Not to mention the ship was still in danger from further attack throughout the night.

Seven minutes after the first attack another kamikaze appeared. First noticed at 1,000 yards, the pilot perhaps figured he would follow up the first attack. He pointed his plane straight at the 52 and closed. The first attack had incapacitated men from every gun crew. Harper called for every man aboard not already at a critical station to man the guns—cooks, stewards, and anyone else he could summons. Just like in movies and recruiting posters, sailors who had never touched a shell or a trigger, carried, loaded, and fired to defend their ship. They willingly answered the call and their efforts paid off. The plane began to take hits from the 52's guns. Harper observed the plane lose altitude and then, perhaps, the pilot lose his courage as well. He veered and drifted away from the ship, continuing to drop toward the water as he disappeared out of sight.

Harper's first obligation was to stay at his post with his fellow LCSs and the two destroyers. There were human lives at stake, though, and he desperately wanted to take his wounded to better medical facilities, which were all back at Okinawa. At last, LCS 114 was reported churning toward RP 15 to replace LCS 52. Harper did not wait for her arrival; at 23:35 he headed toward Okinawa and the hospital ships anchored there. LCS 61 (Call sign BACKSTROKE-61) also left the RP to escort 52 back safely.

It seemed at the moment the communication gang was calling up enemy contact on radar nonstop. At one point during the journey back to Okinawa four planes circled within five miles of the two LCSs. Those four eventually withdrew and conceivably went after bigger or easier pickings. Then at 01:35 hours another bogey appeared on the radar screen at three miles out. The radioman once more began to call distance and direction to the ad hoc gun crews. Harper relayed the information to LCS 61. Harper ordered his ship to increase to full rudder and turned so that he could meet the attack on the port side. He ordered all guns to engage the approaching attacker when it was within 2,000 yards. The guns were fired in short bursts, allowing a moment for the crews to regain their vision and reacquire the plane in their sights. The plane passed the rear of 52, still low and about 600 yards out. It was a mistake on the pilot's part; he placed himself in crossfire between the two gunboats, and punctures began to dot the length of his fuselage. Visible streaks of flame began to shoot out of the engine and holes in the plane. He tried to aim for the bow of the 61 but he no longer had enough control to accomplish his goal. He crashed just short of his target.

Below deck, the only two men onboard trained to save the wounded worked frantically to succeed at their job. Typically, a doctor of medicine was assigned to the ship when they were sent on radar picket. He was present for his temporary station, and LCS 52 was fortunate to have him aboard at this dire moment. He was brought alongside at 13:00 on the 21st by a small boat. He had only been with them for a few days but he was earning his pay.

His name was Dr. Phillip C. Lynch Jr. He was born in Thurston, Washington, to Julia F. McGlinchy and John S. Lynch on 17 October 1917. His father was an attorney. Lynch went to college in Washington but moved to Illinois where he graduated in 1943 from Loyola University of Chicago Stritch School of Medicine in Maywood. He entered the Navy 18 December 1943. As a member of the medical corps, Lynch entered with the rank of Lieutenant Junior Grade. He completed his transitional year at the Naval Hospital, Bremerton, Washington, before going overseas.

The second man who labored over the wounded was Pharmacist's Mate 1st Class Syrian. The ship had no real sickbay and certainly not one large enough to accommodate all the wounded they had from the first attack. The mess hall was the largest open area available and it became the ad hoc hospital. The two-man medical staff worked feverishly for hours after the attack and through the trip back to Okinawa. Their greatest expenditure of energy was attempting to keep the wounded below during the second attack. The men fervently wanted to go topside and man their guns regardless of their injuries. That number included Hawks, the most seriously wounded. Their attention had turned from their own suffering to the task of protecting their buddies. It was a powerful and moving sight.

Larry Cullen was so shaky afterwards he could not sleep. He had been on duty in the wheelhouse for almost twenty-four hours. It was nerve-wracking feeling helpless. He went down to the mess hall where Doctor Lynch and Syrian continued to work on the wounded. He "was appalled at the sight there."[28] He volunteered to help nonetheless. Doing something made him feel better. For days after the attack Cullen found he would shake uncontrollably at the least noise or excitement.

When Virgil Thill was about five years old he and his brother went to the lake to swim. Off by himself, as would always be the case, Virgil was unexpectedly surprised by a giant pig flying ever so casually across the Michigan sky. He watched it with such fascination, becoming ever more excited by its presence, until he had to share the experience with his mother. He returned home at a run and alerted his mother to the appearance of a flying pig. After further investigation, his mother identified the serene flying pig as a dirigible. Virgil would delight in retelling the story of the flying pig, unthreatening, funny even, bringing a bit of happiness to the boring rural setting below.[29] Now, as a seventeen-year-old standing in the blood-filled tub of a 20mm gun, the sky swarmed with angry, deadly, birds of prey. How different his life had become.

SPENCER BURROUGHS
2748 Curtis Way
Sacramento, Cal.
U. of Cal., '43, Pol. Sc.

Spencer Burroughs was one of the most beloved officers aboard *LCS 52*. His rank never seemed to stop him from immersing himself in the dirtiest jobs found in the engine room. While the ship was at sea, he was seldom seen without a grease-stained uniform (University of Notre Dame, Capstan 1945, USNRMS Yearbook).

LCS 114 arrived shortly after midnight on 28 May and joined LCSs 55 and 56 on station at RP 15. Enemy suicide bombers were still out at a distance circling the group. Just before 07:00 hours approximately six kamikazes began their attacks on the two destroyers present. Two enemy planes made their suicide runs against the ships. The destroyers and the CAP Corsairs managed to splash one before it could impact either ship. The second, riddled with bullets, barely missed the *Lowry* but unfortunately maintained enough altitude to stay out of the water. The *Drexler* was not as lucky; the plane struck her, almost by accident. The impact was near the engine room, cutting electrical power and starting fires aboard ship. Chased and engaged by one of the Marine Corsairs, another kamikaze made a run at the crippled *Drexler*. He missed on his first pass, and then turned to point his nose directly at the bow of the ship. He was so close even when the guns hit him; there was no way to stop his crash. The pilot guided his plane into the aft torpedo tubes.[30] The explosion doomed the ship. From the *LCS 114* pilot house the Quarter Master watched the clock; it was a mere forty-nine seconds from the time of impact of the second kamikaze with the *Drexler* until she was completely gone from sight. The ship sank so quickly that most of the men were trapped in the lower compartments. The oil and fuel ignited in a one-mile-diameter ring around the spot where the *Drexler* had last been. Men were forced to swim through the oil and flame; some later died from the attempt. *LCS 114* moved quickly to recover all survivors she could. Approximately 119 of the 199 survivors were pulled from the water by *LCS 114*.[31]

After a nerve-wracking night, Harper arrived at the anchorage off Okinawa around 03:00 hours. The wounded were delivered over to two separate hospital ships. Crowe, Hedger and Jawor were transferred to *APA 179*. Hawks, Payne, De Maio and Gloor were transferred to *APA 21*. The USS *Lauderdale* (APA-179) (call sign, TORONTO) was an auxiliary attack troop transport capable of carrying up to 200 troops or being converted into a 150 bed hospital. The temporary hospital ship, *APA 21* (call sign, LOWLIFE) was formally the USS *Crescent City* (AP-40) converted after 4 March 1945. Once her treatment capabilities were exhausted, she turned her patients over to the USS *Hope* (AH-7).

In spite of every effort possible to save him, James Hawks died the following day from blood loss and subsequent shock. Both Spencer Burroughs and James Hawks were buried in the American Cemetery on Okinawa under standard white Latin crosses.

Few secrets remain secret for very long on a ship. James Hawks was barely transferred to the hospital ship before rumors began to circulate that he had received a "dear John" letter in the mail before the attack.[32] The boys began to wonder, but few spoke the notion out loud, if it had in some way contributed to his death. Questions arose whether at the critical moment, had his mind been somewhere else than in battle. No one would ever know for sure if the

Japanese suicide planes streak past the starboard side of *LCS 52*, off Okinawa (Virgil Thill collection).

deep hurt cast across the vast distance had distracted James. Did it cause him to give up and simply lose the will to live? In such a tightknit community, his shipmates needed to blame something or someone for his death. It was difficult to blame the kamikaze pilot; he was scrambled like a giant egg across the deck.

The morning of the 28th began on a better note. About 09:00 Harper saw two or more landing craft in line, coming into the anchorage site. Each one of the boats, he estimated, would carry up to 100 men. They were each filled with survivors from the *Drexler*. Harper's eyes fell on a familiar figure standing tall and proud on the bridge of the first boat. It was George Hood. He was covered in oil, a sign he had been in the thick of it when the ship went down. Otherwise he was unharmed physically by the loss of his ship. The boats came so close to the 52 as they passed by that the two friends were able to shout back and forth to one another. Harper was curious about the condition of the other destroyer and ships, but George had little information beyond his own ship going down. It was good to see his old friend had also survived the night.

Harper left on a small boat for *LCI 484* at 09:15. At 09:38 a small boat pulled alongside the 52; aboard were Burnette, Hile, and Fields. The three were treated on the hospital ship and released. Having some of the guys back aboard made everyone feel a tiny bit better. Five minutes later another boat pulled up and Commodore T.C. Aylward came aboard. Harper was well acquainted with the commodore; they were in fact close. He was followed shortly by Commander Stone. Jerry Duvendeck was on duty at the time. With the Captain off the ship, it was left to him to address and respond to the brass. The two quickly departed after checking the status of the ship and the men.

Ensign Parker assumed the duty at 16:00 hours and returned the ship to the routine task of making smoke. The crew settled down for the evening. Most had been on G.Qs or at their battle stations for over twenty-four hours. Few had slept at all. They were anchored in semi-safe waters. They could sleep, at least one night, in peace. Lt. (jg) Duvendeck took the last duty of the day. It was uneventful; he ordered the smoke generators cut off at 23:07.

Kikusui Eight, 27–28 May, had put sixty Navy and fifty Army kamikaze aircraft in flight. The last two sorties, Kikusui Nine and Ten, would not be able to mount half of those numbers. Eight was the last massed suicide attack. However, more young men on both sides would die due to suicide attacks before Okinawa drew quiet.

By the last days of May, the men who drove themselves into American ships seemed demonic by action. Their acts of self-destruction went against fundamental beliefs American Christians had based their own wartime actions on. That was in some cases the furthest from a correct analysis of all kamikaze pilots. Ensign Ichizo Hayashi was born in 1922 in Fukuoka Prefecture. He was raised as a Christian and went to his death in early April 1945 believing himself dying in grace. In one of his last letters to his mother he wrote, "We live in the spirit of Jesus Christ, and we die in that spirit."[33] It was not his decision, he wrote in the diary he left behind, to voluntarily commit suicide, the unpardonable sin of Christianity. "To be honest," he wrote, "I cannot say that the wish to die for the emperor is genuine, coming from my heart. However, it is decided for me that I die for the emperor."[34]

Claude Cook wrote Caroline for the first time since they had come off RP duty. It was the evening of the 30th. He was still shaken from the events of three days prior. He could not talk about the events of the week but he so desperately wanted to. "We've had a pretty rough time lately," he said. He assured Caroline he was "still fine and o.k." and that he was doing everything in his power to stay that way. He added that he did not recall what day it was, "Memorial Day" back in the States. He had argued with another crewman about what day it was. It was just another Wednesday, he had concluded. The strain of post trauma was beginning to affect them.[35]

The first of the month was sunny; the rain had stopped for a welcome reprieve. The day went by uneventfully. *LCI 484* tied up alongside off portside and *LCS 53* tied up on the starboard side. Both cast off around 19:00 hours. That evening the boys crowded into the galley, all elbowing for room around the table to write home. Claude Cook gave up waiting on a spot, sat on a bag of clothes, and began writing. It was payday; he had drawn fifteen dollars. With nothing to spend it on except toothpaste, writing paper, and soap, he figured he would be a wealthy man by the time they got some liberty in civilization.

The following day was uneventful as well. The ship remained anchored at the Aagushi harbor site. A movie party was formed and they left the ship at 19:50 hours. Claude Cook was among the party. The men were treated to a comedy, something they could use after three months of being in a combat zone. Claude thought the movie was *Sing Your Blues Away*.[36]

On 3 June, Dr. Lynch was transferred to *LCS 21* without ceremony. That afternoon, at 14:10, a church party departed the ship. Claude Cook noted the chaplain who performed the service was also from Michigan. Claude ran into three of his boot-camp buddies while he was off the ship. He had not seen them since they left Camp Pierce one year before. The day's events and their ties to home and old friends made him feel nostalgic. He reminisced to Caroline that evening in a letter that they had gone on a date during boot-camp leave. He ended his letter with an unusual phrase, seemingly resigning himself to his place in the real world. "The watch must go on."

Things had returned to routine, or as routine as they were going to get in war. On the 5th the ship anchored again at Aagushi anchorage. Duvendeck took the duty at 04:00. He nervously watched the barometric pressure, anticipating a storm gathering. At 07:00 he was informed the storm had missed them.[37]

It was odd in a way how life just went on. The ship and the crew awaited their next assignment. Replacements, both enlisted and officers, came aboard to stand-up for those who had fallen in battle. On the 12th, Ensign Parker reported that four of the crew were to be transferred to *LCS 121*. Those four were J.H. Williams, W.L. Veach, H.J. Vanderpool and G.P. Gallant. Late that afternoon, as a sad reminder of their losses, a small boat pulled alongside carrying replacements. Ensign F.M Kuehne III came on to temporarily fill the shoes of the deceased Ensign Burroughs. With him were eight enlisted men: R.R, Christman, H.L. Clack, J.D.W. Criger, C.C. Darnell, H.J. Goldman, R.E. Hobson, H.E. Kennon and E.W.H. Schultz.

Ensign Fred M. Kuehne III was born in Chicago on 11 July 1922. His parents were Fred Jr. and Vivian Pratt Kuehne. F.M.'s paternal grandfather, Fred Sr., was born in Wisconsin and his grandmother in Norway. Vivian's mother, Josephine Pratt, living with the family in the early 1930s, was born in Norway to Norwegian parents. Vivian's father was born in England.

In 1932 the family opened Kuehne Manufacturing in Mattoon, Illinois. The company specialized in producing fine dinette sets. The town of Mattoon was another community which existed because the railroad came to town. The town, nothing more than a gathering of farms, had been around since the Ohio Valley was first settled. When the Terre Haute Alton Railroad rolled through town in June 1855, the town went by Pegtown—later officially incorporated into Mattoon.

Abraham Lincoln stayed a night in Mattoon's Essex House before he debated Stephen A. Douglas the following day in 1858. The town officially became Mattoon in 1861. That same year, Colonel Ulysses S. Grant mustered the 21st Illinois Volunteer Infantry at Mattoon in the early days of June. He would be promoted to Brigadier General in less than two months. After the Civil War, the community was inundated by Amish farmers who took up residence in the surrounding countryside. When the Kuehne family arrived and began their dinette furniture business it brought jobs and prosperity to the then stagnant economy. Other companies also saw opportunity in Mattoon and soon followed the Kuehne enterprise. Fred Jr. became president of the company and directed the manufacture of wooden dinette sets throughout the war and postwar years. It was a given that his son would take over the business for him.

F.M. Kuehne III enlisted in the Navy on 1 July 1943 at Evanston, Illinois, near Northwestern University, where he then attended. One year later, on 6 July 1944 he joined the crew of *LST 675* (Tank Landing Ship) at St. Andrew Bay, Florida. He had just finished his training at Fort Pierce. *LST 675* was a new vessel, commissioned on 2 June 1944, Lt. L.W. Hamlin commanding. Ensign Kuehne served aboard her during the Lingayen Gulf Landing, early January 1945. The ship was also present for landings during the first stages of the invasion of Okinawa in April of that year. On 4 April, the ship headed for the Okinawa beach to offload. She grounded on rocks and was damaged. She was then targeted by Japanese shore batteries and salvage attempts proved unsuccessful. She was declared unsalvageable and abandoned. Kuehne's first ship was decommissioned 25 August 1945 and left where she beached.

Many of the boys had resigned themselves to the fact they would never see their former shipmates again. Even if they recovered, they would most likely be sent to other ships and fight with other crews. However, the day of 13 June brought some cheer back to the 52, a welcome sight in the form of familiar faces. A small boat pulled alongside at 09:48 to drop off Ensign Strandquist, Crowe and Jawor, all reporting back from the hospital ship *APA 179*. Ensign Parker was there to greet them.

Many of the men of *LCS 52* had some type of military training before serving in the U.S. Navy. Fred Marshall Kuehne III attended Culver Military School from 1937 to 1940. He was in Company B, Infantry. In 1935 he was also listed as attending the Culver Woodcraft Academy. Unlike today, Culver Academies were strictly male when Fred studied there. (Culver Academies, 1940 Roll Call yearbook, Culver, Indiana).

Albert George Parker III gave his parents' address in Hanover, Indiana, as his point of contact on the ship's muster roll. The family had lived on the campus of Hanover College since Albert's father, differentiated from son and father by the "junior," became the president of the college in 1929. Albert Junior, like Albert III, was the son of a Presbyterian missionary minister.

Albert III was born 19 February 1922 to Albert and Katherine Parker in Jinan, China. His father lived in Tokyo from 1917 into mid–1918. He then went to Peking and studied there until 1919. He returned to the States but was ready to perform more of God's work in China by 1920. Albert Jr. applied for reentry to China, listing his travelling companion as Katherine A. McAfee, "wife to be." That application was submitted on 18 May 1920 in Cook County, Illinois. On 10 August the two were married in Chicago, before they departed on the ship *Columbia* from San Francisco. Albert Jr. remained the head of department of Social Science at Shantung Christian University in Tsinan, China, for eight years.

On 18 June 1925, Albert Jr., Katherine, and three-year-old Albert III boarded the *S.S. President Jackson* leaving Shanghai. Under the flags of celebration that accompany Independence Day, the three sailed into Seattle. The stay in America was only temporary. They returned to Tsinan, China, where both of Albert III's sisters, Harriet and Jane Parker, were born. The family would not permanently return to the United States until 1928.

Albert Jr.'s term at the Presbyterian college was a long and progressive reign as president. Under his care, Hanover's enrollment increased dramatically; funding also increased and new construction dotted the campus. The campus overlooked the Ohio River, albeit elevated enough to prevent the frequent flooding suffered by nearby communities. A few miles to the east, also settled on the banks of the Ohio, was Madison, Indiana. Madison, in the 1920–30s, offered the students and faculty markets, banking, and shopping. Further to the west, an hour's drive along the river and across the bridge at New Albany, was Louisville, Kentucky. The campus was otherwise surrounded by table-level fields of corn that in summer seemed to go on forever. The occasional farmhouse broke the monotony of flat ground which often had drainage ditches run along the fields to keep water from pooling. When the Parkers moved in, there were still acres and acres of virgin forest growing along the river as well.

Albert III spent his childhood among the academics and theologians of Hanover. His mother, Katherine was a graduate of Vassar and his father Park College. He and his sisters were immersed in a world of books and thinkers. As a young man, Albert III went off to Lawrenceville Prep School in New Jersey. He then attended Princeton University (his grandfather was class of 1887) and graduated with the class of 1944 with a degree in Economics. Albert was one of those who attended Duvendeck's wedding back in Portland. He was a fine officer and intelligent leader. Like the other officers, Parker was well-liked by the enlisted men.

Kerama Retto over the months had become a repair area for damaged ships. *LCS 52* stopped briefly at the anchorage on 20 June. It felt safe enough to allow a liberty party to go ashore for three hours that afternoon. Their return was followed by storekeeper and mailman, Larry Cullen, bringing a batch of mail aboard. That night they made smoke but all seemed peaceful. Ensign Stewart made only one note for his entire four-hour watch from 04:00 to 08:00—"No unusual occurrences." Things seemed to be coming to a halt, at least on Okinawa.

Virgil Thill was delighted by the liberty time. He went ashore on one occasion and, as was his prerogative, wandered down the beach alone. He came upon a dead Japanese soldier, still lying on the beach. The man's body was bloated, dark and completely covered in flies. He had been left where he fell and no one seemed to have any desire to move or bury him. For Virgil it was an image of war he would hold in his thoughts and dreams for the rest of his life.[38]

The 21st appeared to be going by as uneventfully as the days before. At 15:40 the staff doctor for LCS Flotilla Three came aboard to check out Porter Barron. It seemed Porter would survive. The doc left the ship just as the swimming and liberty parties were coming back aboard.

It looked as if everyone except Virgil Thill had gone below. The boys all liked playing poker for money, but he had been cleaned out by one of the cardsharps early in the war and had no further use of cards. He enjoyed instead sitting on the top deck looking at the anchored ships, the ocean and nearby island. He often saw things that no one else was witness to. On this occasion he caught the movement of a plane approaching the anchorage. It was moving fast and hugging the mountains.

At 18:43 hours, Ensign Parker called *LCS 52* to general quarters. Anchored nearby at the time was the seaplane tender, USS *Curtiss* (AV-4). The *Curtiss* was a survivor of a midget sub attack on 7 December, at Pearl Harbor. She was not so fortunate in avoiding a bomb dropped from a Japanese Val dive bomber that same day. After repairs and extensive combat career in the Pacific campaigns, she arrived in late May to the fighting for Okinawa.

She stuck out like a sore thumb, anchored among the smaller ships at Kerama Retto. Her tall cranes and width painted an inviting silhouette from the air. Unlike many of the days in which typhoons and rain had threatened the ships, that particular Thursday was clear and cloudless.

At first the ships at anchorage received a color red warning by radio indicating that an enemy plane was approaching. A plane was indeed approaching at a high speed. Condition red was cancelled. A brief explanation followed that the plane was merely a friendly observation plane in the area. Before another warning could be sounded, a kamikaze quickly threaded between the mountains of the island and hugged the water at about fifty feet off the waves. It buzzed barely over masts of now unprepared ships, their crews ignoring what they thought to be a friendly plane. The pilot aimed at the bow of the *Curtiss*, ignoring the throng of smaller ships as if they were invisible.

Thill watched the plane as it sped closer to its target. His eyes followed it until it struck. The speed of the plane striking the side of *Curtiss* stripped the wings off on impact.[39] The momentum carried the body of the plane and the bomb through her hull and deep into her starboard side compartments. From *LCS 52*, Thill watched from his vantage point as the bomb exploded within the interior of the *Curtiss*. Fires immediately broke out below deck. Almost as quick, tugs and ships designed to fight fires got underway to assist their wounded sister ship.

The first plane had been a surprise due to the erroneous report that it was a friendly craft. The crews of American ships standing ready at general quarters were not fooled by a second plane following closely behind the first. Three minutes after the plane crash into *Curtiss*, the guns of *LCS 52* and her sister ships opened up with vengeance. It appeared that the second plane was going after the wounded *Curtiss*. The pilot's mistake was climbing to gain speed instead of coming straight in as his predecessor had done. Before he could turn to dive at the big ship, antiaircraft fire from other ships exploded him in midair. Less than a minute later, with the sky clear of aircraft, 52 got underway and sailed toward the *Curtiss* for firefighting duty. They readied their many water hoses and prepared to help extinguish fires threatening the airplane tender. Thanks to quick and innovative actions by the captain of the *Curtiss*, she was not needed. *LCS 52* secured at 19:15 and joined in making covering smoke around the bay.

The *Curtiss* lost forty-one of her crew and had another twenty-eight wounded.[40] Many of the casualties resulted because men were gathered below at the small ships' stores picking up hygiene and other items. Four days after the attack the *Curtiss* was able to sail for the States under her own power. In an instant, things had gone from dull watches and swimming parties to terror and shock for the crew of *LCS 52*.

8

Downfall to Fallout

The ship stayed in the northern waters off Okinawa during June. Her damage from May was minor in comparison to other ships attacked that month. More replacements came; Ensign Albert Moschner came on to permanently replace Ensign Burroughs as the engineering officer.

Albert Moschner was born in Oklahoma on 15 November 1918, a first-generation American. His father, Raymond "Joseph," arrived in the States with two cousins around 1907. Joseph gave his place of birth as Yugoslavia. Albert's mother, Mary C. (Mary, Katherine or Catherine, Amoso) was born in Italy. Mary was a widow who brought three sons to the household.

Albert grew up in McCurtain, Oklahoma, the youngest sibling of three half-brothers and his full brother Henry. Tony, Fred, and Edward Maidic were children of his mother's first marriage.[1] Except for Albert, and Fred who worked as a soda jerk in a drugstore, the men of the family all worked in the local coal mines.

The township of McCurtain, where the Moschner and Maidic brothers grew up, had a diminishing population by 1940. By that year, the town had lost sixty-four of its 934 residents given in the 1930 census. The majority of those families had come there at one time or another to work in the burgeoning coal mines. The community was a coal company town, founded in the late nineteenth-century as Panther. The town was established in the middle of what was the Choctaw Nation—before allotment—in the-then Sans Bois County. When coal was discovered, that made the land something of value that only Anglos could exploit. The company that moved into the area first was the San Bois Coal Company. They built homes for the incoming immigrant miners; three banks, stores, schools and a bottling company soon followed. The coal not only had to be dug out of the earth but it had to be moved to market, so in 1901 Panther was connected to the Fort Smith and Western Railroad line. In 1902 the town's name was changed to McCurtain, in honor of the last Choctaw principal chief.

Things were progressing rapidly for McCurtain until the 1912 mining explosion at the San Bois Number Two, killing seventy-three miners. Among those killed was Anton Maidic, the first husband of Mary C. The company went progressively bankrupt after and the mining population began to exit the area. There were still mines at Kanima, Sans Bois, and Stigler, smaller but employed some of the workers including Joseph. The Moschner family hung on. They, like their neighbors, were faring okay, not rich but comfortable. They owed that status to the mines.

During one of the worst years of the Great Depression, 1934, Haskell County (created from San Bois County) saw eighty-five percent of its citizens receiving government relief. By the time the United States was committed to World War II, the county had also caught the brunt of side effects from the newly constructed dams. The county was flooded by three separate floods in the first years of the 1940s. The people of the county had not seen a single flood, prior to the dams going up, in more than seventy years.

Life in McCurtain was by all accounts pleasant for the five boys of the Moschner family. Henry was probably the most athletic but only slightly. Except for Fred, whose drugstore job pinned him to long hours, the brothers all belonged to the town travelling baseball leagues. They went on the road, hitting every close town that they could drum up a game at. Most towns, regardless of how big or small, had a team.

After high school, Albert attended two years at nearby Connors State Agricultural College in Warner, Oklahoma. Albert, the one member of his family to attend college, chose the most logical way out of the failing area for good. He pinned on the temporary rank of ensign on 11 August 1944. Albert married Virginia Pauline Roebling, from Eureka, California, on 24 January 1945, before shipping out overseas. He would never live in McCurtain again.

Albert was stationed aboard *LC (FF) 423* before coming to *LCS 52*. *LC (FF) 423* was the former *LCI 423*, commissioned on 11 June 1943. She was redesigned *LC (FF) 423* on 31 December 1944. Moschner transferred from her on 2 June and came aboard the *52* on 26 June 1945. Because the ship's fighting days were behind them, Albert only participated in the occupation of Japan while aboard *LCS 52*. According to enlisted crew members, Albert was quiet and kept to himself. No one really got to know him well.[2]

Enlisted men went back and forth to other ships on temporary working parties. Most of the month was spent at Karama Retto generating smoke for anchored ships. Ensign Strandquist was taken off the ship on 20 June, for further treatment of his wounds aboard USS *Gosper* (APA 170), acting as a hospital ship.

Except for the attack on the *Curtis*, the month was peaceful. The day after the *Curtis* was hit, the island of Okinawa was declared secure. The Japanese defenses had bled Allied forces of more than 12,000 men killed and another 38,000 wounded. The Japanese had lost more than 110,000, including Okinawan conscripts. Mopping-up diehard resistance would go on until the end of the war.

On the first of the month, Robert Fields, Joseph May, Oren Tweet, Donald Schultz and Virgil Thill all received their Seaman 1st Class rating back. It looked to be the beginnings of another good month for ships and sailors. Independence Day 1945, *LCS 52* remained off the western beaches making smoke as part of Task Unit 32.9.5. The boys on *LCS 52* received their Christmas packages from the prior December in the mail. The candy was hard as rocks and one package had kept a good-sized colony of bugs alive for months. Claude Cook wrote his Fourth of July letter to Lynn, daydreaming about the past Fourth under a shade tree with her. He imagined transplanting a big tree onto the bow of the ship.[3]

On the 5th, the Philippines were declared secure. The Navy wasted no time. Harper received orders the following day to sail for Leyte, Philippine Islands. The ship fell in column with convoy 00359. The men of *LCS 52* marveled at the bombing raids taking off from Okinawa and headed for Japan as they put the island in the distance. It seemed like an endless stream of planes, one that went on until the ship was too far from the island to see the planes any longer. The other side of that spectacle was that the waters south were free of kamikazes, and that fact made no one sad. The war overall, however, seemed far from over.

Picture of *LCS 52* taken from the deck of *LCS 36*. The convoy of ships on their way to the Philippine Islands met some rough seas. This picture was taken on the Fourth of July 1944 (Nick Stoia collection).

The ships in *LCS 52*'s task unit arrived in San Pedro Bay, Leyte, on the 10th and set in for repairs and rehabilitation. The boys were granted a little shore liberty the next day. Baseball was always at the top of the list for things to do. The ships divided up into teams, enlisted played enlisted and officers played against each other. The officers gave their support by cheering for their boys on the softball field. It was an opportunity for them to put aside rank and just enjoy the skills of those men who had worked so hard for them.

Harper happened to take in the teasing of one particular player from another team. They were calling him "Raysville." Raysville by coincidence happened to be the name of a small town in Harper's home county of Jackson, back in Ohio. As it turned out, the fellow was from his home and another one from another team hailed from another nearby town.[4] It was those small connections that made sailors feel like home was still out there.

Harper viewed the recreation area as "bleak" except for the baseball diamonds. There was a kind of officer's club. The amenities were sparse: canned peanuts, some pretzels and cans of Goebel beer.[5] If one was to believe the advertisements, "Tonight's the night for Goebel Beer." That ad was certainly correct when it was the only beer to be had.

Everyone on the enlisted side got an allotment of two cans of beer. Some, like Virgil Thill, purchased beer allotments from those who did not drink. Claude Cook managed three or four. They all returned to ship too exhausted to even write letters. The 12th was quiet, peaceful; the men wrote letters home and listened to Kate Smith entertain over the radio.

It had been October 1944 since the sailors of *LCS 52* had really seen a town or had liberty off a military base. That last liberty was spent back at Pearl Harbor and it was short-lived. The ship was anchored in the San Pedro Bay, just a few miles south of the city of Tacloban. Upon MacArthur's return to the Philippines, he waded off his stalled landing craft onto Red Beach. Red Beach was located north of the town of Palo. Palo lies approximately thirteen miles south of Tacloban City. During the invasion, the Army's 1st Cavalry Division took the airfield at Tacloban, meeting only light resistance. Since the Allied reoccupation of the Philippines, Tacloban City was turned into a military hub and headquarters.

The city was a major port and had been used heavily by the Japanese. When the Americans returned it remained a major logistics port under new management. Ashore, there were the dirt streets, Quonset huts, plank barracks, large tents and makeshift softball and basketball courts of the American occupation, all the recent work of Seabees and Army engineers. The military establishment was named, simply, Base K. The unmistakable military presence, known as Base K, extended up and down the coast from Tacloban for twenty-five miles.[6] That meant Base K either surrounded or swallowed-up the civilian populations and buildings.

Tacloban City was established as the capital and his headquarters within two days of MacArthur's famous return. The city was founded on a peninsula of Leyte at the confluence of the San Juanico Strait and San Pedro Bay. One mile across the bay was Samar. The city and villages along the shore reminded Lt. Harper of small towns along the California border in Mexico.[7] They were as different as night and day from modern cities such as Manila. The population was mostly poor Catholics, who retained the influence of their colonial Spanish past, made poorer by Japanese occupation. There was no shortage of the traditional bamboo huts along the shoreline. The huts were built on posts which raised them off the ground, in defense of frequent floods. The huts, sometimes mingling with sections of wood plank buildings, pointed to the economic divides between the poor and the extremely poor.[8] It was not uncommon to pass by a river or stream and still see *lavenderas* (washwomen) squatting while they pounded clothes clean with wooden paddles. The streets were lined with open-air merchants displaying meat and poultry without the benefit of refrigeration or regard for pests. Carabao-powered carts with oversized solid wood wheels trod up and down streets, alongside military jeeps and trucks.

The Filipino people had suffered considerably under the Japanese. The Japanese-controlled distribution and storage of foods seldom trickled down to the local population in sufficient quantities. They conscripted human labor for defense projects, and employed torture and murder whenever compliance was not met promptly. That did not stop most Filipinos from taking some part, big or small, in guerrilla activities.

Acts of resistance and defiance by the Filipino peoples continued in spite of the heavy-handedness of the Japanese. The former school teacher, John Harper, would have been proud to know that only ten days after the first American forces landed in 1944, the schools announced their reopening. On the eleventh day, the school in Tacloban opened. The teachers there had been wise enough to bury their American text books in tin cans when the Japanese landed. At the start of the first class absent of Japanese censorship, the Tacloban school children precipitously filled the air with "God Bless America."[9] The jungles, mountains and outlying villages, were in fact, teeming with former defenders of Bataan, escapees from the Death March, and their trusted entourage of Filipino fighters throughout the Japanese occupation. Their intelligence gathering and reporting saved thousands of lives when the Americans returned to the Philippines.

Harper believed that his men had only gone into Tacloban a couple of times while they anchored off the coast and recuperated. To the best of his knowledge that was true. There were also villages on Samar as close, if one or two stealthy liberty hounds wanted to midnight requisition the liberty taxi (whale boat), to get to them. Harper was very much aware of the detriments to health that local concoctions and distilled drinks could bring. He and the men had been informed to drink at their own risk. A particular potent whiskey bore the name Three Roses; obviously the name had been plagiarized off the better-known Kentucky whiskey Four Roses. There were more, ranging from Four Feathers Whiskey to eye-watering fermented coconut and fruit juices. The Philippine liquors were not altered in name only. The locals were about the only humans that could tolerate any of them and it was best not to try.[10]

The 14th of July was almost boring aboard *LCS 52*. Claude Cook got off duty around 15:00 and sat down on a nearly deserted ship to write letters. Most of the boys had gone ashore for liberty. Laton and Keith went ashore and jumped into what Laton deemed a "rough and tumble" ball game. He declared that it was worse than hand-to-hand combat training back at Fort Pierce.[11] Even when the liberty was restricted to the beach areas, men found a way to get to alcohol and women.

The alcohol drew Virgil Thill. He took example from Chief Holland, who had managed to take the whale boat out and covertly negotiate under the roving spotlights one night. It was rumored but never confirmed that Chief's clandestine companion was none other than Laton Burns. The night after Chief's successful operation, Virgil and a buddy made their getaway. They took along a sack of food to be used for bartering liquor. The spotlights from the anchored ships darted and crawled across the water looking for skunk boats. They would have been as content to locate a couple of sailors unauthorized to leave their ship in a stolen whale boat. The Chief had taught them well, though, and they made it to shore undetected. Virgil was astute at locating liquor, even on a Pacific island. It was a miracle when they made it back to the ship half-drunk without anyone being the wiser.[12] It was, after all, still a time of war.

Thill also enjoyed the chance to swim, just as he had done as a boy during the summers in Michigan. He was usually the only one in the water, swimming aimlessly around the ship. A guard with a rifle had to keep watch while anyone was in the water. Sharks patrolled the waters and, just like the dead pilot Thill had seen circled by sharks at Okinawa, they were always looking for easy prey. The waters were otherwise clear, beautiful and warm. He typically swam alongside the ship but one day decided to be adventuresome and dove under the ship, surfacing on the other side. The skipper happened to be watching his dangerous feat at that moment. Harper was not happy, putting it mildly. A messenger was sent to convey the

8. Downfall to Fallout

skipper's fury. That was the first and last time Thill did any UDT training. He had just made his rating back, and he did not need to crawl up the promotion ladder a third time.

The 15th was one of the best days in the Philippines, at least for Claude Cook. He went to have lunch with some buddies from another ship. He barely got back aboard the 52 until he heard his name called for shore liberty. He jumped on the whale (liberty) boat as quickly as his name was called. The guys played basketball and then ended the day with some cards. Claude did not get rich but came out okay for the day, he later confided to Lynn. A movie party included Claude as well. The film was *Jam Session*, a 1944 musical-comedy starring Ann Miller. It turned out to be disappointing only because the guy running the projector had it on the wrong speed. Everyone in the movie was talking so fast no one in the audience could understand what they were saying. Claude climbed into the dingy to return to ship wishing for a bacon, lettuce and tomato sandwich. He did not get one, but, nevertheless, it was a great day.

Laton found time to write Kathleen that same great day. He had to mention that he was very sore from the ball game the day before. It was good to be behind the battle lines and have some rest, though. He mused at the liberty party who were coming back from the beach. They had strings of beads hung around their necks to the extent he thought they looked like the "natives." It all made him think on what they had been through and what might be ahead. "We have been in some terrible battles. I'm not worrying about not coming through [the] rest. After coming this far nothing won't happen the rest of the way. I don't think."[13] The war had humbled him, as it always does. There was no more talk of stars and manly glory. He was no longer the innocent eighteen-year-old who had, only a year before, welcomed the idea of firing his weapon at the enemy.

By the middle of July an armada of navy war vessels shared the San Pedro Bay with the indigenous banca, sail and other fishing and merchant boats. There was hardly an open alley big enough for the larger war ships to travel through. The LCSs all sat still in the waters, going about repairs, logistics and absent of gunnery practice or disaster drills. The men shifted positions more in attempt to avoid the Filipino sun than to exercise. There was a grand purpose for their presence there, however; the Navy was gathering its forces in anticipation of Operation Downfall.

At the southern extreme of Japan's mainland is the island of Kyushu. When viewed on a map, Kyushu resembles a misshapen map of Italy with mainland Japan being the boot and Kyushu filling in for Sicily. The southern beaches of Kyushu were the designated landing areas for the first phase of Operation Downfall, the invasion of Japan.

American planners for Operation Downfall were, overall, Admiral Chester Nimitz, General Douglas MacArthur, Joint-chiefs, Admirals Ernest King and William Leahy, Generals George Marshall and Hap Arnold. After much debate, Operation Downfall was broken into consecutive operations, the first, Operation Olympic was, scheduled for 1 November 1945. Olympic would be the invasion of Kyushu. The second phase of Downfall would be Operation Coronet, the largest planned amphibious operation of World War II, at Honshu. After the landings at Honshu, two armies would drive for Tokyo in a two-pronged attack, hoping that taking the capital would end the war.

It sounded like a feasible plan, yet the planners based a lot of success on sheer luck. While the boys of *LCS 52* were whiling away the hours in the Philippines, the Japanese military was gathering everything that would fly and forming an unprecedented number of

Left to right: Virgil Thill, John Criger and Oren Tweet. While the men's stay off the Philippines was not home, it allowed an allotment of beer, baseball and a bullet-free environment. Criger saw combat aboard *LST 675*. Criger's former ship was damaged beyond repair when she was attacked while offloading at Okinawa. He was subsequently assigned to *LCS 52* in June of 1945. (Virgil Thill collection).

kamikaze. The Allies at Okinawa had twenty-eight ships sunk and hundreds damaged by 2,000 suicide planes. By July, the Japanese had accumulated close to 10,000 planes designated as kamikaze to defend the mainland. Since the ratio at Okinawa was only one hit for every nine kamikaze planes, the Japanese Air Force restructured their operations so that they might achieve a one-for-five ratio. They hoped they could do this simply by targeting lesser armed transports, rather than those ships with better antiaircraft guns, such as destroyers.

It did not take the Japanese long to figure where the most likely beaches for the Allied landing force to mount an amphibious assault were. By the end of July, the Japanese had placed fourteen divisions and their support units at Kyushu. Long-standing military theory stated that in order to guarantee success against a defense, it required three-to-one attackers. With over 900,000 men ready and waiting for the assault forces, it evened the ratio to one-for-one. There was little surprise that American planners estimated between 30,000 and 50,800 casualties the first month.

The Filipinos were being very kind to the sailors. Their liberation was still fresh in mind.

When the boys got liberty, or when they invented their own liberty schedule, they made the most out of the native hospitality. Things were pleasant, carefree, but there was the presence of the inevitable invasion of Japan lying just behind the thoughts of the next liberty party. For the most part, the men knew better than to talk about it, and it was just as well not thought of until it happened. Claude Cook and his buddy Johnny Pfohl found a secluded space in one of the ordnance rooms to write letters. Claude was using Johnny's pen and then was going to hand it back. That was their usual practice for writing, since Johnny owned the only pen.[14]

John Narciso Pfohl was born 21 April 1921 in Chicago, Illinois. He was the son of Walter and Anita Dell Angelica Pfohl. On 14 August 1941 John married Dorothy Pierson, also of Chicago. The two were living on East 73rd Street when Johnny enlisted in the Navy, 27 April 1944.

All the boys aboard had received letters from excited folks back home who had seen *LCS 52* blasting away at the beaches of Iwo Jima on the big screen. Someone had taken footage from the deck of another LCS and it had ended up in Technicolor at the beginnings of feature films across the United States. One of the wives back in Chicago had become so overwrought upon seeing the 52 in action, she screamed until the manger came down from the projector room to see what the problem was. When he learned of her connection to the ship, he promised he would bring her to the projection room to watch the clip again after the feature. He kept his word.

It was 20:00 hours in the Philippines on 16 July 1945 when Claude began his letter. At the same moment, back at Mare Island, California, the 04:00 watch aboard the USS *Indianapolis* (call sign SUPERMAN) was turning over their duties. The ship's crew was already performing the last-minute preparations for its journey to Tinian Island. Her commander had received orders four days prior to carry a top secret cargo to that location, for what purpose was none of his business. Her Captain, Charles V. McVay III, was concerned that his ship, hit by a kamikaze at Okinawa four months prior, was not sufficiently tested after repairs to undertake such a mission. He felt the same about the green crew of 270 officers and men who had joined his ship after the ship's last combat action.[15] The choice to proceed, ready or not, was not his to debate.

More than a thousand miles away from the *Indianapolis*, it was 05:00 at the U.S. Air Force Base in Alamogordo, New Mexico. The base was built in the Jornada del Muerto desert. The name translated appropriately to the Journey of Death desert. The facility at Alamogordo was about to take center stage for the most powerful weapons test ever seen.

For years, groups of scientists had worked feverishly in scattered secret facilities across the United States, from Nigeria Falls, Oak Ridge, Los Alamos and dozens more, to complete an atomic bomb. The operation and research fell under the codename, the Manhattan Project. The scientific director of the project was the brilliant, first-generation American, J. Robert Oppenheimer. Oppenheimer had previously codenamed the Alamogordo site Trinity. The scientists who had labored for so many years on the project referred to the bomb as the gadget.

On that morning no one was tenser than Oppenheimer and his military partner. Oppenheimer's military counterpart was Major General Leslie R. Groves, like Oppenheimer New York born. Groves made his way out into the predawn desert about twenty minutes before detonation. He and other military members with a vested interest in the success of the forthcoming test stretched out on the desert sand. Groves turned his feet toward the direction from which the blast, if it occurred, would come. At 05:30 the bomb went off. The light from the bomb blast was seen almost 200 miles away from ground zero. A window 125 miles away was reported broken by the shock of the explosion. Groves took the initial estimates of the blast equaling 20,000 tons of TNT and included that figure in his first report. He added the results were "successful beyond the most optimistic expectations of anyone."[16] The mushroom cloud that accompanied the blast was measured at some 40,000 feet in diameter at its widest point. It would be a couple of days later before radiation measurements would reach Groves. The witnesses to Trinity were stunned. In a matter of seconds the war and the world had taken a new and inconceivable path.

Back at Hunter's Point Naval Shipyard with its secret cargo loaded, Captain McVay waited for word from Alamogordo. It came quick enough, and the *Indianapolis* sailed under the Golden Gate at 08:00 California time. She sped to an average speed of twenty-nine knots leaving the States. After taking a six-hour layover at Pearl Harbor for refueling, she headed nonstop for Tinian.

The Japanese Imperial submarine *I-58*, a 2140-ton B (3) type sub, commanded by Lieutenant Commander Mochitsura Hashimoto, was at Kure on the morning of 16 July, more than 5000 miles away from San Francisco. The port city of Kure was located southeast of the city of Hiroshima. Submarine *I-58* was launched twenty-two days earlier than *LCS 52*, in September 1944. She had been at the battle of Okinawa as well, but her participation was less than noteworthy. She had managed to endure some fifty American air attacks and was forced to sail for Kure for repairs without ever launching her human torpedoes in battle. She had been at Kure since 29 April and had undergone more aerial attacks while anchored, this time without damage. On the 16 July she was given new orders. She sailed the same day, south to search out and disrupt Allied shipping and prolong an invasion of Japan.

Her unescorted sprint to Tinian put the *Indianapolis* off the Tinian Island beaches on 26 July. The cargo was offloaded and the *Indianapolis* was immediately ordered to Guam. The following day, she arrived at Guam around 11:00 hours. She was issued new orders directing her to Leyte, and she left Guam on the 28th around 09:30, expecting to arrive around the 31st of July for gunnery practice. She was traveling at a much slower pace than her trip to Tinian. She remained unescorted, believing there was no threat of attack that far south.

The 27th of July, Claude Cook perched precariously on top of a life raft, his seat for *Here Come the Waves*, a musical-comedy with Bing Crosby and Betty Hutton. There was a possible second feature, an older silent movie called *The Iron Mask* starring Douglas Fairbanks. While Claude waited, he wrote a letter to Lynn. He penned it with the new pen she had sent him and he had just received. It was nice not having to borrow one from one of the other boys. The big news was he had heard rumors that there might be a peace agreement in the works.[17]

Two days before, *LCS 52* made her first move in almost a month. She sat moored alongside the USS *Sierra* (AD 18) at berth 49, still in San Pedro Bay. The *Sierra*'s mission was to prepare landing craft support vessels for the planned attack on mainland Japan. Coxswain Jordan "Jerry" L. Brantley and Seaman 1st Class Charles Clarence Darnell were loaned out to the *Sierra* on the 29th for temporary duty. Later that day Jordan was transferred to the hospital ship USS *Relief* as a patient. Jordan had apparently succumbed to some accident or illness.

Jordan Lee Brantley was born in Stuckey, Georgia, on 31 May 1914. Jerry, as he preferred, was the sixth of ten children born to Mary Naomi Clements and Christopher Columbus Brantley. Christopher was a farmer working on acreage in Glenwood Township in Montgomery County in the early 1900s. The county of Wheeler was formed in 1912 from parts of Montgomery, incorporating the Brantley family home in the process.

Just before Jordan was born, the family moved to Stuckey. The spot known as Stuckey, Georgia, was never more than a handful of houses, a church and a gas station. Pretty much everyone in the community farmed or had some role in agriculture. By the 1930 census the family had made a big move to Lawtey, Florida. Fifteen-year-old Jordan was working with his father as a farm laborer.

Freda S. Brown was living in nearby North Starke, Florida, in 1930 with her parents. She and Jordan would soon meet and begin a courtship that would lead to marriage. They were married in 1934 in Starke. By 1940 the two were living on what was at the time County Road 48 in Starke and had two children. They were renting a house there for three dollars a month. Jordan was going by Jerry by that time. He was sharecropping a farm and earning around $300 a year. On 5 January 1944 Jerry enlisted in the Navy. Jordan Brantley was among the first crew of *LCS 52*. Jerry returned to the 52 on 3 August from the *Relief* and resumed his duties.

Charles "Chuck" Clarence Darnell was a replacement who came aboard *LCS 52* after the kamikaze diminished her numbers in May. He transferred from *LST 675* on 12 June 1945. Chuck entered service on 22 January 1944 at Cleveland, Ohio. Chuck's first ship, *LST 675*, had a short and tragic life. She was launched the beginning of June 1944 and served in the Lingayen Gulf, Philippines, landings in January 1945. She next sailed into combat in Okinawa. On 4 April 1945 the ship was grounded during typhoon Louise and began to take on water. The incident resulted in damage so extreme that she had to be abandoned. The crew was rescued and taken ashore by other ships. She was decommissioned in August. The hull was deemed unsalvageable and left where she sank until 1957.

Chuck Darnell was born 12 February 1926 in Massillon, Ohio. He was the first son of Wilbur and Florence Hiser Darnell. Wilbert (Wilbur) C. Darnell worked in the steel mills of Massillon as a crane operator for Central Alloy Steel Company and then Republic Steel after the two merged. The steel industry began in earnest in Massillon at the beginning of the twentieth-century. In 1937, Massillon was the scene of tragedy during what was known as the Little Steel Strike. On 11 July of that year, a car failed to dim its lights approaching a police barricade at a strike site. Police opened fire. The incident then sparked a raid and more violence. The night ended with several arrests, three dead and hundreds more wounded.

During the 1930s the town of Massillon encompassed a population of a little over 26,500 people. The Lincoln Highway cut down Main Street and passed the Lions Lincoln Theatre opened in 1915, making it one of, if not the oldest, theaters in the country. The town was a port along the Ohio and Erie Canal and was called the Port of Massillon in the nineteenth-century. The Massillon State Hospital for the insane also occupied a spot in town on a 240-acre campus.

At the time of Chuck's enlistment the family was living at 917 Duncan Street SW, a two-story home built in 1921. The house sat west of the railroad tracks and the Tuscarawas River and just south of Oak Knoll Park. Chuck attended Washington, or simply, Massillon High School. The 1 February 1944 edition of the *Evening Independent* out of Massillon announced that Charles and Massillon resident, and cousin, Donald James Cummings had left for "boot training" at Great Lakes. The two joined the Navy and attended boot-camp together. They returned home for fifteen days of leave after basic training; the two were then ordered to different duties. In early 1945 the two cousins ran into each other in the Pacific, while Chuck was still serving aboard *LST 675*.

Hundreds of ships, of every class, gathered in the waters surrounding the Philippine Islands. The *Indianapolis*, en-route, was about half way between Guam and Leyte by the evening hours of 29 July. The fact that the Japanese sub, *I-58* was operating in the same location was known to U.S. Intelligence but never transmitted to the *Indianapolis*. At fourteen minutes past midnight on the 30th, the captain of *I-58* fired six torpedoes at a ship he knew to be an Allied war vessel. Two of those torpedoes struck and exploded with enough force to sink the ship, later identified to him as the *Indianapolis*. Twelve minutes later, *I-58* quickly moved out of the area feeling redeemed for her lack of success at Pearl Harbor.

The *Indianapolis* carried just short of 1,200 men. It was believed that 900 of those survived the sinking and went into the water alive. Because of her secret cargo she had transported to Tinian, no plan existed to check on her delay. The plight of the sailors of *Indianapolis* would remain undisclosed for four days. Only 317 men were rescued. The survivors shared the horrifying account of the most vicious, prolonged and massive shark attack ever recorded.

Captain McVay was one of the survivors. He was brought before a court-martial in December 1945, charged with and found guilty of hazarding his ship. Although the punishment was dropped by Admiral Nimitz, his career was effectively ruined. In an unprecedented procedure, the commander of *I-58* was brought into the court to testify against McVay. He stated to the court that there was nothing McVay could have done to prevent the sinking. At age ninety-one, Captain Mochitsura Hashimoto, last captain of *I-58*, called the court-martial of Captain McVay "contrived" from the start. In 1968, after decades of threats and humiliation, McVay stepped onto the porch of his home and committed suicide. The *Indianapolis* affair remains one of the most shameful marks on American naval history. It was a slap in the face to the courage and sacrifice made by every sailor who served during World War II. After his death, the shipmates who survived the terrors of four days in the water shared by Captain McVay, fought to have his court record expunged.[18]

Early morning of 5 August on Tinian brought the rumble of a lone B-29 making its way to a bomb-loading pit. The men of *LCS 52* had no interest in what was going on back at Tinian, although they would have been amazed. In a few hours the lone plane would lay the stepping stone into the nuclear age. It and its crew would usher in an event that would leave them and the world in awe.

The bomber was ordinary, if not average, except perhaps for the odd name "Enola Gay" painted on the side. It was the name of the pilot's mother. Colonel Paul Tibbets had flown forty-three combat missions in the European Theater. He had been instrumental in the development of the B-29 Super-fortress, one of which he piloted that morning from Tinian. After Europe he was assigned as commander of 509th Composite Group, a squadron developed for atomic warfare.

The bomb was nicknamed "Little Boy." Only three meters long, it weighed 8,900 pounds. The weight of the bomb required modifications to the B-29 carrying it. The engines were larger than normal and the propellers replaced with a new design. The Enola Gay began its takeoff run down the airfield at 02:45 on 6 August. It was Monday, the start of a new week.

Four possible target cities were chosen because they remained untouched by normal bombing raids. Striking an untouched city was the only way thought to ensure proper measurement of the damage caused by an atomic bomb. When clear weather was reported over Hiroshima, the first choice of the four cities, its fate was sealed.

The Enola Gay left the runway with twelve crewmembers. The man responsible for arming Little Boy was Navy Captain William Parsons. Parsons was involved in the development of the bomb and understood to be the most qualified to arm the bomb in flight. By 03:00, fifteen minutes after takeoff, Parsons had completed that task.

The modified bomb bay doors of the B-29 opened at 08:15, local time. The bomb hurled toward its designated target, Aioi Bridge crossing the Ota River within the limits of Hiroshima. The bomb missed the bridge by a mere 800 feet. The bomb exploded some 1,900 feet above the surface, spreading the blast radius across the city. Estimates showed the red core mushroom cloud to rise as high as 40,000 feet at its peak. The explosion was recorded on film by two trailing bombers to the Enola Gay.

Within a five-mile radius from explosion, the city of Hiroshima was turned to ashes and rubble. Estimates ranged from sixty-nine percent of the city's structures destroyed to ninety percent. The population present in the city was believed to be around 350,000. More than 118,000 would die within a year as a direct result of the bomb. Thousands more would die over a five-year period from exposure to radiation.

The military and political leadership of Japan wavered over possible alternatives to surrender. When capitulation did not swiftly come, another B-29 carrying a second atomic bomb rolled down the runway. On 9 August at 03:40 hours, Major Charles Sweeney piloted his plane named "Bockscar" off the runway on Tinian Island. The plane carried with it a 10,000-pound plutonium bomb nicknamed "Fat Boy." The target city was Nagasaki, Japan. Nagasaki was added to the list of potential targets in the last minutes of selection due to inclement weather over the primary target. Although Fat Boy was a larger and more powerful bomb than Little Boy, Nagasaki sat in a valley surrounded by hills. It was also a port city spread along the coast. These topographical factors reduced the destruction of the bomb. The radius of the bomb's destruction extended out just over two and a half miles. About seventy percent of the city's structures were destroyed, and later estimates placed the total deaths at 87,000 people. As with the figures from Hiroshima it would remain difficult to pinpoint how many people died initially or how many succumbed to radiation poisoning over the decades that followed the two bombs.

Claude Cook was about to step into the shower on the evening of 10 August. The abrupt orchestra of noise a month earlier would have sent the men flying to battle stations. There was something quite different about this commotion, though, and no one bothered to man their guns. The communications gang heard it over the radio but the news was spreading faster than anyone could comprehend. It was about 21:00 when the radio crackled the news. For a few moments things were deathly silent, men trying to process what they had heard. The scuttlebutt was that Japan was ready to surrender, maybe already had. The war was not officially over but it seemed unofficially the powers-to-be had made it so.

The skies of San Pedro Bay suddenly erupted with light from searchlights and pyrotechnics. The flare lockers were emptied of their contents and quickly turned the sky over the Philippine Islands into the 4th of July and New Year's all rolled into one. Ships' sirens blasted and water hoses were broken out to act as canvases for the light show. Streams of water shot into the air and searchlights panned across them creating artificial rainbows. Every fog horn went off at once. The men, too, filled the air with cheers and shouts not heard in those waters for many years. Laton Burns said "it was the most beautiful scene [he] ever looked at."[19] Lt. Harper estimated that there were between 1,000 and 1,500 ships harbored off the coast, all firing their pyrotechnics at once. He called it "a vast display of fireworks second to none that [he] had ever seen."[20] The celebration went on throughout the night.

Things finally began to quiet down the following day. Claude Cook wrote to Lynn, almost in an attempt to get her to confirm or deny the rumor. The anticipation got worse over the next couple days. Men heard rumors about stipulations and negotiations but the million dollar question was, was it really over? Sailors, soldiers and marines were weighing the issues of the Emperor staying in power in every tent and berthing compartment in the Pacific. If the Americans gave in to concessions, what did that mean for the American armed forces in the Pacific?

Finally on the 14th, the announcement came. It was official: Japan had surrendered. That left another question, when would sailors be going home? Claude Cook told Lynn in a letter that evening it did not matter when, they had said the magic words that everyone wanted to hear, "cease fire." There would be no further offensive operations. The war was over, at least for the fighting men. Nothing pleased those fighting men more than the halt of bullets and death. Governments could handle the political side of things, but for the ordinary soldier behind the gun, not pulling the trigger was heaven. Russell Copeland had made a point to write back and forth with Robert Payne, while the latter recovered from the loss of his arm. In one letter according to Copeland, Payne had said, "it was well worth [losing] (sp) an arm to get away from the battles we were in."[21]

That evening Laton closed his letter to Kathleen with the promise, "I'll write you again after V.J. Day." He added something that had been absent through the many letters to her, "Love Laton." There was now room for thoughts of a future beyond the Pacific War.

On the 25th, the ship said goodbye to one of its original members. Abraham Arnold Scurrah, formerly of 540 Ferry Street, Everett, Massachusetts, received his orders to return to the States. He had been in service to the Navy for exactly three years. Abraham preferred to go by Robert or the more traditional short version, "Bob." He had served aboard the 52 as a Fireman 1st Class since joining her on her commissioning. The rating of fireman took its name from the men who worked below decks in the boiler rooms of the steam-powered vessels. In earlier days firemen kept the boilers stoked and generating steam to keep the ship moving. There was no need for that service in modern-era shipping but the firemen remained below pulling maintenance on generators, engines, and electrical wiring. They were the engineering experts of modern seagoing craft.

Abraham was a unique individual even among a unique crew. He was born in Westerly, Rhode Island, on 24 November 1912 to Arnold A. and Agnes Mabel Kirk Scurrah. Agnes was the former Mrs. George E. Fisher of Mansfield, Massachusetts. Agnes entered into the marriage with Arnold bringing four children, two boys and two girls, from her former marriage. Abraham was the first of three more children born to Agnes. He was followed by a brother Herbert and a sister Elizabeth, named after Arnold's mother. Abraham carried the family name of his grandfather Scurrah of Yorkshire, England. Agnes and Arnold were married in Attleborough, on 26 May 1911. Arnold was working as a lineman at the time of his marriage. The two moved around but were back in East Boston by the time Arnold was required to register for the First World War draft. He was thirty-five years old and then working as a machinist at Boston Lockport Block Company, manufacturing tackle-blocks for pulleys used on canal boats, by bridge-builders, and machine-shops. He continued to do machinist work until the early 1940s.[22] On his Second World War draft registration he was then working for the Loyal Order of the Mouse, headquartered at 40 Central Square in East Boston.[23] The family was living in Everett at the address that Abraham later provided as his home address to Laton Burns for his war journal.

The house on Ferry was a three-story frame with six bedrooms built at the turn of the century. It was a huge house but quite necessary for the large family. It sat on a corner and years later, one side would be converted into a commercial establishment. Herbert, also born in Rhode Island, was twenty-four and living in the house with his parents in 1940. He was then working as a machinist helper manufacturing block-tackle.

When sailors were informed that the war was over, every ship's pyrotechnic locker was emptied. The subsequent light show was a once in a lifetime marvel (Virgil Thill collection).

The town of Everett was an industrial hub for manufacturing and shipping at the turn of the twentieth century. In 1870 the southern section of Malden splintered off and became the city of Everett. Everett bordered on the Mystic River and nearby Malden on the Malden River. Everett's mother town of Malden was settled by English Puritans in the early 1600s and named after a sister city in England. Before the factories absorbed most of the land, Everett was woodlands and rolling hill farmland.

One of the most popular and famous Everett residents was Henry Schrow. Schrow was a German immigrant, an Argonaut who panned for riches in California in the early 1850s.

Henry's most renowned adventure, though, began from Norfolk, Virginia, in November of 1852 aboard the frigate *Mississippi* with Commodore Matthew Calbraith Perry. The fleet of U.S. Navy ships arrived in Tokyo Bay on 8 July 1853, for the purpose of launching trade relations with isolated Nippon. The voyage, by one means or another, resulted in the Convention of Kanagawa and trade which lasted until the beginning of World War II between the United States and Japan. Henry returned to Massachusetts in 1860 on the brink of the Civil War. He first joined the Union's 2nd Massachusetts Cavalry. He served throughout the war, fighting at Petersburg, with Sheridan's Army of the Shenandoah, and in many other encounters with Southern forces. After the war, he returned to Everett and made his home at 202 Hancock Street, where he died in 1919. Unfortunately, Abraham never met Everett's most famous son, Henry Schrow. The Scurrah family was still living in East Boston when Henry died.

Abraham, like many of the youthful sailors aboard *LCS 52*, encountered the wrong side of the law as a teenager. In 1930, he was a guest of the state at the Shirley Industrial School for Boys. For the better part of its existence the school was run by Superintendent George P. Campbell. Campbell once classified his inmates into two simple categories (of delinquents), based on his many years of experience. There were boys (and it could be assumed girls too) "with a conscience." These lads had the internal capacity to feel remorse and the weight of their failure to society. They had, according to Campbell, not been able to, for reasons not even known to him, "bring to bear the inhibitory force of their whole selves and [had] fallen into anti-social conduct."[24] He went on to describe the second type of delinquent, those without a conscience, and unable to feel remorse for their acts of misconduct, regardless of the severity. They carried within themselves a blank page where the formula for the difference between right and wrong should have been written. In 1927, prior to young Abraham's incarceration, Campbell noted an increase in the second group of delinquents; they were difficult to cure (but not impossible), he warned. Of course, Campbell attributed both forms of delinquency to "heredity and environment."[25] It was obvious to him that his inmates came from bad blood and bad towns.

At least by the age of twenty-four, Abraham had escaped his environment. He took his twenty-one-year-old brother Herbert with him. The two worked as merchant marines throughout the year of 1936. They were employed by Colonial Beacon Oil Company, purchased five years prior by Standard Oil Company. Everyone who owned a car knew the familiar sight of the octagon-shaped Colonial filling stations with their covered pumps. Standard purchased the company specifically to sell their Esso products in those well-known stations. The Scurrah brothers left the port of Boston on 5 November 1936 for Baytown, Texas. They sailed on what would in the future become one of many tragedies of war, the tanker USS *W.L. Steed*. The master for the trip was Harold Griffiths.

The tanker was built in Quincy, Massachusetts, in 1918. She was in the middle of the Atlantic on her first wartime mission when she was notified that the Armistice had been signed and the First World War had ended. The *Steed* was once again pulled into military service during the Second World War, making forty-five successful runs between 1939 and 1941. She was on her third wartime run of the year on 2 February 1942 when the German submarine *U-103* torpedoed her in her starboard side near her bridge. The crew of thirty-eight, the same number Abraham's crew consisted of, ready at their lifeboats, were ordered to abandon ship after the first torpedo hit. The entire crew occupied four lifeboats in sight of the burning ship. The U-boat surfaced, manned its deck-gun and finished the wounded ship off with seventeen rounds to the stern. The sinking of their ship was only the first page of a tale of horror at sea. The men had rushed into the lifeboats minus cold weather clothing. They had experienced high seas and a bitter snowstorm for the last day with no sign of respite. With no protection from the elements, men began to quickly freeze to death within the boats. The four boats drifted apart in the storm, and it could be assumed that each suffered its own torturous tale. Ill-prepared for the winter conditions, the crew stood little chance if not rescued swiftly.

The first lifeboat located was not discovered by Allied shipping until two days after the sinking of the *Steed*. Only two of the crew were alive and one died after rescue. A second boat was recovered on 6 February with three men who had managed to stay alive by building a small fire in a bucket. The third boat was located on 12 February with four bodies in it. The fourth lifeboat was never seen again after the night the ship went down. Of the crew, only four survived the ordeal.

There were other reasons driving Abraham to stay out of trouble as an adult. He had met a Prince Edward Island-born Canadian named Ruth I. Dyment. The two married in January of 1936 in Portsmouth, New Hampshire. Ruth was a clerical worker. Her parents were George and Ellen "Jennie" Dyment. George entered the country one year prior to bringing his family. Jennie brought eight of their thirteen children into the country in August of 1916, via Maine, with her final destination of Malden. The Dyment family made a home in Malden, where George Dyment worked as a ship's carpenter. George apparently died sometime around 1921. In the 1930 census, Jennie and Ruth were taking on boarders in their home and showing no other means of income. Jennie gave her marital status as widowed.[26] Ruth was living with her mother through 1935 and took the clerk job she maintained through her marriage to Abraham. After they married, Ruth and Abraham rented at 271 Eastern Avenue in Malden. The two then moved to Holyoke Street. Abraham was working as a driver for Malden Supply Company. Abraham enlisted in the Navy on 21 August 1942. Seven days later, his younger brother, Herbert Holdsworth Scurrah, enlisted in the Army.

The transfer of Abraham back to the States was bitter-sweet. On one hand, it meant that the Navy was keeping its promise to hold men only for the "duration of the war." On the other hand, there was always a bit of jealousy from those who had to remain behind. Their turn would come, based on the departure of Abraham, but it would never be soon enough.

The ship anchored aimlessly, with all the rest, in harbor off the Philippines. There was nothing to do except wait for the war to end, dream about home, write home and drink beer when the opportunity arose. The men prepared the ship for inspection—the inspection came and went. Right after the inspection, Larry Cullen took a trip ashore. He had only one thing in mind to accomplish while there, and it was not to play baseball. He located his allotment of beer and downed it. The usually cool, both physically and emotionally, Cullen lamented to his folks in a later letter about the heat. "This is the place they use for bragging purposes when they say it is as hot as."[27]

He shared the details of their exploits and tragedies with his folks in their first uncensored letters. His shipmates were showing the first signs of succumbing to tropical diseases. Rashes from the heat and humidity were tormenting some. Larry wrote about his fear of getting some form of "jungle rot" or "creeping crud." Everything stayed wet in the heat of tropical climate. Watch bands rotted off the wrist. Larry had lost three to the rot in the short months they had been there. He debated whether he should continue to replace them with the "two-bit" cloth bands or spend the money for an expensive seven-dollar stainless-steel band.[28]

Everyone on the ship was coming to the point where they felt obligated to tell their families back home something about what they had been through. They procrastinated because most did not know how. There were no words that would describe fully the terror and there was no reason to share misery with loved ones. The solution, as it turned out, came from the most obvious and likely source. Larry Cullen, the scholar that he was, drafted a letter which was reproduced and distributed across the gamut of hometowns and states of 52 men. The letter addressed kamikaze attacks and spun the glory of shooting the enemy down with the ease of a Hollywood movie. Most importantly it redundantly reassured that the war was over and those left standing were alive and un-maimed. It was, to hear Larry portray the last two years, one big adventure and a duck-shoot against a cunning but inferior evil empire. By this method, several families in the States all unknowingly received the same upbeat and comforting letter.

Larry Cullen was also returning to his former humorous outlook on life. He wrote a letter to his Pop and shared that he had been receiving several editions of various newspapers from the States, a welcome change from *Stars and Stripes*. There was only one small glitch; the papers that were now arriving in abundance had what Larry called "historical value only." He informed his dad that it looked as though the Russians were about to take Berlin and he would not be surprised if the Germans gave up soon. It was, of course, 26 August 1945 when he felt so blessed by the good news in Europe. It was a certainty his dad was never fooled by the yesterday's news charade.

The formal Japanese surrender was signed on the top deck of the USS *Missouri* on 2 September 1945. *LCS 52* was still anchored in the Philippines. Life aboard ship had become so monotonous some of the boys reminisced about the busy days of combat. It was hard to go directly from a sprint to a chair. Claude Cook mostly continued to sit around and write Lynn. He too reminisced more and his letters were filled with underlying frustration to be home. He wrote a long letter on the 9th explaining who did what on the guns.

Claude was in one of the ordnance rooms, what had been one of the busiest places on the ship a month before, enjoying the solitude. Lincoln "Smithy" Smith came by to share some pictures his sister, Zerma, had sent him from home. Zerma was about a year and a half Smithy's junior and, like him, born in the rural unincorporated township of Rutherford, North Carolina.

Smithy was a likeable "kid" and had endeared himself to the crew since their gathering in Washington, D.C., to get on the cross-country train. Lincoln Smith was born to Jesse H. and Callie L. Smith on 21 June 1926. He was their first child. The family moved in the 1930s to Cramerton, N.C. Lincoln worked at the nearby Cramerton Mills. The Mills were founded in 1906 along the Southern Railway lines at the edge of the South Fork River. Major Stuart W. Cramer, Jr., U.S. Army, the owner's son, was the original developer of a new kind of khaki uniform in 1929. Those uniforms, known as Cramerton Army Cloth, continued to roll off the looms through World War II. Mr. Cramer graciously loaned the design to other manufacturers during the war years. Stuart Cramer, Jr., took over the business in 1940 after his father's death.

Jesse Smith also worked through the Depression as a laborer in the cotton mills. With the war's increased demand for textile products, Jesse took up a position as an electrician in

From left to right, back row, Robert Payne, L.E. Parham, and Laton Burns; center row, Gerald Davis and Hanford Cazee; seated in front, Lloyd Keith. Taken in Hawaii before any of these men had ever experienced the terror of war. Smiles this genuine would not appear again aboard 52 until the ceasefire (Virgil Thill collection).

one of the local cotton mills of Cramerton. The family was living at 249 8th Avenue in Cramerton when Smithy joined the Navy on 5 March 1943. He met Claude Cook at Fort Pierce and they had been friends since. Smithy left Florida on 29 July and trained through 11 August 1944 on the USS *Wyoming*.

At twenty-one years old, Smithy was the gun captain of the single forward 40mm, the gun that Burns and Keith worked. When Cook described him in his letter, he gave his rank as Gunners Mate 2nd Class. He was promoted to that rating on 18 December of the prior year. Smithy, called the "good kid," would not keep it much longer.

The following day, things did not pick up. Cook and three others retreated to the ordnance room again and stretched out on the deck for a nap. Rest did not come easy, if at all; the heat of the Philippines was sweltering. Claude finally gave up and decided to write a letter. He had forgotten his pen and paper in his locker and rather than go all the way back to the compartment be was loaned writing gear by Smithy.

With mail no longer censored, the crew vented their pent-up frustrations in their letters. Claude had been eligible for his next rating since July. He never received it because the captain required promotions to be based on Navy tests. Through April to the end of July the men had been a little too busy swatting off kamikaze attacks to hit the books. The fire control rating that Claude was up for consisted of a series of nineteen tests. With the war over and nobody sure what was coming next, the most plausible scenario was the Navy would freeze promotions. All the hours of studying would be for naught. The consensus in the end, for those up for promotion, was to just forget about it.

Claude Cook carried a different, but no less respected, heroism into battle. He was a ranking Michigan State Patrolman before the war who had also taken on the responsibility of full-time care of his elderly, infirm grandparent. After the war Cook returned to his job as a trooper (Mike Kaloz collection).

Claude was no stranger to having men follow him into hairy situations. Having been a supervisor of troopers before the war, Claude was usually slow to judge others with the responsibility of leadership in combat. However, there was no longer any combat to use as an excuse. Other ship's captains were issuing out "spot promotions" across the board. Claude and the other enlisted members of 52 had taken note of those generous examples. "If the Old Man [Captain] was a square shooter, he'd give them on spot ratings," he bemoaned. No one else was forcing their men to take tests. Claude made a deriding reference to the captain teaching third grade back in Ohio before the war. He was holding back saying outright that the Old Man was treating his crew like third graders.

It was no secret the captain was a strict disciplinarian; he had been that way since the crew met him. It was not a new or acquired trait. It could be construed that he ran his ship by the same letter-of-the-law firmness as he had run his midshipman classrooms at Notre Dame, probably not his third grade classes. If 52's "Report of changes" each month were compared to those of other LCSs, their captains issued obviously fewer captain's masts, deck courts and other punishments. The crew's actions in combat clearly indicated the 52ers were not a bad bunch. There was also no denying that they were a mischievous lot when they had, or made, the opportunity to be so, but probably no more than any other crew. It was not the captain or officers who made a man and his buddies return two days late from shore liberty. That was the choice of a few men who knew the consequences and did the crime anyway. Nevertheless, the enlisted men saw only the excesses and extremes of punishment; many would go to their graves believing they were petty sentences. Some of the problems were generic to a small vessel. If the same man had been running an aircraft carrier, most of the crew would have never had the chance to salute him, let alone interact with him on a daily basis.

What enlisted men seldom, if ever; saw was the fragile state a ship existed in. LCS ships, as a group, had some of the youngest, most inexperienced captains in the fleet. Most were thrown into the fray without ever having the courtesy of tutelage under experienced captains. No LCSs were ever lost during the war because of a captain's failure to do his job correctly. Most importantly, men of any rank did not have to like the way the captain held his ship together. They simply had to obey orders.

There was another side that the Old Man never allowed the enlisted men to see. After the wounded were evacuated for treatment, he frequently went by to check on their progress. He wrote to them and stayed in contact for many months, always desirous to know how they were doing. He alone was left to attempt to find some words of comfort for the two mothers who had lost sons on his watch. He alone had to make what seemed to be a senseless death into a heroic parting for one's wife. It was a burden few men bore and none cherished.

The lazy days in the tropical clime were taking a toll on the men. Some had come down with dysentery and even malaria. Claude Cook had his bout with dysentery shortly after his candid letter to Lynn was mailed. He began getting symptoms while on watch. Weakness set in and he was put on a regimen of unidentified pills by the Pharmacists Mate. The pills came by the handful, ten to twenty at a time. It took him five days before he was feeling strong enough to even write another letter. By the time he was up and moving again, the ship was headed north.

9

Ex-Kamikazes and Mysteries of the Orient

Landing Craft Support Group Seven under command of Lieutenant-Commander Stone, consisting of *LC* (FF) *484, LCSs 31, 32, 34–36* and *51–57*, departed Leyte on the 17th. They formed up with LCS Groups Thirteen and Fourteen and headed toward Okinawa, where they would refit for the journey to Japan. It was the mission they had dreaded for so long while the war raged. Now, it was the mission they welcomed, knowing the end of their fighting and dying had come. It was almost too good to comprehend. They were entering Japanese home waters as an occupying force, not an invading force.

LCS 52 and her group returned to Okinawa on the early morning of 21 September. For the first time since they had left the States, they sailed the entire way with all their lights lit. Claude Cook saw the island of Okinawa as that "same desolate piece of land that we left last July 6th."[1] There was little time on this stop to revisit old ghosts, though; the ships set sail the following day for Japan. Only twelve ships the 52 arrived with were ordered to proceed on to Japan, leaving the bulk of the convoy at Okinawa. En-route the ship's radio picked up Radio Tokyo. The boys heard through that source that the vets of Iwo would occupy Wakayama. They were the vets of Iwo. Their reputation preceded them even to Japan.

The Navy moved quickly to get ships into harbors for security and other occupation missions. Led by the United States, the Allied occupation would last from August 1945 to April 1952. The *LCS 52* sailed into harbor at Wakayama, Japan, on 25 September. While Americans had limited contact with Japanese soldiers during the fighting, they had even less with Japanese citizens. American sailors arriving in Wakayama had no idea what the citizens believed about the war or what they had endured during the war. Lillian Natsue Uehara Morgan later described what her hometown of Wakayama looked like before and then just after the bombings ceased. As far as the eye could see, there was only the "rubble of burned-out buildings, homes, and department stores." Two multi-story department stores were located in the city, one was five floors, Morgan recalled. "It now stood with twisted steel frames sticking up into the heavens," she sadly remembered.[2]

The 52 approached their harbor site with all guns manned and at the ready. "While nothing actually happened that caused us any real alarm we were at battle stations and ready to defend ourselves or shoot our way into and out of any harbor," Lt. Harper said.[3] The apprehension did not last long. The people were just as tired of the war as the American armed forces were. No uprisings or underground resistance activities materialized and tensions soon eased.

The only consolation the Japanese received in the Potsdam Declaration ensured the Emperor would remain in place. It was, in the end, a good decision. His efforts went far in quieting any potential underlying animosity to the occupation. In his speech of 15 August, he mandated his people to accept the occupation forces with humility and integrity. The Emperor's voice reverberated from loudspeakers and radios, imploring his people:

> Beware most strictly of any outburst of emotions which may engender needless complications, and refrain from fraternal contension [sic] and strife which may create confusion, lead ye astray and cause ye to lose the confidence of the world.[4]

The people complied. Across Japan, citizens walked humbly, all the while fearing that their army's atrocities throughout a decade of war might be visited upon them by the conquering forces. Their compliance was reciprocated with none of the rape and vengeance they expected.

"The fact we could sail into the harbor of Japan without a shot being fired and take over the city made the fact that we had won the war seem much more realistic," Claude Cook said about their arrival in Wakayama.[5] The ship was anchored near shore. Sailors aboard the 52 watched as a seemingly endless stream of soldiers disembarked from transport ships to take up the physical occupation of their old enemy's country. From the ship, the boys could clearly see and consider the damage done by bombing raids. Most of the buildings along the shore, the port industrial section, had gaping holes in their roofs and sides. Windows were rarely seen intact. Almost to the last they had been broken and shattered by bombings. In the far distance sailors could see the residential parts of the city. It was less damaged as far as they could tell but not exempt from the effects of collateral damage. The structures which seemed to survive along the industrial section were the concrete and steel-framed buildings—former warehouses.

The harbor was peppered with mines. Transports were cautiously approaching the docks. In spite of the wary entry, one of the LSTs struck a mine and was badly damaged. The Allies could not blame their old enemy for the accident. The irony was, the mines had been dropped there by American planes.

Dropping mines in the waters surrounding Japan began 27 March. The purpose was to deny the Japanese shipping debarkation and departure of military supplies. It was hoped, under the best circumstances, the effort would cut off warfighting necessities including oil, food, munitions, reinforcements and general resupply to Okinawa. If ships engaged in the transport of those items happened to go to the bottom in the process that was an added benefit. The code name for the operation was appropriately, Starvation I and II. Responsible for carrying out the dropping of thousands of mines were the B-29s of the 313th Bombardment Wing, stationed in the Marianas. Most of the shipping in 1945 passed through the Shimonoseki Straits. The Straits therefore held the number-one spot on the target list. The mines used were of three types, acoustic, magnetic, and pressure. The first two types each came in either 1,000 or 2,000 pounders. A B-29 held an average payload of 12,000 pounds. The first sortie of Operation Starvation I included ninety-two bombers. The first flight took off on the night of 27 March 1945. The last runs came the day before the ceasefire on 14 August. In total, fifteen sorties planted 3,578 mines in Japanese waters.[6] For all the hindrance they created for the Japanese military, they created just as much for the occupying forces.

Aboard the 52, the first evening in Japanese home waters ended uneventfully. It was a life swiftly approaching boring, compounded by so many days in the serene waters of the

Philippines. With hostilities over, there was also time to complain about the old standby thorn stuck in everyone's craw, no mail. Mail had not gone out or come in since they left the Philippines. If that was not bad enough, an inspection of the ship was in the works. All servicemen who had spent time in combat zones dreaded one thing about a peacetime existence: the brass looked for ways to fill large blocks of time. That was always the attitude and perspective of the trigger pullers and wrench turners anyway.

The next three days were spent painting and tidying up the ship. Cook spent all day the 28th repainting his gun director, among other things. They were tired and recalling before the war when those vacant blocks of time were filled with make-work. Those thoughts subsided quickly as *LCS 51* pulled alongside to drop off bags of mail. Men were happy again and had something other than grumbling to do.

Deeper in the heart of Japan, the aftermath of surrender was still a pill too bitter to swallow for ultra-nationalist factions. As Cook and the other boys painted and scraped rust, members of the ultra-nationalist organizations steadily approached the palace of Emperor Hirohito. There, they committed suicide by the traditional method of self-disembowelment.

With less than a week in country, 52's officers discovered an electric train which ran from Wakayama to Osaka. It was an adventure too good to pass up. They divided up into small groups for liberty. Some stayed back so that the ship would remain properly manned at all times. The touring liberty officers found that a new officers' club was having its grand opening the first night they made it to Osaka. The club played American music and served Japanese beer and rice wine. A month earlier that night was unimaginable.

In other clubs, geisha girls stood by to dance or accompany the soldiers and sailors to the *benjo* for special attention. The benjo, or bathroom, was usually nothing more than a hole in the floor over a pit where one squatted. While it may have been a suitable place to conduct commercial amour for the Japanese, it did not conform to even the saltiest sailor's expectation of a proper whorehouse. An LCSer told his gal back home, "These Jap women do not appeal to me." He did admit that most were clean, in spite of the deficiency of soap in postwar Japan. He added in his letter, "The things I could say about them [Japanese women] are unprintable and is not allowed now."[7]

What surprised the men most was the poverty and hunger of the Japanese people. The war had taken a toll on the average citizen just as it had taken a toll on the sailor. "We were surprised and saddened [at] just how destitute they were," Harper said.[8] Sailors ran across workers who, if they had anything for their lunch at all, had a roasted sweet potato, seaweed, or a little rice flavored with fish heads.

Lt. Harper recalled that they went to Osaka and took along their own military rations. By that stage in the logistical operations they were being issued surplus Army rations. The rations had "some hard rolls and some jelly in them." The officers, Harper said, became too embarrassed to eat in front of the Japanese workers. They begged for a bit of roll or jelly to take home to their "bebes." "Like all humans all over the world, they thought the world of their children," Harper wrote.[9] The people had stepped out from behind the shadow of their fanatical military and were suddenly visible to the officers and men as simply human beings. For the most part, all the men found the Japanese likeable and got along just fine with them.

Between all the readying for inspection, the ship moved off the shore of a smaller town named Wakanoura. Ten men at a time were allowed to go ashore for liberty. Among those ten was Claude Cook. It was his first time on Japanese soil. He noticed that the people clearly

9. Ex-Kamikazes and Mysteries of the Orient

had no resentment toward the Americans. They looked and acted more like a "liberated race, rather than a conquered one," he wrote to Lynn.[10]

Former Dutch, Filipino, Australian, British and American Prisoners of War trickled into Wakanoura via the railway which connected the city to the interior. The first Allied ships arrived early in the month to care for and liberate their erstwhile POWs. Hospital ships arrived to take on the more seriously ill ex-POWs. The majority of former prisoners had worked as forced labor in Japan proper. The ex-POWs were transported to Dejuma Wharf and loaded onto transports. The POWs were priority and each respective country moved to have them off Japan and headed home by 14 September. The hospitals within the city where they had been treated still cared for patients, who were often observed by occupation forces peering down from windows.

The city was crowded and living space for the people was almost as rare as it was on a LCS. The streets were narrow and usually dirt, packed by continuous use. Bicycles were the most common form of transportation. Young mothers carried their babies around strapped to their backs by cloth cords, as did older siblings at times. All genders and ages wore open-toed wooden sandals. Westerners were not known to be xenophiles in general. While the culture was curious, Americans were not particularly accepting of many Japanese customs. That may have had more to do with the lingering memories of encounters with Japanese combatants than the physically undistinguishable citizen.

The enlisted liberty party discovered, as the officers had before, the people were destitute. They attempted to sell any little souvenir or trinket to the sailors. The sailors understood they could not offer currency for the items legally, but they often fell prey to the relentless hawking of goods nevertheless. Items, if sold, might mean the difference between survival, or not, in some cases. Invariably, those who succumbed to the salesmanship attributed their discretion to charitable indulgences.

If the use of money was prohibited, then buyers and sellers turned to the ancient trade practice of barter. Cigarettes, candy and soap became currency. In return the sailors packed off handcrafted dolls, chinaware and garments of all manners. It was a buyer's market, at first. A pack of smokes bought anything the Japanese had to offer. As more and more sailors lined the streets, the little town began to look more like San Diego or Honolulu east. Then an economic upswing occurred, and the law of what price the market would bear began to apply. "The Japs aren't so dumb," Claude Cook conceded, as he monitored the skyrocketing prices over the length of the day.[11] Fear that the shelves would soon be void of souvenirs encouraged soldiers and sailors to become the proverbial wastrels locals had relieved of currency, from Tijuana to Manila.

If the sailors put forth a smile, the people grinned and laughed. They seemed to delight in the Americans' friendly gestures toward them. It was a chore to try to communicate with the Japanese, but the boys made the effort. The towns were beginning to receive their own soldiers back as they were being demobilized as well. Their attitudes toward the Americans were far from the deference the general citizens showed. There were no exchanges of smiles or bows, and angry stares seemed to extend out to both factions. Cook's ire percolated to the surface when his group passed a Japanese soldier wearing a pair of sniper's climbing boots. Shortly thereafter they passed a group of soldiers staring down at them from a hospital balcony. Those men had all seen the same bloody war that they had left, Cook realized. They "would gladly have cut our throat," Cook later wrote. He was ready. If they left him alone, then okay, but if they were spoiling for more war, he was ready and waiting for the slightest provocation to continue the fight. They obviously hated the Americans' presence, and he admitted the feeling was mutual.[12] Nothing compelled the two sides to engage in further hostilities, though, and both satisfied themselves with contemptuous stares.

The days were pleasant and warm. The nights were chilly with a soft breeze. It reminded some of the boys of the approach of fall back in the States. It only made them more homesick and lured them to think of a life that seemed long ago, drives in the country and pretty girlfriends in black dresses. They still wrote pounds of letters to friends and loved ones, but the mail had not yet moved off the ship since they left Okinawa.

With the big inspection done, the boys on ship lounged about in the most leisurely manners available to them at the time. It was already 30 September, and for the most part the days were filled with whatever was thought up to occupy time. After lunch, five or six of the boys passed around hunting and fishing magazines. Talk turned to hunting mishaps and other pre-war excitement with guns. The conversations and stories went on for three hours. Reveille still went at 05:30, but few seemed to care.

Idle time also produced copious amounts of scuttlebutt. Rumor had it that the 52 might move up near Tokyo as early as the following day. The most prevalent subject of gossip was when the Navy would start releasing men to go back to the States. Cook had heard that first to go would be married men with children and those sailors under eighteen years of age, which included his good friend Johnny Pfohl. Johnny's daughter had arrived into the world while the 52 was still battling it out with kamikazes off Okinawa.[13] One way or another, the men had to face the fact that many of the old crew would be looking at lots of new faces soon, faces that had not shared the horrors of combat. The bottom line, though, was everyone simply wanted desperately to go home.

No one was going home just yet. Events were tying the 52 to a postwar mystery which would not be solved. On 2 October a Navy PBM-5E Mariner took off from its anchorage near its mother ship, USS *St. George*. The aircraft belonged to Patrol Squadron 205 (VP-205) and was piloted by Lt. Gilbert D. Lizer and co-piloted by Ensign Kazimer Olenski. Aside from its seven enlisted crewmembers the plane carried two high-ranking naval officers. For reasons that would remain ambiguous, Admiral William Sample and Captain Charles C. McDonald jumped aboard the plane as it left that morning. The plane never made a single radio check, and it was last seen fifty-three minutes and thirty miles north of Wakayama, its take-off site. That route placed the plane flying away from Tokushima Prefecture.

A wide scale search began after the plane failed to appear at its scheduled return time. On the 4th the weather grounded air searches and the search was resumed by ships of the fleet. With a typhoon approaching, most of the ships turned to run from the storm on the following days. The search went on through the 13th with no sightings of debris or the plane. The hunt for the Mariner was called off and all passengers and crew were declared missing.

Logs and radio traffic of the USS *Suwanee* (call sign LOCUST) for the morning of the 16th was typical of all crafts and commands. "Jap authorities from Tokushima Prefecture reported on 16 October the finding of a body washed up on the beach of an 'aviation colonel, approximately 20 days dead.'"[14] The *Suwanee* was Captain McDonald's new ship. The commander of 5th Fleet reported that "the body of an unidentified American aviation Colonel had been found on the beach at SETO MOCHI in TOKUSHIMA Prefecture. ComPhibGroup Eight was directed to investigate." Amphibious Group Eight further clarified "LCS 52 with

Army and Navy representatives departed for TOKUSHIMA, SHIKOKU, to investigate circumstances of death and identify body of Army Colonel or Navy Captain which washed ashore and was buried by Japanese," With the slightest variation, the insignia of an Army colonel and a Navy captain (a silver eagle with wings spread holding arrows in its talons) looked identical to the untrained eye. No one had to include the obvious in their messages: Captain McDonald would have been wearing such an insignia.

Ensign C.L. Stewart had the midnight to 04:00 watch the morning of the 15th, anchored next to *LCS 51* in Wakanoura-Wan. The crew was mustered at 08:00 and the ship made way to come along USS *Wasatch* (AGC-9). *Wasatch* was a ship designed specifically to be an Amphibious Force Command Ship. At 09:55 Lt. Harper went aboard the *Wasatch* for a conference on the mission. Before the skipper could return, a small boat came alongside 52 and offloaded Army personnel—part of an investigating team. Lt. Harper, Comdr. Stone, Comdr. Ryan and Lt. Hollis boarded 52 five minutes later. Towing a Landing Craft, Vehicle and Personnel (LVCT), commonly called by its designer's name a Higgins boat, the 52 got underway to Tokushima just before noon.

The city of Tokushima sat along the Shinmachi River. Along its banks, warehouses had once housed the harvest of a thriving indigo trade. Only their scorched concrete walls remained. The city was almost leveled by bombing raids still fresh in the memories of the survivors. The damage to the city was the result of July incendiary bombings by the 330th Bombardment Group (very heavy).[15] The air raids on the city were determined by existing technology, directed against industrial complexes only. The death total for the city was 1,000, with twice as many injured. The mass of bombers the crew of the 52 had witnessed on 4 July as they left Okinawa were, in fact, the same bombers who had brought devastation to Tokushima and numerous other Japanese cities.

A few days after the bombings which left a handful of buildings standing in the scorched city limits, American planes dropped leaflets instead of bombs. They read, "Face an ugly death in vain or choose to surrender with honour!" As many leaflets as could be located were gathered up by police. Citizens were forbidden to read or have in their possession a leaflet.[16]

During the war, Tokushima had been a patriotic enclave. School children practiced military maneuvers, learned to don gas masks and celebrated the enlistments of older boys. In the early years of the war, large groups of citizens turned out to wave goodbye to soldiers departing from the train station. Most of the women belonged to the Great Japan National Defense Women's Association. They recycled, collected care packages for their troops and in many ways mimicked the efforts made by Americans on their home-front.

The city had also been the home of the Tokushima Air Group, formed in 1942. They were tasked with training navigators on *Shiragiku* trainers. By the early months of 1945 the situation on the warfront had become desperate. The standing air assets were depleted and invasion of Japan proper appeared imminent. The old trainers were turned over to the newly formed Tokushima Shiragiku Unit, five squadrons of kamikaze. The first squadron left for the Battle of Okinawa on 25 May two days before *LCS 52* was hit. The other squadrons followed the first and all fought in the waters around Okinawa. One-hundred-eight men from the former Tokushima Air Group died during the war.

The only person who wrote down any information on the briefing the crew of 52 received as they got underway came from Laton Burns. According to his journal:

> Went to [Tokushima] to pick up a dead pilot. His plane crashed at sea about [three] weeks before we got him. Japs got him on Oct. 14, and buried him on land.

The ship arrived at the entrance to the breakwater at 15:40 and put a small boat in the water to reconnoiter the depth and bottom. Twenty minutes later, 52 was heading up the channel. As the ship made its approach, a throng of civilians gathered along the docks. After what the crew had seen of the common-folk Japanese citizenry, it was easy to attribute the gathering to nothing more than curiosity. The ship grew closer to the harbor, and an eerie dissolving of the crowd occurred. The dock was left bare of people except for the small party of Japanese authorities.[17]

The ship anchored in two fathoms (twelve feet) of water. From there the LVCT had to take the investigating parties ashore. The crew waited to see what would happen next. It was almost 18:00 when the LVCT brought the skipper and the investigators back. There was no body. For whatever reason, the Americans had agreed to pick it up the following morning.

Lt. Harper, Lt. Comdr. Stone and the investigators headed back to shore early on the 16th in the LCVP. At 09:10 they returned, bringing the remains of the flyer with them. Before bringing the casket (described as a box) aboard the ship, it was ordered opened to verify the contents. Thill was one of the men who went down to meet the transport party and to lift the box aboard. He assisted in removing the lid. What they found was more gruesome and malicious than Laton's censored entry. They were shocked to see that the man had been decapitated. Only the body was present. Thill stated that the body lacked decay, and it seemed to him that the pilot had been recently killed. He noticed blood on the cut and the neck area looked like fresh red meat. He was familiar with such sights from his days on the farm. He barely noticed the flight suit the man was wearing.[18]

There was nothing to be done, other than bring the body aboard. No one aboard 52 ever knew the identity of the man. Those who had verified the contents had only peeked in. None had ever seen a man with his head cut off before; it prompted a quick look and that was all. The enlisted men would never recall what service branch the flyer came from. Lt. Duvendeck, at the conn at the time of the boat's return, did make a telling entry on the log, "Small boat [LVCP] returned bringing remains of Army Colonel."

Everyone was in a hurry to get underway. Luck turned against them, and the anchor cable became entangled in the port shaft, stalling the engine. One of the boys had to don shallow-water diving gear and go under to disentangle the cable. After some makeshift repairs, the ship got underway but only under the power of the starboard quad engine. They churned in to Wakayama Fleet Anchorage at 17:40 and the LCVP took the investigating party and the "body of Army Colonel ashore."

The following day, 17 October, CINCPAC reported:

> Com5thFleet reported that the body of the American colonel found on the beach at SETO MACHI (reported in yesterday's summary) was unidentifiable owing to the absence of head and hands. It is thought that this incident may have a possible relationship to the "missing Mariner"; the parachute and insignia are being traced to determine whether there is any connection between the two incidents.

The mystery of Captain McDonald's disappearance grew. Another mystery formed. If the body was not that of the Navy captain, then where had the Army colonel come from and when? They were both high-ranking officers (O-6 pay-grade), and the two services had managed to misplace both of them within days of each other. Stranger still, it appeared on face value that someone had gone to extremes to make sure the "colonel" was never identified. The only other conclusion was that he had been taken alive and purposefully mutilated or tortured prior to death. Either way, if that were true, the heinous acts occurred long after the surrender was signed.

After the body was dropped off on shore, the incident was set aside. The crew of the 52 were left to wonder who the man in the box was. If he had been murdered, who had done such a thing? The people of Japan had been mandated by their emperor to avoid outbursts of revenge and anger toward the occupying forces. While decapitation was a common practice in Japanese military culture, cutting off hands was not. There was the possibility the hands had been removed as torture prior to the man's death, but it seemed more feasible that they had been removed to avoid identification. It was also hard to imagine that the flyer had been in the water for one or more weeks, and the condition of the body did not reflect that level of deterioration. He, whoever he was, became another unknown soldier, at least to the crew of *LCS 52*.[19]

The ship's next move came on 24 October, their destination Nagoya, Japan. Nagoya was the third-largest city in Japan. The population prior to the war reached close to one and a half million people. The city covered nine square miles by 1945. Nagoya was also the largest center for manufacturing aircraft in Japan. It was estimated that her aircraft factories put out over fifty percent of Japan's war planes. Nagoya was the site of the enormous Mitsubishi electric works and Chigusa plant on the Nagoya Arsenal. Along with aircraft production, Nagoya made everything from ball bearings to food rations. The city had an effective railway and a port capable of docking up to thirty-eight ships, making it Japan's second-largest port. The city housed a number of "shadow" factories as well.[20]

Nagoya (Aichi Prefecture) was headquarters for several POW camps scattered within the city and Japan proper. The main camp was commanded by Lt. Colonel Michiji Otake and opened 5 April 1945. The main camp, built on the site of Nagoya Cattle, was headquarters for the branch camps in the Tokai Hokuriku areas. The camp never held prisoners; it burned after the bombing raids of 14 May and was moved to Minamisotoboricho, Sakae-ku, Nagoya City.

Each sub-camp, or branch, supplied forced labor for mines, ironworks and other, regularly cruel, manual labor. The work was made cruel by the poor diet, harsh physical treatment and the notion the POWs were to be worked relentlessly until they died. The camps were liberated in mid–September 1945. Many of the prisoners, such as Lyle Harlow and Kenneth Hourigan of Company D, 192nd Tank Battalion, were taken prisoner in April-May 1942 at Bataan and Corregidor. Company D was made up of men from Harrodsburg, Kentucky. Both Harlow and Hourigan ended their captivity at Nagoya # 9 POW camp, working as stevedores on the docks.[21]

The path to liberation began when B-29 bombers took off from Guam, Tinian and Saipan on 14 May. They arrived over their target at 08:15. For ninety continuous minutes over 500,000 fire bombs rained down on Nagoya. The city was hit again on 16 May. More than 113,000 buildings were leveled, including the ancient Nagoya Castle, before Japan's surrender. The stream of bombers flew their sorties unmolested and without fighter escort.

On 25 October 1945 *Landing Craft (Flotilla Flagship) 484* led LCS (L)s *31, 34, 51, 52, 54, 55* and *57* into the harbor at Nagoya. They left Wakayama the day before on orders to perform further occupation duties in that city.

Liberty call was a common feature during the first months of the occupation of Japan. William John Mason, a member of *LCS 86*, wrote in an interview that the Japanese men and women stepped aside and allowed the sailors to pass, bowing to the Americans as they did so. Mason also said that the Americans were given explicit orders not to harass the Japanese citizens.[22] Lt. Harper echoed those instructions to his officers and men.

The Mitsubishi aircraft plant, pummeled by bombing raids, was one of the main destinations for exploration by the crew. Despite the blown-out walls, windows and doors, the factory remained covered by the greater portion of its roof. One of the boys was adept at metalwork and made a rather fine suitcase out of sheet metal he located inside the factory. Everyone wanted one, and he was soon inundated with orders for the popular item. Virgil Thill acquired enough sheet metal and had a proper souvenir crafted, an object he would keep and treasure his whole life.

Several bars still functioned in Nagoya, to the delight of Thill and the other drinkers. Thill was in one of the watering holes near the former aircraft factory when he ran into an English-speaking young man. The two struck up a conversation which went on for a couple hours. The irony of the situation was the timing of the meeting. Just before the surrender, the young Japanese flyer had finished his training as a kamikaze pilot. Thill, of course, was the American lad who thrilled at firing his 20mm AA gun at enemy planes. Had the Japanese lad been two months earlier with his graduation from flight school, they could have met under very different and deadly circumstances.

The two boys, both still young men who should have been in high school were it not for the war, shared a drink and a common character. The kid who was recruited to give his life unconditionally for his country sat with another who had volunteered to give his for his own if necessity dictated. They were bright and friendly to everyone they met. The former pilot gave the sailor a picture of himself and two of his fellow pilots. He signed it "kamikaze pailet [sic], Y. Furuta."[23] They wore the uniform of the Imperial Japanese Navy. All three were non-commissioned officers (NCO) and they were young. All were likely fairly fresh graduates of one of the twenty basic academies included in the Yokaren enlisted training programs. Late in the war, and designated for home defense, they would have most likely been slotted as Ōka (Ohka) pilots.[24] As basic flight training cadets, their particular Yokaren School was eight months long. While the academic side of the Yokaren schools included subjects on flight and communications, the cadets received a liberal dose of physical training and assaults by the cadre. The physical assaults were as much a part of the curriculum as math. It hardened the cadet to endure physical pain and psychological suffering. In American service bootcamps of the 1940s there was no denying recruits received the occasional smack or punch, but for the Yokaren boys that was a good morning kiss.

After graduation from a Yokaren program they were taken to one of the naval air stations for Flight Basic Training. The most *stick-time* they might have received prior to this would have been a few seconds airborne in an antiquated glider. They were candidly told on their first day at the course that no student among them should expect to see the war's end. They should immediately accept the fact they were walking dead men. Equipment was so scarce by 1944–45 the young men attending flight training were started on wooden cockpits—a contraption resembling a child's go-cart. As training went on, they, of course, had to graduate to real trainers, whatever leftover that might be. If they had not heard rumors already, they were introduced, by one method or another, to the secret weapon they would pilot one-way into battle.

The Ōka (Cherry Blossom) was basically a light, wood-framed bomb with a cockpit. It was carried to the battlefront by a mother plane and released to fly under its own power the short distance to a target. It was assisted in speeding to the target by three solid-fuel rockets enclosed in the tail section. Aside from the rocket-booster's short-term help with extending flight time or speed, the Ōka was essentially a glider. Unlike its kamikaze predecessors, the Ōka was incapable of landing, at least safely. For Americans, the Ōka conjured up an image of an unstoppable machine, operated by an implacable man, trained in mechanical vengeance. As frightening to Allied sailors as the idea of a human guided bomb was, the wartime effectiveness of the Ōka was deficient in all its limited encounters.

Young Ōka pilot Furuta had, by all probability, never seen combat. He wore the uniform associated with light-duty Japanese Home Island defense. His air station would have been in some remote location outside the cities.[25] That would have kept him reasonably safer than the average citizen facing the persistent B-29 bombing strikes. In essence, Furuta was more absent from the ugly face of war than an urban worker or housewife. His new American friend had seen that face close up and he wished its appearance on no man.

The picture also revealed a soldier who cherished the friendship and brotherhood of his mates. They were young men who obviously loved life like all other men. It was an image difficult to reconcile with the suicide-driven fanatics American sailors had encountered off Okinawa.

It is the nature of men, regardless of culture, to fear and frequently scorn those they do not know and understand. Thill was not one of those Americans. The chance meeting allowed him to see the side of the Special Attack Squadron pilots that very few outside their families were ever privileged to observe.

Before the first American had walked upright onto the beaches of Okinawa, the Japanese high command, minus a few delusional zealots, understood the war was lost. The kamikaze pilots understood also that their last acts would not turn the tide of war to Japanese victory. Their purpose was to bleed the Allied forces; the crux of that effort was simply to obtain a better deal in defeat. The pilots were just as disillusioned as the general public was, but they were honorable, patriotic and driven by tradition to follow orders. Often, that did not dissuade them from showing their contempt for giving their lives for a lost cause. One pilot, lifting-off for his last mission, strafed his own command post before heading out to sea.[26] By the closing days of the battle for Okinawa, the majority of suicide pilots were draftees, the pool of volunteers having nearly dried up. No soldier wished his death to be in vain.

They were a breed apart. Special Attack Force (tokkōtai) pilots were often poetic, spiritual and passionate souls. It was common practice to write doting final letters to their families. In these last letters were instructions to their children, confirmation of their eternal love, reassurance to their parents and often apologies for not having been better progenies. Even Admiral Takijiro Onishi, the brainchild of the kamikaze squadrons, and fanatic to the end, often voiced the gamut of his emotions in haikus and letters.

The average pilot, in spite of the finality of the circumstances, somehow held on to the hope that some miracle would manifest itself, and he would return. "I want to see you grow up to be a splendid bride, but even if I die…" wrote Uemura Masahisa to his infant daughter before his death in October 1944 in the Philippines. Furukawa Takao wrote in his last letter to his pregnant wife in April 1945, "Wait for me. I will return without fail." In the end, there was no desire to die if it could be avoided. The few flyers who were recovered or had their bodies recovered wore lifesaving gear, such as parachutes and life vests.[27] Considering the goal was crashing full speed into a ship, these devices would have seemed pointless to the hopeless. The only other explanation for the lifesaving equipment was it belonged to pilots assigned to escort aircraft, not kamikaze. However, kamikaze pilots were, on rare occasion, observed bailing out under canopy.

Being a kamikaze pilot amounted to paying the ultimate sacrifice for one's country. Yonetsu Yoshitaro wrote to his stepmother, "All that is left is to carry out the duties for which I've been trained and to fulfill the Imperial mandate." Yonetsu died November 1944 off Luzon.[28] Young men would, however, continue to reluctantly die to the bitter end because of extremists such as Onishi. He barged into a war council as late as 13 August, four days after the second atomic bomb had been dropped. Onishi declared to his listeners that if Japan was willing to commit its 20,000,000 people to the concept of "special attack," then the war could still be won.[29]

Onishi was not the last surviving fanatic to believe in the miracle of Kikusuis (floating cherry blossoms). Admiral Matome Ugaki accepted the position as commander of the Fifth Air Fleet (designated suicide) back in February of 1945. Ugaki was a survivor of the Battle of Leyte Gulf and dozens of other encounters. According to witness reports, Ugaki listened to the Emperor's capitulation speech made to the people of Japan by radio. The fact that the Emperor's mandate was no longer sending men to fling themselves at ships did not sway Ugaki's earlier affirmation to be the last kamikaze. On 15 August, Ugaki gave a motivating speech to approximately twenty-three pilots stationed at an airbase on Kyushu. There was open derision for the idea of killing more young men after surrender, but he cowed several into volunteering. He managed to mount a plane (he was not a pilot) to piggyback with another flyer. What happened after takeoff became an Amelia Earhart-style mystery. Ugaki reportedly sent his last radio message at 19:24 that evening. It was presumed by the content of the message he was over Okinawa. Sixteen minutes later, seven or more aircraft strafed an anchored ship, *LST 296*. The crew returned fire and downed all attackers. Like most mangled kamikaze crews, no evidence, bodies, parts thereof, or personal items led back to Ugaki.

That was the core of the most perpetuated legend of the last kamikaze. The Japanese witnesses are hard to discount; Ugaki and his flyers probably did get off the ground. Ugaki was not given a posthumous promotion, which had been awarded automatically to all previous kamikaze. He had disregarded the Emperor's directive and had caused other men to disobey it as well. The lack of official recognition was probably another indication that he did, in fact, takeoff.

The real problem with the story begins at the end. Only one ship and crew seem to have been present for the final kamikaze attack; hundreds of Allied ships were still anchored off Okinawa on the 15th of August, but no other ship reported a sighting. It was quite a battle, one lightly armed LST against seven or eight suicide planes.[30] Quite a battle indeed, especially for a ship number that never existed. Back in September of 1942 when LSTs were being commissioned hand-over-fist, the order for hull numbers LST 296–300 was cancelled. The postwar ghost kamikaze attack apparently was thwarted by a ghost ship.

The story of the last kamikaze never came up in conversation between Thill and Furuta. They would honor their countries by living to rebuild. Furuta preferred to hear about the United States and what life was like there. They talked about the war and their thoughts on it. The subject was sure to come up, but it was speaking of history now. What they had been was not what they were. They parted company, never to see or hear from each other again.

The personality and interests of each sailor were reflected in the souvenirs they sought out and purchased. Laton Burns focused on seeing Japan from a cultural point of view. He filled a photo album with those interests. Of the eight postcards Laton Burns picked up on liberty in Japan, four were from the Kimii Temple (Kimiidera) in Wakayama Prefecture. When Burns viewed the Kimii, the temple had survived many wars, including the last, and was at the time 1200 years old (Hoki Era 770). The name itself roughly translates to "The temple with three fountains." One postcard showed a long, stone staircase. The caption made reference to "a hundred stone stairs" and claimed that the steps were the "longest in Japan."

According to another postcard, which survived the later years in his photo album, Burns visited the fountain which pours from the mountain and never dries up. "Water fall is located at center right of stone stairs," the caption read in Japanese. The other two postcards are of the bridge and cherry blossoms in full bloom at the temple. The temple boasts that the blossoms bloom first here. All of the postcards from the Kimiidera were photographed by Mitsunori Terai. Terai left no lasting mark on history, aside from the survival of his postcards.

Burns picked up several postcards from Yashima, Japan. Yashima was the site of a defining battle between the Genji and Heike clans in the year 1185. The

The photograph presented to Thill during his encounter with pilot Furuta (center) after the war ended underscored the learned respect young sailors had for one another (Virgil Thill collection).

battlefield was easily toured by curious Americans at the end of another war eight centuries later. The city today is almost a ghost town, having lost most of the tourist trade it depended on. In 1945, though, the crew, if allowed ashore long enough, could have visited the lava plateau which overlooks the town nearly 300 feet below. Another of the main attractions was the Yashima-ji Temple and its adjoining gardens and shrines.

The one postcard, which stood out as an oddity from the others, was the photo of a boy holding an obviously heavy bale with his teeth. The young man was a minor sumo wrestler. If he survived to see the end of the war he would have been in his late-fifties. The postcard bore no date and could have been produced originally in the early 1900s. The lad pictured went by what Americans might have considered a ring or stage name, Adachiyama. Perhaps he borrowed the moniker from the mountain of the same name in the Fukuoka Prefecture. As a young competitor the sumo community had high hopes for the bulky Adachiyama. In an article of *The Japan Times*, he was listed as one of two teenage up-and-comers, though he had yet to enter a ring:

> The eldest son of one Masutaro Sekine living in Osato-mura, Kita-Adachi district, Saitama prefecture, and his real name is Seisaku.
> He is now 14 years old, but he is said to weigh as much as 22 kwan 500 me (about 190 pounds) and to possess a bodily frame powerfully built and of dimensions in proportion to his weight. This year the promising lad in question was, under the professional name of Adachiyama, admitted as one of the disciples of the retired wrestler Tomozuna.[31]

Burns undoubtedly enjoyed touring shrines and ancient sites. He bought more postcards of waterfalls, cherry trees heavy with white blossoms, and ordinary people going about their daily lives in his trek across the Orient, than any other attractions. It was a far cry from the mountains surrounding Oneida, Kentucky, but the beauty was there and he took it all in. With the dangers of war absent, paid sightseeing was compensation for the trouble of being away from home.

Another piece that ended up in his war album was a picture of a saddle with "Halsey" engraved the length of the fender. The saddle was obviously sitting in a room aboard a ship. That ship happened to be the USS *Missouri*, and the date the picture was taken was around 2 September 1945. The location of the ship was Tokyo Bay. The reason Admiral Halsey had a saddle and other horse riding accouterments in his room went back to March of that year. That month, "Bull" Halsey made a statement to the effect that he would ride, or like to ride, the Emperor's white horse down Tokyo's Ginza. The press thought the remark just the kind of thing that defined American hubris. It cried vengeance for the multitude of dead from Pearl Harbor to Bataan to Bastogne and a thousand points in between. The Admiral was soon inundated with every kind of riding equipment.

At the time of the comment, Operation Iceberg was still on the planning table. War bonds were a big part of the funding for what might still be a long conflict to subdue Japan. To further promote the next bond drive, the City of Reno, Nevada, arrived at a banner idea. The Chamber of Commerce commissioned a local business, Bools & Butler Saddlery, to create a custom saddle for the admiral to use on his victory ride. Not to be outdone, the Pyramid Lake Paiute Tribe, northeast of Reno, handcrafted a pair of buckskin riding gloves. The admiral was going to encompass the image of the stereotypical true western American when he rode down the conquered street. The saddle arrived aboard the battleship that would soon accept the surrender of the last belligerent of the Axis sometime in August. It was far from the only piece of horse riding gear that made it that far. Admiral Halsey remarked that his quarters were looking like a tack room. The silver-inlayed saddle took center stage. Postcards of the saddle displayed in the admiral's room were made and sold around the world. Curiously, someone (perhaps an ordinary sailor with access to the quarters) reproduced their own pictures of the saddle. Laton Burns acquired one of the copies.

Virgil Thill had acquired a working knowledge of Japanese. He was often asked by his fellow shipmates to translate something or make conversation with the locals. He was also a wheeler-dealer. Virgil understood the consequences of taking food off the ship. It was against regulations and that meant confinement, if he were lucky. The best plan of action was, do not get caught. Virgil took the food and traded it for wristwatches. He then returned to the ship and sold watches to the boys. It did not matter the price, it was all profit to him. He became the man to see for good wristwatches and earned the rather derogatory nickname of Isaac Jacob Thillberger.[32] It was all in fun, and things were not as politically correct in 1945 as they would be later.

The 52 was next sent to Jinsen (Inchon), Korea. Laton's journal compressed the whirlwind back and forth schedule the 52 operated on after the war ended. On their first trip to Jinsen they departed Nagoya, Japan, on 12 and arrived in Jinsen on 17 November.[33]

The Navy was being vague about the purpose of the trip to Korea. Lt. Harper was not as worried about the intrigue as much as the unaccommodating tides accompanying the coastal city of Jinsen. At high tide, frequently between ten and sixteen feet rise occurred, and an ordinary dock could not therefore be used. To refuel, a floating dock created from a ship had to be employed. Taking on any supplies, in fact, presented problems at Jinsen. Simply handling the ship in the strong currents and heavy winds at Jinsen caused steering and mooring headaches for any vessel, especially a small one.

The Japanese annexed Korea in 1910 and it remained in their control until September 1945. Jinsen (Inchon) is located approximately thirty miles southwest of Seoul. While the Russians rushed south to seize Korea north of the thirty-eighth parallel, American troops landed at Jinsen on 8 September. The following day, formal surrender of Japanese forces was accepted in Seoul.

The first concern of the Allies at Jinsen was to repatriate the remaining 168 prisoners of war at the Jinsen P.O.W. camp. The camp was located in the southeast side of Jinsen almost a quarter of a mile from the railroad. It had been the prison for more than 250 British and Australian P.O.W.s until mid–April of 1945. That month the first Americans arrived from camps in Japan. When the four-acre camp was liberated, there were 138 surviving Americans. Only thirty of the Brits and Aussies remained, most having been shipped to camps in China prior to the end of the war. The majority of men imprisoned at Jinsen were officers. The small contingent of enlisted men served as a labor force to perform tasks considered by the Japanese to be beneath officers. Because it was an officer's camp, the treatment of the men there was considered better, if by only slightly, than other camps. The camp at Jinsen provided prisoners with hot and cold running water, bath houses, and regular access to those facilities and fair medical care. The men still slept on wooden bunks and straw sleeping mats, in overcrowded barracks. A hot bath did not a resort make.

The 52's five-day trip to Korea from Japan was broken up only by a couple of stops to refuel along the way. When the ship arrived they were briefed on their less-than-lofty mission. The 52 had become a recreational taxi—an over-armed liberty boat. She was to load up between fifteen and twenty officers at a time and transport them to China, where they could experience liberty and better chow. The officers were mostly destroyer and destroyer-escort guys who had been suffering in Korea while the crew of 52 lived it up in the decimated and poverty-stricken Japan.

The LCS was tight quarters under the best of circumstances, but with ordnance rooms and bare decks, they could accommodate cots for the passengers. It was Navy orders and, somehow, regardless of comfort, they would make do. Before they loaded up, there was no reason not to sample what the little town of Jinsen had to offer. As usual, the enlisted and officers not standing watch went their separate ways.

Harper commandeered some Navy trucks to take a party to Seoul, only a couple hours' ride away. Between the roads and the old trucks, the ride was as rough as any storm endured on the ship. Seoul, the capital, was better than they expected. The DD officers were trying to get out of Korea. After Japan, the men of 52 were happy to be in. Unlike Nagoya, there were actual operational restaurants. A sailor could sit down and order something off a menu and have it served on a plate. The menu may have been sparse, but it included meat and chicken commonly, plenty of fresh vegetables, roasted chestnuts and even fruit. It seemed like a feast in comparison to feeling ashamed for eating military rations in front of starving Japanese citizens.[34]

On the 21st, loaded with its steerage passengers, *LCS 52* left for China. They crossed over the Yellow Sea and arrived at the mouth of the Hai River on 23 November. In Stoia's journal he referred to the river as the Pieping River. Lt. Harper called it the Wang River. Before the ship could get upriver they had to cross the Taku Bar. The Taku Bar, developed over centuries by sand deposits carried downstream, was rough water and only passable by low-draft vessels. The mud was so dense at certain places in the bar that the 52's propellers slowed as they churned the mire. They "could hardly cut through the mixture and [we] had to move very slowly," Harper said.[35] No ship larger than about 300 feet in length crossed the bar. LCSs and LCIs, by design, were perfect in length and draft for moving people and supplies up and down river from the port city of Taku, though. Taku was a small village, but the real logistical hub, and most accessible pier, to China's interior lay seven miles beyond the bar at Tangku. The town of Tangku was the river gateway to Tientsin, 52's ultimate destination for its liberty-starved passengers.

The Navy started putting the 1st Marine Division (in force) ashore at Tangku on 30 September. The Navy filled nearly every warehouse and open pier in Tangku their first day. More than 440 tons of equipment, supplies and vehicles flooded the city. The marines quickly fanned out to seize railway posts up and down the line. From Tangku, Peiping-Mukden Railroad followed the river to Tientsin and beyond. All along the rail line Japanese regulars or their puppet counterparts still guarded the tracks and stations. To the last, they simply wanted to surrender to the Americans and go home. They were still under frequent attacks by the Chinese Communist forces. There were recurrent firefights and constant harassment. A month after the rest of their countrymen had laid down their arms, they were still fighting to survive a war that was not even their own.

Japanese forces, around 50,000, surrendered at Tientsin on 6 October. With an honor guard, a band, and General Keller E. Rockey acting as the representative for Chiang Kai-shek, the surrender of China-based Japanese forces was anticlimactic compared to that in Tokyo Bay a month prior. The Japanese delegates marched out across the plaza at the former

French Municipal Building (now the IIIAC Headquarters) to the sound of the Marine Corps' Hymn. With that, the Japanese, both civilians and former military, were officially in the care of the Marines.

Once past the Taku Bar, the trip up river to Tientsin took less than two days. Laton Burns reported in his journal that the ship arrived on the 23rd but no time of day was given. The city had played the part of prison for the marines, sailors, soldiers and civilians captured on Wake Island and China after Pearl. The Japanese took control of the city (1938–1945) during the war but prior to that it was in the hands of several Western powers. The architecture the crew of the 52 experienced there clearly reflected the better side of Western concessions. Lt. Harper noted that the streets bore the names of English queens and the like.[36] Americans, for the first time in a long time, were guided around the city by signs posted in English.

Tientsin was declared an open trading port by the British in 1860. From that year on the city was a concession of France, Germany, Britain, Japan, Russian, Austria-Hungary, Belgium and Italy. *LCS 52*'s and the visiting officers located the Belgian, French and White Russian quarters during their visit. Herbert Hoover wrote of the city while living there, "Tientsin is a universal city, like a world in miniature with all nationalities, all architectural styles, all kitchens."[37] On their first visit, Harper believed, Tientsin was a city of around three-million. With the Japanese and Korean refugees, the ubiquitous American marines, and the displaced Chinese, it might have come close to that figure.[38]

Tientsin remained a universal city until the Japanese invaded in 1938. The city suffered under their oppression until 1945, when liberated. Thill also recalled the 52 arrived in Tientsin on 26 November. The memory of young children living in cardboard boxes and eating food out of garbage cans stuck in his mind. The Navy had regulations against giving the children hand-outs, even though they begged for food. The sailors circumvented the policy by drawing extra rations at mealtime and then tossing the leftovers in the trashcans. The homeless urchins then recovered the food without further law-breaking.[39]

Tientsin had always been a city of the haves and have-nots. The well-to-do gathered at the expansive horse racetrack, which was operating when the officers visited it in late November 1945. The restaurants were not much for ambiance but they did quench the appetite for fresh milk, vegetables and meat the tin can officers had come so far to locate. The establishment they picked served roast duck and an unidentifiable brand of stout vodka to wash it down. When Harper and some of the others began to spit out buckshot from the meat, they assumed the lead was evidence of its freshness. The group dined in the same place later and was served a bottle of vodka with a fly floating prostrate on the surface. For fear of receiving the same tainted bottle back after the critter was removed in the kitchen, they ordered a quart. The huge jug arrived at the table insect-free.[40] With the war and its culinary deprivations a memory, the officers could afford to be a little discerning about their grub.

As would their sailors, the officers found the availability and mystique of rickshaws fascinating. Since the rickshaw taxis were human powered, a fully loaded vehicle would take fifteen to twenty minutes to take its passengers one mile. The currency rate of exchange was about 2,700 yen to one dollar. A one-mile ride cost around four dollars or 10,000 yen.[41]

While sailors were living it up in the universal city, the marines were staggered along the roads and railways of China. The marines had already suffered six wounded from communist snipers and ambushes and one pilot killed.[42] The day Tientsin received the Japanese surrender, three were wounded twenty-two miles outside the city attempting to dismantle a roadblock. The Nationalist forces were scattered and unequipped to even assume guard posts along the roads and rails. In many places, the Americans split the duty with Japanese soldiers who remained armed and on duty after their surrender.

The situation was delicate at best. President Harry Truman did not want American military mixing it up in China's "fractional conflict."[43] However, Truman made few efforts to hide the fact he supported and wanted the Nationalists to triumph and China to form a democracy. What that did for troops on the ground, outside the occupied cities, was to handicap them with untenable rules of engagement. The day before *LCS 52* left Korea, Gen. Albert Wedemeyer (Commander, U.S. Forces China Theater) suggested it was either time for all U.S. Armed Forces to leave China or provide them with workable rules of engagement sufficient to achieve their original objectives.[44] That recommendation would be tabled, and American servicemen would remain under harassing and deadly attacks for years to come.

Leaving China on 30 November, the 52 returned to Jinsen, Korea. There, they dropped off their liberty party of officers. The crew made a liberty call of their own while in Jinsen. Virgil Thill did not venture further than the docks. He was out of money and nothing thwarted a good time in port like being broke. He instead trained his keen sense of curiosity toward the extremes of the tide. At low tide, he observed, the 52 rested entirely in mud. As the tide returned, she rose to meet the level of her mooring dock.[45] The world never ceased to amaze the farm boy in Virgil.

The 52 taxi departed Korea on 5 December, loaded once more with another group of officers bound for Chinese attractions. On 7 December *LCS 52* arrived in Tsingtao, China. It was cool, extremely different from the Philippines, in both climate and culture. The boys went on liberty wearing their pea coats buttoned up tight and gloves. The men of *LCS 52* were all still spellbound by the rickshaws. Laton Burns had his photo taken in one. Some of the rickshaws, like the one Burns hired, were powered by the operator walking or running within a frame harness. The operators were accustomed to the strenuous exercise and sped the customer to their destination with seemingly little effort.

Virgil Thill hired a bicycle-powered rickshaw. He was already drunk by the time he decided to go for a ride. Riding leisurely did not suit Thill's fancy. He begged the driver to allow him to operate the leg-powered taxi for himself. "How about me doing the driving and you riding in the back?" he proffered.[46] After much consternation the driver finally gave in and switched places. Thill took him on a reckless ride down a steep hill, at speeds the rickshaw was not built for. The displaced driver was in the back, screaming and hollering for a halt, but none came quick enough. Surprisingly, the two survived without crashing. The driver seized control of his vehicle and furiously gestured Thill away. As usual, Thill had gone his own way and the 52 pack had gone theirs. There was no one around to marvel in his daring.

The city was surprisingly modern to Virgil Thill. He went into a huge, multi-story furniture store, just to look around. Then he went to an upscale restaurant, had a good meal and drinks.[47] It was ironic that the city could serve the well-to-do in one building and the poor lived on the street next door.

Tsingtao (Qingdao in Chinese) was a city that went all out to welcome their Western liberators. Bars and clubs of every proclivity swung open their doors to thank the GIs at an affordable price. The crew of 52 found it easy to locate their pleasure, as business-type cards for these establishments floated about the streets in abundance. Such a card for "The Jeep Bar" (with a drawing of an American army jeep on the front) instructed the GI to present it

Officer or enlisted, the boys found the Chinese rickshaws fascinating. Laton Burns with an unidentified Tsingtao driver was the only *LCS 52* sailor to have his picture taken with one. Virgil Thill chose a bicycle-powered rickshaw. He coaxed the owner into allowing him to drive. The breakneck downhill speeds he managed to attain would have seriously injured or killed both him and the owner in a crash, but he pulled it off safely (Diane Burns Brads collection).

to their rickshaw driver and he would carry the customer straight to the door. At "Jimmy's Bar" they would find Hawaiian and Spanish guitar, "genuine drinks," along with "Hill Billy" and "Boogie-woogie" music. The "Texas Bar" wisely offered the biggest draw to a homesick American—"girls." Other such hang-outs were the "Dreamland Café," "Rudy's American Bar," to name a very few, swinging establishments. The Chinese bars and girls, all painted in American fads, unknowingly made the battle-weary GIs undoubtedly more homesick.

Since the Chinese Communists also moved in to take over the city from the Japanese in August, American sailors and marines could enjoy a drink alongside their Communist allies. That drink had to be quick, though, as communist control of the city only lasted until October, when Chiang Kai-shek's forces moved in to the city and they moved out. After the war, an American naval base remained in Tsingtao until June 1949. The *LCS 52* left the port of Tsingtao on 11 December 1945. They were not headed back to Korea. It was, at last, the trip everyone had dreamed of.

The *52* left China and headed to Saipan. The ship remained off the now-familiar island from the 21st through the 27th. They were once more missing the Christmas season at home. Still, this Christmas for the 52ers, spent with no one shooting, was better than the last. They made another stop at Eniwetok and celebrated New Year 1946 there.

A little less than a year before, 29 January 1945 at 08:00, the ship sailing west, they had crossed the International Date Line—many for the first time. Lt. Phillip Jacobson, on watch at the time, recorded in the ship's log, "Now in—12 Time Zone, having crossed the International Date Line." There had been no festivities, no appearance of King Neptune and no sacrifice made to ensure good sailing.

According to ancient seafarers, not making sacrifices to the gods of the sea (usually goats and sheep) could get ships into deep distress. Although the belief in Neptune faded over the centuries, the rites and rituals of crossing certain positions at sea (formerly believed to be the locations of sea god temples) continued into the twenty-first-century. The grandfather of all sea fraternities was the Order of the Shellback. A sailor or marine became part of that brotherhood after undergoing examinations and negotiating certain rites of passage. There were other fraternities, Northern Domain of the Polar Bear or the Royal Order of the Blue Noses, Mossbacks, Golden Shellbacks and many more. Those unlucky enough not to be accepted into an order were considered lowly and disenfranchised landlubbers.

While the rites of passage were a tightly-held secret, *LCS 52*'s crew joined one of the more sought-after orders.[48] No waters possessed more allure than those of the ancient and mysterious Orient. Along the 180th Meridian of those waters, the Golden Dragon was ruler and gave favor or indifference to ships and sailors in their passing. On 8 January 1946 the ship crossed into the domain of the Golden Dragon, at Latitude 1634 and Longitude 180°00. With permission, the ship's X.O., Clifford L. Stewart—himself well-traveled in many a domain of various sea gods—stood in for the Golden Dragon. One of the sailors who was "inspected and found worthy, [and] was initiated into The Sacred Order of the Golden Dragon" that day was Laton Burns. He placed the card in his wallet with the other important pieces of identification.

They arrived at Pearl Harbor on 15 January and remained there for eight days, refitting and relaxing at their old haunts. Before allowed liberty call, Ensign Stewart ensured that each man was properly attired with the military accouterments which identified him as a combat veteran of the Pacific War. Each of the original sailors were given an official card to carry in their wallet or on their person which stated they had earned the World War II Victory Medal, Asiatic-Pacific Medal with two stars, Philippine Liberation and the American Theater Ribbon. Those men who had been wounded in combat added to their list the Purple Heart Medal.

Leaving Hawaii, they pointed their bow toward San Francisco. With every turn of the screws eastward, her crew knew they were growing closer to home. The ship's official "Report of Change" sheet began to reflect the parting of the old crew. On 1 February, William Barber, Ervin Bennett, Gerald Bilton, Russell Blough, Laton Burns, Hanford Cazee, Joe Chavez, Russell Copeland, Larry Cullen, Robert Fields, Hugh Goldman, Anthony Jawor, Victor Klein, Galan Libby, James Linn, Donald Olney, Howard Poindexter, Carl Reed, Harry Tucker, Carl Wertz and Howard Williams all received orders to their respective separation centers. They parted in masses such as this, in accordance with their points accrued. The same day as the old-salts got their tickets punched for home, Chief Holland received his transfer orders. His journey was only beginning. Laton Burns made his final entry in his war journal, "Arrived in the States Feb. 1st 1946." According to Virgil Thill, the remaining crew was given thirty days of leave from San Francisco; once they returned to duty the ship was "put in mothballs" in Oregon.[49]

Again, it is always interesting to look into what caught the interest of persons of a certain era. Within Laton's photo album he placed a card from a club in San Francisco, Bobby's Club, located at 72 Eddy Street. There is little evidence of the club's existence today. The owner of a matchbook cover from Bobby's Club was selling it on eBay at the time of this writing. The matchbook added to the club's story only in the fact that three veterans either owned the club or at least worked there. In a time when civilians in San Francisco were less than friendly to GIs, that would have meant a lot to battle-worn sailors looking for a safe haven to blow off steam. Laton's cousin, Ambrose, a 7th Army Division veteran of Okinawa, hated to hear the name of San Francisco spoken in his presence.[50] He stated that he frequently encountered signs posted in business windows which read

Jordan Brantley (left standing), Anthony Jawor (right standing) and Eugene De Maio (sitting) with unknown woman. Photograph taken in Hawaii before departing for the war zone (Virgil Thill collection).

"no dogs or GIs allowed." Regardless of how many veterans operated Bobby's Club, the club seems to have faded quickly into obscurity after the war. Prior to the war, the 1920s, the location was a cigar store that also served soft drinks. Today, the ground where Bobby's once sat is covered by a parking garage and a Barbary Coast coffee shop. The last time that the location offered drinking and dancing, two amenities that would have guided young soldiers and sailors there in the day, was over sixty years after the war when it was known as "The Trapp," a gay bar. That would have certainly drawn a bit of sarcasm from the World War II veterans.

The men who came to *LCS 52* after the last shots of the war were fired were not always the snot-nosed youths who got caught by the last draft numbers called. The majority of the boys may have been fresh from basic occupational training; others were seasoned veterans who had seen more than their share of combat. Fireman 1st Class Chester Paul Swisher, Jr., was reassigned to *LCS 52* from the receiving station at Shoemaker, California, on 9 February 1946. He started his career in the Navy on 16 October 1939. The following day his hometown newspaper, *The News-Palladium* of Benton Harbor, Michigan, shared with their community of readers the exciting news of the six local boys who had just been officially accepted into the U.S. Navy. It was worthy of front-page publication. Chester was one of those six. The paper went on to explain that the boys would be taken to Detroit and sworn in. Then they would be sent to the Naval Training Station at Newport Rhode Island, for twelve weeks of training. There, according to the understanding of the civilian writer, they would be instructed in "nautical and military subjects before being transferred to sea duty." When Chester shipped off for his basic training, he was barely eighteen years old.

Chester "Chet" Swisher, Jr., was born on 22 September 1921. He was the first son of Chester P. and Vema Swisher. Chester Sr. and his first wife were married in September of 1919. Chester Sr. was born in Indiana and raised in Mill Township, Grant County. He, as did almost every adult male in his neighborhood, worked in the nearby rubber factories. Before Chester Jr. was born, the couple moved to Michigan. Chester Jr. was born in Benton Harbor and grew up in Hartford. After the death of his mother he was raised by his step-mother, Lullia Reed Swisher. The Swisher home of Chester's youth was a lively place, accommodating up to sixteen siblings, biological, half and step, plus parents, at any given time during the 1930s. By the time he arrived at his first ship, USS *Maryland* (BB-46), on 29 March 1940, having completed his basic at USNTS Great Lakes, he was used to tight living quarters.

During the last years of the Great Depression, Chester Sr. worked for the Works Projects Administration (WPA) constructing sewer systems.[51] Chester Jr.'s next youngest brother, James, was employed with the CCCs, performing brush removal to help with prevention of soil erosion. Their step-mother was working on a farm and their step-sister, eighteen-year-old Opal Reed, was working as a waitress in a local restaurant. Chester Jr.'s decision to enlist, whatever his underlying reason, was good financial timing.

The Colorado-class battleship *Maryland* earned the nicknamed, "Fighting Mary" for her World War II service. She was commissioned on 21 July 1921, almost three months to the day of Chester's birth. During her first two decades at sea, she was used as a diplomatic showpiece. The first time she fired her arsenal of weapons at an enemy was shortly after 08:00 on 7 December 1941.

On that Sunday morning, *Maryland* was moored on Battleship Row along with the other battlewagons that would become household names over the next four years. The *Maryland* was tied alongside the starboard side of the USS *Oklahoma*. The ships and crews had discontinued training and other operations to prepare for an Admiral's Inspection on the following Monday. Everyone was up, some preparing clothes for Sunday church services to be held aboard the *Oklahoma*. Working parties were taking on provisions on Sunday morning before the attack, including 2,000 pounds of ice. The first indication of trouble, for anyone working or resting below the main deck of the *Maryland*, was the sound of explosions from bombs hitting nearby Ford Island. Horns sounded the alarms and the crews rushed to General Quarters (07:52).[52]

A Japanese plane dropped a torpedo which subsequently struck the *Oklahoma*. The first was followed by two more torpedoes striking the *Oklahoma* on her port side. She immediately began to take on water and list to port. Only the aft machinegun got into action before the deck was too covered with oil and water to load the guns. That single gun was quickly put out of action by Japanese bombs and strafing. The battleship listed further to port as between three and five more torpedoes punched new holes in her hull so large jeeps could have driven through them. The lines, cables and gangplank began to snap as the *Oklahoma* began to roll over at a one-hundred-thirty-five-degree angle. A torpedo plane targeted the *Maryland* as well. Though only struck once in the hull, with a small hole to show for the pilot's trouble, she began to take on water.[53]

The fate of *Oklahoma* was evident within the first ten minutes of the attack. She was not to be saved or could not be defended. The abandon ship call went out, and sailors and marines went into the oil-covered water. Most tried to reach the *Maryland* and many were rescued by her crew. *Oklahoma* survivors, with revenge in their hearts, it is certain, lifted themselves off the deck and began assisting ammunition parties supplying bullets to the guns of the *Maryland*.

Unlike most of her sister ships, the crew of the *Maryland* found ammunition for their weapons and began to fight back. A quick-thinking ensign broke the lock off the ammo locker and started a supply line feeding the *Maryland*'s guns. Wayne D. Ring, another *Maryland* sailor, rushed to his battle station after General Quarters was sounded:

> Our guns didn't go into action for 10 minutes because all of our ammo was locked up.... I saw the Oklahoma capsize, and as she rolled over she jammed us against the quay. A week later they had to dynamite us to get us out.[54]

Fires broke out after bombs hit the *Maryland* on her forecastle and bow. The fires were quickly abated and the ship was never in danger of being sunk. The crew of the *Maryland* fought off three enemy attacks as they watched, stunned, as the ships around them absorbed attack after attack. The *California* was in front of the *Maryland* and moored some distance from the other ships in column. Behind *Maryland* were the *Tennessee* and *West Virginia*, moored side by side. Behind them was the *Arizona* tied alongside the *Vestal*. Moored alone, to the stern of the *Vestal*, was the *Nevada*. The Japanese planes came across Hickam Field in a northwestern direction, placing the *Oklahoma* and *Maryland* directly in front of their first approach. The *Vestal*, tied alongside the *Arizona*'s portside and despite being struck by two bombs, got underway and sailed away from the sinking *Arizona*.

There was plenty below deck to be done during the attacks. The men working in Chester's area were attempting to get the boilers up and made ready to get underway. Air compressors were rendered inoperative, electrical wiring insulation was damaged throughout the compartments where the bomb had penetrated and gauges were busted and inoperable.

It was a fireman's worst nightmare. Still, the men below decks of the *Maryland* somehow managed to restore power enough to get the engines going and get the ship moving, only to discover the ship was pinned by the *Oklahoma*. Understanding the petrifying fear of not knowing what was happening above deck, the ship's command elements turned on the loudspeakers and kept the below decks personnel informed of the "progress of events visible to those on topside stations."[55] The two sections which carried the most damage when the attacks ended were the engineering and the gunnery departments.

The aftermath was hard to stomach. The days after the attack were filled with the sight and smell of gas and oil blanketing the surface of the harbor. Bloated bodies arbitrarily rose to the top and floated among the wreckage or were carried by current to shore. Working parties used large nets to scoop bodies and parts of bodies from the oil slick. Perhaps the worst was the unknown numbers of survivors trapped in compartments below the waterline of the *Oklahoma*. Rescue divers and wielders were able to cut escape holes in the section of the bottom of the ship above water and save a few, but most were unreachable. The tapping of SOS signals against bulkheads went on for days before their air ran out and they died in the dark of their steel coffin.

The hull of the *Maryland* was patched up, and along with the *Tennessee*, she sailed to Washington State for repairs. After twenty-three days at sea, the patch broke near the coast and the crew pumped water frantically to keep her afloat. The *Maryland* returned to duty after repairs and fought in combat operations in the Gilberts, Kwajalein, and Okinawa. Chester's last day aboard the *Maryland* was 23 May 1942. He was transferred on that date to a course of instruction at NRS, Norfolk.

MoMM2c Swisher reported aboard *APC 38* (Small Coastal Transport) on 29 January 1943, the day of her commissioning. All eighty-nine APCs built during the war were one-hundred-feet long wooden crafts, armed with four single 20mm guns. They were manned by six officers and a crew of twenty-two enlisted men. *APC 38*, like the majority of her sisters, served in the Pacific.

Chester's next ship was *LST 354*. He joined that ship on 25 August 1943. The ship had just finished occupation operations on Vella Lavella, ending on 21 August. His first combat with *LST 354* was the occupation of Cape Torokina, which lasted through 17 November. He returned to *LST 354* on 12 December 1943 from Base Hospital # 7. There was no change of report indicating how long or the reason he was at the hospital. Chester was present on *LST 354* for the Green Island landings in mid–February and the landings on Saipan on 15 June 1944. It was during the invasion of the Marshalls that *LST 354* took a hit from enemy shelling. Many of the crew were killed. Chester was at the helm of the ship when the shell found the 354. On 4 September 1944, Chester received a change of rating to fill a vacancy aboard ship. He was designated to "CMoMN (AA) (T)." He was acting in that capacity during the ship's participation of the landings on Iwo Jima in 1945. His last combat operation aboard *LST 354* was during Operation Iceberg, the assault on Okinawa. Chester was given emergency leave on 25 October 1945 and sent back to the States. After more than four years in a combat environment, there was no doubt he needed the rest. His next assignment was with *LCS 52*. Chester's duties there were mundane in comparison to his prior assignments, the largest of which was mothballing the old girl.

10

Rebuilding Lives

Tom Brokaw coined the title the *Greatest Generation* to describe the men and women who came into adulthood during World War II.[1] Helping defeat the Axis powers was only a minute part of their earning that esteemed description. Between 1945 and 1947 some 12,000,000 servicemen were demobilized. Many of the boys came home to find their former employers had filled their pre-war position with someone else. With no further need for the glut of military materiel manufactured during the war, millions of jobs simply went away. The possibility existed that the country could easily fall backwards into the economic abyss of depression. Miraculously, that did not happen.

Technologies previously developed for military uses found their way into homes and offices. Mechanical analog and digital computers, developed during the war, found their place in postwar business and science. Television replaced radio as the most popular means of entertainment and collective social instruction. The modern refrigerator replaced the bulky, cantankerous iceboxes of the 20s and 30s. Following the war, the amount of electricity use doubled every decade thereafter. Aircraft technology developed during the war morphed into passenger and cargo careers. The secret science of radar converted into traffic and weather control instruments and made sense out of the increased jumble in the skies. Of course, the energy produced by atoms which ended the war turned on the lights for millions of homes. In the "buy-on-time," demand for the latest gadget America, it all came down to someone had to build it.

After the war servicemen left their units, airplanes, and ships behind. For the most part they were proud of their service. It was the public face, patriotism, pride and courage. What they had done in war was a tightly held secret, though, and some moments were too taboo to speak of even among wartime comrades. There were ample humorous stories told over drinks at the VFW and at reunions, but seldom did the tight lips of the secret-holders ever open for family or civilian friends. It seemed impossible to try and share the terror and sorrow of war, and there was no logical or sane reason to do so. The innocent notions of noncombatants deserved to remain intact.

Men who had been family to one another in battle sometimes drifted apart in postwar society, sharing secret horrors that only seemed worse when looking in the face of an accomplice. Some could never bring themselves to reunite, the emotional wounds after half a century still raw. It took years in other cases for members of a unit or ship to decide to get together and share their lives and families once more. For two of the 52's shipmates, they would have no lives to share.

James Lee Hawks bled to death after being severely wounded by the kamikaze explosion on the 27th of May 1945 off Okinawa. He was awarded the Purple Heart and the Asiatic-Pacific Medal posthumously. In May of 1949 his remains were taken from the American Cemetery on Okinawa Island and shipped to the National Memorial Cemetery of the Pacific, located in the Punchbowl, Oahu, Hawaiian Islands. The origin of the Punchbowl's name is believed to be from the Hawaiian word "Puowaina," meaning the "Hill of Sacrifice." James' date of interment in Hawaii was 10 March 1949. He was buried in section M, grave number 795, under a flat granite tombstone displaying a Latin cross. His grave is to the right of the flagpole and near the main entrance to the cemetery.[2]

James was in actuality a junior. His father had died in November of 1933 from an infection, the result of an amputation of his left leg after an auto accident. James Sr. was a veteran of World War I and was also buried under a military headstone, in Greensboro, North Carolina. Five years old at the time of his father's death, it was left to his mother, Rhoda Alberty Hawks, to raise James. Rhoda never remarried and lived out her life in Cabarrus County, North Carolina. She passed away in March of 1976 at the age of eighty-nine.

The remains of Ensign Spencer Burroughs, also buried on Okinawa, were returned to the United States. Spencer was interred in Arlington National Cemetery, Washington, D.C., on 13 May 1949. His grave is located in section 34 and his grave number is 3942. In 2011 Spencer's younger brother Geoffrey Burroughs wrote a book titled *Destiny Answers* to honor his brother's sacrifice.[3] The task at the time of Spencer's death, of writing a letter from the command to the family, was of course that of Lt. Harper. Below is the text of the original letter:

Dear Mrs. Burroughs:

It is with heavy and saddened heart that I undertake to tell you of the death of your husband in action aboard this vessel last May twenty-seven. You have my utmost and sincerest sympathy in your bereavement. We who are left to serve on are doing so with saddened spirits and a real feeling of loss. Every officer and man of this vessel is with me in the knowledge that we have lost a very dear friend and comrade, that you have lost a loving and devoted husband, and that our country has lost an admirable, able, and brave officer.

Sunday, May twenty-seven, had begun as a fine day for us, though we knew that enemy action might come at any moment. During the afternoon we received our mail, including packages of books and phonograph records for Spencer. After having admired the books and listened to the records we were called to general quarters as enemy planes were sighted.

Spencer was at his battle station supervising the firing of our after guns when an enemy plane loaded with explosives dived at us in a suicide dive. Though it was a dark night the guns gave a good account of themselves and the plane was forced to change its course and approach from astern. This put the whole burden of our defense on Spencer's gun. The men on the gun, inspired and encouraged by your husband, courageously kept up a heavy and effective fire despite the fact that the enemy plane was diving upon them at utmost speed.

When the plane was almost upon us their fire succeeded in detonating the bombs it carried, thus destroying the plane. The courage of your husband in facing this attack saved the lives of many, many of his shipmates, but cost him his own. He was struck in the temple by shrapnel from the exploding plane and was killed instantly. The Medical Officer and I were at his side almost immediately, but he passed away quietly and without suffering. A great sense of loss descended upon us at that moment, and will remain with us whose lives he saved until the time we can no longer feel loss or pain.

Spencer was buried with military honors on an Eastward slope of the military cemetery in this area. Close by is the grave of one of our men who perished with him. Had it not been for the unflinching courage of your husband in the performance of his duty those two graves might well have been twenty.

With this letter I send my prayer for the Divine to ease your grief and grant peace to your heart.

Sincerely,
John O. Harper

Spencer was a man of quality and none of his shipmates ever forgot him; he was well liked and admired throughout their long lives. His father, Ephraim Spencer Burroughs, died in 1948. Spencer's mother, Olga Adelia Wemple Burroughs, lived until 2000. Brooke, the only sister of Spencer, left a letter for the public at Olga's memorial service describing her. Brooke said at the time of Spencer Jr.'s death that her mother gave up all of her political and social activities she had been so involved in throughout her life. Olga unplugged the telephones and wanted no contact from the world. She remained in that reclusive state for three years before returning to her work.

The surviving members of *LCS 52* returned to lives as diverse after the war as those they had before the war. Most of the men went back to the same jobs, or at least similar jobs, as they had left. In some cases they also returned to the same troubles their lives were mired in before the war. To compound the problems of readjusting to society, they carried with them the psychological trauma of the battlefield.

Virgil Thill, still a young man, went back to the farm on the Upper Peninsula and tried once more to be content tending dairy cows. He soon found that life on the farm had not improved for him. After being a seventeen-year-old operating a Navy ship in a war zone, the farm held even less attraction than it had before the war. He soon left for Detroit.

In the city he took up his old habits of heavy drinking. He went to work but only showed up about three days out of a week. The rest of the time he was too drunk to attend or too busy getting drunk. For the first time in his life, he admitted to himself that he was an alcoholic.[4] He tried Alcoholics Anonymous and for a while attended every meeting. During the time he put his faith in AA, he also encountered their recommendation to have faith in someone bigger than one's self. Virgil was not prepared to do that and they were not prepared to instruct him on that path.[5]

After about a month of being sober, he and an acquaintance decided to make their fortunes in California. California lacked the anchor that both men needed to stay tethered to sobriety. They backslid into their old drinking habits and ended up in jail. The State of California agreed to release them under the condition that they would leave the state. There was little choice but to accept the offer.

Virgil returned to Detroit and lied to get a factory job. His cover was just as quickly blown and he was let go. His only option was to return home to the farm. There, he was no better off. Girls he had grown up with crossed the street to avoid him. It was the same with his other old friends. His parents who had caused his problem belittled him for it. His father told him he was a disgrace to the community. At home he gave church another shot. He went but never heard about Christ or saw Him appear in his life. His situation did not improve over the year, and the following fall he left for Detroit.[6]

He joined the other dregs and drunks on Skid Row. The only welcoming faces were those of the barkeeps in the scattered taverns. It was not long before his survival depended on the handouts of a mission soup kitchen. When he could manage a meal at the mission, it consisted of watery soup and moldy bread. In post–World War II America the missions operated on shoestring budgets and they stretched the soup so that everyone might get a little. The bread, also courtesy of other charitable individuals, suffered from a lack of preservatives, unavailable in those years, and always bore distasteful mold.

He worked the streets from Detroit to Chicago. He bummed money and worked an odd job until he made it to payday. All the while he promised himself not to take another drink. As payday neared he readjusted his vow to steak and a beer. When the money was in hand, his night ended with a belly full of beer, and that was all. Virgil spent two years close to starvation and plagued by alcoholism on the Row.

One day, that "special day," Virgil was standing in line at the Detroit City Rescue waiting for the one o'clock serving of that watery soup he detested. The usual preaching was going on; the stuff that he typically ignored or slept through. Somehow, the message, Isaiah 53:6, did not deflect from his usually effective barrier. It went straight into him like a bullet fired from a 20mm gun, "All we like sheep have gone astray; we have turned everyone to his own way; and the Lord hath laid on him the iniquity of us all." Virgil Thill, hell-raiser, alcoholic, and bum, had heard the words of Christ.[7]

Things were still not easy for Virgil. A lifelong addiction was not kicked to the curb cold-turkey. Virgil did his best to stay sober but among his friends on Skid Row he found a brotherly bond he was not finding in churches. After about six weeks he went back to his old ways, the ways of the Skid Row drunk. He landed back in jail. This time, he fought the DTs for forty-five days while locked up in Detroit's correctional facility. After he got out, he met one of his old friends from the street who was in need of help using up a rich girlfriend's money. The two went on a binge through the Christmas and New Year's holidays. Virgil was only twenty-two years old.

Once again, something began to lead him back to the mission. He was met by a man who worked and preached at the mission, who made him so uneasy he would sometimes leave without eating to avoid him. His name was Andy Roseluke.[8] His stare during services made Virgil so anxious it caused him almost physical pain. Virgil found the courage to stay in Andy's presence. Andy, in turn, rented Virgil a room. It was near the Ward Memorial Presbyterian Church where Andy happened to attend. Andy stuck by Virgil during the hard days ahead. He loaned Virgil money to live off of until he got a job. Virgil had found the Christian and friend he had not encountered before.

Virgil took odd jobs washing dishes at first. He found a suit at a pawn shop, one appropriate to wear into church. That did not change anything within the church. To his dismay, Virgil found that the people in that church treated him the same whether he wore that suit or the T-shirt and blue overalls they were used to seeing him in. He started going to meetings with other young people his age at the church. To his surprise, the girls there did not cross the street to get away from him like back home.

Virgil went back to the factory and this time was hired, even though they knew who he really was. He worked there during the day. His evenings were filled with classes at Detroit Bible College and the classes required to complete his high school diploma. One day he walked into Detroit Edison Electric Company and applied for a job. He told them everything. He shared his poor work record, his struggle with alcohol, and his trouble with law enforcement. He had never done that kind of work before but he promised them he would learn. He told them about his faith that Christ had saved him from himself and the bottle. Under normal circumstances, a company who could pick and choose from the best employees in the state would have never hired him, but nothing in Virgil Thill's life had ever been normal. They agreed to employ him. He worked for many years on the underground lines. His last five years with the company he went to businesses and homes where their debt to the company had become so delinquent it required personal collections. As with his first years, he enjoyed his job. Virgil worked for Edison for thirty-five years and retired as an honored employee.[9]

One day in the early part of July 1950, Virgil was headed up the steps of Ward Church when he noticed one of the girls in his youth group standing at the top. He mustered the courage to walk right up to her and ask her out on a date. Her name was Lois Mary Cockburn. She was the daughter of James and Janet, Scottish immigrants. Lois, born in Michigan in 1932, was first-generation American. Her parents had recently agreed that she might date if she could find a nice boy.

At the time Pearl Harbor was bombed, the Cockburn family was living in Detroit. Lois, nine years old, heard the news of the attack on the radio. She later remembered too clearly that her family back in Scotland wrote of the depredations they were experiencing in Europe before the United States entered the war. Her parents listened to the news religiously because of their ties overseas. At five o'clock that December Sunday they turned on the radio. Upon hearing the news of the Japanese attack, her mother remarked to her dad, "We're going to be in the war from this."[10] She was right. Now, Lois stood on the steps of a Detroit church contemplating a date with a veteran of that war.

They dated for almost a year. The two decided to marry in August but the church was booked. When they agreed to marry in July, her mother vetoed, July being too hot. It came down to June and all things fell into place. Lois and Virgil were married 9 June 1951 at a ceremony at Ward Church. Virgil, still close to destitute, wore his two dollar and fifty cent suit he had bought from the pawn shop to wear to church. Lois wore a seventy-five dollar wedding gown—a sizable purchase for the day.[11] The two newlyweds spent one week of their honeymoon on the Thill farm in the Upper Peninsula. Honeymooner or not, Virgil's dad woke him up each morning at five to milk the cows. He was far from the callow boy who had left the farm in 1944 but he still had not evolved into a farmer.

Lois worked at the Ford Motor Company in Dearborn during the day, in the payroll department. Before they married, she was attending the Walsh Institute of Accounting at night. After they were married, she transferred over to Detroit Bible College with Virgil. They recently celebrated their sixty-third anniversary together.

Virgil eventually bought a sailboat and stood at her wheel, as he had done on the 52 as a teenager. He sailed her up and down the Detroit River for thirty years. When he began to have heart problems he was no longer able to perform the strenuous labor of handling ropes and sails. Losing the boat was a small matter to Virgil; he had a lifetime of travel, companionship and loving family to catch up with.[12]

After raising four sons, Lois and Virgil began to travel around the country. They visited all fifty states and toured some, like Alaska three times. They looked up old shipmates and gathered boxes of pictures, letters, and souvenirs from the war years. Once, shortly after they were married, they accompanied Claude Cook and his wife to a reunion of Michigan-only, 52 veterans. The idea of a reunion stuck, but Lois and Virgil wanted to do it on a big scale. They solicited survivors from the lists of addresses and phone numbers they had accumulated and broached the idea of a ship's reunion. In 1994, shipmates of *LCS 52* gathered at Wright-Patterson Air Force Base in Dayton, Ohio. The men and their wives shared stories, showed off their kids and grandkids, and played practical jokes on one another. Pop Hile was fooled into believing the meal for the event was S.O.S.[13] He was wolfing the specially made dish down when someone finally let him in on the joke. He enjoyed the real meal as well. Only sixteen members of the crew could make the first reunion. Virgil was nobody's drinking buddy this time. Regrettably, several of the crew had already passed away.

Following the reunion, 1995 was the fiftieth anniversary of the Battle of Iwo Jima. Lois and Virgil were invited to attend the ceremony on the island. Their son James, a Wisconsin doctor, promptly and selflessly paid their way there. The two skipped across the Pacific, touching down at old haunts such as Saipan before arriving on Iwo. On Saipan, Virgil showed Lois some of the places he had experienced during the war. They toured the jailhouse where Amelia Mary Earhart had purportedly spent her last days. The two went around the island, stood on the Suicide Cliff, and visited the monuments.[14] After a night on Saipan, they boarded the plane for Iwo Jima.

Ownership of the Island of Iwo Jima was restored to Japan in 1968. The United States has control of a communications site there, but the last members of the U.S. Coast Guard stationed on the island departed the year before the fiftieth anniversary of the battle. The airstrip on Iwo Jima is maintained by members of the Japan Maritime Self-Defense Force (JMSDF). There are approximately 400 Japanese soldiers and sailors stationed on the island. Except for memorial ceremonies, the island is off limits to tourism and visitors.

The island still lives up to its literal name, meaning *Sulfur Island*. At the time of the

The first reunion, in 1994, brought together some of the original crew. From left to right: (standing) Tweet and his son, Prendergast, Keilty, (possibly) Hile, Strandquist, Burnette, and Reed; (kneeling) Stoia, Bauer, Bledsoe, Thill, and Gardner (Virgil Thill collection).

American landings, there were infrequent volcanic eruptions, and the smell of sulfur was so thick it was nauseating. What looked to be black sand on the beaches of Iwo Jima was really semi-powdered lava rock. It was a nightmare for the marines to negotiate or dig into on 19 February 1945. From the miles of manmade and restructured natural caves on the island the Japanese defenders soaked it red with marine blood. Aside from the wounded and killed, twenty-two marines and five sailors earned the Medal of Honor on Iwo Jima.

Only a little more than 1,000 defenders ever left their caves alive. Nearly all of the 22,000 Japanese defenders were entombed within the sealed-off caves. That number included the over-all Japanese commander during the battle, General Tadamichi Kuribayashi. Before the battle, he had written a series of letters to his wife. Against his wishes they became public after his death. He wrote, "Do not plan for my return. Do not be surprised when you hear that I have died."[15] He issued his last known words of farewell to his troops on 23 March 1945.

On the half-century anniversary of the battle, Kuribayashi's widow, Yoshii, sat respectfully under an umbrella, shielded from the sun. Her son and daughter accompanied her on the journey. Virgil and Lois made acquaintance with her and quickly became friends. They were given a picture of her, which she signed without hesitation. Some of the Marine veterans had a hard time, being in such close proximity to Japanese veterans who had killed and maimed their buddies. The anxiety was two-fold. Virgil just wanted the ceremonial speeches to cease so he could go to the top of Mount Suribachi. Before he went to find a ride, he and Lois stopped and talked with some of the visiting Navajo Code Talkers who had served on Iwo.

Virgil, like all the veterans, was treated with celebrity status by the young marines who constructed the infrastructure of the ceremony. They came to him asking for his autograph and he obliged by signing the backs of their t-shirts or whatever object they brought to him. He probably seemed even more invincible when he informed a young Marine lieutenant of the lack of organization in setting up the event. He struck hard, telling the Marine officer, if the battle fifty years before had been run with such poor organization, the Marines would have lost. Then he informed the Marine general that he came there to go to the top of Mount Suribachi and he intended to go. The general commissioned a five-ton truck to immediately take him there. Lois, clad in her fine dress, climbed into the cab next to the driver like an old salt marine grunt. Virgil mounted the truck in the seat next to her, but did not seem to draw the attention of onlookers that she had with her agile entry. Witnessing marines felt compelled to admire and compliment her on the feat.

Only two *LCS 52* reunions were ever held. Both were planned by Lois and Virgil. After that, Virgil became the unofficial historian for *LCS 52*. He collected boxes of memorabilia from the time the ship sailed through the later, postwar years of the sailors' lives. Lois too, researched without benefit of computers, the whereabouts of former 52ers. Mostly using nothing more than a phonebook and phone, she was able to locate the majority of survivors or next-of-kin.[16]

The two still live in Farmington Hills and maintain contact with the known survivors of the original crew. During the research of this book I had the opportunity to talk frequently with Lois and Virgil. I made a two-day trip to their home and was greeted with such courtesy we became quick friends. Virgil has taken up the hobby of recovering objects that others leave on the street to be taken away by the city. He enjoys repairing and making those discarded items function once again. Collecting was a fitting metaphor for a man who was once broken and discarded but was ultimately found and repaired.

Jack Denzil Gloor, after being wounded in action on 11 May 1945, never returned to *LCS 52*. He was taken back to the States, where he recuperated from his wounds. On 15 February 1946 he joined the crew of the USS *Alvin C. Cockrell* (DE 366) for temporary duty. Jack was promoted to Gunners Mate 3rd Class on 1 May while serving aboard the *Cockrell*. The following day he was dropped off at San Diego for separation and discharge. Jack returned to his former hometown of Hicksville, Ohio.

Jack became part of the Hicksville Fire Department after the war. He left a legacy of being a great fireman and man. He served as the Hicksville Fire Chief from the beginning of 1972 to the beginning of 1978. He retired from the department in that year. Jack died 23 October 2009 and was buried in the Forest Home Cemetery in Hicksville, near his parents, sister, Wanda, and brother Rex.

Galen C. Libby was sent to the separation center at Boston, Massachusetts, on 1 February 1946. Galen married Joy C. Kirkpatrick of Dover-Foxcroft, Maine, on 12 June 1946. She was a recent graduate of the Foxcroft Academy. Joy was the daughter of John D. and L. Pearl Kirkpatrick.

Galen and Joy made their first home together in Bangor. Their two children were born there. The family moved to Lincoln and then to Brewer. Galen worked as a salesman for the Standard Register Company and in 1965 was the proprietor for the Industrial Park Esso. Joy worked those years for the Eastern Corporation. In 1966, Joy and Galen moved back to Lincoln. Then in 1970 they resided in South China. When the two retired in 1986, they began to spend their winters in Tucson, Arizona. Galen died 17 April 1994 in Bangor, Maine. Joy Libby passed away on 13 October 2005.[17]

In 1944 the Servicemen's Readjustment Act, known commonly as the G.I. Bill, was passed. The G.I. Bill provided a never-before-possible opportunity for former servicemen to attend an institution of higher education, regardless of their economic status. In the decade that followed their discharges, 2.2 million went to college. Another 5.6 million returnees attended vocational or technical schools.

Several of the men from *LCS 52* joined the ranks of those attending or returning to institutions of higher education. Laton Burns took classes in agriculture, pursuing his dream of being a better farmer. The skipper, John Harper, Jerry Duvendeck and Albert Parker all went back to college after the war and earned graduate degrees. They were the norm, not the exception.

Jerry Paul Duvendeck returned to Michigan and received a Master of Science degree in zoology from Michigan State College on 28 November 1951. He was living in Kalamazoo at the time. His mother and father were also living there. Marquerite M. Duvendeck was working as a saleswoman. Jerry's sister, Anne E., was single, living on her own in Kalamazoo and going to school as well.

After he completed his education, Jerry was a tireless biologist for the Michigan Department of Conservation. His studies on deer acorn diets and several books on natural resource management are renowned in the state. The following were some of the books he wrote in that field: *Oak Management and Acorn Crop Forecast for Deer in Michigan's Lower Peninsula*, *The 1957 Acorn Crop in Region II*, *Basic Formula: Oak Management for Game*, *The 1967 Deer Season, Bois Blanc and Beaver Islands*, and *The 1966 Extended Ruffed Grouse Hunting Season on Garden and High Islands*, to name a few. His wife, Isabelle Frances Duvendeck, passed away on 23 July 1986 at their residence in Denton. Jerry passed away on 9 March 1996 in Flint, Michigan. His last residence was still in Denton, Michigan.

Laton Burns returned to Kentucky. He and Kathleen Dezarn married 23 November 1946. They moved to a farm adjacent to his father's in Crab Orchard, Kentucky. Things went well for the newlyweds until they had their first child, Diane, in the winter of 1947. She was followed by a son, Dan, the following winter. With two small children, the little farm enterprise was insufficient to produce a respectable income.

Laton ceded his dream of being a farmer and moved his family to Ohio in 1950. His brother Milton was living in Ohio at the time and the two families initially merged into one house. Milton was working at Frigidaire, one of the largest employers in the area. Laton was soon hired on as well. Once Laton had regular income coming in, he moved his family to an apartment in Franklin, Ohio. They did not remain there long. They then moved to another apartment but in the country, a place more appealing to the two Eastern Kentuckians who had grown up surrounded by open-space.

On weekends the family loaded into the car and took drives through the countryside, typically looking at and admiring farms. Laton always harbored the hope that he would one day own another farm.[18] By the time Diane was ready for school, Laton moved the family to Germantown and bought a home there. The house was in a "plat," the forerunner to a subdivision. The plat where Laton purchased was filled with a majority of World War II vets all chasing the American Dream. Most of the residents were Kentuckians and Tennesseans who had immigrated to the north seeking factory work. The Burns family remained there while the kids attended school.[19]

Their next move came when they purchased a larger home and rented the smaller one as investment property. In spite of living and working around other veterans, Laton and Kathleen seldom socialized with outsiders. All of Laton's family moved to Ohio over the years as well as two of Kathleen's brothers. They often gathered with one or all of the family, as they had been accustomed to in Kentucky. They played Rook, shared dinners, holidays and summer picnics. The family attended the Germantown First Baptist Church. Laton sang in the choir. He still loved sports and played for the church baseball team.

If Laton had learned anything from the Depression, it was frugality. He saved enough money for both of his kids to attend college. He also instilled in his children the absolute presumption they would attend college. It was a given that they would do well in all school work, including college. When his children came of college age, Laton created notebooks in which he kept meticulous accounting records of school expenses. Each column denoted, penny for penny, tuition, room and board and pocket cash. He saw in college the opportunity to excel above the social status one was born into.[20]

On Labor Day, 7 September 1970, Laton suffered a fatal heart attack. He died knowing that the following month his son would graduate from college. He had witnessed his daughter graduate from college and walked her down the aisle at her wedding before he passed away. Through the postwar years, he returned to Kentucky on occasion and visited with his friend Lloyd Keith. In his wartime photo album he wrote on Keith's picture, "My closest friend in battle."

Lloyd "Clements" Keith was transferred to the separation center at Great Lakes on 16 May 1946. He returned to his home in Manchester, Kentucky, after discharge from the Navy. He married his local sweetheart, Evelyn Sparks, who had attended school with him.[21] She was a freshman at Eastern Kentucky University during 1945, while he was serving off Okinawa.

Upon his return, he was hired at the main post office in town and served for many years as a friendly, out-going and well-known postman. Many of the World War II veterans chose the postal service as a career. They all viewed the carrier positions as a welcome transition from military service. In 1950 Clements was included on a list of registered football officials by the Kentucky High School Athletic Association. He never lost his love of sports. He ultimately did what so many Kentuckians do to avoid harsh winters. He retired to Florida. There, he ran a successful service station in Orlando through the 1960s-70s.[22] Clements passed away in Volusia, Florida, on 29 August 2006. His wife passed away days short of three years prior to him.

Ensign Albert G. Parker III had been on a path to the pulpit since the day he was born. He returned from service and attended McCormick Theological Seminary, earning his divinity degree. He continued his education and earned a master's degree from the University of Illinois. His ministry took him all over the country. Before he retired in 1985, Albert served as the minister for Presbyterian churches in the states of Illinois, Kansas, Michigan, Arizona, Colorado and New Mexico. He was pastor over the church in Grand Haven, Michigan, for fourteen years. Albert's church there served a member who was a State Trooper acquainted with Claude Cook. He served as pastor for the First Presbyterian Church, Lawrence, Kansas, from 1953 until 1961. His last church was the White Rock United Presbyterian Church in Santa Fe. He was installed as pastor 3 October 1981 and remained there until he retired.

On 14 August 1949 he married Joanne Lindberg in Portland, Oregon. Joanne was born in Washington State and the family moved to Portland from Bellingham in the late 1930s. She was familiar with the docks and company where *LCS 52* was manufactured.

Albert's father, only six months from his retirement date, died-while president of Hanover College in March of 1958. Albert's sister, Jane, was a familiar face at Hanover College until the day she died there in November 2008. Today many of the buildings at the college bear the names of Albert III's mother and father. They left an iconic legacy at Hanover.

Before Albert died, Adler Strandquist and his wife stopped in to visit with the Parkers at their home in Albuquerque. The Strandquists were snowbirds in Arizona during the harsh winters in their home of Minnesota. The two old "salts" entertained their spouses with tales of LCS adventures. Albert was tasked with performing the final inventory of the *LCS 52* in Astoria during her decommissioning. He recalled all of the mementos sailors had taken from her. He admitted that his only keepsake was the leather cribbage board from the wardroom. He played on it for years after.[23] Albert passed away on a Sunday, 1 March 2009. He and his wife were living on Indiana Street, Albuquerque, New Mexico, at the time.

Claude Harris Cook was transferred to USNCT Great Lakes, Illinois, on 5 March 1946 for processing out of the Navy. After his discharge he returned to his former job as a Michigan State Policeman. In 1946 Caroline Artman and he were married. On 13 December 1953 he was promoted to Sergeant and took over as Post Commander of Troopers at Centerline, Michigan. By 25 May 1958 he had worked his way up through the ranks of the MSP. He was promoted to Captain that day and took over as head of Operations and Communications in East Lansing. In that position, he created the police blockade system that was used across the United States for almost fifty years. It was common to see newspapers, like the *St. Clare Sentinel*, praising his work. He was a rising star, and in April 1965 Claude was placed in the position of acting Commander of the Uniformed Division. His distinguished career ended on 15 October 1965, when forced to retire after suffering a heart attack.

Claude went back to work as a liaison between his new employer, Associated General Contractors, and the Michigan State Police. In that capacity he supervised assets and resources which would abate the damage from natural disasters.[24] The position was a forerunner to commanders who would one day coordinate emergency management planning. He worked for AGC until 1972. After his second retirement Claude welcomed a chance to relax, and did so until he passed away 2 June 1978 in his hometown of Lansing. He had served his state and his country selflessly for just short of fifty years.

Benjamin L. Beittel was separated from service on 4 November 1945. He returned to his family in Carlisle, Pennsylvania. Ben became a dynamic figure in the community. At one time in his postwar life, he worked as an assistant warden for the Cumberland County Prison on East High Street.[25] Ben also belonged to the Union Fire Company, Carlisle's volunteer fire department since 1789. The fire company had worked out of a station on West Louther Street since 1889. Ben's last employment was fulltime at the Carlisle Barracks Post Exchange. He retired from that job and devoted himself to his family and community. His youngest daughter recalled how she returned to nursing classes from breaks at home and her classmates gathered anxiously to hear Ben's latest jokes and songs.[26]

After the war Ben rejoined the congregation at St Paul's Evangelical Lutheran Church where his son had been confirmed. He remained a member there until his death. In 1978 Ben and Grace lost their oldest son, Ben Jr., to a heart attack. Ben Sr. passed away on 12 October 1989 at eleven in the morning. He was buried near his son at Westminster Memorial Gardens, North Middleton Township, Pennsylvania.

Some of the men could not bring themselves to part with a life they had, in spite of war, grown to love. Many of the original 52 crew remained in the Navy.

Gerald "Jerry" E. Bledsoe was transferred to the separation center at Great Lakes on 24 April 1946 for release from active duty. He returned to the home of his parents in Moline, Illinois. Civilian life did not suit him the way the Navy had. He returned to school during 1947 in Moline but soon after reenlisted. He served aboard the USS *Wiltsie* (DD-716), stationed out of San Diego, in 1948. He received orders to report to Bainbridge, Maryland, for prep for entry into the Naval Academy. He admitted to his old skipper and friend, Lt. Harper, "I did not pass one subject on the entrance exam."[27] Gerald remained in the Navy as an enlisted man.

After Jerry's attempt at the Naval Academy, he was sent to Boston and assigned to another destroyer. Jerry married a hometown girl around this time, Joan, and she followed Jerry across the country. The couple lived in New London and Groton, Connecticut, in the early years of Jerry's naval career. While there, Quartermaster 2nd Class Bledsoe applied for submarine school in New London. He was accepted and passed sub school with no problem. He was subsequently assigned to the USS *Spikefish* (SS/AGSS-404), a Balao-class submarine, for five years. As a training sub, the *Spikefish* made trips to Cuba, the Mediterranean, Bermuda, Scotland and dozens of other ports during Jerry's time aboard her.

In 1958, he was back at Rock Island but serving as the Officer in Charge of Navy recruiting there. His father, Frank, was working at the welfare office at the time. Jerry served as a recruiter for two years, next door to his and Joan's hometown and their families. He then was sent to Charleston, South Carolina. He was assigned to the USS *Darter* (SS 576), an improved Tang-class Submarine used for refresher training.[28] Jerry was reassigned to the submarine staff at Charleston. He remained at Charleston for the next four years. Jerry was transferred from the east coast to Litchfield Park, Arizona. Jerry retired from the Navy in 1965. He retired as a Petty Officer 1st Class.

After a distinguished military career, Jerry worked as an engineering consultant in Phoenix. He remained with them for twenty-five years and retired in 1991 at age sixty-five. Jerry was a member of the Sun City West PRIDES (Particular Residents Involved Doing Environmental Services). The organization members donate their own time to pick up trash, sweep gutters, curbs and sidewalks, and trim along public routes.

Jerry was also a member of the Fleet Reserve Association. The group is the oldest enlisted association in the United States. Its mission is to lobby and fight to retain the rights and benefits earned by enlisted members of the Navy, Marine Corps and Coast Guard. The organization serves active duty, retired and reserve personnel in those branches.

He was a member of the Prince of Peace Catholic Church in Sun City West, Arizona. On 23 November 2014, Gerald E. Bledsoe passed away. He was eighty-eight years old. He left behind his wife and two sons. After he retired, Jerry reconnected with Lt. Harper. The two talked on the phone and wrote letters to each other. Harper later had this to say of the then seventeen-year-old signalman who served with him on his first and only ship. "He [Bledsoe] had been a bright young man, serious and dependable, and we had been close friends since the signalmen were usually assigned to the

Gerald Bledsoe was one of the signalmen aboard *LCS 52*. He is demonstrating flag semaphore, the method by which ships communicated with one another over distances while at sea. The flags are read when in the fixed position. Flags were used during the day and lights after dark. Semaphore is still used in emergency situations today (Nick Stoia collection).

conning tower." Harper, though a stickler for by-the-book performance, never reprimanded his officers for fraternizing with the enlisted men.[29] Before Ensign Burroughs was killed, he and Larry Cullen had been best friends. Harper also made unsanctioned friendships with enlisted men in close proximity to him, such as Jerry. As it turned out, he would never reprimand someone for doing what he himself was doing.

Clifford Stewart left *LCS 52* in July of 1946, decommissioning her from service. He took command of *LCS 92* from July to November of 1946. In 1947, Stewart was assigned to the USS *Cacapon* (AO-52) as the Gunnery Officer. During the Korean War, Stewart served as the Operations Officer aboard the USS *Sticknell* (DD-888).

He was assigned to the CIC Team Training center in San Diego as an instructor for two years. It was during the early 1950s that he met his wife, Dorothy, in San Diego. He was a Lieutenant Commander when they met. Dorothy was living in nearby La Jolla. After they married they continued to live at 8231 Paseo del Ocaso in La Jolla. They raised a son and daughter together, as they travelled the world with the Navy.

Stewart also served as the Executive Officer aboard the USS *Carpenter* and then took command of the USS *Foss* (DE-59). From 1957–1960, Stewart worked at the Bureau of Naval Personnel. He left there to command the USS *Thomason*. He was promoted to Captain 1 July 1965.

During Vietnam, Captain Stewart commanded the Coastal Surveillance Force (CFT 115) from April 1966 to March 1967. Stewart received the Legion of Merit for his part in developing the concepts of coastal inshore warfare during the early years of the Vietnam War.

Stewart retired at Hunter's Point Naval Shipyard, California, in 1974 as a Captain and commander of that instillation. His career spanned thirty-two and a half years and encompassed three wars. He and his wife purchased a thirteen-acre ranch in Healdsburg, California. They raised sheep and planted apple, walnut and almond trees, an operation his daughter describes as a "small family ranch." Stewart continued his service by involving himself in his civilian community. Among other positions, he served on the Sonoma County Planning Commission, Board of Zoning Adjustments and North Coast Regional Water Quality Board.[30]

He lost his wife in 2013. Captain Clifford Stewart (RET) turned ninety-eight in 2014. He continues to live in his home on his ranch and explores his property on a golf cart. The Stewart family attended the ceremony when *LCS 102*, the only surviving landing craft support, was returned to the United States. When asked about specific sailors, Stewart says there were too many commands and too many faces to recall his two years aboard *LCS 52* these days. There was a visit from Lois and Virgil Thill in 2007. They stayed with Dorothy and Cliff at their ranch. Captain Stewart and Nick Stoia have spoken on the phone.[31]

Although Albert Moschner was not part of the original crew, he served as engineering officer after Burroughs was killed. He was also another of the crew who felt compelled to remain in service. He and his wife, Virginia, were living in San Diego in 1950 and resided at 3322 Gunther Lane. The couple was then stationed in Norfolk in 1958; the two lived on Chester Street. In 1961 he returned to San Diego for duty. He and Virginia lived at 5043 ½ Del Monte that tour. After more than twenty years of dedicated service to the Navy, Albert left service and took a job at the Santa Rosa, California, Sears store as a warehouseman. The two were living at 1121 Slater at that time in 1965. Albert passed away on 28 January 1992 in Santa Rosa.

Frank Maidic, Albert and Henry's half-brother, joined the Army Air Force on 17 October

1942. Frank followed his brother Edward "Adie," who enlisted 21 March 1941. Albert's older brother Henry also served in the Army during World War II. He did not complete a full tour, his service cut short. He never spoke of the incident and the family only knew he was involved in a jeep accident. He never drove after his return from the Army. Henry returned to McCurtain, Oklahoma, and worked in the coal mines. He, his father Joseph, and mother Mary were buried in the Miner's Cemetery, one mile west of the ghost-town-like McCurtain.

Albert remained in the Navy and rarely returned to the Oklahoma town where he was born and raised. He was promoted to Lieutenant (jg) on 1 April 1946 and retired at that pay grade.[32]

Oren C. Tweet left the 52 temporarily on 6 April 1946 for the hospital at Mare Island. He remained there until 15 April and returned to LCS 52. Oren was transferred to the Columbia River Group Pacific Reserve Fleet on 7 May. He joined the crew of *LSM 289* on 3 June 1946 at Portland. On 24 September 1946, Oren reported to the post demobilization and separation center in Seattle. His last ship, *LSM 289*, was decommissioned on 15 November.

Not one to sit idly by, Oren filed with the United States Patent Office for a patent on an invention on 29 October 1946, a device described as a combination ashtray and saucer of "ornamental design." The patent was granted 21 June 1949, "Des. 154,224."

During his time at Tongue Point (extensive piers were constructed to berth mothballed ships, including LCSs), he was arrested one night for possessing an officer's blanket. It was the same blanket he had been given as a replacement for the one he gave the wounded on 27 May 1945. Although he was cleared of all charges, the incident left a bitter taste. He gave up on the notion of making the Navy a career.

His time at Tongue Point was not all disappointing. While taking in the local entertainment at the Grange Hall in nearby Svensen, he danced with a young lady named Ellen Aho to a schottische with a Scandinavian twist.[33] Ellen grew up in Svensen, an unincorporated town on the Columbia River.[34] The town had even closed its post office in 1944. The two fell in love and were married on 26 October 1946 in Longview, Washington. They lived in Puyallup, Washington, while Oren went to night school and worked in a body and fender shop. He studied auto painting. In 1948 the couple moved back to Ellen's hometown of Svensen, where Oren worked at Lovell Auto Company. In 1949 he was living at Route 4, Astoria, Oregon. He was an up-and-comer in the auto repair industry. In 1950, Oren moved to Westport and owned and operated Westport Auto Body and Fender. In 1953 Ellen was also working at the Westport Body Repair Shop. Oren purchased the Pontiac dealership in 1955 and it became Oren Pontiac Company in Westport. In 1957 the couple moved to Clatskanie.

Ellen and Oren lived in Clatskanie, about thirty-five miles east of Astoria, for the rest of their lives. It was there that Oren left his legacy as one of the finest human beings to walk the streets of postwar America. In the 1960s, Oren owned and operated Oren's Insurance Agency and Tweet's Blue Ribbon Cleaning Center, along with other commercial real estate. He was a volunteer fireman for sixteen years and City Council member for almost thirty-two years. He was a member of the Masonic Lodge and the Scottish Rite. When he was not Grand Marshaling the 4th of July parade, he was cooking up his famous Oren's North Dakota Ho-Bo Stew to raise money for the Doernbecher Children's Hospital. Oren also flaunted his culinary skills each year on Memorial Day by cooking pancakes, eggs and sausage for the community's annual breakfast. He was a long-time member of the American Legion, the Veterans of Foreign Wars, Al Kader Shrine, Kiwanis Club and the Odd Fellows. He seemed to be tireless in his efforts to better his community. He served a term as treasurer for the Masonic Lodge, acted as noble grand for the Odd Fellows and the list went on. In 1993 the city of Clatskanie awarded him the first-ever Oren Tweet Community Service Medallion. The award was issued for civic duty above and beyond. It stands as the city's highest honor for a deserving citizen today.[35]

In his spare time, if there was such a thing, he collected and displayed miniature antique farm machinery and replications of farming scenes. He enjoyed woodworking, photography and videotaping. Oren and his family were longtime members of the Faith Lutheran Church. In early-February of 2006, Oren was hospitalized. Oren C. Tweet passed away on the 12th day of February in Portland. He was so well-thought-of his funeral service had to be held in the high school auditorium. He was buried in the Murray Hill Cemetery of Clatskanie.[36]

Abraham "Bob" Scurrah was not absent from the ocean for long. In August of 1947 the destroyer USS *Charles H. Roan* received him aboard from the training center in San Diego. He still carried the rank he left the 52 with, Fireman 1st Class. He remained aboard until 3 October 1947, when he and six shipmates were transferred to the USS *Spokane*. He served on the *Spokane* through January 1949. In the Malden, Washington 1945 through 1948 directories, Ruth and he were listed at 19 Garfield Terrace. His occupation was "USN." Ruth and Abraham separated and divorced sometime after.

In 1950 he married for the second time, Barbara A. Scurrah from Boston. The two lived on Pleasant Street in Malden in 1958 through 1960; Abraham was the foreman of Kaulback Reality Company. His father, Arnold, became an American citizen in May of 1945, days after Germany surrendered. Arnold died in Everett in 1954. Herbert Scurrah, Abraham's brother, passed away in 1986. He served from 1942 to 1946 in the U.S. Army.

Abraham died on 20 January 1997 in Malden. He was buried in the Forest Dale Cemetery.[37] Descendants of the Scurrah family still reside in the same house in Yorkshire, England, where Abraham and Herbert's great-grandparents lived. The Shirley Industrial School for Boys where Abraham was an inmate in his youth was closed in 1972. Some former inmates who survive retain kind memories of their rehabilitation, while others recall few experiences there they did not loathe.

Ulysses Johnson, the only African-American among the 52's original crew, was transferred to the USS *Rankin* (AKA 103) on 2 November 1945, the same day the *Rankin* left Nagoya, Japan, and headed toward the U.S. to drop off passengers who had earned separation from service. Johnson returned to his home in Memphis. Ulysses and his wife, Dorothy Faye Shannon, raised eleven children together. Dorothy passed away in 1985 and Ulysses followed on 16 October 1999. His honorable service during the war was inspiration to his children, several of whom served in the armed forces. One of those children retired from the Army and another retired from the Navy.

Jordan "Jerry" Lee Brantley was transferred to the USS *Hansford* (APA 106) on 5 October 1945. After discharge, he went back to his family in Florida. He and Freda had three more children together. It is possible Jerry worked as a driller with the Industrial Drilling & Boring Corporation in 1949. The company as a relative startup venture was incorporated only two years prior. He was living on Starke Street, in Jacksonville, Florida, that year, if he indeed worked for Industrial. Jerry had a son, Roger A. Brantley, who passed away in 2004. Roger retired from the "ecology drilling business" according to his obituary. Jerry's obituary in the 4 March 1989 *News-Journal* out of Daytona Beach, stated that he was a retired geologist.

He and Freda were divorced in December 1972 in Bradford County, Florida. He later married Ethel "Jerry" Rogers. Jerry was living in Zephyrhills, Florida, in the early 1980s. He moved to Orange City sometime around 1988. In a letter from his second wife to Virgil Thill, she stated that Jerry had been in a wheelchair for the last twelve years of his life. She listed only two sons and two daughters as his children. Jerry passed away at West Volusia Memorial Hospital, Deland, Florida on 2 March 1989. Jerry's ashes were scattered in Starke.

MoMM2c John T. Keilty enlisted on 15 December 1943 at age fifteen under clandestine circumstances. John was advanced to MoMM2c (LC) (T) on 1 May 1945 while aboard the *LCS 52*. On 22 May 1946 he transferred to Columbia River Group, 19th Fleet, for assignment. On 14 June 1946 he was transferred to the U.S. Naval Amphibious Base, Coronado, California. He was shown present for duty on *LSM 437* for the quarter ending 30 June 1946; he was shown mustered aboard that ship on 14 June of that year. On 14 March 1947 John was transferred to "Navy #3700 Ponape, FFT to Guam Navy # 926, FFT to nearest R/S continental U.S. for discharge. Expiration of enlistment."

Laton Burns recorded in his journal that John was living on Garden Street, Bellingham, Washington, before the war. John returned to Washington and was awarded a General Educational Development (GED) diploma in 1947 from Bellingham High School. He married Shirley Stamatis on 4 November 1950 in San Mateo, California. The two were divorced in Nevada in 1973. John graduated from the University of San Francisco in 1953 with a degree in Business Administration. He moved to Woodacre, California, in 1956 and became a ubiquitous presence in community affairs. He was the manager for the Household Finance Corporation in San Rafael and then a home builder in Woodacre. John served on the Lagunitas School District Board for three years. He was a charter member of the San Geronimo Valley Lions Club and served a term as president. In 1964 John ran for a spot on the county board of supervisors.

John Keilty died in Lake, California, on 15 October 1998.[38] Edward Jr., the brother whose identity he borrowed to enlist in the Navy, passed away on 4 May 1961. Edward was buried in Holy Cross Cemetery, in Spokane, Washington.[39]

Charles "Chuck" Darnell was transferred to Great Lakes for separation on 24 April 1946. From there he returned to his hometown of Massillon, Ohio. Chuck married Patricia Ann Marchand, a resident of Massillon since the late 1930s, when she, her older sister and mother moved in with her maternal grandparents. Chuck worked for Tyson Bearing Company for twenty-seven years, retiring in 1985. He attended St. Barbara's Catholic Church all of his life. He coached the St. Barbara's school fifth and sixth grade football teams for twelve years. He bowled on an area team, often setting records, played leading parts in the St. Barbara's annual minstrel shows, and was active after the war in the American Legion and VFW.[40] Chuck and Patricia ventured back across the ocean in July of 1972, but to England that time. There, they attended the wedding of their son, stationed in London with the U.S. Navy. The couple married in Standmore, England, and most of the Darnell family attended.

Chuck passed away at his home on Saturday, 23 January 1999. He was buried in the Brookfield Cemetery in Massillon. He had fought a good fight against a prolonged illness and was in the care of hospice when he passed.[41]

Nick Stoia returned to his hometown of Alliance, Ohio. He worked for a door company,

Seneca Manufacturing, for over fifteen years. After that, he became a city building inspector and housing inspector for Alliance. He married Helen Codrea, a local girl he had known for the majority of his life. Helen's parents, as were Nick's, were immigrants. Helen and Nick attended Alliance High School together. "We went to the same church together, [grew] up together and finally made it together," Nick said.[42]

Nick left school in the twelfth grade to join the Navy. When he returned home, he made it a priority to finish high school. American History was the only subject he had failed to complete before he enlisted. He took that during the summer and received his diploma in 1947. He and Helen were then married in 1952. "We've been married a long time," Nick said, "we worked together."

Nick's younger brother Ralph also joined the Navy during the war. He was assigned as the storekeeper to a sub-tender out of the home port of New London, Connecticut. Nick summed up his own time in a war zone. "It was rough duty" when you look back on it. "You know at seventeen, I wasn't really—my mind wasn't really quite right yet."[43] Helen and Nick still live in Alliance. They stay in touch with Virgil and Lois Thill by phone.

Lt. John O. Harper, wartime commander of *LCS 52*, returned to his home state of Ohio. He resumed his education at Ohio State and obtained a law degree. John graduated in 1948 having achieved the honors of being a member of Delta Theta Phi, Phi Rho Pi, Kappa Delta Phi, the editor of the Ohio State Law Journal, and Secretary and President of the Student Bar Association. He said in his memoirs when speaking of his and his wife's undying devotion to better education, "We have supported education in every way we know how."[44] No one could argue against that statement. After graduation, Harper took up residence in Springfield, Ohio. John served on the City's Board of Education for eight years. Many of those same years he sat on the Board of Education for Clark County Joint Vocational School. He later helped with the founding of Clark State Institute of Technology and was on the institution's first Board. He taught business law at Antioch College, while simultaneously serving as the college's attorney. He later became a member of the Board of Trustees for Urbana University. He was also the founder and the first chairman of the Ohio Council of School Board Attorneys. He served the city and citizens of Springfield and the State of Ohio in a legal capacity for twenty-five years. He negotiated disputes and suits for agencies and individuals throughout his career, including firemen, teachers and police officers. He was employed at Martin, Browne, Hull & Harper PLL until 2005. In 1995, Harper recorded his life's story on twelve audio tapes. With few exceptions his memory of events, places and people was close to perfect. John Harper died in a Springfield nursing home at 05:15 on 14 February 2006. He was buried in the Ferncliff Cemetery in Springfield, Ohio.

Chester P. Swisher, Jr., remained on *LCS 52* until 7 May 1946. He was transferred to the Columbia River Group, 19th Fleet for assignment. He then reported aboard the USS *Perkins* (DD 877) in June. He worked on the *Perkins* through 1948. It was only the beginning of a very long and distinguished career in the Navy.

On 3 January 1958, Chester married Cleo A. Heyer, the woman he would spend the rest on his life with, in a Los Angeles, California, ceremony. The two apparently had a second ceremony in Las Vegas, Nevada, in June of 1962. Chet and Cleo raised three children together. Chief Petty Officer Swisher said farewell to the Navy in July of 1961. He opened an insurance agency in San Diego as his second career.

After his retirement, Chester and Cleo remained in the Navy city of San Diego. Chester was active in community and veterans organizations, especially those related to the survivors of Pearl Harbor. In 1995, Chester was voted San Diego County veteran of the year. In 2006 he returned for the sixty-fifth anniversary to Pearl Harbor. Only a handful of survivors were still physically able to make the trip. Tom Brokaw was the keynote speaker for the ceremony. Brokaw stated, "It was here the greatest generation was forged."[45] Since that time, formal anniversary ceremonies for Pearl Harbor survivors have ceased. The detriments of age on the veterans have forced the promoters to consider the toll that the trip takes on the survivors as not worth the risk.

The prior year, on the sixtieth anniversary of V-J Day, the Director of the San Diego Veterans Memorial Center, Chet Swisher, also attended and sat proudly as President George W. Bush thanked him for his service. In his address, the President spoke of the thousands of men who never knew of one another but joined the military ranks to fight a common enemy to the free world. They met, fought together, suffered together and sometimes died together on now forgotten islands such as Kwajalein, Tarawa, Saipan, Iwo Jima and a hundred others. "The men and women who served in World War II belonged to a generation that kept its faith even when liberty's ultimate triumph was far from clear," the President added.[46] That was certainly true in the minds of the elderly men who sat listening to the president's speech as their thoughts, most assuredly, drifted back to the sights and sounds of 7 December 1941. The Navy men who fought on separate ships, but together, were oftentimes introduced to one another by being added to a ship's roaster. Like Chester, many had met, at one time or another, during their time aboard *LCS 52*.

Chester Paul Swisher, Jr., died on 3 April 2009. His brother, Art, who followed him into the Navy during World War II and then served in the Army during Korea, survived him. Chester and the men who served on ships like *LCS 52* were the toughest the country had to offer; they fulfilled their obligation to freedom and guaranteed it in blood.

11

Death of 52

Landing Craft Support Ships first saw combat during the liberation of the Philippines (October 1944–August 1945). On 15 February 1945 LCSs faced an attack directed specifically at them by thirty or more suicide boats. Three of the LCSs (*7, 49* and *26*) were hit by suicide boats while acting as a screen to Mariveles Harbor, Corregidor Island, that day. A fourth, *LCS 27*, claimed five enemy boats sunk, but was damaged to the extent that it was forced to beach in order to prevent its own sinking. The LCSs *7, 49* and *26* all sank as a result of their damage by enemy boats. Seventy-six LCS sailors from the four damaged ships lost their lives during the attack. By the end of the day, only two LCSs remained to provide close support for ground operations on Corregidor.

Twelve LCSs, including *LCS 52*, engaged enemy shore defenses and supported American landings on D–Day, Iwo Jima, on 19 February. Easter Sunday 1945 marked the beginning of operations against the Japanese-held Island of Okinawa, codenamed Operation Iceberg. That campaign lasted until 22 June 1945. A total of eighty-six LCSs saw combat off Okinawa before the war ended. Only twenty-one of the total one-hundred-thirty LCSs escaped combat duty during the war.

The bulk of combat for the LCSs was experienced during the Okinawa campaign and particularly on Radar Picket duty around that island. The table of organization for Okinawa consisted of Flotilla Three made up of LCSs *11–25, 29, 31, 33–40, 51–57* and *109–112*. Flotilla Four was made up of LCSs *61–69, 81–95*, and *114–123*. Flotilla Five included LCSs *2, 4, 70–74, 96–101, 102, 104*, and *125*. Duty time on Radar Picket was usually between ten to twelve days. LCSs first assumed these duties due to heavy losses of destroyers in the first days after they took the RP stations alone. Eighteen destroyers were sunk by kamikazes before LCSs were sent to support the remaining destroyers. Unofficial estimates credit more than one-hundred-fifty kamikazes downed by LCS gunners. With the help of the LCSs' firepower, the numbers of destroyers lost on RP was greatly reduced. It was likely at no other place or time during the Pacific War that that firepower was more appreciated.

Flotilla One was sent to support the amphibious assaults by the Australian I Corps, during the Borneo Campaign (1 May-21 July 1945). Their participation in that campaign began on 7 June. LCSs involved in combat at Borneo were *8, 28–30, 41–48, 50* and *58*.

During combat operations across the Pacific, five LCSs were sunk. Those, in numerical order, were LCS *7, 15, 26, 33* and *49*. Eight LCSs were damaged in combat to the extent they were out of action for repairs for longer than a month. Those eight were *27, 36, 37, 57, 88, 116, 119*, and *122*. Eleven LCSs were damaged but repaired within thirty days. They were *8,*

14, 20, 25, 31, 33, 51, 52, 57, 93, and *121*. A total of one-hundred-thirty-three sailors lost their lives while serving aboard LCSs.

Ships, as do the seemingly iron men who drive them, eventually grow too old to meet the needs and demands of warfare. The United States, shortly after war's end, began to modify, scrap, or rid themselves of vessels no longer having missions they were originally designed for. The *LCS 52* was a close-fire-support gunboat designed for a specific purpose in a specific kind of beach warfare; she fell quickly from grace. On 28 February 1949 she was reclassified as USS *LSSL-52* (Landing Ship Support Large). She served in that capacity until 29 July 1953. She made a familiar trip back to Japan, where she was loaned to that nation's new postwar navy. She was renamed *JMSDFS Sasayuri*. She was returned to the United States 29 August 1958. Sometime thereafter she was struck from the Naval Register.

December 1958—The old girl rose and ebbed with the crest of each wave. Otherwise she was motionless, her engines meticulously drained of their life's blood, oil and fuel. Below her main deck, where sailors of two nations had laughed, slept and read letters from home, stillness was broken only by the creaking of her bulkheads. The conning tower, pilot house and wardroom, too, all empty of any sign that men had once called her home. The tubs where her powerful guns had once sat lay vacant. Her teeth and claws jerked from their base, she was helpless against attack.

In the distance the whistle of large shells hurled from modern American fighting vessels could be heard as they closed with her. No alarms sounded, no one beat to quarters. She was alone, accepting of her execution. The shells pierced her skin with a speed and accuracy her first crew could have never imagined. The sea rushed through the punctures, bringing balance to nature. The attack continued for as long as she remained in sight.

The water quickly covered the mess deck, the spot where Ensign Burroughs' body had once lay in view of his many mates. The table where James Hawks had fought for life soon disappeared under the salty foam. She sank to the bottom, becoming a submerged monument to them both. Others, James Linn and Anthony Jawor, were already waiting on their old ship on the other side, their lives cut short after surviving the war.

Those old sailors who busily went about their daily lives knew not of her demise. The captains and officers did not know to order her crew to her rescue. Perhaps, had they been alerted, they would have done just that, formed a good defense and negotiated her salvation. They would have surely taken her to safe anchorage and moored her in a place of hallowed honor. The reality was, most passed away many years behind her never knowing her fate. She was a forgotten relic of a time that most never spoke of or wished to think of again. The close ties they had formed during that time at war remained throughout their lives but few acknowledged the over-sized can that had brought them together.

She served her mother country one last time and was sunk while acting as a target for naval gunfire practice. The *LCS 52* sits now somewhere on the bottom of the ocean, a home for shellbacks and pollywogs of a non-human sort. Her sisters, who were returned to the United States, all met the same fate. It is unknown if some old LCSs remain in some foreign dock or not. One for certain survived and lives in testimony to the gunboat men of World War II, who went down to the sea in Mighty Midgets.

12

Roll Call *LCS 52*

Commissioning Crew, September 23, 1944

Enlisted

Allard, Ernest T. (ser.no. 855-10-18):

Radioman 3rd Class **Ernest Thomas Allard** enlisted in the Navy on 23 October 1943 in Chicago, Illinois. Allard was transferred to the Hospital Ship USS *Relief* AH-1 on 14 July 1945. He was returned to *LCS 52* on 9 August 1945. He was aboard the *52* on 5 November 1945 and received a Captain's Mast that day. On 20 November 1945, Ernest was transferred to the USS *Torrance* (AKA 76).[1] He was listed in Laton's war journal as "Et" Allard of S. Racine Avenue, Chicago, Illinois. He was probably born 14 October 1917 and died in Cook County, Illinois on 9 September 1989.

Barron, Porter, Jr. (ser.no. 570-06-62):

Seaman 1st Class **Porter Barron, Jr.**, enlisted at Great Lakes, Illinois on 21 October 1942. He was advanced in rank on 1 December 1944 aboard *LCS 52*.[2] Porter returned to Nelsonville, Athens County, Ohio after the war. When Laton entered him in the war journal he had a home address on Grosvenor Street in Nelsonville.[3]

After the war, he worked for the U.S. Forestry Service and then later retired from the Tri-county Vocational School. Porter passed away on 15 April 1991 at 10:38 p.m. in Doctors Hospital of Nelsonville, Ohio. He married Elizabeth Ann Fisk, who died on 23 May 1999. The couple had two sons. Both Elizabeth and Porter were buried in Greenlawn Cemetery in Nelsonville.

Bauer, Clarence A. (ser.no. 869-87-66):

ETM 1st Class **Clarence Antone Bauer** enlisted 23 April 1943 at Mankato, Minnesota. He was advanced to RT1c (T) (LC) on 1 June 1945 ("Auth: BuPers C/L 297-44").[4] Laton's journal gave 923 N. 5th Street, Mankoto, Minnesota as his home. He was transferred to the separation center at Minneapolis on 5 March 1946.

Clarence was born 17 October 1924 in Blue Earth, Minnesota. He was working as a mechanic in 1948 and living at 923 N. 5th Street in Mankato. He married Mary Pat Amberg on 11 July 1953. The two lived at 517 E. Lafayette. Clarence retired from Northwestern Bell Telephone Company in 1991 after forty-three and a half years of service as an electronics technician. Mary and Clarence had one son and two daughters. His hobbies were fishing, and playing on his computer. He also enjoyed remolding and woodworking. Clarence died on 20 September 2013 and was buried at the Calvary Cemetery in Mankato, Minnesota.[5]

Beittel, Benjamin L. (ser.no. 922-71-63):

Radioman 3rd Class (LC) **Benjamin "Ben" Leonard Beittel** enlisted 5 April 1944 in Harrisburg, Pennsylvania. He was advanced to RdM2c (T) (LC) on 1 June 1945.[6] He was recorded as living at 364 W. North Street, Carlisle prior to the war in Laton's journal. At the end of March 1950 he applied for and received a pension based on his Navy service. He listed Franklin Street, Carlisle as his address. He stated that he was separated from active duty on 4 November 1945 at Bainbridge, Maryland. Ben passed away on 8 October 1989. He was buried at Westminster Memorial Gardens in Carlisle, Pennsylvania. He was married to Grace E. Harbach.

Bennett, Ervin (ser.no. 949-55-15):

Seaman 2nd Class **Ervin Bennett** enlisted in the Navy at Great Lakes, Illinois on 28 April 1944. Ervin was advanced in rank on 1 December 1944 aboard *LCS 52*. He was listed in Laton's war journal at East 96th Street, Garfield Heights, Ohio. On 1 February 1946 he was transferred to the separation center in Toledo, Ohio. In the 1940 Census Ervin was listed as an eighteen year old living at the same address he gave Laton. He was living with his parents Kenney and Kate Bennett. The census showed his birthplace as West Virginia and his birth year around 1922.

Bilton, Gerald P. (ser.no. 952-80-77):

Boatswain Mate 2nd Class **Gerald Patrick Bilton** enlisted on 24 May 1944 at Great Lakes, Illinois. Laton listed Gerald on Roger Street, Melvindale, Michigan at the beginning of the war. He was advanced to Seaman 1st Class on 16 November 1944. He received a Captain's Mast on 12 July 1945. He was transferred to the separation center at Great Lakes on 1 February 1946.[7] It was difficult to locate firm information on Gerald after the war. He may have lived his life in Alpena, Michigan, about five hours from where he was living when the war started. If so, Gerald holds three patents all pertaining to "method for controlling caliper and edge and corner delamination of hardboard." Records showed that he was born on 2 November 1918 in Alberta, Canada and died 24 December 2002 in Alpena.

Bledsoe, Gerald E. (ser.no. 727-06-68):

Seaman Third Class **Gerald E. Bledsoe** enlisted on 5 January 1944. He was listed in Laton's journal at 6th Street, Moline, Illinois before the war. Gerald was advanced to SM3c (T) on 15 January 1945 and then to SM2c (T) on 1 November 1945. He was transferred to Great Lakes on 24 April 1946 for release to inactive duty. Gerald was received for duty aboard USS *Wiltsie* 4 September 1948. Gerald was transferred from the USS *Wiltsie* (DD-716) on 30 September 1948 to "No. 411 to CO, Naval School, Acad, and College Prep, Bainbridge, Maryland."[8] He died in Sun City West, Arizona, on 23 November 2014 while this book was being written.[9]

Blough, Russell J. (ser.no. 949-49-49):

Motor Machinist's Mate 3rd Class **Russell Jay Blough** enlisted in the Navy on 25 April 1944. He was advanced in rank to "F1c" on 15 January 1945. On 5 October 1945 he was made a Motor Machinist's Mate 3rd Class (MoMM3c). He was transferred to the separation center at Toledo, Ohio on 1 February 1946.[10] Russell was born 6 October 1914. He died on

27 August 1962 and was buried in Woodlawn Cemetery in Wadsworth, Ohio. Russell was married to Bernice M. Blough.

Brantley, Jordan L. (ser.no. 831-12-84):

Coxswain **Jordan "Jerry" Lee Brantley** enlisted in the Navy on 5 January 1944 in Strake, Florida. He was transferred to the USS *Sierra* (AD 18) on 29 July 1945 along with Seaman Darnell. Jordan was sent to USS *Relief* (AH1) on 29 July 1945. He returned to the 52 from the USS *Relief* (AH1) on 3 August 1945. Jordon returned to *LCS 52* and was present for the quarter ending 30 September 1945. He was again transferred to the USS *Hansford* (APA 106) on 5 October 1945.[11] Jordan passed away on 2 March 1989 in Orange City, Florida.

Brashers, Albert L. (ser.no. 876-76-59):

Electricians Mate 3rd Class **Albert Lewis Brashers** enlisted on 6 October 1943 in Denver, Colorado. Albert received Captain's Masts on 13 October 1944, 22 August, and 5 November 1945. Albert was transferred to Shoemaker, California for release to inactive duty on 16 May 1946.[12] He was listed in the journal of Laton Burns as "Albert Brashiers, Route 1 Wiley, Colorado." Albert Brashers was born 16 June 1925 in Texas. He was the seventh of nine children born to Leroy Clark and Ethel M. Brashers. Leroy was a farmer who moved his family frequently. The family lived in Texas, Colorado and Missouri during Leroy's lifetime. Albert reenlisted in November 1948 and served through the Korean War. His service number was changed to "RA 17-240-164." The RA indicated Regular Army. He was listed as holding the rank of Sergeant First Class (SFC). He served until June of 1952. Albert was married to Florence Marie (probably Archuletta), of Gunnison, Colorado. After his second military tour, Albert worked as an electrician for Storey Electric in Grand Junction. He and Florence lived at 2881 F Road. Albert died 3 October 1960. He was buried in the Masonic and Odd Fellows Cemetery in Gunnison, Colorado.[13]

Burnette, Horace C., Jr. (ser.no. 893-55-75):

Signalman, 3rd Class **Horace C. "Smiley" Burnette, Jr.,** was from Norman Park, Georgia. He was born on 6 July 1925 in Cartersville, Georgia and passed away 5 March 2012 in Thomasville, Georgia. He was nicknamed "Smiley" and sometimes "Frog." Horace was married to Frankie Page Burnette. His parents were Horace Clinton, Sr., and Margurette R. LeFur Burnette. After his years in the military, Horace returned to Georgia and made a career as a maintenance supervisor at Georgia Power Company, from which he retired. He was buried at Deep Bottom Cemetery in Norman Park, Georgia.[14] As one of the signalmen onboard the 52, Burnette was trained to communicate with other ships and land-based units through flag semaphore, visual Morse code through signal lamp flashes (signal projector), and flag-hoist signaling. In the U.S. Navy, flagmen were often called by nicknames such as "Flags" or "Skivvy Waver." His home address in the journal was Norman Park, Georgia.

Burns, Laton (ser.no. 958-84-28):

Seaman 1st Class **Laton Burns** returned to his home state and married his sweetheart. He moved to Ohio where he worked for many years and raised his two children. He passed away on 7 September 1970.

Cazee, Hanford H. (ser.no. 955-75-70):

Seaman 1st Class **Hanford H. "Hank" Cazee** enlisted 28 April 1944 at USNTC Great Lakes. He was the subject of a Captain's Mast, 7 October 1944; no disposition was given.

Hanford was transferred to the separation center at Great Lakes on 1 February 1946.[15] He was recorded in the journal of Laton Burns at RR # 5, Bloomington, Indiana before the war. Hanford was born on 5 March 1918 in Monroe County, Indiana and passed away on 10 April 1987. He was buried at Clover Hill Cemetery in Harrodsburg, Indiana. Hanford was married to Beulah R. Cazee, who passed away 23 November 2010; she is buried next to Hanford. In the 1940 census they were living in Clear Creek, Indiana and Hanford was listed as a "labor." Hanford was the son of Logan and Lillian M. Lemon Cazee.[16]

Chavez, Joe F. (ser.no. 876-97-36):

Motor Machinist's Mate 3rd Class **Joe Floyd Chavez** was born 23 September 1925 and passed away on 27 April 2007. He enlisted in the U.S. Navy on 27 January 1944 in Denver, Colorado and was sent to USNTC Great Lakes. Joe was advanced to Fireman 1st Class (LC) on 1 May 1945 aboard the 52. He was transferred to the separation center at Shoemaker, California on 1 February 1946.[17] He was buried at Virgil Cemetery in Virgil, Colorado. Joe was listed in the wartime journal of Laton Burns at Box 5, Weston, Colorado. The 1981 city directory showed Joe living in Weston.

Cook, Claude H. (ser.no. 952-37-56):

Seaman 1st Class **Claude Harris Cook** enlisted at Great Lakes, Illinois on 26 April 1944. The following day he reported for his basic training at Great Lakes. Claude was sent to Fort Pierce, Florida for training on 13 June 1944 from NTC Great Lakes, Illinois. He was advanced in rank on 1 December 1944 aboard LCS 52 to Fire Controlman, 3rd Class.[18] His Personal Record Book (PRB) recorded his operations as "invasion and capture of Iwo Jima, 19 February to 8 March 1945; invasion of Okinawa, Ryukus, 1 April to 21 June 1945," and the "Occupation of Southern Honshu, Japan, 25 September 1945." His records also showed that he was aboard the USS *Consolation* (APH-115) from 1 November to 23 November 1945. He was sent from there to "a U.S. Naval Hospital Continental United States for further treatment and disposition." His records stated that he was a "third class" swimmer. On 5 March 1946 he was transferred to Great Lakes for the purpose of processing his discharge.[19] Claude passed away in Lansing, Michigan on 2 June 1978.

Russell Copeland was one of the old men aboard. He was fascinated by the life seventeen-year-old Virgil Thill had lived prior to the war and often talked of writing a book of Virgil's exploits (Virgil Thill collection).

Copeland, Russell S. (ser.no. 924-97-14):

Seaman 1st, Class **Russell S. Copeland** entered service on 15 May 1944 at Great Lakes. Russell was advanced in rank on 1 December

1944 onboard the 52. Laton had his home address in the journal on Scott Drive, Dravosburg, Pennsylvania. On 1 February 1946 Russell was reassigned to the separation center at Sampson, New York.

After the war he resettled in Oklahoma. According to his obituary, Russell spent his postwar years working in real estate and for General Electric. He passed away on 2 September 1999. Russell was married to Betty Copeland. Russell was buried in the Israel Private Family Cemetery in Yukon, Oklahoma.[20] He was a graduate of McKeesport High School in Pennsylvania, a small community near Boston.

Crowe, Wilford C. (ser.no. 283-51-81) W.I.A.:

Fireman 2nd Class **Wilford Carl Crowe** enlisted on 25 February 1941 in Cleveland, Ohio. He was received at the receiving station, NOB Norfolk, Virginia from the USNR Signal School at Chicago on 22 May 1941. Wilford was received aboard the USS *Matagorda* (AVP 22) on 18 March 1943 at Guantanamo Bay, Cuba. A Report of Changes was submitted from the *Matagorda* on 22 March 1943 which showed several of the crew transferred, including Wilford, but the transfer location was not included.

He was wounded in action during the attack of 27 May 1945. He was at that time transferred to the Hospital Ship *APA 179* on 28 May for treatment. Wilford returned to *LCS 52* on 13 June 1945. He was present for duty aboard the USS *Trippe* (DD 403) on the quarters ending 1 March through 1 July 1946. Wilford was advanced to Electrician's Mate 1st Class on 1 April 1946 while aboard the *Trippe*. Wilford was next transferred to the USS *Clymer* (APA 27) for "FFT nearest RecSta Cont. U.S." on 20 August 1946. That action was noted on the decommissioning report of the *Trippe* dated 28 August 1946. Wilford then joined the crew of the USS *Eugene A. Greene* (DD 711) on 6 January 1947. He was transferred from USS *Gearing* (DD 710) "for duty." On January 23 he was transferred again to "Tran. RS. Norfolk, Va. for discharge" from USS *Eugene A. Greene*.[21]

In the register of Ohio men wounded in action, Wilford's parents were given as Mr. and Mrs. Jesse Curtis Crowe, of Mingo Junction. Wilford was born 29 July 1922 and passed away 1 June 1979. His last residence was given as Mingo Junction, Ohio. His son, Wilford C. Crowe, Jr., passed away in 2009 and was buried at Oakland Cemetery in Mingo Junction; it is very likely that Wilford Sr. was therefore buried nearby. Wilford's marriage to Anna M. Crowe appears to have ended in divorce at the end of April 1979 after twenty-seven years. This was only weeks before Wilford passed away. Anna later remarried Kenneth J. Dahlem of Mingo Junction. When Kenneth passed away, Wilford Jr. was listed as a deceased stepson.

Cullen, Charles L. (ser.no. 838-67-04):

Storekeeper, 2nd Class **Charles Lawrence Cullen** was born 13 November 1906 and passed away on 30 June 1998.[22] Larry was advanced in rank to SK 2nd Class on 1 May 1945. He was transferred to the separation center at New Orleans on 1 February 1946. He was married to Alma Milholland Cullen, who passed away in 2004. Larry's parents were Harold D. and Bessie M. French Cullen. Larry and Alma were buried side-by-side in Foley, Alabama. When Laton recorded Larry's address in his journal sometime in late 1944, his home of record was South 18th Street in Birmingham, Alabama.

Larry, as he was known to his family, was a very interesting and diverse man. He wrote poetry, and loved to read. After the war he returned to Alabama. One of his favorite things to do was fish. He visited the coast as often as possible and enjoyed going in June in particular.

He had his own small boat and rowed it around the bay sporting his white Navy cap atop his head. His daughter said that he loved to catch speckled and white trout, and redfish. He also gigged at night for flounder, using a light in the water to lure them near, and then struck at them with the gig while standing on the prow of his skiff. He eventually got a very small outboard motor, which he considered an exciting addition.[23]

He had his own wood turning lathe at home and made many of the furniture pieces for the family. His daughter said that he often turned out end tables but was just as good at hobby chests and other designs. "Dad could fix anything," his daughter said. Along with fishing and woodworking, Larry loved his Alabama football and listened religiously to the Saturday afternoon games.[24] Larry was a mischievous sort growing up and his sense of humor never departed him.

Davis, Gerald (ser.no. 929–01–70):

Seaman 1st Class **Gerald "Pops" Davis** was born 18 May 1910 in Doddridge County, West Virginia and died 17 May 1987 in Harrison County, West Virginia. He was the son of Wilson and Bessie Davis Davis. He was married to Iva Davis, who passed away in 1991. Gerald was buried at the Odd Fellows Cemetery, Salem, West Virginia.[25] Gerald entered service on 14 April 1944. Gerald was listed in the war journal on Water Street, Salem, West Virginia. He is shown released from active duty on 10 November 1945—he was listed under "casualties."

Del Castillo, Felix (ser.no. 817–00–70):

Seaman 2nd Class **Felix Del Castillo** enlisted on 20 December 1943. Felix was the subject of a Captain's Mast on 1 November 1944; no punishment was recorded. He was transferred to the "U.S. Naval Base Saipan, Auth: Med. Form G." on 14 February 1945.[26] That was the day that *LCS 52* left for Iwo Jima. Apparently, Felix suffered some catastrophic injury or illness that ended his navy career. He never returned to active duty again. Because he never made it into Laton's journal there is no way of knowing for certain where he was living before the war. Felix enlisted at NTS Sampson, New York. A Felix Del Castillo was located who had a social security number issued out of New York before 1951. That SSN matched a Navy World War II veteran born 4 January 1909 and who passed away on 26 June 1987. Records indicated that he enlisted on 27 December 1943 and was released on 11 October 1945. His last known residence was Tampa, Florida. He was buried at Hillsboro Memorial Cemetery in Brandon, Florida. Felix was buried next to his spouse, Carmen V. Del Castillo, who died in 1997.

De Maio, Eugene A. (ser.no. 924 -97–22) W.I.A.:

Seaman 1st Class **Eugene Albert De Maio** enlisted 15 May 1944 from 1325 Gibbon, Pittsburgh, Pennsylvania. He was advanced to Seaman 1st Class on 1 December 1944. He was among the crew wounded by the suicide plane on 27 May 1945 while on picket duty. He was transferred to the Hospital Ship *APA 21* on 28 May. Eugene was shown transferred to the Hospital Ship USS *Solace* on 30 May from the USS *Crescent City*. On 4 June he was then transferred from the *Solace* to "USN Base Hospital NO. 18, FFTMT & DISP."[27]

Eugene Albert Demaio was the son of Vincent (Vincenzo) and Josephine Bertolozzi Demaio. Vincent came to the U.S. in 1913 as a twenty-three-year-old laborer from Castellarano, Italy. Eugene's mother also arrived from Italy. The family was living at 1313 Seitz Street during the early 1940s. Vincent had worked as a construction worker for most of his time in the States. He certainly had been at Booth & Flinn Company since he registered for the World War I draft in 1917 and through 1942 when he registered for the World War II draft.[28] He most likely had a hand in the building of two of Booth & Flinn's more noteworthy construction projects in Pittsburgh, the Armstrong (1926) and Liberty Tunnels (1924). When he registered for the World War II draft he stated that he had one glass eye. In 1940, Pietro, Josephine's brother, was living in the house and working as a cook.

Eugene reported for duty on the USS *Missouri* (BB-63) on 18 March 1946. He was separated from service on 3 June 1946 at PSC Lido Beach, New York. He applied for a veteran's pension in 1950. At the time he was living in Carnegie, Pennsylvania. On that application, Eugene stated that he also did naval service on the USS *Charger* (CVE 30) from 16 January to 11 March 1946. No musters of that service could be located (most likely due to another form of his name being used). He listed his dates of service on the *Missouri* as 18 March to 31 May 1946.[29]

In 1981 he was shown in the directory at Briscoe Street in Pittsburgh. Eugene was recorded on a veteran's burial form as born on 15 February 1926 and died 9 October 1987. He was buried at the Calvary Cemetery in Pittsburgh.[30] On military records, his name was listed under three different spellings. In the 1980s, Eugene was living at 44 Rhodes Avenue, Pittsburgh. Gloria A. De Maio continued to live at that address throughout the 1990s. She was a couple of years Eugene's junior and it could be assumed (but not verified) they were married.

Di Priter, John (ser.no. 924-97-34):

Seaman 2nd Class **John Di Priter** enlisted 15 May 1944 at McKeesport, Pennsylvania. He was listed in the Burns journal as John Depritter of 500 George Street, Turtle Creek, Pennsylvania. John was the subject of a Captain's Mast on 1 November 1944. On 1 May 1945 John was promoted to SC 3rd Class while aboard *LCS 52*. He was shown on a report of changes, advanced to SC 2nd Class (T) on 15 November 1945. On the 20th of that same month John was transferred to the USS *Torrance* (AKA 76).[31]

He was living in Allegheny, Pennsylvania at the time of the 1920 census. In May of 1950, John applied for compensation through the state of Pennsylvania. He gave his birthday date as 22 September 1913 and his place of birth as Wilmerding, Allegheny County, Pennsylvania. He was still residing at 500 George Street, Turtle Creek when he applied for his service compensation.[32] John was a first-generation American. His parents, Angelo and Mary Di Priter were both born in Italy. In the 1920 census they were shown as living in a rented home in Wilmerding, Pennsylvania. The father was recorded as immigrating to the U.S. in 1906. However, on the same census John's mother was shown to have been born in Brazil and immigrated to the U.S. in 1902. Both parents seem to have come to America from Italy, indirectly in his mother's case.

Fields, Robert R. (ser.no. 293-51-88):

Seaman 1st Class **Robert R. Fields** enlisted on 7 April 1944 at Indianapolis, Indiana. He was advanced to 1st Class on 1 July 1945 aboard the *52*. Robert was transferred to the separation center at Great Lakes, Illinois on 1 February 1946.[33] Roberts is shown in the journal as having a prewar address on Backaman Street in Indianapolis.

Gaham, Jack C. (ser.no. 293-51-92):

Seaman 1st Class **Jack Carlton Gaham** enlisted 7 April 1944. He was listed in the war journal at Lesale Street, Fort Wayne, Indiana. Jack was transferred to Great Lakes for release from active duty on 16 May 1946. He returned to the Fort Wayne area after the war.

Jack's father was the son of a Montana farmer. Jack's biological father was Ralph J. Gaham. His mother was the former Imogene E. Hire. Jack Carlton was born in Fort Wayne, Indiana in 1926. He was the only son out of six children. The family lived in a house at 1632 Boone Street. While Ralph was with the family, 1930s, he worked as a wire drawer at Dudlo Manufacturing in Fort Wayne. The hair-thin enamel wire made by the company went into detection systems the British used to thwart the German U-boat problem during the Great War. The Fort Wayne branch of the company shut down in June of 1933 and Ralph went looking elsewhere. By 1935, Ralph and his new wife, Sue, were living in Grass Valley, California. Ralph and his twenty-five-year-old stepson were working as miners in a gold mines. Grass Valley, Nevada County, came in a close second in the 1848 California gold rush. Its second most profitable time was between 1930 and 1940. In those years, two mines, Idaho-Maryland Mines and Empire-Star, employed 4,000 miners and pulled out of the ground more than fifty-million-dollars' worth of gold.

Meanwhile, back in Indiana, Jack's mom married Robert L. Whitehouse in October of 1937. Robert was an automobile salesman. Jack, four of his sisters and two of Robert's sons, from his first marriage, lived under the same roof. Robert was well-off enough to employ a live-in servant to help with the household tasks; Imo later married John T. Pasko.

Jack married Madonna R. Rice of Jefferson, Indiana. He retired from International Harvester in 1978 after giving that company thirty years of dedicated service. He was an avid fisherman and bingo player. Madonna and he raised eight children together over their sixty-seven years of marriage. Jack passed away on 20 December 2013. He was buried in the Highland Park Cemetery, Fort Wayne. During the years he spent in the military, he changed the spelling of his surname to "Gaham" instead of "Gahan" as his father used.[34]

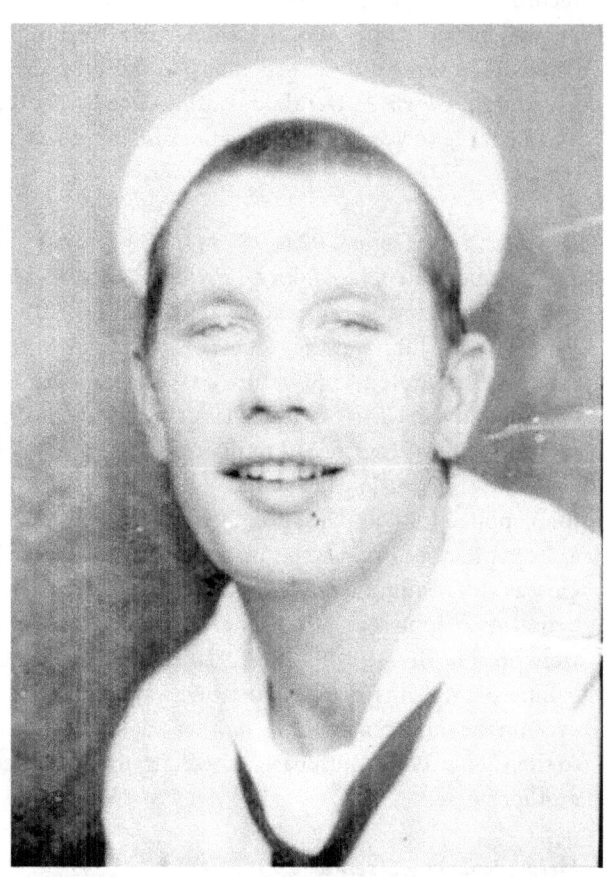

Jack Gaham flew under everyone's radar. He seldom ended up in liberty stories, photos or trouble. Jack was, nevertheless, one of the original crew. He grew up under three father figures and went on to play a part in rebuilding postwar America (Virgil Thill collection).

Gardner, William E. (ser.no. 609–27–73):

Seaman 3rd Class **William E. Gardner** enlisted on 11 January 1944 in Rochester, New York. He was listed in the journal as W. Garner, P.O. Box in Natural Bridge, New York. William was advanced to SM3c (T) (LC) on 1 June 1945. William was born in Clayton, New York. He returned from the war and settled in Liverpool, New York. He married Gertrude and worked at Crucible Steel until he retired. William passed away at the Community General Hospital on 19 October 2008. He was buried in Our Lady of Peace Cemetery in Liverpool. He was eighty-one years old at the time of his death. One of the means by which William's identity was confirmed was from the postings of pictures on a pay genealogy site. One of the pictures had William and a shipmate clad in grass skirts on a Pacific island. Those were identical, down to the palm trees, to the ones in Laton's photo album. Among the pictures of William was one of him wearing what appears by insignia to be a Natural Bridge Fireman's dress uniform. There was no mention of him being a fireman in his obituary; however, it may have been a short-lived career.

Gloor, Jack D. (ser.no. 293–54–34) W.I.A.:

Seaman 1st Class **Jack D. Gloor** entered service on 19 April 1944 at Great Lakes. While on *LCS 52*, Jack, Jim Nelson and Ralph Prendergast all received a Captain's Mast on 21 March 1945.[35] Jack was transferred 11 May 1945 to the Hospital Ship *APA 21* and showed a status of "wounded in action."[36] He was received aboard the *Alvin C. Cockrell* (DE 366) from "USN RecSta., T.I. San Francisco, Calif. for temporary duty" on 15 February 1946. Jack was transferred to a station in California on 2 May 1946.

Hailman, William T. (ser.no. 293–51–89):

Seaman 3rd Class **William Taylor Hailman** resided on N. Main Street,

Carl Reed (left) and William Gardner trying out their hula skills (Virgil Thill collection).

Frankfort, Indiana before the war. Hailman enlisted in the Navy on 7 April 1944. William was the subject of a "Deck Court" on 19 October 1944; no punishment recorded. William T. Hailman was advanced to next rank on 15 February 1946. He was transferred to PSC, Great Lakes, for release to inactive duty on 16 May 1946.[37] He was born on 5 June 1926 in Frankfort, Indiana. He died 6 September 1995. His footstone reads, service aboard USS *Suwannee* from 1944–1946, but no records of his presence on that ship could be located.[38] According to his obituary, he worked at Nickel Plate Railroad in signal maintenance for twenty years. He also worked at Butler Service Station as a mechanic. He first married in 1946 but divorced in 1969. He married Emily Noe Blackstone on 12 June 1979. His parents were Charles M. and Cecile O. Hailman. He was buried in Scotland Cemetery, Frankfort, Indiana.

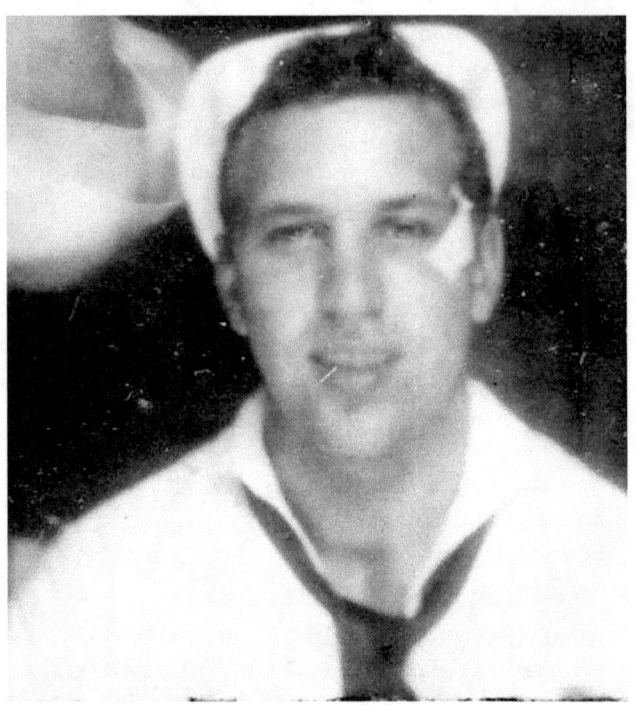

A shipmate could not bear not sailing his Dixie Cup cap into William Hailman's picture (Virgil Thill collection).

Hall, James S. (ser.no. 928-85-53):

Fireman 1st Class **James S. Hall** was the son of Lace and Lille White Hall of Logan, West Virginia. His parents were married in 1915 in Logan. Lace made a living doing whatever he could find. He was not a lazy man. At age sixteen, Lace was working on a coal tipple in Logan County. James ("Sam") was the oldest child and shortly after he was born, Lace registered for the World War I draft. He was working as a packer in the Logan Grocery Store at the time. By the time Lace had to register for the World War II draft he was working at the Pure Oil Company as a driver. When he was required to answer if there was any reason he should not be drafted for the Great War, Lace replied, "have family to support."[39] When he died in 1962 he was a merchant.

James entered service on 24 March 1944 at Logan, West Virginia. James was advanced in rank on 1 May 1945 to F1c (LC) onboard *LCS 52*. He was entered in the war journal at a box number in Logan, West Virginia. He was married to Vaudna Virginia Peck when he entered service. The two were married 13 January 1934; James was seventeen. James owned and operated a store in Logan after the war. He and Vaudna played host to Lois and Virgil Thill in April of 1994.[40] James was born 14 March 1916 and died 17 August 2003. He was buried at Forest Lawn Cemetery in Pecks Mill, West Virginia.

Hanning, Paul A. (ser.no. 313-90-76):

Fireman 1st Class **Paul A. Hanning** enlisted 26 April 1944 at Great Lakes. He was changed to Fireman 2nd Class on 1 December 1944 from Seaman 2nd Class. He was advanced in rank 1 May 1945 to F1c (LC) while aboard the *LCS 52*. He was advanced to MoMM 3rd Class on 24 January 1946. He was transferred to PSC, Great Lakes, for release to inactive duty on 16 May 1946.[41]

A Paul Arthur Hanning was born in Michigan 1 June 1926 and died in Clearwater, Florida, 4 May 1989, but that information could not be corroborated with the sailor from *LCS 52*. However, his Navy service dates for enlistment and release are close to that of F1c Hanning of *LCS 52*. There was a Paul A. Hanning (abt. 3 years old) living with Paul H. Hanning and Erma M. Hanning at Royal Oak, Oakland, Michigan in the 1930 census.

Hawks, James L. (ser.no. 263-97-87) K.I.A.:

Seaman 2nd Class **James Lee Hawks** was born to James Lee, Sr., and Rhoda Alberty Hawks on 14 March 1928 in Cabarrus, North Carolina. James enlisted in the Navy on 1 March 1944 at Raleigh, North Carolina. He transferred from "ATB, Ft. Pierce, Fla." on 29 July 1944 to the USS *Wyoming* at Norfolk Naval Yard, Portsmouth, Virginia. He was present aboard the *Wyoming* on the month ending 31 July 1944. He was then transferred to "ATB. Little Creek, VA." on 11 August 1944. On 28 May Lt. Harper reported James as transferred to the hospital ship *APA 21*, "Wounded in action."[42] James died of his wounds sustained during the attack of 27 May, after being evacuated from Okinawa. Lieutenant Harper said after his death that, "Hawks was a Carolina lad, cheerful, polite and a splendid man to have aboard."[43] James was first buried in the American cemetery on Okinawa and then moved to the National Memorial Cemetery of the Pacific, Honolulu, Hawaii on 10 March 1949. He was re-interred in "sect or plot 'M'" in "Grave or lot '395.'" James was listed as a Protestant on his military records.

Hedger, Donald C. (ser.no. 635-38-22) W.I.A.:

Seaman 2nd Class **Donald C. Hedger** enlisted on 1 March 1944. Donald Hedger was listed with a prewar address at RR.3 Taylor Mill Road, Covington, Kentucky in Laton's journal. He was the subject of a "deck Court" on 19 October 1944. He and Hailman both received the same on that day; it might be assumed whatever indiscretion was committed was done with a buddy. Donald was transferred to the Hospital Ship *APA 179* on 28 May 1945. He was listed on that report as "wounded in action."[44] He did return to the 52 after being treated.[45]

Donald was born 7 April 1926 in Kenton County, Kentucky. His parents were Helen Lakeman and Raymond C. Hedger. After the war, he returned to the Covington area and was listed in the 1948 directory as working as a clerk for David D. Fisk. He married June C. Cornelius and the two raised a family in Fort Mitchell, Kentucky. Donald passed away in April 1987.

Henry, Austin J. (ser.no. 808-36-92):

Gunners Mate 3rd Class **Austin J. Henry** entered the Navy on 20 December 1943 at New Haven, Connecticut. He did his training at Fort Pierce, Florida. He then trained aboard the USS *Wyoming* from 29 July to 11 August 1944. Austin was advanced to Gunners Mate 3rd Class on 1 December 1944 onboard *LCS 52*. He and Richard Hile were transferred to the USS *Hansford* on 5 October 1945.[46] He was listed in the journal of Laton Burns, residing on Green Street, Hartford, Connecticut before the war.

He may have also lived in Middletown before the war. The 1932 directory showed an Austin J. Henry as an attendant at the Connecticut State Hospital (CSH). His age was listed on the 1930 census as about thirty-three and employment at CSH. His occupation status

Donald Hedger (left) and Harvey Schroder with unknown women. The boys of 52 enjoying the amenities of the Hawaiian Islands (Virgil Thill collection).

changed in 1937 to fireman at CSH. Also working there throughout the time Austin was employed at CSH was Bertha Henry, who was listed as a barber. Only two Navy veterans could be located in the VA death index by the name of Austin Henry. The first was born 27 June 1911. The second was born 23 October 1925. In the 1962 Hartford directory, Austin J. was listed as married to Helen E. and they were living on Baltic.

Hile, Richard F. (ser.no. 872-24-54) W.I.A.:

Seaman 1st Class (QM) **Richard Francis Hile** enlisted 15 November 1943 in Lincoln, Nebraska. He was advanced to QM3c (T) (LC) on 1 June 1945. On 5 October 1945, Richard was transferred to the USS *Hansford* (APA 106). His prewar address was RR#1 Lincoln, Nebraska. Richard returned to the 52 after being wounded on 27 May. He was transferred to the USS *Hansford* on 5 October 1945 and finished his service aboard her.

After the war, Richard returned to his wife and children in Nebraska. The family lived in Lincoln at 3041 N. 46th Street. Richard worked for the Chicago, Burlington & Quincy Railroad (CB&QRR) as a timekeeper through the fifties and sixties. He and Helen raised two daughters and three sons together.

His brother Donald, after being wounded aboard the *Hadley* on 11 May, recovered and went on to serve on the USS *General J.C. Breckinridge* (AP176). After his service Donald worked for Continental Oil Company for thirty-seven years. Donald married his wife Shirley in 1949. Both brothers loved to play golf. Richard enjoyed bowling and dancing and Donald liked to travel. Richard was described as a diehard Nebraska Huskers supporter. Richard passed away on 13 November 2005 and was buried in Lincoln Memorial Park.[47]

Hill, Harry Lee, Jr. (ser.no. 816-62-57):

Gunners Mate 3rd Class **Harry Lee Hill, Jr.**, was born 29 January 1915 and died 23 July 1961. He was buried in the Old Fellows Cemetery in Milford, Delaware. Laton listed him living on South Walnut Street in Milford, Delaware before the war. He enlisted in the Navy on 20 December 1943 at Camden, New Jersey. On 1 December 1944 he was advanced in rank to Seaman 1st Class. Harry was advanced to GM3c on 1 December 1944.[48] Though this is unconfirmed information, Harry's mother who was working in a powder plant in Milford apparently died in an accidental explosion in that factory in the 1940s. Her name may have been Louise Knipp Hill. This particular record is thin evidence for that event in Harry's life, as his mother's name was listed in other (unsubstantiated) records as Minnie Fleetwood. Harry is listed by this source as being married twice and having one daughter by each of those spouses.

Holland, Muscoe C., Jr. (ser.no. 223-73-63):

Muscoe C. Holland, Jr., enlisted 13 June 1940 at NRS New York. Holland had a long and distinguished career as a sailor. He was aboard the USS *Kearny* on 13 September 1940, when she set sail. He received a change of rating to "Sea2c" on 13 October 1940. He was promoted to Seaman 1st Class on 1 May 1941 while aboard the *Kearny*. He received a change of rating to Coxswain on 4 January 1942. Holland was transferred to the USS *George Clymer*, transferred from Headquarters, 8th Naval District, New Orleans on 21 June 1942. On 1 August 1942 Holland was appointed "Boatswain's Mate Second Class." Holland was then transferred to "Commander Landing Craft Flotilla, South Pacific for duty" on 24 May 1943. From there, Holland was received aboard the *LCI (L) 23* on 29 May 1943. He was received onboard the *LCS 52* on 23 September 1944. He was transferred to ConWest SeaFron on 1 February 1946. It appears that he may have gone to another ship, *DD-696* around 1 October 1946.[49] He retired from the Navy and lived in California for the remainder of his life. He died in San Diego on 22 July 1977. His wife was Virginia W. Holland. They had a son, Muscoe Coleman Holland III.

Jawor, Anthony D. (ser.no. 952-19-92) W.I.A.:

Seaman 1st Class **Anthony David Jawor** enlisted 11 April 1944 at Port Huron, Michigan. He was transferred from the USS *Wyoming* after training to ATB Little Creek, Virginia. He was listed as advanced to S1c on 1 December 1944 per "Report of Change" for the month ending 31 December 1944. The Report of Changes for the month ending 31 May 1945 reflected that Anthony was transferred to Hospital Ship *APA 179* with a status of "wounded in action," the result of the suicide plane attack of 27 May 1945. On 13 June 1945 Anthony was received back aboard *LCS 52* from *APA 179*. Another entry showed him received from *LST 675* on 12 June 1945. He was transferred to the separation center at Great Lakes, Illinois on 1 February 1946.[50] Laton listed him in the journal at Sturges Street, Port Huron, Michigan before the war. He was also listed in the register of Michigan wounded in action on 3019 Sturges Street, in Port Huron. His spouse was given as Alfreda Helena Jawor. They were married on 1 September 1939. Anthony David Jawor was born on 31 August 1918 and passed away on 18 December 1953. He was buried in Mount Hope Cemetery in Port Huron, Michigan.[51] Anthony was aboard a civilian passenger liner, the *Iris*, which arrived in Boston from Padloping Island, New Brunswick on 2 December 1943. The manifest listed his place of birth as Detroit and included his address in Port Huron, as well as his birth date. He gave his age as twenty-five during that trip. There was no further information as to why or how long he had been out of the country.[52]

Johnson, Dewane L. (ser.no. 961-55-38):

Seaman 1st Class **Dewane L. Johnson** enlisted on 10 December 1943 in Omaha, Nebraska. Dewane was advanced to the rank of Seaman 1st Class on 16 November 1944. He was transferred to the Separation Center at Minneapolis, California on 5 March 1946.[53] Dewane married Beverly A. Holling on 5 November 1949 and they owned a farm near Storla, South Dakota; Dewane loved farming. He was an avid fisherman and poker player. His wife recalled that he told of many hours aboard ship playing card games with his friends. The real tragedy, Dewane survived combat but was later killed in a tractor accident while doing the job he loved the most. Dewane L. Johnson passed away on 9 February 1992, and his last residence was Letcher, South Dakota. Dewane was buried in the Victor Lutheran Cemetery in Mount Vernon, South Dakota. Beverly stated that they attended the ship's reunion together and she attended one after Dewane's death.[54]

Johnson, Ulysses, Sr. (ser.no. 967-18-31):

Steward's Mate, First Class **Ulysses Johnson, Sr.,** enlisted on 27 April 1944 in Memphis, Tennessee. He was advanced to StM1c on 1 June 1945 while aboard the *52*. The Report of Changes reflected that Johnson was the subject of a Captain's Mast on 4 August 1945. Ulysses was transferred to the USS *Rankin* (AKA 103) on 2 November 1945. On that same date he was listed aboard the *Rankin* for the purpose of transportation to the States for separation.[55]

Keilty, John T. (ser.no. 386-90-94):

John T. Keilty was advanced in rank on 1 May 1945 to MoMM 2nd Class. On 22 May 1946 he was transferred to the Columbia River Group, 19th Fleet, for assignment. He was then received at the Naval Amphibious Base, Coronado, California on 14 June 1946. He was picked up by USS *LSM 437* in June of that year. He served aboard that vessel until 14 March 1947, when he was sent to Guam to be transported home to the States for discharge.

Keith, Lloyd C. (ser.no. 958-84-270):
Quarter Master 3rd Class **Lloyd C. Keith** enlisted on 29 April 1944 through NRS Louisville, Kentucky. He received a Captain's Mast on 5 November 1945; there was no disposition recorded. On 1 December 1944 Keith was advanced to S1c and on 15 February 1946 he was advanced to QM3c while aboard the 52.[56]

Kochanowicz, Charles J. (ser.no. 244-89-07):
Gunners Mate 3rd Class **Charles J. Kochanowicz** entered service on 19 November 1942 at Philadelphia, Pennsylvania. He was aboard the USS *Sloat* (DE245) 30 September 1943 through 31 March 1944. He was advanced to GM3c on 1 December 1943 while aboard the *Sloat*. The ship left Casablanca, French Morocco on 7 December 1943—to sea. He was transferred to Fort Pierce, Florida on 22 May 1944 from the *Sloat* at Norfolk, Virginia. He was shown received at Norfolk Training Station on 16 August 1943.

Charles was advanced in grade from Seaman 1st Class to GM2c on 1 December 1944 aboard *LCS 52*. On the Report of Changes ending the month of 31 July 1945 he was "Reduced" on 24

July 1945 to GM3c. The report entered the following explanation, "Capt's Mast. Reduced to GM3c, Negligence of Duty." On the Report of Changes for the month ending 31 August 1945 Charles had three separate entries. They were listed as follows in the order stated on the report. On 15 August he was the subject of a Captain's Mast but no punishment was recorded. The following day, the 16th, he was transferred to "Receiving Station Navy No. 3964."[57] On 27 August 1945 Charles was received back aboard *LCS 52* with the notation, "Receiving Station Navy No. 3964." Based on the short length of time his absence was noted and that he left on the heels of a Captain's Mast, he may have been sent to the land base for punishment. Charles was transferred to the USS *Torrance* (AKA 76) on 20 November 1945.[58] According to the journal, "C.J. Kochanowitz" was living on Tulip Street in Philadelphia before the war. Indications were that Charles sold a home on Susquehanna Street in Philadelphia in 2001. Public records stated that he died in 2002 at the age of eighty-seven.

Libby, Galen C. (ser.no. 823-30-73):
Gunners Mate 2nd Class **Galen Carl Libby** entered service on 15 February 1943 at NRS Bangor, Maine. He was received aboard *LST 242* on 29 July 1943 from ATB Solomons, Maryland. Galen received a promotion to S1c on 1 September 1943. His rating was changed on 1 December to GM3c. He joined the crew of *LCS 52* on her commissioning day. Laton Burns listed GM1C Libby in his journal with a residence in Garland, Maine. He was advanced in rank to Gunners Mate 2nd Class on 1 December 1944 aboard *LCS 52*. He was advanced to Gunner's Mate 1st Class on 15 November 1945. He was sent to the separation center at Boston, Massachusetts on 1 February 1946.[59]

Linn, James L. (ser.no. 655-94-91):
Motor Machinist's Mate 3rd Class **James Lee Linn** was living at "R. # 4" Albany, Oregon, before the war. James was born 25 December 1925 in Albany. James was the son of Simon P. and Georgia F. Small Linn. He was married to Glorian Z. Gladhart. He was transferred to the separation center at Bremerton, Washington on 1 February 1946. After surviving the war James died in a tractor accident on his farm at Route # 4 on 23 April 1954. He was buried at the Riverside Cemetery in Albany, Linn County, Oregon.[60] Linn along with John Keilty, Joe

Chavez, Russell Blough, and Lloyd Keith, also at one time or another rated as machinist mates, were responsible for mechanical maintenance and operation of a number of machines aboard ship. Their tasks could have included everything keeping the ship alive and moving from turbines, engines, and all things with moving parts.

May, Joseph H. (ser.no. 962-59-23):

Seaman 2nd Class **Joseph Harold May** enlisted on 28 April 1944. On the Report of Changes for May 1945 Joseph was advanced to S1c on 1 July 1945 while aboard the 52. That same report showed that he enlisted in Fostorio, Ohio. Laton showed him at a prewar address of R. # 3, Sycamore, Ohio.

Joseph was named after his grandfather. His own father was William Thomas May and his mother was the former Elizabeth Miller. Joseph was born 6 June 1911 in Marion County, Ohio. His father was a farmer who settled in the rural township of Sycamore. Joseph shared his boyhood home with five older sisters, one older brother and a younger sister, Viola. After Joseph's father died in 1923, the children departed the home. By 1930, eighteen-year-old Joseph had taken the responsibility as head of the household for his widowed mother and younger sister. Joseph was working as a laborer for the Stand Pottery Company. He married Alice Kunkle on 8 September that same year. With the war looming, Joseph was taking care of five of the seven children he and Alice would have together. The family was also host to two nephews residing there. Joseph was still working in the manufacture of pottery as a caster.

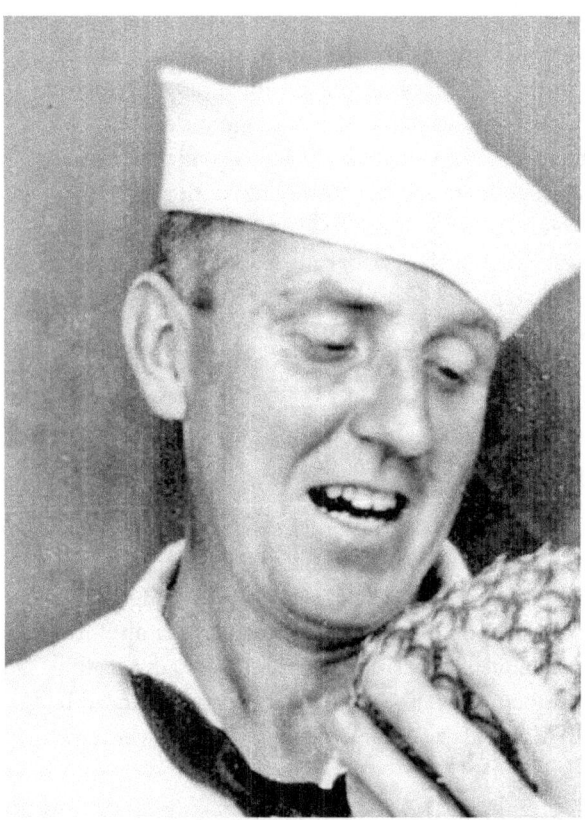

Joseph May, like Gaham, came from a large family. He lost his father at age twelve and became the man of the household for his widowed mother and sisters. He lost his youngest sister to complications from surgery one month after LCS 52 sailed for the war zone. He was, of course, unable to return home for her funeral. In Hawaii, he did manage to make friends with a pineapple, though (Virgil Thill collection).

Only a month after LCS 52 was commissioned, Joseph's sister, Viola, entered the hospital to have her gallbladder removed. She died five days later from complications, as her father had from his acute gallbladder problems.[61] Heading into battle, the death of his younger sister was a heavy blow to Joseph. Joseph left the service in November of 1945. He returned to Ohio, where he farmed and took a job at American Standard in Tiffin, Ohio. He worked there for ten years. He was employed with the Ohio Department of Transportation for fifteen more years. Joseph passed away on 17 April 1992. His wife, Alice, preceded him in death in 1981.

He was buried in the Pleasant View Cemetery, Wyandot County, near his parents and sister Viola.[62]

Nelson, Jim (ser.no. 552-53-47):

SC2c (LC) **Jim Nelson** enlisted 2 July 1942 at Charleston, West Virginia. Jim was picked up at the receiving station, San Francisco on 15 November 1942. He was assigned to LCT (5) Flotilla Seven that date. On 15 December 1943 Flotilla Seven formed with the assault forces off the beaches of Arawe on the southern cost of New Britain. Jim was a part of Flotilla Seven's landings of equipment and supplies on the beachhead of Peleliu Island. The LCTs were also engaged in picking up soldiers adrift in rubber boats from the failed landings at Umtingalu (Blue Beach). Initially, the transports were meeting with small, but surmountable logistical and planning problems. At 08:55 the first waves of Japanese planes slipped through the CAP. Flotilla Seven's commander recorded fifteen dive-bombers and seven fighters targeting his ships. The ships managed to maneuver and avoid damage. Throughout D–Day, only one sailor was injured. During the following days, the echelons of Flotilla Seven were under almost constant aerial attack. On the 17th, the formations were bombed and strafed by an estimated forty to fifty Vals, Zekes and Nates.[63] The result was three direct hits on *APC 21*(Small Coastal Transport), which sank her. The battle for Arawe would last through most of February the following year. Echelons of Flotilla Seven landed 3,100 troops, 6,287 tons of supplies and 451 vehicles and guns. They offloaded while they and their escorts fought relentless air attacks.

Jim was transferred to USS *Pollux* (AKS4) on 7 May 1944. That vessel made convoys throughout the South Pacific. She ran supplies and wartime equipment from Australia to New Guinea and to the Philippines. It was necessary and dangerous duty. He was transferred to the new crew of *LCS 52* and sailed with her on her commissioning voyage. Jim served aboard the 52 through the battles of Iwo Jima and Okinawa. He received a Captain's Mast on 21 March 1945 while the ship was anchored off Saipan. No punishment was listed. "Report of Changes" for month ending 30 June 1945 indicated him as transferred to USS *LC (FF) 484* for duty; authorized by commander LCS Group Seven. *LC (FF) 484* was a LCI that was redesigned as the Flotilla Flagship on 31 December 1944. Jim joined the USS *Helena* (CA-75) on 3 July 1946. Jim got into trouble and was brought before a Deck court on 5 August 1947. He was reduced to "SC2." He was transferred to the USS *Los Angeles* (CA-135) on 26 November 1947. On 9 April 1948 Jim was transferred from the USS *Los Angeles* to the USS *Crescent City*. He was then transferred to USNH Oakland on 28 April for unstated reason.[64] Nelson was not listed in the war journal, which made it impossible to verify with any accuracy any activity beyond his military service.

Nufrio, Anthony J. (ser.no. 706-37-09):

MoMM2c (LC) **Anthony J. Nufrio** entered the Navy 7 August 1942 at Newark, New Jersey. He served aboard the USS *Harry Lee* from 21 September 1942. He was assigned to the USS *Calvert* on 24 October 1942. He was sent to the Navy Hospital at Norfolk on 6 December and returned on the 17th of 1942. He was promoted to Fireman 2nd Class on 1 February 1943. He was received aboard the USS *Charles Carroll* on 28 March 1943 from ATB Camp Bradford, Virginia. He had reported to Camp Bradford on 12 March. He then went to the USS *Elizabeth C. Stanton* on 25 April 1943. He made his F1c on 1 May, while aboard the *Elizabeth C Stanton*. His rating changed to MoMM2c on 1 July. He and several of his fellow shipmates were sent to amphibious training at Little Creek, Virginia on 30 November 1943. He reported to the USS *Clay* (APA-39) on 23 December from ATB Little Creek. On 11 April 1944, Anthony was transferred to the "Diesel Classification Center at San Francisco." His next duty was with the newly commissioned *LCS 52*. Anthony was transferred with Jim Nelson to *LC (FF) 484* on 30 June 1945. He was sent to the States on 25 November of that year for separation.[65] Nufrio is not listed in the Burns war journal. It was impossible to determine any history beyond military service.

Olney, Donald D. (ser.no. 960-93-42):

Seaman 2nd Class **Donald Dee Olney** was born on 12 May 1921. He enlisted on 11 December 1943. He was transferred to the separation center at Great Lakes on 1 February 1946. Laton recorded his pre-war address as Duncan Falls, Ohio. Donald passed away on 14 August 2004 and was buried at Harmony Cemetery in Claysville, Ohio. According to his obituary in the *Daily Jeffersonian* of Cambridge, Ohio, Donald died at his home in Beverly, Ohio. He was the son of Vernon Lee and Weltha Welch Olney. Donald's occupations after World War II included coal miner and school bus driver for Franklin School system. He was listed as a Mason. He enjoyed several hobbies, including fishing and square dancing. He also played guitar, enjoyed country music and raised beagles. He was married to Shelba Callahan Gregg Olney on 25 August 1993 who survived him.

Olsen, George E. (ser.no. 817-02-79):

Gunners Mate 3rd Class **George E. Olsen** was born 5 February 1918 and passed away on 30 June 1994. He was buried in the Long Island National Cemetery in Farmingdale, New York. He was listed in the war journal at 1349 East 54th Street, Brooklyn, New York. The house at 54th Street was built in 1940. There was no further information located on George's family or life after the war.

The ship's report of changes for 31 December 1944 showed that George enlisted on 21 December 1944 in New York City. He trained aboard the USS *Wyoming* in July and August of 1944. He was advanced to GM3c on 1 December 1944 onboard *LCS 52*. George was transferred to the Naval Hospital on Oahu on 22 January 1945. No indication of illness or injury was given. He was back aboard the *52* by March. He was transferred to the USS *Torrance* (AKA 76) on 20 November 1945.[66]

Parham L.E. (ser.no. 952-43-52):

Seaman 1st Class **L.E. Parham** was born to L.E. and Elah (sp) Parham on 22 June 1917 in Tennessee. L.E. Jr. was the second child and second son of the couple. L.E. Sr. was a farmer by trade but worked highway construction during the Depression. Zula, née Lowery, ten years his senior, married L.E. Jr. on 2 November 1935 in Carroll County, Tennessee. Zula brought a daughter to the marriage and two sons followed before his enlistment. In 1940, L.E. was working as a "carder" in a textile mill in Milan, Tennessee. The family lived on Harris Street. Laton Burns recorded L.E. Jr. as living on Home Street in Muskegon, Michigan before L.E's enlistment. He was listed in the city directory for 1944 living at 890 Home. He was married to "Julia" and working in the factory of CM Corporation.[67] In the 1946 Muskegon directory, L.E. was listed at the same residence but employed with the "USN." His wife was then listed as Zula, not Julia.

L.E. enlisted on 28 April 1944 at Muskegon, Michigan. He trained aboard the USS

Wyoming during July and August of 1944. He was the subject of a Captain's Mast on 7 October 1944. He also received a Captain's Mast on 1 July 1945. L.E. was released from service on 7 November 1947. Zula Annabelle Parham filed for divorce in Missouri in October of 1947. She passed away on 19 February 1993 and was buried in Springfield. She retained her married name on her headstone. He passed away on 17 November 1991 in Sacramento, California.[68]

Payne, Robert G. (ser.no. 962-58-03) W.I.A.:

Seaman 1st Class **Robert G. Payne** enlisted in the Navy on 27 April 1944 at Great Lakes, Illinois. He was transferred from the USS *Wyoming* to ATB, Little Creek, Virginia on 11 August 1944. Laton showed him living in Costalio, Ohio at the time of the war. Laton probably meant Castalia, Ohio. Robert was advanced to S1c on 1 December 1944 onboard the 52. Robert was transferred to the temporary hospital ship *APA 21* on 28 May 1945 as "wounded in action."[69] His injury was the result of the suicide plane attacks of 27 May.

Prendergast, Ralph J. Jr. (ser.no. 293-58-31):

Seaman 1st Class **Ralph J. Prendergast** was recorded as living on Wood Avenue in Hammond, Indiana in the 1940s. Ralph was born 14 May 1926 and passed away on 17 June 2012. He was married to Margaret Reed. He was seventeen years old when he joined the Navy. He started as a gunner but later became one of the cooks aboard ship as well. Ralph was advanced in rank to Seaman 1st Class 16 November 1944 while aboard the 52. He received a Captain's Mast on 21 March 1945; no disposition recorded. Ralph was transferred to PSC, Great Lakes, for release to inactive duty 16 May 1946. After his military service he became a graduate of Bryant Stratton Business School. Ralph was an accountant by profession and worked with his wife at the Visiting Nurses Association. It was noted in Ralph's obituary that among his other hobbies he enjoyed singing in a barbershop quartet. He had a great sense of humor and liked to entertain those around him with stories, his daughter added.[70]

Pfohl, John N. (ser.no. 944-92-11):

Seaman 1st Class **John Narciso Pfohl** enlisted on 27 April 1944. He was received aboard the USS *Wyoming* on 29 July 1944 from ATB, Fort Pierce, Florida. After training aboard the *Wyoming*, he was transferred to ATB, Little Creek, Virginia on 11 August 1944. He was advanced to Seaman 1st Class on 1 December 1944 aboard *LCS 52*. John was transferred to the USS *Hansford* (APA 106) on 5 October 1945.[71] In Laton's war journal he appears as "Johny" on East 73rd Street in Chicago, Illinois. He died 24 January 1990. He and his wife were buried together in Sunset Memorial Cemetery, Benton County, Washington.

Poindexter, Howard R. (ser.no. 932-04-63):

Seaman 1st Class **Howard Raymond Poindexter** enlisted in the Navy on 26 April 1944. He was advanced to Seaman 1st Class on 1 December 1944 while aboard the 52. Howard was transferred to the separation center at Norfolk, Virginia on 1 February 1946.[72] He was born 18 July 1922 and passed away on 14 March 1990. Laton listed his prewar address as 1111 22nd Street, Newport News, Virginia. On his draft registration card, Howard listed his prewar address as Siloam, Surry County, North Carolina. He also listed the same town as his place of birth. He gave his prewar occupation as shipbuilding in Newport News.

Reed, Carl L. (ser.no. 942-04-63):

Quarter Master 3rd Class **Carl L. Reed** enlisted on 6 December 1943. Carl was advanced in rank to QM2c on 16 August 1945 while aboard *LCS 52*. Carl received a Captain's Mast on

5 November 1945. Carl enlisted at NRS Chicago, Illinois. He was transferred to the separation center at Great Lakes, Illinois on 1 February 1946.[73]

Carl Reed was born 13 February 1921 and died 12 November 2006. His parents were James E. and Lucy Catlett Reed. He was born in Sidell, Illinois. He married Cathrine Bradford in 1941. Cathrine passed away in 2001. Carl is buried in the Greenwood Cemetery in Danville, Illinois. In the war journal Carl gave his prewar address as RR.4 in Danville, Illinois. According to *The Commercial-News* of Danville, Cathrine and Carl celebrated their sixty-fifth anniversary together on 17 July 2006. He was listed as a member of the Masonic Lodge, VFW, and American Legion in 2006. Both of them travelled extensively before their deaths and the paper listed a visit by the couple to Pearl Harbor.[74]

Schroeder, Harvey W. (ser.no. 869-55-15):

Radioman 3rd Class (T) **Harvey W. Schroeder** was born 5 October 1925 in Wisconsin to Hubert and Leona M Schroeder. He enlisted 30 November 1943 at Beaver Dam, Wisconsin. He was the subject of "Deck Court's" held on 1 November and 5 November 1944. No punishment was listed. He was transferred to the USN Base Hospital No. 8 on 19 January 1945. Another Change of Report indicated that he went to the Naval Hospital on Oahu that same date. His release date from service was 11 May 1946.[75] He passed away on 9 June 1979 in Beaver Dam.

Schultz, Donald H. (ser.no. 293-54-29):

Seaman 1st Class **Donald H. Schultz** enlisted on 19 April 1944. He was present for the quarters ending 30 September 1944, through 1 April 1946. Donald was advanced to S1c on 1 July 1945 while aboard *LCS 52*. On the "Report of Changes" for 1 March 1946 Donald was shown advanced to S1c on 15 February 1946 while aboard the *52*. There is almost eight months difference in the entries for promotion to S1c. It would be difficult to say why he was promoted twice to the same rank, unless he was reduced once. He was among the group of three who received a "Deck Court" on 19 October 1944. It could have been some administrative mistake or perhaps one made by him. He was the subject of a Captain's Mast on 5 November 1945 and the disposition indicated was "Reduced to S2c."[76] Laton listed him in the journal with a middle initial of "D," however all of his records indicate "H." He was shown in the journal living on North Edy [Eddy] Street in South Bend, Indiana at the beginning of his service.[77] Donald was apparently born on 12 December 1926 in South Bend. He died on 4 December 1979 at the age of fifty-three in the Memorial Hospital of South Bend. His obituary listed him as a former owner of Stewart Optical but did not indicate he was an optometrist. The records further stated that he was a member of the Masonic Lodge. He married Dorothy Miller in 1959. Dorothy passed away in 1980.

Scurrah, Abraham A. (ser.no. 607-58-57):

Fireman 1st Class **Abraham Arnold Scurrah** enlisted 21 August 1942 in Boston, Massachusetts. He received a "Deck Court" on 12 October 1944. The Report of Changes for the month ending 31 August 1945 reflected that Abraham was transferred to "NRS Navy No. 3964 for transportation to U.S." on 25 August 1945.[78]

Smith, Lincoln W. (ser.no. 826-59-31):

Gunners Mate 2nd Class **Lincoln W. Smith** enlisted on 5 March 1943. He was advanced to Gunners Mate 2nd Class on 1 December 1944. He received a Captain's Mast on 5 November 1945, which showed a disposition of "Reduced to GM3c."[79]

After the war Lincoln "Smithy" Smith returned to his home in North Carolina. He attended the Woodrow Wilson College of Law in Atlanta and graduated in the spring of 1950. Although he had his law degree he had no intention of practicing in the near future. He continued to work as a salesman at Victory Dodge and Motor Company. He was still working as a salesman in 1955 and living in Atlanta. He was married to Mary H. Smith in 1955 but that union did not last.

Stoia, Nick (ser.no. 285-76-30):

Seaman 1st Class **Nick Stoia** enlisted 19 April 1944 at Canton, Ohio. On 15 January 1946 he was promoted to RdM3c. After the war Nick (b. 1926) returned to Alliance and was married to Helen. He still resides in Alliance.

Swartout, Donald J. (ser.no. 313-88-16):

Seaman 1st Class **Donald Jerry Swartout** was born 19 April 1927, the first child of Alpha Jerome and Addie Mae Seaton Swartout. Donald enlisted on 20 April 1944. Donald was advanced in rank to Seaman 1st Class on 1 December 1944. Donald was transferred to the USS *Wilkes-Barre* (CL 103) on 29 November 1945. He

Nick Stoia saw an opening for radio striker and took it. Nick was one of the youngest men aboard, with the exception of Keilty, who forged paperwork to enlist at fifteen (Nick Stoia collection).

was listed in the Burns journal as Don J. Swartout of Washington Avenue, Lansing, Michigan. In 1946 a Donald Swartout was renting at 1609 S. Washington and employed at the Hager School of Music. The next entry in the directory for that same year showed Donald J. renting at 611 N. Francis Avenue and working as a clerk at Bean Manufacturing. In the 1948 directory Donald (no middle initial) was still living at [1]609 S. Washington Avenue. In 1949, Donald J. was renting at 612 Avon and was working as an attendant at Harry's Service Station. No other Donald was listed again. Two of his brothers were then living at 611 Francis.

On 7 November 1952, Donald married eighteen-year-old Joyce Elaine Johnson of Mason, Michigan.[80] Throughout the mid–1950s, Joyce and Don lived at a home on Pearl Street in Lansing. He was a driver for Savant Cleaners. In the late 1950s, Don worked as a salesman for Capital Laundry and Dry Cleaning. He and Joyce apparently moved in with a spinster aunt, Maryaleen R. Swartout, who had lived at the home on Francis most of her life. She would outlive Donald J. by nine years. He passed away on 19 May 1970. His father, Alpha (Alfred), outlived him by four years. Don was buried in the Chapel Hill Memorial Gardens in De Witt, Michigan (sometimes confused with being in Lansing). Buried near Don is his father who served in the U.S. Army. His brothers are also buried nearby. Victor K. served in the Army and Roger served in the U.S. Marine Corps in Korea.[81]

Syrian, John A *(ser.no. 560-39-01)*:

Pharmacist's Mate 1st Class ***John A. Syrian*** was listed in Laton's journal with an address in Mt. Clare, West Virginia. Syrian entered service on 12 October 1942. He was promoted to PhM 1st Class on 1 December 1944. As the only medical person shown on the 52's muster rolls during that time, Syrian was responsible for the daily health, safety, and preventive medicine of the crew. During combat operations John was responsible for tending to any severity of wound and stabilizing the wounded sailor until he could be transferred to one of the hospital ships for tertiary care. John Syrian served the men in both these capacities during the battles of Iwo Jima and Okinawa. The designation of Pharmacist's Mate was replaced after the war by that of Hospital Corpsman. No man aboard ship and especially those attached to a Marine ground unit is more highly regarded than the "Doc." The doc's mission is one of the most difficult in the Navy—keep as many men, at as many guns, as many days as possible. John was transferred to the USS *Terry* (DD 513) on 30 October 1945. The 52's muster roll for the month ending 1 January 1946 listed Pharmacist's Mate 1st Class *Carl E. Wertz*.[82]

John did not fail to answer the call of duty again; he was on the musters as a Hospital Man 1 (HM1) in July 1951 supporting Marine Corps personnel in Korea. He was assigned to Co D 1st Medical Battalion, 1st Marine Division, FMF (using the same service number issued in World War II). He was present for duty in D Company on the muster rolls for June, October 1951 and January 1952. In April 1952 John was listed at "Casuals Mb Us Ns Treasure Island, San Francisco, California." He was also listed as holding the rank (pay grade) of E-6. The Department of Veterans Affairs listed his second enlistment on 27 February 1951 and his release as 12 June 1952.[83]

John's brother, Pete J, appears to have enlisted in 1942 "for the duration of the war" as well. John was a first-generation American. He was known for his athletic abilities while in high school and was the first of his family to graduate. He was an avid golfer throughout his life.[84]

Thill, Virgil E. *(ser.no. 306-80-05)*:

Seaman 1st Class ***Virgil E. Thill*** enlisted in the Navy on 26 April 1944. He was advanced to Seaman 1st Class on 1 July 1945. He received a Captain's Mast 15 July 1945. He received a Captain's Mast on 5 November 1945, where he was reduced to Seaman 2nd Class. Virgil was advanced to the next highest rating on 15 May 1946 while aboard *LCS 52*. He was transferred to PSC, Great Lakes for release to inactive duty on 16 May 1946.[85] He and his wife, Lois, live in Farmington Hill, Michigan. The couple raised four sons together. The Thills have traveled the world since retirement and have been instrumental in keeping records of the men of USS *LCS 52*.

Tweet, Oren C. *(ser.no. 960-98-95)*:

Motor Machinist's Mate, 3rd Class ***Oren Clifford Tweet*** entered service 28 April 1944. He was received aboard the USS *Wyoming* on 29 July 1944 from ATB, Ft. Pierce, Virginia. On 11 August 1944 he was transferred to ATB, Little Creek, Virginia, presumably after training. Oren was the subject of a Captain's Mast on 5 November 1944. Oren was advanced to S1c on 1 July 1945 while aboard *LCS 52*. He was advanced to F1c on 15 December 1945. He was advanced in rank again on 15 February 1946 to MoMM3c. On 20 May 1946 Oren was transferred to Columbia River Group, 19th Flt, for assignment. On 3 June 1946 he was received aboard *LSM 289* from ComPort Sub-Grp, 19th Fleet, Portland, Oregon. *LSM 289* was the LSM Division "Baker" Flagship, 19th Fleet. Oren was then sent to the Post Demobilization Separation Center receiving station in Seattle, Washington on 24 September 1946.[86]

Van Buren, Donald A. *(ser.no. 800-76-67)*:

Gunners Mate 3rd Class **Donald A. Van Buren** enlisted 23 August 1943. On 15 November he was advanced to GM2c T and then on 20 November 1945 he was transferred to the USS *Torrance* (AKA 76). Both those entries showed him enlisting at Johnston, New York. He was listed in Laton's war journal at Washington Street in Sloverville, New York before the war. The town of Sloverville could not be located in New York. The town he was probably from was Gloversville, in Fulton County, New York. There in Broadalbin-Mayfield Rural Cemetery, Broadalbin, Fulton County there is a grave marker for Donald Van Buren who was born in 1919. He was married to June A. on 4 July 1942. She passed away in 1989 but Donald's death date was left blank as of 2010. He was probably born on 2 July 1919 and passed away 11 April 2013.[87]

Williams, Howard J. *(ser.no. 907-97-66)*:

Fireman 1st Class (LC) **Howard J. Williams** was born in Yonkers, New York on 10 January 1918. He was the son of Johanna "Hannah" Marie Cleary and Edwin Joseph Williams. He was the seventh of their eight children. Edwin worked for the famous Otis Elevator Company in Yonkers for twenty years as one of their foremen. On 9 March 1921 he was in his office when he had a heart attack and died.

Howard "Bill" Williams enlisted 21 March 1944 at Great Lakes. He was advanced in rating from Seaman 2nd Class to F1c (LC) on 1 May 1945 while aboard *LCS 52*. He was transferred to the separation center in Lido Beach, New York on 1 February 1946. He was listed in Laton's journal at West Lincoln Avenue, Mt. Vernon, New York. He returned to Mount Vernon where he married Marie Prosch, born and raised in that city. The two were married on 3 July 1948. Bill worked as a machinist for Hertlein Special Tool Company for thirty-two years. He was a proficient tennis player and taught the game to community children. He was an active member of the local Veterans of Foreign Wars post. Bill passed away on 8 August 1996 at Northern Dutchess Hospital in Rhinebeck, New York. The following summer, Marie also passed away. Both were buried in the Kensico Cemetery in Valhalla, New York.[88]

Officers

Harper, John O. *(ser.no. 227 928)*:

Lieutenant **John Oral Harper** was born in Ohio on 5 September 1917 and passed away at 5:15 am on 14 February 2006 at the nursing home in Springfield, Ohio. In his college yearbook photo of 1948 his large smile is the thing that stands out the most.

Duvendeck, Jerry Paul *(ser.no. 256 814)*:

Lieutenant, Junior Grade (jg) **Jerry Paul Duvendeck** was the executive officer for *LCS 52*. His picture was located in the "Scotsman" yearbook for 1942, in which he was listed in the junior class. Jerry was very active at Alma; he was the assistant head waiter during the

1942 school year, responsible for service in the school dining hall. The waiters were hand-picked based on their academic performance and other qualities. Jerry was also a member of Delta Gamma Tau and described as volunteering for "special fields" in military services.[89] It went on to say that Jerry was the first man from the college to be accepted to the Navy V-7 program.[90] After the war, Jerry returned to school and received a Master of Science degree in zoology from Michigan State College on Wednesday, 28 November 1951. According to the commencement booklet he was from Kalamazoo. The 1947, 48, 50, 55, 56 and 1960 Kalamazoo city directory showed a Mrs. Marquerite M. Duvendeck (saleswoman) living in that city and her spouse was Raymond H. Oddly, there was a second commencement booklet for 1952 from Michigan State College, Sunday, 8 June, which listed the same names for a Master of Science degree, including Jerry. The only additional information was it listed him from Portsmouth, Ohio. Jerry was born on 11 December 1921, most likely in Portsmouth, Ohio, albeit maybe Michigan. He passed away on 9 March 1996 in Flint, Michigan and showed a last residence of Denton, Michigan. His father's name was listed in one record as Ray "Dwendeck" and his mother's Marguerite. He began his time as a commissioned officer in the Navy around 20 June 1943. He was certainly on *LCS 52* on her maiden voyage; he signed the muster roll for 30 September that year. He also signed as executive officer the muster roll of 31 December 1944 as an ensign. Then on the 31 March 1945 muster roll he signed as Lt. (jg) indicating he had been promoted. On 30 June 1945's Jerry signature block on the muster roll was left blank and only Lt. Harper signed. This was at the end of the Okinawa campaign and might mean that he took leave or was assigned temporary duty somewhere. Jerry signed the muster roll on 30 September 1945 and forwarded it up the chain from "Waka-no-ura, Japan." Interestingly, on the muster roll for 3 January 1946, from Pearl Harbor, Jerry signed as the captain of the ship and Lt. (jg) C.L. Stewart as the Executive Officer. He was released from duty around 4 April 1946. Jerry remained in the Naval Reserves throughout the 1950s.[91] After he completed his education, Jerry was a tireless biologist for the Michigan Department of Conservation. His studies on deer acorn diets and several books on natural resource management are renowned in the state.

Burroughs, Spencer (ser.no. 313–688) KIA:

Ensign **Spencer Burroughs** was born to Spencer E. Burroughs and Olga (Wemple) Burroughs on 15 August 1920 in Susanville, Lassen County, California. His father was a well-known attorney. Spencer grew up with three siblings, Olga, Trent and Geoffrey. Spencer graduated from Sacramento High School and then went on to Stanford. He enlisted in the University of California's V12 training program and then received his commission from Norte Dame, in South Bend, Indiana at the age of twenty-four. He married Elaine Eleanor Baker on 23 January 1944 at a home wedding in Sacramento, performed by Judge Annette Adams.[92]

Many of the crew who knew Spencer gave descriptions of his presence and character. He was a trusted officer. Lt. John Harper spoke of the night on picket duty when Spencer was killed. He stated:

> Ensign Burroughs, a former student of mine, serving as Engineering Officer aboard, received a package of new phonograph records and we were playing them in the wardroom that evening when the general alarm went wild again.... When I reached the fantail of the ship I found the damage control party already at work. Mr. Burroughs had been killed instantly by shrapnel from the blast. A gunner forward was killed.... We arrived at the anchorage at dawn the next morning and transferred our

wounded men. Mr. Burroughs was buried in the military cemetery at Okinawa as was Hawks, the other man killed by the plane.... Though the loss to the Japs was heavy our own loss was great. Mr. Burroughs was a splendid fellow. He was a leader in his Midshipman class at Notre Dame and was doing a fine job out here.

Cullen, in a letter home in 1945, also spoke of Spencer:

> The officer we lost, Ensign Burroughs, was a swell fellow, and he and I had lots of interesting talks together. We argued books and philosophy (he was more of a true student than I, who only too well recognize myself as a dabbler). We had planned to write a story about the amphibs together—that was only a couple of days before his death. I sure did hate to see him go.

Spencer's name was included with those of seventy-seven other graduates in the 9th Notre Dame USNRMS *Capstan* of 1945, who gave their lives in combat.

Stewart, Clifford L. (ser.no. 357 987):

Ensign **Clifford Lee Stewart** remained in the Navy for most of his adult life. He rose to the rank of Captain before retiring. He still resides on his small ranch in California.[93]

Parker, Albert G. III (ser.no. 357 805):

Ensign **Albert George Parker III** hung up his Navy uniform after the war. He became a minister, as his father and grandfather had been. He shepherded churches throughout the United States before settling in New Mexico.[94]

Strandquist, Adler W. (ser.no. 370 190):

Ensign **Adler Wilhelm "Swede" Strandquist** was the son of Andrew Emmanuel and Lilly T. Strandquist, born in Minnesota on 12 June 1921. Ensign Strandquest was wounded during the kamikaze attack on 27 May 1945. He carried in his arm the shrapnel from that attack for the rest of his life. He was listed in the U.S. Navy Casualties Book, and his wife, Bernice Alice, was living at 605 N. Main, Parks Rapids, Minnesota at the time. He died on 19 December 2007. He is buried at Fort Snelling National Cemetery, Minneapolis, Minnesota. Adler's headstone reads, "LTJG US Navy World War II." He was married to Bernice A., the girl he had met in high school, for most of his life. The two parted company on 26 October 1976. On 26 May 1979, Adler remarried to Ruth J. Barnes in his home county of Hennepin.[95]

Replacements

Barber, William George (ser.no. 667-17-93):

William George Barber enlisted on 1 March 1943 at NRS Springfield, Massachusetts. William served aboard *LCI 484* before coming to *LCS 52*. He joined that ship on 21 October 1943 from the separation center at pier 92, New York, New York. He was present for duty on the *484* for the quarters ending 21 October through 31 December 1943 and 31 March through 31 December 1944. On 1 June 1944 a report of change was submitted which listed William and the action taken was "fill compliment." William was present on the rolls for a muster submitted on 11 January 1945 and the quarter ending 31 March 1945. On 5 June 1945 Barber was received aboard *LCS 52* from the *LCI (F) 484* "for duty." "Auth. LCS Grp.7" He was shown on the muster roll for *LCS 52* for the quarters ending 30 June through 31 December 1945. He was transferred to the separation center at Boston on 1 February 1946 from *LCS 52*.[96]

Before the war, he was listed at 33 Cleveland Street, Greenfield, Massachusetts in Laton's journal. The Massachusetts birth index showed a William George Barber born in the year 1925 in Greenfield, but gave no other details. The state's marriage index showed a William George married in the year 1947 in Greenfield. The 1940 census had his family living at 28 Cleveland Street in Greenfield. The head of household was shown to be Gladys Barber, thirty-eight years of age. In the 1945 Greenfield directory, William was listed at 33 Cleveland and having the occupation of U.S. Navy. In the 1956 through 1963 Greenfield directories a William G. was shown at Willmark Avenue and married to Persis A. Barber. His occupation was "mechanic." After 1963 they no longer appear in the directory and may have moved out of state. Persis died in 2001 in Nassau, Florida. William G. Barber, born in Massachusetts 26 November 1925, also died in Nassau, on 18 September 1999. There was a William Barber and a Gladys Lee married in Nassau, Florida in 1929. It is difficult to say with certainty how William George the *LCS 52* veteran connected to the Barbers of Florida or if they did at all.

Christman, Russell Richard (ser.no. 819-31-86):

Seaman 1st Class **Russell Richard Christman** enlisted 8 December 1943 in Allentown, Pennsylvania. Russell was received aboard *LST 738* on her commissioning day of 9 May 1944 from ATB, Camp Bradford, NOB Norfolk, Virginia. He was transferred to the U.S. Naval Hospital at New Orleans on 8 June 1944 from *LST 738*. He was received aboard the *LST 675* on 28 July 1944. Russell was sent to the "Dispensary" in New Orleans on 29 July 1944 from his new ship the *LST 675*. He was promoted to S1c on 1 May 1945 while aboard *LST 675*. He was received aboard the 52 on 12 June 1945 from *LST 675* ("Auth: *LCS 52*'s visual 120315"). He was listed present for duty aboard *LCS 52* for the quarters ending 30 June through 31 December 1945. He was transferred to the U.S. Naval Hospital, Mare Island, California on 19 March 1946. He was back aboard *LCS 52* at the time of transfer, returning from Mare Island on 3 April 1946. He was then transferred to Bainbridge, Maryland separation center for release to inactive duty on 11 April 1946.[97] Russell applied for a veteran's pension through Pennsylvania in 1950. On his application he stated he was living at R.D. # 2 in Lehighton. Russell was born 4 October 1925 and passed away at his home in Lehighton, Pennsylvania on 30 April 2004. His obituary listed his wife as Arlene Hartranft Christman. He was still living in Lehighton, Pennsylvania, where Laton's journal recorded him living in the 1940s, at the time of his death. He is buried in the Lehighton Cemetery, Carbon County. His parents were Eugene Elmer and Amelia Feist Christman.

Clack, Harold L. (ser.no. 834-17-42):

Seaman 1st Class **Harold L. Clack** enlisted 25 November 1943 at Raleigh, North Carolina. Harold was aboard *LST 980* on her commissioning voyage of 26 February 1944. The Report of Changes stated that Harold was received from "USN Rec. Sta. Boston, Mass." On 6 March 1944, Harold left the *LST 980* and was sent to the U.S. Naval Hospital, NOB Norfolk. No disposition was given for his transfer to the hospital. Harold then sailed with *LST 742* on her commissioning voyage of 27 May 1944, his second new ship. He was received from "NRU, C.I.T. Pittsburg, PA." He was sent again to a hospital on 23 June 1944, this time from *LST 742* to Lakefront Naval Hospital, New Orleans. Harold was present for duty aboard *LST 675* for the quarter ending 30 September 1944. That muster listed him as coming aboard on 24 June 1944. A later Report of Changes for 29 July showed that he was picked up in New Orleans by the *675*. Like his former ship *LST 742* that dropped him off, *675* was headed for Panama

From left to right, (top row) Unknown, Clack, Gaham; (bottom row) Darnell and Hobson. (Virgil Thill collection).

when it picked him up. Harold was on the muster for *LST 675* for the quarters ending 31 December 1944 and 31 March 1945. He was next transferred to *LCS 52* "for duty" on 12 June 1945 from *LST 675*. He was listed as present for duty aboard *LCS 52* for the quarters ending 30 June 1945 through 1 April 1946. On 11 April 1946 Harold left the *52* for Camp Shelton, Norfolk, Virginia to be released to inactive duty.[98]

Laton showed his address prior to the war as R2 Clinton, North Carolina. His draft registration card showed his address as Route # 2 Clinton (South Clinton) Sampson County, North Carolina. He was born in Sampson County on 12 September 1925. He gave his employer's name as "A.S. Clack" also at Route # 2.[99] In the 1940 census he was living with Alvis Clack (43) and Annie Clack (38). Alvis Sterling Clack and Annie Lee Loftis Clack were his parents. Harold passed away on 10 May 1983. He was buried at the Rowan Baptist Church Cemetery in Clinton, near his parents.

Criger, John D. W. (ser.no. 758-82-05):

Seaman 1st Class **John D. W. Criger** enlisted 24 February 1944 at Baltimore, Maryland. He was sent to the receiving station at Norfolk on 29 April 1944 from the USS *New York*. John was present for duty aboard *LST 675* on her commissioning voyage 24 June 1944. John was received from ATB Camp Bradford at Norfolk, Virginia. He was listed present for duty for the quarters ending 31 March through 31 December 1944. He received his Seaman 1st

Class rating on 1 January 1945. John was received aboard the *LCS 52* on 12 June 1945 from *LST 675* ("Auth: LCS 52's visual 120315"). On the muster rolls of *LCS 52*, John was listed as present for the months ending 30 June (marked as "D.H.") through 31 December 1945. He was transferred to the receiving station at Treasure Island on 26 March 1946 from *LCS 52*. John was born on 22 February 1927 and passed away 17 February 1996 in Baltimore, Maryland.[100] Laton showed him living in Mount Savage, Maryland, prior to the war.

Darnell, Charles Clarence (ser.no. 285-61-13):

Seaman 1st Class **Charles Clarence Darnell** was born 12 February 1926 and died 23 January 1999. He attended Massillon High School in Ohio. His father was Wilbur Darnell, listed at 917 Duncan Street, Massillon. Charles' religion was given as Catholic. Charles enlisted 25 January 1944 in Cleveland, Ohio. He was an original member of the *LST 675* crew on her commission date of 24 June 1944. He received advancement from S2c to Seaman 1st Class on 1 September 1944, aboard *LST 675*. He signed aboard the *52* on 12 June 1945 from *LST 675*. He is another one of the crew that has very little postwar information available. He was listed as present for duty for the quarters ending 30 June through 31 December 1945. He was transferred to the USS *Sierra* on 29 July 1945. The USS *Sierra* was at that time assigned to repairing LCSs and destroyers for the invasion of mainland Japan. He was also present for duty aboard *LCS 52* for the quarter ending 1 April 1946. Charles was transferred to Great Lakes, Illinois for "release to inactive duty" 24 April 1946.[101] He was listed in the war journal as C. Darnell of Dancun Street in S.W. Massillon, Ohio. He was buried in Brookfield Cemetery in Massillon, Stark County, Ohio.

Downey, Jessie W. (ser.no. 287-29-66):

CMOMM **Jessie W. Downey** enlisted in the Navy on 8 or 9 May 1939 at Louisville, Kentucky. His first ship was the USS *San Francisco* and he sailed aboard that ship on 14 September 1939. He was transferred to the USS *Vega* on 10 November 1939. Jessie was promoted from Fireman 3rd Class to Fireman 2nd Class on 16 May 1940 while aboard the *Vega*. Jessie appeared to be aboard the *Vega* through 30 September 1942. However, he showed up on the *Vega* on the quarter ending 31 March 1943. On 9 April 1943 Jessie was transferred from the *Vega* to "Submarine Training School, Sub-base, New London, Connecticut for course of instruction." His records are slightly ambiguous. He was received on *LCI 482* on 19 October 1943, leaving Barber, New Jersey. The Report of Changes from *LCI 482* that month showed Jessie as enlisting in 11 May 1943 at Richmond, Virginia. He was transferred from *LCI 482* on 11 January 1944 to the U.S. Naval Hospital in San Diego, California. Jessie was received back on *LCI 482* on 25 February 1944. He was then transferred to the *LCI 728* on 26 February 1944. Jessie was transferred to ATB, Solomons, Maryland on 30 September 1944. He was received aboard *LCS 52* on 2 November 1944. He was listed as "Donny" on that report.

Jessie was present aboard the *52* for the quarters ending 31 March 1945. He was transferred to *LC (FF) 484* on 10 April 1945. Jessie was shown present for duty aboard *LST 904* on 30 June 1946; he was received aboard on 6 June 1946. Jessie was then shown on leave in Bowling Green, Kentucky starting 20 July 1946. He returned from leave to *LST 904* on 20 August 1946. He was received aboard *LST 1119* from USNAB, Coronado, California, 1 October 1946. He was transferred from *LST 1079* to "RecShip, San Francisco, FFT NRS Detroit, Mich., for re-habilitation leave and reassignment…" on 3 February 1946. He was then received on 15 February 1946 to RecSta, Shoemaker, California. He was transferred back to *LST 1096* on 14 March 1946. He was then back aboard *LST 1110* for 2 March 1947. He then was aboard *LSM 378* on 16 July 1947 through 24 February 1948. His last record was on *LSM 378* for the muster 15 June 1948.¹⁰² However, he may have remained in the Navy through 1952.

Doyle, Patrick (ser.no. 314-87-73):

Seaman 2nd Class **Patrick Doyle** enlisted 2 March 1945 in Detroit, Michigan. He was received aboard the 52 on 4 August 1945 from *LST 614* ("Com. LCS(L) Flotilla THREE"). He was present for duty on *LCS 52* for the quarters ending 30 September through 31 December 1945. On 10 December 1945 Patrick was transferred back to *LST 614*. He was mustered onboard *614* for the quarter ending 1 April 1946. He was aboard the *LST 614* when she was decommissioned 18 June 1946.¹⁰³ His address was 1615 Infantry Street, Detroit, Michigan, prior to the war.

Edwards, Vance, Jr. (ser.no. 286-24-46):

Fireman 1st Class **Vance Edwards, Jr.,** enlisted 6 February 1945 in NRS Akron, Ohio. He is listed as W. Edward at Winter Avenue, Akron, Ohio in the war Journal. On the Report of Changes for August 1945 he was shown "Received" on 4 August 1945 aboard *LCS 52* from "Com. LCS (L) Flotilla THREE." Vance was present for duty in *LCS 52* for the quarters ending 30 September 1945. He was transferred to *LST 614* on 10 December 1945. He was shown present for the quarters ending 1 January through 1 April 1946 aboard *LST 614*.¹⁰⁴ Because of the common last name, too many records exist to confirm any further information. The 1940 census listed a Vance Jr. in Akron and gave his age at about thirteen. The census listed his birth place as West Virginia. The family was living on Samuel Avenue. A Vance Edwards was later married to Doris L. Zimmerman; he was born 14 February 1927. They were married on 25 April 1953 in Summit, Ohio. The Veterans Administration recorded Vance Edwards, born 14 February 1927 and died 29 December 1987. He had a first enlistment of 16 March 1945 to 19 August 1946, which matches closely with his muster sheets. The VA then listed a second enlistment from 22 March 1951 to 19 July 1952 in the Navy. No records could be located for that period of service and it was assumed that he was using a different name or service number.

Gaudette, Harold Edwin (ser.no. 804-75-74):

Seaman 1st Class (RM) **Harold Edwin Gaudette** enlisted 31 October 1944 in Worchester, Massachusetts. Harold was received aboard *LCS 52* on 4 August 1945 from "Conn. LCS (L) Flotilla THREE." He was advanced in rank to Radioman 3rd Class on 1 December 1945. Harold was present for duty aboard the 52 for the quarter ending 30 September 1945. He was transferred to *LST 952* on 10 December 1945. It appears from *LST 952*'s Report of Changes that the transfer was accomplished while both ships were in Tsingtao, China. He was present for duty aboard *LST 952* during the quarters ending 1 January through 1 July 1946.

Harold was listed under the following entry in the war journal: "Harold Guadette, Pleasant Street, Warchester (sp), Massachusetts." In that city's directory before the war there were listed Lucien C., Harold E., and Howard B. living at apartment 241 on Pleasant Street. Harold was probably born 9 February 1926 and died 25 August 2004 in Worchester, Massachusetts. He was listed in the city directory at Woodway Drive in Worchester around 1989. He was shown to be an accountant at Eastern Oil that year. His wife was listed as Alice M. Harold.

He was listed in an earlier directory as an accountant for Eastern Climate Control Corporation. No spouse was listed at that time. A Massachusetts marriage index gave his year of marriage as 1950. His parents were listed in a Massachusetts census as Lucian C. and Hazel B. "Gandette." Harold's wife Alice died in 2002 and was also buried at the Mountain View Cemetery in Shrewsbury, Worchester County, Massachusetts.[105] In the "Bridges" Winter 2004 newsletter for Becker Junior College, Harold E. Gaudette, [class of] 49 was listed in the "In Memoriam" section. Apparently Harold, like the majority of the returning servicemen, took advantage of his GI education benefits and returned to school after the war. No further information could be located on his attendance at Becker.

Goldman, Hugh John (ser.no. 907-74-28):

Seaman 2nd Class **Hugh John Goldman** enlisted 10 March 1944 in New York City. He was on the original crew of *LST 675* on her commissioning date of 24 June 1944 and received aboard from ATB Camp Bradford, Norfolk, Virginia. He was shown present for duty aboard *LST 675* for the quarters ending 30 June 1944 through 31 March 1945. He was present for duty on *LCS 52* for the month ending 30 June 1945. Received aboard the *52* on 12 June 1945 from *LST 675* ("Auth: LCS 52's visual 120315").[106] Hugh was transferred to the separation center at Lido Beach, New York, 1 February 1946 from *LCS 52*. Laton's journal recorded him at #15 Claremont Bonnet Street, New York.

Griffin, John M. (ser.no. 670-19-80):

EM 1st Class **John M. Griffin** enlisted 19 February 1942 in Oklahoma City, Oklahoma. He was received aboard the *LCS 52* on 2 November 1944 from LCS (L) Group Seven. He was shown present for duty for the quarter ending 31 December 1944. John was the only member of the original crew who came aboard *LCS 52* after her commissioning voyage. John was transferred to *LC (FF) 484* on 10 April 1945 from *LCS 52*. He was a member of the "LCS (L) Group Seven Staff" and shown on the 1 October 1945 report of changes for that unit as transferred to the "Continental U.S. FFT to Separation Center for discharge" on the 14th of the month.[107]

Hobson, Ralph E. (ser.no.753-34-80):

Seaman 1st Class **Ralph E. Hobson** enlisted 11 March 1944 in Springfield, Illinois. "Report of Changes" for the month ending 30 June 1945 showed Ralph "received" from *LST 675* on 12 June 1945. Ralph was shown present onboard the *52* for the quarters ending 30 June 1945 through 1 April 1946. He is listed in the war journal as "R. Hobson" of Box 78, Paris, Illinois. He was born on 2 August 1926 in Redmon, Illinois, which is less than eleven miles from Paris. Ralph died at the Illinois Veterans Home in Quincy at eighty-three years old on 30 March 2010. Ralph was an independent carpenter after the war. His obituary stated that he also loved gardening and horses. He is buried in the Sunset Cemetery in Quincy, Illinois.[108]

Kennon, Harold E. (ser.no. 845-78-85):

Seaman 1st Class **Harold E. Kennon** enlisted on 31 July 1943 in Chattanooga, Tennessee. He was marked as "on leave, expected to return" on 18 July 1944 and he returned to his *LST 675* on 22 August 1944. He was shown as present for duty aboard *LST 675* for the quarters ending 30 September 1944 through 30 September 1945. He was promoted to Seaman 1st Class on 1 May 1945. Listed present for duty on *LCS 52* for the month ending 30 June 1945 after being received aboard the 52 on 12 June 1945 from *LST 675*. ("Auth. LCS 52's visual 120315.").[109] He resided at 2 Belmont Apts, Nashville, Tennessee before the war.

Puckett, John R. (ser.no. 836-33-89):

Ship's Cook, 3rd Class **John R. Puckett** enlisted on 20 February 1943 in Washington, D.C. Laton showed him living at R # 2, Gladys, West Virginia. The Report of Changes for 30 June 1945 stated that Puckett was received aboard the 52 on 18 June 1945 from the *LC (FF) 484*—authorized by verbal orders of the commander LCS Group Seven. John was promoted to SC2c (T) on 15 December 1945 while aboard *LCS 52*. Puckett was transferred to the separation center at Norfolk, Virginia on 20 February 1946.[110]

Robbins, Glenn, Jr. (ser.no. 357-79-46):

Seaman 2nd class **Glenn Junior Robbins** enlisted in the Navy on 28 November 1944 at Fort Worth, Texas. He joined the crew of *LCS 52* on 23 August 1945. He was transferred to *LST 614* on 10 December 1945. Glenn was present for duty aboard *LST 614* for the quarters ending 1 January through 1 April 1946. The captain submitted a Report of Changes on 7 May 1946 which stated that they were leaving Hulutao, Manchuria for Shanghai, China. Then on 18 June 1946 the captain sent a list of the crew and stated that they departed Minami Daito Jima for Okinawa. On 20 June 1946 the captain of *LST 614* sent in a "Final Report" which stated that no personnel were aboard due to decommissioning.[111] Glenn was listed in Laton's journal as Gllen J. Robins, Rt.1, Ponder, Texas.

Schultz, Earl W.H. (ser.no. 306-71-55):

Coxswain **Earl W.H. Schultz** enlisted 16 March 1944 at Milwaukee, Wisconsin. He was listed present for duty for the month ending 30 June through 31 December 1945. He was received aboard the 52 on 12 June 1945 from *LST 675* ("Auth: LCS 52's visual 120315"). Earl was advanced to the rank of "Cox (T)" on 1 November 1945.[112] Laton recorded him at 924 North Union Street, Appleton, Wisconsin before the war.

Tucker, Harry E. (ser.no. 928-98-80):

Radioman 3rd Class **Harry E. Tucker** enlisted 11 April 1944 in Charleston, West Virginia. He was listed in the journal at a P.O. Box in Webster Springs, West Virginia before the war. Tucker appears on the Report of Change for month ending 30 June 1945 as a SC2c (RM) and showed that he was advanced to S1c (RM) on 1 June. He was received aboard *LCS 32* on 20 January 1945 and then immediately transferred to *LCS 52* on 21 January 1945. The entry for this on the 52 change showed him received from "RB, Oahu, T.H. (Auth.: AdComPhibsPac)." He was transferred to the separation center at Bainbridge, Maryland on 1 February 1946.[113]

Officers

Kuehne, Fred M. III (ser.no. 330449):

Ensign Fred Marshall Kuehne enlisted in Evenston, Illinois on 1 July 1943. He was picked up from Fort Pierce, Florida on 6 July 1944, aboard *LST 675*. Fred attended the Culver Military School, Culver, Indiana, during the 1937–1940 (summer and winter) sessions. He was on Culver's soccer team, which took Regimental honors two of the years he played. He made Corporal and became involved in motorized infantry, a talent that would be of little use on the sea. Nicknamed, "Smilin' Fred," a mark of his cheerfulness and humor, Fred carried those traits to his grave.

He was born in Chicago on 11 July 1922. He attended Northwestern University in Chicago before entering the Navy. He moved his family, wife Jayne Patterson, to Texas in 1963.[114] Fred passed away on 16 February 2005, in Dallas, Texas.

Moschner, Albert (ser.no. 356-64-30):
Ensign Albert Moscher was born 15 November 1918. He passed away on 28 January 1992 in Sonoma, California.[115] He began his career in the Navy as an enlisted man. He enlisted in Dallas, Texas on 2 August 1941. His first ship was the USS *North Carolina* Albert joined that crew on 5 February 1942 from Norfolk NTS. Albert was given, what was to be temporary, ensign's rank on 11 August 1944. However, Albert retired as a Lieutenant (JG) in July of 1971.[116]

Postwar Crew

Bagdonas, Paul J. (ser.no. 320-79-41):
Paul J. Bagdonas enlisted 22 July 1942, NRS Chicago, Illinois. The USS *Cole* (155) received him on 3 October 1942 as a coxswain. He served on that ship until 20 April 1943, when he was transferred to the USN Hospital at Charleston. The record only indicated "for treatment." It appears that Paul reenlisted on 13 December 1945. Paul was received aboard *LCS 52* on 7 February 1946 from "Rec. Sta. Shoemaker, Calif." *LCS 52* then transferred him to the Columbia River group, 19th Fleet on 22 May 1946. He was received from the USS *Agenor* (ARL-3) to the USS *Atlas* (ARL-7) on 20 July 1946. On 9 September 1946, he was transferred to Sub Group 19th Fleet at Swan Island, Portland. He was assigned to USS *LSM 476* on 19 September. On 30 January 1947 he was picked up as a crewmember aboard the USS *Henry W. Tucker* from the receiving station at Treasure Island, California. Paul was the subject of a Deck Court on 21 April and was reduced in rank from Boatswains Mate 1st Class to BM2. Paul and several of his crewmates were received aboard the USS *John A. Bole* on 26 April 1947. He was transferred to the USN Hospital at San Diego on the 30th of the month. He next returned to duty aboard USS *PC 564* on 4 February 1948. On 18 May 1948 he was transferred to USN Hospital Charleston for treatment. On 4 June he returned to his ship from the hospital. BM2 Bagdonas was transferred to the USN Training Station at Newport, Rhode Island on 17 June 1948.[117]

Bradshaw, Robert W. (ser.no. 338-57-72)
Seaman 1st Class **Robert W. Bradshaw** enlisted 13 November 1943, NRS St Louis, Missouri. He was assigned to the USS *Alshain* (AKA-55) on 15 April 1944 from ATB Fort Pierce. Robert was received aboard *LCS 52* on 7 February 1946 from "Rec. Sta. Shoemaker, Calif." He was transferred to USN Hospital, Mare Island, California on 4 March and received back aboard *LCS 52* on 15 March 1946. He was present for duty aboard *LCS 52* the quarter ending 1 April 1946.[118]

Coviello, Andrew J. (ser.no. 908-03-34):
Seaman 1st Class **Andrew Joseph Coviello** enlisted 23 March 1944, NRS New York, New York. Andrew joined the crew of the USS *Wilkes-Barre* (CL-103) on 1 July 1944 from

NTC Newport, Rhode Island. He was tried for Absent without Leave on 13 August 1944 while aboard the *Wilkes-Barre*. He was found guilty and sentenced to three days confinement and a fine of $20.00. On 13 June 1945 another offense occurred and Andrew was sentenced to ten days confinement and a loss of pay of $16.00. He came aboard LCS 52 on 29 November 1945. He was advanced in rank to S1c on 15 February 1946. On 24 April 1946, Andrew was transferred to Lido Beach, New York for release from active duty.[119]

Andrew was born in New York on 14 January 1926.[120] He was the first son born to John and Anna Marie Coviello of the village of Port Chester, Township of Rye, New York. John was born in Italy and arrived in the United States with his parents in 1907. Anna was born in New York but both of her parents were also from Italy. John grew up in Port Chester with his parents, Andrew and Christina, who sometimes went by Sadie. When he registered for the World War I draft he gave his permeant point of contact as "Sadie." The family was living at 64 Purdy Avenue, where Andrew and Christina would remain for several years. John worked as a retail grocer for most of the 1920s and 30s. Andrew and his younger brothers grew up in the house at 73 Townsend in Port Chester. He was employed as a machine operator at one of the town's many factories, Russell Burdsall and Ward (RB & W Nut and Bolt Works) according to the 1940 census.

Andrew J. returned to the area of Port Chester after the war. Because of a conflict in two identical names from the town it was impossible to verify any further postwar history.

Dandridge, Marvin M. (ser.no. 605-16-53):

Pharmacist Mate 2nd Class **Marvin M. Dandridge** enlisted 30 November 1945, NRS Birmingham, Alabama. He was received aboard LCS 52 on 5 February 1946 from "Rec. Sta. Shoemaker, Calif." Present for duty aboard LCS 52 the quarter ending 1 April 1946. Marvin was transferred to the USS *Intrepid* (CV-11) on 23 May of that year. Marvin remained in the Navy after the war ended.

He served as a Pharmacist Mate 2nd Class with the Headquarters Company, 1st Battalion, 5th Marines after the *Intrepid*. He was promoted to PM1c while serving with that unit. The official designation for Corpsman was changed to Hospitalman, in 1951. HM1 Dandridge moved across the country and joined Headquarters 1/8, 2nd Marine Division. His last locatable military record showed Marvin assigned to the H&S Battery, 4/10, 2nd Marine Division in July of 1957. Records indicated that Marvin retired as a HM1.[121] He was married to Kathleen Eugenia Dandridge who passed away 6 June 1999. Marvin followed her 28 August 2004. They are both buried in Cheltenham Veterans Cemetery, Maryland. Marvin was living on Bayfront Drive, in Chesapeake Beach, Maryland at the time of his death.

Marvin "Danny" Dandridge was most likely born on 21 February 1923 in Alabama. His parents were Stanley "Charlie" and Nellie Dandridge of Toulminville and Prichard, Alabama. Both parents worked in the cotton mills throughout their adult lives. As soon as the children became able, they joined their parents there. Marvin was the second oldest child and the second son. Leonard was two years his senior and James followed Marvin three years later. By 1939–40, everyone in the family with the exception of sixteen-year-old James and fourteen-year old Joyce held some job in the cotton mill. They were living in a rented home at 64 Mill Village, Prichard, at the time. The mill where they worked probably was that belonging to J.C. Saunders and called Saunders Cotton Mill. All of the homes located in Mill Village were shot-gun style houses. Leonard and Marvin probably attended Barker School for their elementary studies.[122]

Charlie passed away between 1940 and 1942. Leonard had moved out and the remainder of the family was living at 156 Kate in Prichard. Marvin was still a battery hand at the cotton mill. James was employed in 1942 at the National Youth Administration (then run by the War Manpower Commission). The NYA ended in 1943.

Gaston, Victor E., Jr. (ser.no. 247-45-47):

Fireman 1st class **Victor Edmond Gaston, Jr.,** enlisted in Darby, Pennsylvania on 23 February 1945. He was advanced to F1c on 1 December 1945, while aboard *LCS 52*. He was transferred to *LST 614* on 10 December 1945.

Victor was born 16 August 1927 in Philadelphia, Pennsylvania. He was the first son and second child of Victor Sr. and Eva Rose Gaston. Their children were raised in Upper Darby Township. Victor Sr. made a living working in leather and later as a projectionist. He died in 1960 in Darby. The family was living at 1240 Wycombe Avenue when Victor Jr. joined the Navy.

The township of Upper Darby borders West Philadelphia. Victor Jr. and his siblings probably attended Upper Darby High School, opened in 1895. In 1940, Upper Darby was a large urban township, with 56,883 citizens calling it home. Darby is also home to the Lower Swedish Cabin, believed to be the oldest building in Pennsylvania.[123]

Victor and his wife, Valerie, moved to Hollywood, Florida after his military service. He became a city police officer there and retired from that occupation after twenty years honorable service. He passed away on 8 February 2005 in his postwar hometown of Hollywood.

Green, Robert D. (ser.no. 301-26-83):

Seaman 1st Class **Robert D. Green** (Ser.no. 301-26-83) enlisted on 22 February 1944 at Chicago, Illinois. Robert was received aboard *LCS 52* on 7 February 1946 from "Rec. Sta. Shoemaker, Calif." He was transferred to *LCS 45* on 29 August 1946.[124]

Hildebrandt, Eric G. (ser.no. 960-47-90):

Fireman 2nd Class **Eric G. Hildebrandt** enlisted 1 August 1945 at NRS Milwaukee, Wisconsin. Eric was received aboard on 9 February 1946 from "Rec. Sta. Shoemaker, Calif." Eric was sent to the PSC Washington, on 16 May 1946 for release from active duty. He returned to his home state of Wisconsin after the war and passed away on 10 June 1973.[125]

Eric George Hildebrandt was most likely the son of George P. and Mary Hildebrandt. He was born in Canada on 13 July 1921. The family moved officially to the United States in 1923. Eric and his older sister, Verna, arrived with their mother after completing an inspection on the Canadian side on 23 March of that year. His father was born in Simferopol Laurian, Russia. His father worked as a farmer in Canada. Thirty-one-year-old George was living with his parents in Canada in 1916. He married for the first time two years after. He listed his year of immigration as 1911 on the Canadian census. Eric's mother was born in Germany but the entire family listed their race as German, including George. When Mary and her two children arrived in the States they met their father in Eastport, Florida. However, by 1930, the family was living in Milwaukee, Wisconsin. There were three additions to the family, Evlyian, Dorthy and Wallace Hildebrandt.

In 1940 the family was living at 2032 N. 9th Street, Milwaukee. George was working as a watchman, or gatekeeper, for a steel corporation. Lincoln High School was located approximately two and a half miles from their home. It was probably there that Eric attended school.

Eric became a citizen of the U.S. on 20 November 1946. He was living at 2345 S. 77th Street in West Allis when he was naturalized.

Eric made the front page of the *Orland Park Herald*, Illinois on 20 October 1960. Four days earlier he found himself flying a two-seater plane from Alabama to West Allis. He was only a student pilot and not certified to fly after dark. With dusk and fog setting in, he decided to set the plane down in a farmer's field outside of Frankfort, Illinois. Unfortunately, the field was freshly plowed and upon landing the plane flipped, causing considerable damage. Eric, on the other hand, escaped injury.

Homberoff, Albert L. (ser.no. 293-07-15):

Seaman 1st Class **Albert L. Homberoff** enlisted 9 November 1945 in Guam. Albert was received aboard on 7 February 1946 from "Rec. Sta. Shoemaker, Calif." He was transferred to U.S. Naval Hospital, Mare Island, California on 2 March and received back aboard *LCS 52* on 20 March 1946. Present for duty aboard *LCS 52* the quarter ending 1 April 1946.[126]

Jakovich, Joseph F. (ser.no. 251-25-97):

Seaman 1st Class **Joseph Frank Jakovich** enlisted 24 February 1944 in Philadelphia, Pennsylvania. He came aboard *LCI 454* on 21 August of that year. Joseph was transferred from *LCI 454* to "Commander, Western Sea Frontier on 9 October 1945. He was received aboard on 7 February 1946 from "Rec. Sta. Shoemaker, Calif." He was then transferred on 2 May to the Columbia River Group, 19th Fleet. He was sailing aboard *LSM 118* in December of 1946. In March of 1947, he was transferred to the Columbia River Group Reserve Fleet.[127]

Joseph was born on 1 March 1926. His mother's maiden name was Ribarich. After the war he returned to Johnstown. He was married to Elizabeth L "Betty" Kinback. In 1951 he was working for Bethlehem Steel Company and the two were living at 225 Lincoln in Johnstown. He later married as his second wife, Cecelia A. Jakovich. He passed away on 10 September 1960 at his home in Redondo Beach, California. His body was brought back to Pennsylvania and was buried in the Grandview Cemetery, Johnstown.

Klein, Victor Deldon (ser.no. 881-27-61):

SF 3rd Class **Victor Deldon Klein** enlisted 12 June 1944 in Calaveras Altadena,, California. He was received aboard *LCS 52* on 21 November 1945 from *LCS Gr.7*. He was transferred to the separation center at Terminal Island, California on 1 February 1946.[128]

McClement, Donald A. (ser.no. 372-53-71):

Fireman 1st Class **Donald Arthur McClement** enlisted 18 June 1943 at Denver, Colorado. He was assigned to *YMS 267* on 26 October 1943. *YMS 267* was assigned to the San Francisco bay and coastal area. She swept the Bay each day for mines and patrolled the northern coast until sent to the Pacific. Donald was promoted to F1c on 12 April 1944 while serving on *YMS 267*. He was also transferred on that date to *YMS 317* for duty. He just missed taking part in the Guam landings in July with his old ship. On 3 May, *YMS 317* also headed for the Pacific. She performed minesweeping and convoy escort duties around Eniwetok, Kwajalein and Saipan. On 1 April 1945, Donald's rating was changed to S1c. Donald was sent to the nearest receiving station in the U.S. for assignment on 27 November 1945. He was received aboard *LCS 52* on 7 February 1946 from "Rec. Sta. Shoemaker, Calif." He was transferred to U.S. Naval Hospital, Mare Island, California on 16 March 1946. Donald served aboard the

USS *Warrick* (AKA 89) until transferred to "RS, YBI" San Francisco for terminal leave and discharge on 18 February 1947. He had been with that ship since 26 April 1946.[129]

Donald was born 24 May 1926 in Nebraska. In the 1930 census, his mother, Gladys, sister and he were living with his grandparents, H.H. and Grace McClement. The family was living in Taylor Village, Nebraska. H.H. was serving as town marshal at the time. Then, in 1940, the family had moved to Shasta County, California. Donald's father, William H., was employed as an ironworker. The family lived in rural Eagle County, Colorado in the mid–1930s, the 1940 census indicated. According to the *Pueblo Chieftain*, Donald passed away 19 July 1999. He was married to Betty L. and had five children. After the war, Donald worked for Colorado Fuel and Iron Company (CF&I). He and his family lived in Pueblo.

Mercer, Roger H. (ser.no. 294-01-76):

Seaman 1st Class **Roger Holmes Mercer** enlisted 13 February 1945 at Indianapolis, Indiana. Roger was received aboard on 7 February 1946 from "Rec. Sta. Shoemaker, Calif." He was transferred to the Columbia River Group on 22 May 1946.

Roger was born 27 March 1927, in Indianapolis to Charles W. "Jack" and Ruby F. Mercer. He was an avid and skilled sportsman in his youth. He loved to play and watch baseball. After the war, Roger worked as a salesman of restaurant equipment. He married Marilyn Joan Prather on 30 July 1949. The couple had five children together. He continued to play sports and coached throughout his life. Roger passed away on 30 September 2010. He was buried near his parents at Forest Lawn Memory Gardens in Greenwood, Indiana.[130]

Morse, John G. (ser.no. 619-56-94):

ETM 3rd Class **John G. Morse** enlisted 27 January 1945. He joined the crew of 52 on 2 March 1946 from the receiving station at Shoemaker, California. He was present for duty aboard *LCS 52* for the quarter ending 1 April 1946.[131]

Nicola, Francis J. (ser.no. 286-43-19):

Seaman 1st Class **Francis J. Nicola** enlisted 29 November 1945 at Portland, Oregon. He was received aboard on 7 February 1946 from "Rec. Sta. Shoemaker, Calif." Present for duty aboard *LCS 52* the quarter ending 1 April 1946.[132]

Oakley, Gerald P. (ser.no. 619-60-63):

Seaman 2nd Class **Gerald P. Oakley** enlisted in Longmont, Colorado on 17 March 1945. He was received aboard *LCS 52* on 3 December 1945 from "ComLCS Flot. 3," then transferred to *LST 952* on 10 December 1945. On 5 April 1946 Gerald was transferred to the USS *Scribner* for transport to the West Coast for emergency leave and reassignment. He was serving aboard *LST 614* located at Haiphong, French Indo China, at the time of the transfer. He had been with that ship since 4 January 1946.[133] Gerald's home address in Longmont in 1946 was listed as 712 9th Avenue. He returned there after his service and was listed as a watch repairman.

Owens, Fred L. (ser.no. 263-53-40):

Seaman 1st Class **Fred L. Owens** enlisted 1 January 1942 at Raleigh, North Carolina. He was received aboard *LCS 52* on 7 February 1946 from "Rec. Sta. Shoemaker, Calif." Present for duty aboard *LCS 52* the quarter ending 1 April 1946.[134] Fred was most likely born 13 September 1921 and passed away 3 July 1972 in Philadelphia, Pennsylvania.

Parrish, Robert R. (ser.no. 357-93-28):
Fireman 1st Class **Robert R. Parrish** enlisted in Dallas, Texas on 11 December 1943. He reenlisted 4 October 1945 at Seattle, Washington. He was received aboard USS *Epping Forest* (LSD 4) on 20 May 1944 from "Amphibious Training Center—Tulagi." He was then transferred to RS Seattle on 29 October 1945. He was received aboard *LCS 52* on 7 February 1946 from "Rec. Sta. Shoemaker, Calif." Robert was transferred on 9 February 1946 to USNH Treasure Island. He was received back from Treasure Island on 16 February 1946. Robert was transferred to the Columbia River Group on 21 May 1946. On 19 June, Robert was received on *LSM 262*. By December of 1946 he was working aboard *LST 850*. Robert was transferred back to the Columbia River Group on 27 December.[135]

Racine, Eugene B. (ser.no. 301-34-75):
Seaman 1st Class **Eugene B. Racine** enlisted 26 December 1944 at Chicago, Illinois. Eugene was received aboard *LCS 52* on 7 February 1946 from "Rec. Sta. Shoemaker, Calif." He was present for duty the quarter ending 1 April 1946.[136]

Ramsey, Clyde B. (ser.no. 295-93-43):
Gunners Mate 2nd Class **Clyde B. Ramsey** enlisted 11 February 1941 at Nashville, Tennessee. He served aboard the USS *Washington* through 1941–42. On 1 March 1942, Clyde was charged with leaving his post without permission. He was fined $92.00 on the 5th during a Summary Court Martial. Clyde was the subject of a second SCM in October when he was found asleep on watch on the 17th of the month. He was fined $18 for two consecutive months. He was received aboard *LST 475* on 21 May 1943. Clyde was received aboard *LCS 52* on 7 February 1946 from "Rec. Sta. Shoemaker, Calif." GM2c Ramsey was transferred to the Columbia River Group on 22 May 1946. He was received aboard *ATA 206* on August 30 but transferred off due to disciplinary actions on 5 September 1946. He was sent back to the Sub-Group, 19th Fleet at Portland.[137]

Although Clyde's pre-war information could not be verified with certainty, he was probably the son of Henry M. and Martha Ramsey. Clyde was born in Virginia but was living with his family in Carter County, Tennessee by 1930. His father was a blacksmith working at a "silk mill." By 1940, Martha was listed as a widow. The family's income was coming from the oldest son, Lee, and daughter, Hope, working in a textile plant.

Samons, Richard M. (ser.no. 287-44-11):
Gunners Mate 2nd Class **Richard M. Samons** enlisted 4 September 1940 at Louisville, Kentucky. He was received aboard the USS *Idaho* on 10 November from NTS, Great Lakes. He served aboard the *Idaho* as an "Able Sailor" until 6 December 1940. His next assignment was on the *Chicago*. He was transferred from USS *Chicago* on 15 November 1941. He was temporarily aboard the USS *San Francisco* while she was at Pearl Harbor that month. Richard was received aboard USS *Chaumont* (AP5) on 21 November 1941 and sailed from Pearl Harbor on the 29th. He was listed as a "passenger" aboard her during January of 1942. His transfer orders listed him as going to "Langley FFT Trinity for duty." He was received on the USS *Trinity* (AO 13) on 20 January 1942. He was advanced to GM3c on 1 November 1942. On 1 June 1943 he was advanced in rating to GM2c. He was the subject of a Captain's Mast on 7 July 1943. He was reduced in rating to GM3c. He had kept his rank barely over a month.

He was sent to the "Mobile Hosp #9 for trtmt via Derreck" on 17 December 1943.

Richard was put aboard the USS *Mizar* (AF 12) on 20 December as a passenger from the R/S at San Francisco, California. He was received aboard the USS *Yukon* on 5 April 1944 from "RS, Pier 92, NY, NY." On 1 June he received his GM2c rating back. He was transferred to the "NavTraSta (Gunner's Mates and Select. Hyd) Wash. D.C." on 27 June. He served on the *Grafton* (APA 109) from 5 January 1945 through January 1946. Richard was transferred, "To: On emergency leave (30 days delay enroute) to report to NRS, Louisville, Ky." on 2 January 1946. Richard was received aboard *LCS 52* on 24 February 1946 from "Rec. Sta. Shoemaker, Calif." He was transferred to the Columbia River Group on 22 May 1946.[138]

Richard's military records used the single "m" spelling of his name. Richard was probably the ten-year-old who showed up in the 1930 census in Floyd County, Kentucky. He was the son of W.L., ("Lewis") and Sally C. Music Samons. Richard was born in Paintsville on 8 November 1921. His father and older brothers worked in the coal mines of Floyd County. By the time Richard reached adulthood, twenty, according to the 1940 census, he too was working in the mines. It appeared that his way out of the Kentucky mines was the Navy. Richard passed away on 14 March 1976 in Martin County. He was returned to his old homestead and buried in the Salisbury Cemetery at Hunter, Kentucky. There was a discrepancy between the Veterans Administration and Kentucky death records. The VA listed him as passing away on the 11th of the month. They also spelled his name "Sammons."

Schmidt, Paul E., Jr. (ser.no. 953-88-86):

Fireman 2nd Class **Paul E. Schmidt, Jr.,** enlisted 30 October 1945 at Detroit, Michigan. Paul was received aboard *LCS 52* on 9 February 1946 from "Rec. Station Shoemaker, Calif." Present for duty aboard *LCS 52* the quarter ending 1 April 1946.[139]

Swisher, Chester P. (ser.no. 311-36-27):

Chester P. Swisher Jr. Received aboard on 9 February 1946.[140]

Thiel, Edward J. (ser.no. 960-50-29):

Fireman 1st Class **Edward J. Thiel** enlisted 23 August 1945 at Milwaukee, Wisconsin. He was received aboard on 9 February 1946 from "Rec. Sta. Shoemaker, Calif." He was advanced to F1c on 15 May 1946. Edward was transferred to the Columbia River group, 19th Fleet on 22 June 1946.[141] A World War II sailor's grave was located in Willow Springs, Illinois with the epitaph "Edward John Thiel." He was born 25 December 1923 and passed away 17 April 2000.

Wertz, Carl Eugene (ser.no. 279-98-46):

Pharmacist's Mate 1st Class **Carl Eugene Wertz** (ser.no. 279-98-46) enlisted in the Navy on 21 May 1942 in Cincinnati, Ohio. He was on the commissioning report of the USS *Hendry* (APA-118) on 29 September 1944. He was promoted to HA1c on 1 February 1945. Carl was sent to the USS *Ozark* (LSV-2) for temporary duty on 11 February 1945.[142]

He joined the crew of *LCS 52* on 29 October 1945 for "independent duty." He was present for duty aboard the 52 on 31 December 1945. He was transferred to the separation center at Toledo, Ohio on 1 February 1946. Two records of veterans by the same name were located but it is more likely that Carl is buried in the M.J. Dolly Cooper Veterans Cemetery in Anderson, South Carolina. He was born on 21 June 1924 and died 21 October 2009. He is recorded as being a Navy veteran of World War II and holding the rank "PHM1."

West, Charles C. (ser.no. 258-31-36):

Gunners Mate 2nd Class **Charles C. West** enlisted 19 November 1940 at Baltimore, Maryland. Charles was received aboard on 7 February 1946 from "Rec. Sta. Shoemaker, Calif." He was present for duty aboard *LCS 52* for the quarter ending 1 April 1946.[143]

Williams, Joseph (ser.no. 582-41-45):

Steward's Mate 2nd Class **Joseph Williams** enlisted on 28 November 1945. He joined the crew of the 52 on 6 March 1946 from the receiving station at Shoemaker, California. He was transferred to the USN Hospital at Astoria, Oregon on 15 May 1946 "for treatment." He next appeared on the rolls of *LCS 24* for December 1946. He was transferred to "SubDiv 2" on 21 December 1946 by authority of the Commander Pacific Reserve Fleet. Joseph Williams enlisted in Columbia, South Carolina. Due to the common nature of the name, it was impossible to locate further records. There were three different Joseph Williamses aboard LCS ships during 1946–47. All three of those served as steward's mates.[144]

Williams, Robert J. (ser.no. 553-91-78):

(Indiscernible) **Robert J. Williams** enlisted (no date given) February 1944 (ser.no. 553-91-78) at NRS Santa Fe, New Mexico. He was received aboard on 6 February 1946 from "Rec. Sta. Shoemaker, Calif." He was present for duty aboard *LCS 52* for the quarter ending 1 April 1946.

Yoder, Don L. (ser.no. 650-63-02):

Fireman 2nd Class **Don L. Yoder** enlisted 28 September 1945. Don was received aboard *LCS 52* on 9 February 1946 from "Rec. Sta. Shoemaker, Calif." He was transferred to U.S. Naval Hospital Mare Island, California on 26 February 1946 and received back aboard on 20 March 1946 from the U.S. Naval Hospital, Mare Island, California. Present for duty the quarter ending 1 April 1946.[145]

Chapter Notes

Introduction

1. Tin can is a nickname among sailors for destroyers and the smaller destroyer escorts; however, it is used here in reference to the literal household object.
2. Nick Stoia, telephone interview by author, Alliance, OH. 2 June 2014.
3. Claude H. Cook, *Memoirs of Claude Harris Cook* (unpublished, undated). In possession of his grandson, Mike Kaolz.
4. John O. Harper, *Memoirs* (unpublished, 1994). In possession of his daughter, Carol Harper Marsh.

Chapter 1

1. The Joint Board, consisting of Army and Navy planners, was a predecessor of the Joint Chiefs of Staff.
2. William Manchester, *American Caesar: Douglas MacArthur 1880–1964* (New York: Dell, 1978), 448.
3. Manchester, *American Caesar*, 393.
4. Although American and Australian forces took Buna, New Guinea, a month before Guadalcanal fell, American forces were not committed in New Guinea until seven months after the Canal landings began.
5. Vice Admiral Turner nicknamed them "Mighty Midgets," as his fleet sailed toward the landings on Saipan, and the infamous Tokyo Rose called them "Miniature Destroyers."
6. Maury Klein, *A Call to Arms: Mobilizing America for World War II* (New York: Bloomsbury, 2013), 537.
7. Stoia, Interview, 2 June 2014.
8. Claude Cook to Caroline Artman, 22 August 1944, letter.
9. Cook to Artman, 22 August 1944.
10. *Ibid.*
11. Cook, *Memoirs*.
12. *Ibid.*
13. Harper, *Memoirs*.
14. *Ibid.*
15. *Ibid.*
16. *Ibid.*
17. *Ibid.*
18. *Ibid.*
19. Laton Burns. *Wartime Journal* (unpublished, 1944–1946). In possession of his daughter, Diane Burns Brads.
20. Diane Burns Brads, various email messages to author (2009–2014).
21. Foundation School records, Laton and Polly Burns. Berea College Special Collections & Archives, Berea, KY.
22. Brads to author.
23. *Ibid.*
24. *Ibid.*
25. Laton Burns to Kathleen Dezarn, July 1944, letter.
26. Burns to Dezarn, July 1944, letter.
27. *War Diaries*, LCS 52, September 1944.
28. Harold Cullen's obituary states "1911." However, the general consensus is 1912.
29. Norma Cullen Vines, various email messages to author, 2012–2014.
30. IV Corps of the Fifth Army, *Order of Battle* (9 April 1945).
31. Vines to author.
32. *Ibid.*
33. *Ibid.*
34. *Ibid.*

Chapter 2

1. "In The Navy" was released 30 May 1941, prior to United States involvement in the war.
2. Franklin D. Roosevelt, *Development of United States Foreign Policy: Addresses and Messages of Franklin D. Roosevelt* (Washington, D.C.: Government Printing Office, 1942), 120–125.
3. Theodore Roscoe, *United States Destroyer Operations in World War II* (Naval Institute, 1953), 37.
4. *World War II Draft Cards (Fourth Registration) for the State of New Jersey*. State Headquarters, ca. 1942. NARA Publication: M1986. NAI: 2555983. The National Archives at St. Louis, MO.
5. Oliver A. Gillespie, *The Official History of New Zealand in the Second World War, 1939–1945: The Pacific*. Edited by Howard Karl Kippenberger (Wellington, NZ: Historical Publications Branch 1952).
6. Steve Estes, *I Am a Man! Race, Manhood, and the Civil Rights Movement* (Chapel Hill: University of North Carolina Press, 2006), 28–29.

7. Angus Konstam, "Hero of Pearl Harbor: Doris Miller," *Naval Miscellany* (New York: Osprey, 2009).

8. A term used in one sense to refer to blacks who accept their social and economic relegation as destiny and feel there is no point in attempting to fight the corrupt and unsympathetic system.

9. Jimmie Meese Moomaw, *Southern Fried Child in Home Seeker's Paradise* (Bloomington, IN: AuthorHouse, 2010), 188.

10. Laura Pride quoted in Michael Keith Honey, *Black Workers Remember: An Oral History of Segregation, Unionism, and the Freedom Struggle* (Los Angeles: University of California Press, 2001), 50.

11. Virgil Thill. Interviews with author. Personal interview, Farmington Hills, MI. 23–24 June 2014.

12. Thill. Interviews, 23–24 June 2014.

13. *Ibid.*

14. Virgil Thill to author, various telephone interviews, 28 April–10 October 2014.

15. James L. Mooney, ed., *Dictionary of American Naval Fighting Ships*, Vol. III (Washington, D.C.: Government Printing Office, 1969), 161.

16. Virgil Thill, personal interview, 24–25 June 2014.

17. *Ibid.*

18. *Ibid.*

19. Saundra Syrian Goss to author, telephone interview, 10 June 2014. Mrs. Goss is the daughter of John Syrian.

20. John T. Edge, "Fast Food Even Before Fast Food," *New York Times*, 30 September 2009, D1.

21. West Virginia Archives and History, Division of Culture and History (2014). http://www.wvculture.org/history/government/immigration05.html.

22. S. Thomas Bond, "The Oldest Things I Know About Our Land" in *Farming as I Have Known It: 60 Years in Central Appalachia* (2011), http://www.lhfwv.com/book/show.php?chapter=title-page-i.

23. Department of Commerce, U.S. Census data, 1930 and 1940, Grant District, Harrison County, WV. Sheets 3B and 14-B.

24. Henry W. Francis, "Report, Clarksburg, West Virginia," November 25, 1934, Franklin D. Roosevelt Library, Hopkins Papers, Box 66.

25. Goss to author, 10 June 2014.

26. *Ibid.*

27. *Ibid.*

28. Cook, *Memoirs*.

29. In his memoirs, Claude Cook wrote "Henry Gibson." He probably transposed the 1960s comedian's first name in the moment. Hoot Gibson was the co-actor of the day with Carey and Mix. All three were stars of the early, silent and talking, western genre.

30. Cook, *Memoirs*.

31. *Ibid.*

32. *Ibid.*

33. *Ibid.*

34. Cook, *Memoirs*, 17.

35. Ibid, 20.

36. Mike Kaloz to author, various email messages, 2013–2014.

Chapter 3

1. *Fourth Registration Draft Cards (WWII)*. Ohio State Headquarters, ca. 1942. NAI: 623234. The National Archives at St. Louis, MO.

2. Ancestry.com. *U.S., School Yearbooks, 1880–2012* [database online]. Provo, UT: Ancestry.com, 2010.

3. *Deck Log*, LCS 52, 6 October 1944.

4. *World War I Selective Service System Draft Registration Cards, 1917–1918*. Washington, D.C.: National Archives and Records Administration. M1509, 4,582 rolls.

5. Clifford Stewart, telephone interview by author, 14 October 2014.

6. Paul Zarbock, "Interview of James G. Paterson" *World War II: Through the Eyes of Cape Fear* (University of North Carolina at Willington: Trans. No. 501, 9 July 2003), http://library.uncw.edu/capefearww2/voices/Paterson_James501.html.

7. Paterson misidentifies the *Exhibitor* as the *Excalibur* in his oral history. He also later identifies this ship, not the *Fairport*, as the ship that was sunk. Interview of James G. Paterson, 9 July 2003.

8. Stewart to author.

9. Franklin J. Hillson, "Barrage Balloons for Low-Level Air Defense," *Airpower Journal* (Summer 1988).

10. Captain Kenneth Wing of the *Beaconhill* stated he departed New York in a convoy of six ships on 4 January.

11. There is some discrepancy in the number of ships in the Atlantic convoy, ranging from 18, 19, 25 and 30. The convoy leaving Scotland was probably the 30 ship convoy.

12. Justin F. Gleichauf, *Unsung Sailors: The Naval Armed Guard in World War II* (Annapolis, MD: Naval Institute, 1990), 210–218.

13. Russian Ministry of Communications and Mass Media.

14. Scott Ostler, "Cliff Stewart, 97, Made Baseball History in Ria During WWII," *San Francisco Chronicle*, http://www.sfgate.com/sports/ostler/article/Cliff-Stewart-97-made-baseball-history-in-5503225.php#photo-6346748.

15. Stewart, interview, 14 Oct. 2014.

16. *Ibid.*

17. Cook to Artman, 8 October 1944, letter.

18. Burns to Dezarn, 27 October 1944, letter.

19. Burns to Dezarn, 27 October 1944, letter.

20. Harper, *Memoirs*.

21. Vines to author. Norma recalled that her dad told her everyone went by "Mac."

22. Vines to author. Norma felt that her dad and Burroughs were best friends, in spite of the rank difference.

23. United States Census, 1940. Sacramento, CA. Roll: T627_286; Page: 8A; Enumeration District: 34–131A.

24. Geoffrey Burroughs to author, email, 22 June 2014.

25. Burroughs to author.

26. *Ibid.*

27. *Ibid.*

28. Elaine Burroughs to Geoffrey Burroughs, email to author, 22 June 2014.
29. Elaine Burroughs to Geoffrey Burroughs, email to author.
30. *Ibid.*
31. *Ibid.*
32. *Deck Log*, LCS 52, 8 November 1944.
33. *War Diary*, LCS 52.
34. Harper, *Memories*.
35. Operation Forager, invasion of the Mariana Islands.
36. Thill to author.
37. Harper, *Memoirs*.
38. Albert Parker to Virgil Thill, circa 1996, letter.
39. The photographs give the spelling of "Demayo" but all official records show Eugene De Maio.
40. Chet Cunningham, *The Frogmen of World War II: An Oral History of the U.S. Navy's Underwater Demolition Units* (New York: Pocket, 2005), 207–8.
41. From Japanese report: Annansaki, 22 August 1944, Special Report, GOTTO Unit, Intelligence Office (JOKOSHITSU).
42. *Genealogical and Personal History of the Upper Monongahela Valley, West Virginia* (Baltimore: Genealogical Publishing, 1978), 443–445.
43. The city directors for Fairmont listed him as a "Barber bsmt" throughout the 1920 and 1930s. While the abbreviation for "basement" is used often in this context, I could find no connection to the terms joined together in this manner or what it meant.
44. The grade of "Striker" is usually reserved for those who have completed a technical school. A technical field such as radioman was given the title of striker to differentiate them from regular seamen.
45. Stoia to author.
46. Deborah D. Moore, *GI Jews: How World War Two Changed a Generation* (Cambridge, MA: Belknap Press of Harvard University Press, 2004), 32.
47. *Ibid.*
48. *1930*; Census Place: *Cincinnati, Hamilton, Ohio*; Roll: *1807*; Page: *5A*; Enumeration District: *0039*; Image: *448.0*; FHL microfilm: *2341541*.
49. Timothy Snyder, *Bloodlands: Europe Between Hitler and Stalin* (New York: Basic, 2012), 143.
50. Saul Friedlander, *The Years of Extermination: Nazi Germany and the Jews 1939–1945* (New York: HarperCollins, 2007), 225.
51. All figures courtesy of American-Israeli Cooperative Enterprise, *WWII Statistics on Jewish American Soldiers*, www.jewishvirtuallibrary.org/jsource/ww2/jewstats.html.
52. Louis V. Plant, *A Brief History of LCS 55* (unpublished narrative), www.navsource.org/archives/10/05/050055h.htm.
53. Harper, *Memoirs*.
54. Ernie Pyle, *Ernie's War: The Best of Ernie Pyle's World War II Dispatches*, edited by David Nichols (New York: Random House, 1986), 372; Captain Sakae Ōba surrendered, along with his 49 surviving troops, 16 months after the battle for Saipan and 90 days after V-J Day. *The Daily Target*, 2 December 1945: "Remnants of Japanese Forces on Saipan as they Surrendered Yesterday."
55. Thill to author.
56. Thill to author.
57. Statement of Lt. Harper. The frames are simply the ribs of a ship. Bulwark is the strake of shell plating above a weather or shelter deck. It helps to keep the deck dry and also serves as a guard against losing cargo or men overboard.

Chapter 4

1. Thill to author.
2. *Ibid.*
3. *Ibid.*
4. *Ibid.*
5. Stoia to author.
6. Vines to author.
7. Lois Thill to author. Personal interview, 23 June 2014.
8. Beverly Johnson to author, 16 April 2014, letter.
9. James D. Hornfischer, *The Last Stand of the Tin Can Sailors* (New York: Bantam-Dell, 2004), 213.
10. Alfred Tennyson, *Poems of Alfred Tennyson* (Boston: J.E. Tilton and Co., 1866), 441.
11. Subsequently the letters ended up in the archives of the National Pacific War Museum. The pinup picture was excluded only because all information as to artist and copyright could not be located.
12. Ray C. Hunt and Bernard Norling, *Behind Japanese Lines: An American Guerrilla in the Philippines* (Lexington: University Press of Kentucky, 1986), 65.
13. Hunt, *Behind Japanese Lines*, 48.
14. Harper, *Memoirs*.
15. Cook, *Memoirs*.

Chpater 5

1. Burrell argues that in a seven-month period, out of 2800 bombing raids on Japan, only nine bombers were shot down and this reasoning for taking Iwo was irrelevant. Robert S. Burrell, *The Ghosts of Iwo Jima* (College Station: Texas A&M University Press, 2006), 105.
2. Emma Belle Petcher, "The War," directed and produced by Ken Burns and Lynn Novick, Florentine Films, 2007.
3. "Scout Awards Go to 105 at Honor Court." *Hammond Times*, 17 February 1939, Page 24.
4. *Selective Service Registration Cards, World War II: Fourth Registration*. Records of the Selective Service System, Record Group Number 147. National Archives and Records Administration.
5. Hammond High School "Dune" Yearbook 1944.
6. *Applications for Headstones*, compiled 01/01/1925 06/30/1970, documenting the period ca. 1776–1970 ARC: 596118. Records of the Office of the Quartermaster General, 1774–1985, Record Group 92. National Archives and Records Administration, Washington, D.C.
7. Jimmy Carter, future president of the United States, served with her last crew as an ensign.

8. John, Harper, Virgil Thill and Larry Cullen, *A Short History of LCS 52* (unpublished).
9. Bill D. Ross, *Iwo Jima: Legacy of Valor* (New York: Vintage, 1985), 60.
10. "Walking" fire, or rounds, refers to an adjustment of rounds after each impact until they are on target. In this case, the rounds are being adjusted so that they stay in front of advancing friendly ground forces and do not remain in one location until they land on those friendlies. It is used as a method of keeping the enemy's head down while the attacking force advances.
11. William S. Bartley, *Iwo Jima: Amphibious Epic* (Washington, D.C.: U.S. Government Printing Office, 1954), 53.
12. *War Diary*, LCS 52.
13. Derrick Wright, *The Battle for Iwo Jima 1945* (Gloucestershire, UK: Sutton, 1999), 35.
14. "Iwo Like a Pork Chop Sizzling on Yank Skillet," *The Brooklyn Daily Eagle*, (New York), 19 February 1945, 2.
15. *A Short History of LCS 52*.
16. Thill to author.
17. Bartley, *Iwo Jima*, 129–130.
18. The term "marking" targets was not used until many wars later and was usually accomplished by the use of a laser marker on the target, put there by a special operations team hiding nearby. I have included the term in the text to better describe the procedure.
19. After Action Report, Gunboat Support Group.
20. V Amphibious Corps Landing Force "Special Action Report, Iwo Jima Campaign" (30 May 1945).
21. The 40mm guns aboard the 52, and all other ships, were designed by the Swedish company AB Bofors.
22. Thill to author.
23. Albert Parker, *Notes* to Virgil Thill, March 1998.
24. Thill to author.
25. Theodore Roscoe, *United States Destroyer Operations in World War II* (Annapolis, MD: Naval Institute, 1953), 364–366.
26. Stoia to author.
27. For a closer look at Lt. Col. Dillon's awards: http://militarytimes.com/citations-medals-awards/recipient.php?recipientid=8293.
28. *Ships Log*, LCS 52.
29. Letter from Claude Cook to Caroline Artman 15 March 1945.

Chapter 6

1. Grandson of Genghis Khan.
2. Bill, Sloan, *Ultimate Battle* (New York: Simon & Schuster, 2007), 92. Sloan gives no reference to the origin of these figures, and it is impossible to determine if this includes allied vessels lost or damaged by kamikaze attacks as well.
3. Sloan, *Ultimate Battle*, 94.
4. The investigation after the attack did not indicate any ammunition exploding. Harper probably saw the explosions from the engine room and two of the three enemy bombs that went off. Or, over the years he recalled one of the ships hit the following night and morning and the two memories merged.
5. Harper, *Memoirs*.
6. Ibid.
7. Ibid.
8. Marty Roberts, *Memoirs*, "Part 5 of 8: YMS-468 in Battle, Up to Japan's Surrender." http://yms299.org/archives/1088.
9. Harper, *Memoirs*.
10. Danielle Glassmeyer, "The Wisdom of Gracious Acceptance: Okinawa, Mass Suicide, and the Cultural Work of Teahouse of the August Moon," *Soundings: An Interdisciplinary Journal* 96, no. 4 (2013), 398–430.
11. Dennis Warner, Peggy Warner and Sadao Seno, *The Sacred Warriors: Japan's Suicide Legions* (New York: Van Nostrand Reinhold, 1982), 218.
12. "Flash Red": Air attack imminent, enemy aircraft in vicinity. All ships set Condition 1. "Control Green": All guns hold fire on air targets.
13. "Control Yellow": All guns fire on any air targets.
14. Harper, *Memories*.
15. *Ship's Log*, 19 April 1945.
16. *War Diary*, LCS 52.
17. Thill to author.
18. Mefferd. Action Report, 11 May 1945.
19. Ibid.
20. Robin L. Rielly, *Kamikazes, Corsairs, and Picket Ships: Okinawa, 1945* (Havertown, PA: Cassmate, 2008), 239–240; Morgan Winget, "WWII Veteran—Art Martin: Sharing their Stories" *Orrviews*, Orrville, OH: September 11, 2009, Pg. 7.
21. Thill to author.
22. *A Short History of LCS 52*.
23. *Report of AA Action off Okinawa Jima, Ryukyu Islands*, 5/11/45, LCS 109. Micro No.: 129233, Reel: A1708. The National Archives, Washington, D.C.
24. Baron J. Mullaney, Action Report, 15 May 1945. Hugh W. Hadley (DD-774) Memorial Web Site. http://www.hadley.com/Hile.htm. Accessed 27 March 2015.
25. Statement of Donald Lee Hile (unknown date), Hugh W. Hadley (DD-774) Memorial Web Site. http://www.hadley.com/Hile.htm. Accessed 27 March 2015.

Chapter 7

1. Hatsuho Naito, *Thunder Gods: The Kamikaze Pilots Tell Their Story* (New York: Kodansha, 1989), 176.
2. Harper, *Memoirs*.
3. William Crawford Eddy, Archibald Hart Brolly, Eugene Smith Pulliam, Elmer Charles Upton, and George William Thomas, *Wartime Refresher in Fundamental Mathematics* (Upper Saddle River, NJ: Prentice-Hall, 1943).
4. Deborah Martinez, "Ward Island Was Hush-Hush Radar School," *Corpus Christi Caller-Times*, 7 March 2000. http://www.caller2.com/2000/march/07/today/local_ne/1801.html.
5. A. Hoyt Taylor, "The Vocabulary of Radio," in

Radio Reminiscences: A Half Century (Washington, D.C.: U.S. Naval Research Laboratory, 1948).

6. "Jacob E. Trimmer Dies in Carlisle Hospital," *New Oxford Item* (PA), 2 January 1958, 2.

7. Information on the history of Carlisle from Dr. George P. Donehoo, "History Past & Present" (Historical and Museum Commission, 1981), http://www.ccpa.net/DocumentCenter/Home/View/7176. Accessed 4 June 2014.

8. Elizabeth Beittel Hilliard to author, 24 July 2014, letter.

9. Frank's brother Joseph was brought back to the States in 1944 from his original burial place in France, where he fell.

10. Stoia to author.

11. Lawrence B. Smith, *Aboard LCS 11 in WW II: A Memoir by Lawrence B. Smith* (Bloomington, IN: Xlibris, 2011), 32–33.

12. Warner, *Japan's Suicide Legions*, 237–238.

13. In Harper's Action Report he recorded the time of attack at 22:23 hours.

14. Russell Copeland to Virgil Thill. 9 February 1994, letter.

15. *Ibid.*

16. Copeland to Thill, letter.

17. Hoffman, *Daily Astorian*, 12 January 2007. Janine Manny, "Clatskanie's Oren Tween Served His Town Well," *Longview Daily News*, 16 February 2006. Deborah Steele Hazen, "His Name Is Synonymous with Community Service in Clatskanie," *Clatskanie Chief*, 28 June 2001, 1, 6 and 7.

18. Larry Cullen to Harold D. Cullen (father), 26 August 1945, letter.

19. The buckle was later passed on to Virgil Thill and remains in his possession.

20. Filial: of or due from a son or daughter. Translation Mordecai G. Sheftall.

21. A first lieutenant in the Navy heads the deck department, made up of boatswain's mates who maintain the exterior of the ship's surfaces, anchor and moor the ship, man the rescue and assistance lifeboats, and monitor underway replenishment. United States Naval Reserve Intelligence Program, *Ready-for-Sea Handbook* (San Diego: 1999), http://www.fas.org/irp/doddir/navy/rfs/part04.htm.

22. Official Website of Warren Minnesota, http://www.warrenminnesota.com/index.asp?Type=B_BASIC&SEC=%7B0460851E-007E-40EA-B360-6B32DC21BB70%7D. Accessed: 28 May 2014.

23. The decathlon is an accumulation of points collected over ten track and field events during one season. Warren High School Yearbook, 1942, "Ponier." Ancestry.com. *U.S. School Yearbooks* [database online]. Provo, UT: Ancestry.com, 2010.

24. Vernon Finn Grinaker, "Concordia Sports—The First One Hundred Years," http://wwwp.cord.edu/dept/sports/sportsbackup/finn/ch5a42.html, Accessed 28 May 2014.

25. The following year the name was changed to the War Training Service. *Moorhead Daily News*, "Concordia Students Finish CAA Course," 7 February 1942.

26. Copeland to Thill, letter.

27. Thill to author.

28. Larry Cullen to his father, letter.

29. Thill to author.

30. E. Andrew Wilde, Jr. editor, *The USS Drexler (DD-741) in World War II: Documents, Photographs, Recollections* (Needham, MA: Self-published, 2003).

31. Rex Davis, *May 28, 1945—Another Day of Infamy*, http://www.kamikazeimages.net/stories/lcsl114/index.htm.

32. Thill to author.

33. Rikihei Inoguchi and Tadashi Nakajima, "The Divine Wind" Japan's Kamikaze Force in World War II (Annapolis: United States Naval Institute, 1958), 203–205.

34. Emiko Ohnuki-Tierney, *Kamikaze Diaries: Reflections of Japanese Student Soldiers* (Chicago: University of Chicago Press, 2006), 163.

35. Cook to Artman, letter. 30 May 1945.

36. Cook to Artman, letter.

37. *Ship's Log*, LCS 52, 5 June 1945.

38. Thill to author.

39. *Ibid.*

40. Robin L. Rielly, *Kamikaze Attacks of World War II: A Complete History of Japanese Suicide Strikes on American Ships, by Aircraft and Other Means* (Jefferson, NC: McFarland & Company, 2010), 293–294.

Chapter 8

1. The 1930 and 1940 Federal Census listed their names as "Maidic." However in a 1961 article, in which Edward contributed, his and his father's name was given as "Madic."

2. Thill and Stoia to author.

3. Cook to Artman, letter.

4. Harper, *Memoirs*.

5. *Ibid.*

6. Alvin P. Stauffer, *US Army in WW 2: The Quartermaster Corps: Operations in the War Against Japan* (Washington, D.C.: Government Printing Office, 2004), 90.

7. Harper, *Memoirs*.

8. Hunt, *Behind Japanese Lines*, 4.

9. "School News Digest," *The Clearing House* 19, no. 6 (1945): 382.

10. Harper, *Memoirs*.

11. Burns to Dezarn, letter.

12. Thill to author.

13. Burns to Dezarn, letter.

14. Cook to Artman, letter.

15. Dan Kurzman, *Fatal Voyage: The Sinking of the Indianapolis* (New York: Broadway, 2001), 14.

16. General Leslie Groves, *Memorandum for the Secretary of War*, July 18, 1945. Harry S. Truman Library, Papers of Lansing Lamont. http://www.pbs.org/wgbh/americanexperience/features/primary-resources/truman-bombtest.

17. Cook to Artman, letter.

18. In July 2001 the Secretary of the Navy exonerated Capt. McVay of the loss of his ship and crew. The conviction still remains in his official record and requires a presidential order to expunge it.

19. Burns to Dezarn, letter.

20. Harper, *Memoirs*.
21. Copeland to Thill, letter.
22. *World War I Selective Service System Draft Registration Cards, 1917–1918*. Washington, D.C.: National Archives and Records Administration. M1509, 4,582 rolls.
23. *Selective Service Registration Cards, World War II: Fourth Registration*. Records of the Selective Service System, Record Group Number 147. National Archives and Records Administration.
24. Francis Martin, "Delinquency of Adolescent Boys," *The Journal of Education* 106, no. 14 (1927), 357.
25. *Ibid.*
26. George, according to Internet genealogy sources, may have married again and died in 1945 in Massachusetts; however, no primary documents link the two men. It is more likely Jennie was a widow by the 1930 census.
27. Cullen to father, letter.
28. Cullen to his father, letter, 26 August 1945. Rob Reilly collection, National Museum of the Pacific War, Fredericksburg, TX.

Chpater 9

1. Cook to Artman, letter.
2. Lillian Natsue Morgan, *Made In Japan: Lillian Natsue Uehara Morgan's Life Story* (Bloomington, IN: Xlibris, 2011), 112–113.
3. Harper, *Memoirs*.
4. Douglas MacArthur, *Reports of General MacArthur: Japanese Operations in the Southwest Pacific Area*, Vol. II—Pt. II. (Washington, D.C.: Government Printing Office, 1966), 728.
5. Cook, *Memoirs*.
6. Wesley Frank Craven and James Lea Cate, eds., *The Army Air Forces in World War II*, Vol. V (Chicago: University of Chicago Press, 1953), 666, 672–673.
7. Lt. Toxey H. Smith to Ida Newsom, 19 August 1945, letter. National Museum of the Pacific War Archives and Special Collections, Fredericksburg, Texas. LT. Smith was a crewmember of *LCS 113*.
8. Harper, *Memoirs*.
9. *Ibid.*
10. Cook to Artman, letter.
11. Cook, *Memoirs*.
12. Cook to Artman, letter.
13. *Ibid.*
14. *Ship's Log*, USS Suwanee, 16 October 1945.
15. Maurer Maurer, ed., *Air Force Combat Units of World War II* (Washington, D.C.: Government Printing Office, 1983), 210–11.
16. Austin Smith, *Tokushima Air Raids Digital Archive*. http://impressionsofeastasia.com/tokushima-air-raids-digital-archive.
17. Thill to author.
18. *Ibid.*
19. After making contact with the National Archives, Maxwell AFB (holders of World War II Army Air Corps records), the Army Historical Center and several other government agencies—all claimed to not have, or be able to locate, the incident. Once the body was moved to shore, he seems to have disappeared from record.
20. Shadow factories were those non-military producing factories which were converted over to make military equipment for the war effort. Every country, including the U.S., refitted factories to manufacture war materials. The name has nothing to do with covert operations. In Japanese urban areas, machines were often hidden inside the homes of the workers.
21. These two accounts of the Harrodsburg Tankers are included here as an example of Americans who spent the longest duration in Japanese prisons. I grew up listening to firsthand accounts of the Tankers' experiences in prison camps and quote them as such.
22. Ensign W. C. Warren III, *A Brief History of LCS 86*, http://www.navsource.org/archives/10/05/050086h.htm; Mason, William, telephone interview by author, 6 June 2014.
23. Thill to author.
24. M. G. Sheftall, *Blossoms in the Wind: Human Legacies of the Kamikaze* (New York: NAL Caliber, 2005), 141. Ōka was the Japanese name derived from its proposer, Lt. Masakazu Ōta. Officially, the Ōka was known as the Project Marudai Special Attack Craft.
25. Interpretation of pilot's uniforms and probable backgrounds courtesy of M. G. Sheftall, Ph.D., author of *Blossoms in the Wind: Human Legacies of the Kamikaze*.
26. Naito, *Thunder Gods*, 25.
27. Robin L. Rielly, *Kamikaze Attacks of World War II: A Complete History of Japanese Suicide Strikes on American Ships, by Aircraft and Other Means* (Jefferson, NC: McFarland, 2010), 27–28.
28. "Last Letters of Kamikaze Pilots," *Manoa* (Summer 2001), 120, 121, 122.
29. Evan Thomas, *Sea of Thunder: Four Commanders and the Last Great Naval Campaign 1941–1945* (New York: Simon & Schuster, 2006), 338. Paraphrased quote from "Statements" of Togo # 50304.
30. By 1945, an LST would have been armed with no more than four 40mm guns and two 20mm guns.
31. "Young Promising Wrestlers," *The Japan Times*, 24 January 1901.
32. Thill to author.
33. Burns gave the dates of 13 and 18. In other accounts, such as Ensign Parker's, the dates are 12 and 17 for departure and arrival in Korea. It is more than likely Ensign Parker is correct, having access to the log entries.
34. Harper, *Memoirs*.
35. *Ibid.*
36. *Ibid.*
37. It seems impossible to track the quote to its exact date and place. Hoover was a mining engineer working in the local area when the Boxer Rebellion brought him and his new bride into the fray in June 1900. Hoover, not quite twenty-eight years old, was cited for his bravery and the assistance he gave the military and civilians during the months he was captive to the siege of Tientsin.
38. An estimated half-million Japanese soldiers and civilians were eventually evacuated back to their homeland after the war.
39. Thill to author.

40. Harper, *Memoirs*.
41. *Ibid*.
42. Michael Parkyn, "Operation Beleaguer: The Marine III Amphibious Corps in North China, 1945–49," *Marine Corps Gazette* (July 2001), 36.
43. Benis M. Frank and Henry I. Shaw Jr., *Victory and Occupation: History of the U.S. Marine Corps Operations in World War II*, Vol. V (Washington, D.C.: Government Printing Office, 1968), 533.
44. Henry I. Shaw Jr., *The United States Marines in North China 1945–1949*, 2d ed. (Washington, D.C.: Government Printing, 1962), 2.
45. Thill to author.
46. *Ibid*.
47. *Ibid*.
48. In former times, hazing was a large part of the ceremonies and sometimes took a cruel turn. In 1997 the U.S. Navy, while recognizing the value of naval tradition, put official limits on activities which could result in physical or emotional harm to a sailor or marine. *SecNav Instruction 1610.2*, 1 October 1997.
49. Thill to author.
50. Ambrose Burns Jr. to author, various conversations.
51. Originally called the Works Progress Administration, the name was changed in 1939 to Works Projects Administration.
52. *War Diaries*, 1941–1945, National Archives Identifier: 4697018, Record Group 38. The National Archives at College Park, MD.
53. *War Diaries*, CINCPAC, 4697018, Group: 38. The National Archives at College Park, MD.
54. Fred Rasmen, "Maryland Survived Pearl Harbor Attack Battleship: A Week Later 'Fighting Mary' Was Able to Sail Away for Repairs and Later Lived Up to Its Nickname as the U.S. Pushed Japan Back in the Pacific," *Baltimore Sun*, 7 December 1997.
55. Action Report of Captain D.C. Godwin for 7 December 1941, *Maryland*, prepared 15 December 1941.

Chapter 10

1. Tom Brokaw, *The Greatest Generation* (New York: Dell, 1998).
2. *Honolulu, Hawaii, National Memorial Cemetery of the Pacific (Punchbowl), 1941–2011*. Interment Control Forms, 1928–1962. Interment Control Forms, A1 2110-B. Records of the Office of the Quartermaster General, 1774–1985, Record Group 92. National Archives, College Park, MD.
3. Geoffrey Burroughs, *Destiny Answers* (Charleston, SC: CreateSpace, 2011).
4. Thill to author.
5. *Ibid*.
6. *Ibid*.
7. *Ibid*.
8. Andrew Charles Roseluke served as a combat engineer from 1950 through August 1951. He was born in Pennsylvania, a first-generation American, in 1924. He died in 1957.
9. Thill to author.
10. Lois Thill to author, personal interview, 24–25 June 2014, Farmington Hills, MI.
11. Lois Thill to author.
12. Virgil Thill to author.
13. Commonly referred to by military members as "Shit on a Shingle" (SOS). It is a breakfast dish served in mess halls and consists of a thin textured beef gravy covering an ordinary piece of toast. The blandness of the concoction defies description.
14. Laderan Banadero (Suicide Cliff) is located on the northern end of Saipan, where hundreds of civilians jumped from to avoid the horrors, they were told by Japanese propaganda, would happen to them at the hands of the Americans.
15. Richard F. Newcomb and Harry Schmidt, *Iwo Jima: The Dramatic Account of the Epic Battle That Turned the Tide of World War II* (New York: Henry Holt, 1965), 57.
16. Lois Thill to author.
17. Obituaries, http://bangordailynews.com/2008/09/25/obituaries/joy-k-libby.
18. Brads to author.
19. *Ibid*.
20. *Ibid*.
21. Clay County Historical and Genealogical Society, Manchester, KY.
22. *Ibid*.
23. Parker to Thill, letter.
24. Kaloz to author.
25. Now known as the "Old" Cumberland County Prison, it operated from 1854 to 1954.
26. Elizabeth Hilliard to author, various email messages, 2014.
27. Gerald Bledsoe to John Harper, letter March 1997.
28. Not to be confused with the USS *Darter* (SS-227), grounded and then purposefully sunk in August 1944.
29. Jerry Bledsoe to John Harper, letter.
30. Stewart to author, interview, 14 October 2014.
31. *Ibid*.
32. *United States Military Registers, 1902–1985*. Salem, OR: Oregon State Library.
33. The place of origin for the dance is thought to be Bohemia, but the dance was accepted and varied throughout Europe. It is a partnered folk dance, slower than a traditional polka.
34. Nancy Hoffman, "Oren Tweet Watched the Flag Being Raised on Mount Suribachi," *Daily Astorian*, 12 January 2007. http://www.dailyastorian.com/20070112/oren-tweet-watched-the-flag-being-raised-on-mount-suribachi. *Daily Astorian*, "Obituary," 16 February 2006.
35. *The Clatskanie Chief*, 1 November 2012, http://www.clatskaniechiefnews.com/2012/10/31/november-1-2012-6/.
36. Hoffman, "Oren Tweet."
37. National Cemetery Administration. *U.S. Veterans Gravesites, ca. 1775–2006*. New Hampshire, Marriage and Divorce Records, 1659–1947. 1940; Census Place: Malden, Middlesex, MA; Roll: T627_1609; Page: 5B; Enumeration District: 9–264.
38. *U.S. Social Security Death Index. California Mar-*

riage Index, 1949–1959. U.S. Social Security Applications and Claims Index, 1936–2007. U.S. School Yearbooks, 1880–2012. 1940; Census Place: *Spokane, Washington*; Roll: T627_4387; Page: 13A; Enumeration District: 41–101.

39. *Applications for Headstones for U.S. Military Veterans, 1925–1941.* Microfilm publication M1916, 134 rolls. ARC ID: 596118. Records of the Office of the Quartermaster General, Record Group 92. National Archives.

40. Obituary of Charles Darnell, Massillon Public Library.

41. *Ibid.*

42. Stoia to author.

43. *Ibid.*

44. Harper, *Memoirs*.

45. Mike Gordon, "Attack on Pearl Harbor: 65 Years Later," *Honolulu Advertiser*, 8 December 2006.

46. George W. Bush, *Remarks of the 60th Anniversary of V-J Day in San Diego, California August 30, 2005* (Washington, D.C.: Government Printing Office, 2005).

Chapter 12

1. *Muster Rolls of U.S. Navy Ships, Stations, and Other Naval Activities, 01/01/1939–01/01/1949*; A-1 Entry 135, 10230 rolls, ARC ID: 594996. Records of the Bureau of Naval Personnel, Record Group Number 24. National Archives at College Park, College Park, MD.

2. *Muster Rolls of U.S. Navy Ships, Stations, and Other Naval Activities.*

3. *Death Certificates and Index, December 20, 1908–December 31, 1953.* State Archives Series 3094. Ohio Historical Society.

4. *Muster Rolls of U.S. Navy Ships, Stations, and Other Naval Activities.*

5. *U.S. Cemetery and Funeral Home Collection* [database online]. Provo, UT: Ancestry.com.

6. *Muster Rolls of U.S. Navy Ships.*

7. *Ibid.*

8. *Ibid.*

9. Lois Thill to author.

10. *Muster Rolls of U.S. Navy Ships.*

11. *Ibid.*

12. *Ibid.*

13. *Applications for Headstones for U.S. Military Veterans, 1925–1941.* Microfilm publication M1916, 134 rolls. ARC ID: 596118. Records of the Office of the Quartermaster General, Record Group 92. National Archives at Washington, D.C.

14. *United States Obituary Collection* [database online]. Provo, UT: Ancestry.com.

15. *Muster Rolls of U.S. Navy Ships.*

16. *Monroe County, Indiana, Obituary Index, 1899–2011* [database online]. Provo, UT: Ancestry.com.

17. *Muster Rolls of U.S. Navy Ships.*

18. Responsible for operating new fire control systems, as well as maintaining and repairing them as necessary.

19. *Muster Rolls of U.S. Navy Ships.*

20. Pennsylvania. World War II Veterans Compensation Applications, circa 1950s. Records of the Department of Military and Veterans Affairs, Record Group 19, Series 19.92 (877 cartons). Pennsylvania Historical and Museum Commission, Harrisburg.

21. *Muster Rolls of U.S. Navy Ships.*

22. The storekeeper is responsible for operating a stockroom or store, or an accounting system, and/or the handling of fiscal and materiel accounting, under supervision of supply officer.

23. Vines to author.

24. *Ibid.*

25. *Find A Grave*, http://www.findagrave.com/cgi-bin/fg.cgi.

26. *Muster Rolls of U.S. Navy Ships.*

27. *Ibid.*

28. *World War II Draft Cards (Fourth Registration) for the State of Pennsylvania*; State Headquarters: *Pennsylvania*; Microfilm Series: *M1951*; Microfilm Roll: 73.

29. Pennsylvania. World War II Veterans Compensation Applications, circa 1950s. Records of the Department of Military and Veterans Affairs, Record Group 19, Series 19.92 (877 cartons). Pennsylvania Historical and Museum Commission, Harrisburg.

30. Pennsylvania Historical and Museum Commission, Harrisburg; *Pennsylvania Veterans Burial Cards, 1929–1990*; Series Number: *Series 3*.

31. *Muster Rolls of U.S. Navy Ships.*

32. Pennsylvania. World War II Veterans Compensation Applications, circa 1950s. Records of the Department of Military and Veterans Affairs, Record Group 19, Series 19.92 (877 cartons). Pennsylvania Historical and Museum Commission, Harrisburg.

33. *Muster Rolls of U.S. Navy Ships.*

34. *United States Obituary Collection.*

35. When the Command alleges that a military member is guilty of committing a minor violation of the Uniform Code of Military Justice (UCMJ) it may impose on the sailor a nonjudicial punishment (NJP). The Command is authorized to deal with minor violations or infractions of the UCMJ in this manner. In the Navy and Marines, the Article 15 or NJP procedure is called a "Captain's Mast."

36. Formally the *Crescent City AP-40*. She was converted on 25 February 1945 to a temporary hospital ship. She began receiving casualties from Okinawa on 6 April 1945 and continued that mission until the end of the war. Patients were in general transferred from AP 21 to the *Hope*.

37. *Muster Rolls of U.S. Navy Ships.*

38. *Find A Grave.*

39. *World War I Selective Service System Draft Registration Cards, 1917–1918.* Washington, D.C.: National Archives and Records Administration. M1509, 4,582 rolls.

40. Lois Thill to author.

41. *Muster Rolls of U.S. Navy Ships.*

42. *Ibid.*

43. Harper, *Memoirs*.

44. The *APA 179 Lauderdale* was a 10,000-ton Attack Personnel Auxiliary troop transport during the battle for Okinawa. It was converted into a 150-bed hospital ship.

45. *Muster Rolls of U.S. Navy Ships.*

46. *Ibid.*

47. *Find A Grave.*

48. *Muster Rolls of U.S. Navy Ships.*
49. *Ibid.*
50. *Ibid.*
51. *Applications for Headstones for U.S. Military Veterans, 1925–1941.* Microfilm publication M1916, 134 rolls. ARC ID: 596118. Records of the Office of the Quartermaster General, Record Group 92.
52. *Passenger Lists of Vessels Arriving at Boston, Massachusetts, 1891–1943.* Micropublication T843. RG085. 454 rolls. National Archives, Washington, D.C.
53. *Muster Rolls of U.S. Navy Ships.*
54. Johnson to author, letter.
55. *Muster Rolls of U.S. Navy Ships.*
56. *Ibid.*
57. The Receiving Station may match the post office codes which would be 3964 SF Tacloban, Leyte, Philippine Islands.
58. *Muster Rolls of U.S. Navy Ships.*
59. *Ibid.*
60. *Find A Grave.*
61. *Death Certificates and Index, December 20, 1908-December 31, 1953.* State Archives Series 3094. Ohio Historical Society, OH.
62. Ohio Obituary Index, 1830s-2009, Rutherford B. Hayes Presidential Center.
63. All aircraft figures are taken from the Preliminary Report on Operation, Commander B.C. Allen Jr. 10 January 1944.
64. *Muster Rolls of U.S. Navy Ships.*
65. *Ibid.*
66. *Ibid.*
67. Cannon-Muskegon Corporation. The founder of CM Corp., George William Cannon Jr., was a lieutenant in the Navy during WWII and commanded PT 108 in the Pacific Theater.
68. *California Death Index, 1940–1997.* Sacramento, CA: State of California Department of Health Services, Center for Health Statistics.
69. *Muster Rolls of U.S. Navy Ships.*
70. *U.S. Cemetery and Funeral Home Collection.*
71. *Muster Rolls of U.S. Navy Ships.*
72. *Ibid.*
73. *Ibid.*
74. 13 July 2006 edition, http://commercial-news.com/anniversaries/x212468502/Mr-and-Mrs-Carl-Reed/print.
75. *Muster Rolls of U.S. Navy Ships.*
76. *Ibid.*
77. *U.S. City Directories, 1822–1995,* South Bend, IN.
78. *Muster Rolls of U.S. Navy Ships.*
79. *Ibid.*
80. *Michigan, Marriage Records, 1867–1952.* Michigan Department of Community Health, Division for Vital Records and Health Statistics.
81. *Find A Grave.*
82. *Muster Rolls of U.S. Navy Ships.*
83. *Muster Rolls of the U.S. Marine Corps, 1798–1892.* Microfilm Publication T1118, 123 rolls. ARC ID: 922159. Records of the U.S. Marine Corps, Record Group 127; National Archives in Washington, D.C.
84. Information from Saundra Syrian Gross via the "John, Kathleen and Sharon Syrian/Donald T Goss Fund" site, of the Tucker Community Foundation. http://tuckerfoundation.whatsupwv.com/endowed-funds/grants/john-kathleen-sharon-syrian-donald-t-goss-fund/.
85. *Muster Rolls of U.S. Navy Ships.*
86. *Ibid.*
87. *Find A Grave; Social Security Death Index, Master File.*
88. *Find A Grave; Sixteenth Census of the United States, 1940.* Washington, D.C.: National Archives and Records Administration, 1940. T627, 4,643 rolls.
89. *U.S., School Yearbooks, 1880–2012; Fifteenth Census of the United States, 1930.* Washington, D.C.: National Archives and Records Administration, 1930. T626, 2,667 rolls. *Beneficiary Identification Records Locator Subsystem (BIRLS) Death File.* Washington, D.C.: Department of Veterans Affairs.
90. For more on Navy College Training Program, V-7, see: http://en.wikipedia.org/wiki/United_States_Naval_Reserve_Midshipmen's_School Navy College Training Program, V-7.
91. *United States Military Registers, 1902–1985.* Salem: Oregon State Library.
92. "Home Wedding Unites Couple," *Reno Evening Gazette,* 14 February 1944. http://newspaperarchive.com/reno-evening-gazette/1944-02-14/page-8.
93. *U.S. City Directories, 1822–1995,* San Diego, CA; *United States Military Registers, 1902–1985.*
94. Lists of Chinese Passenger Arrivals at San Francisco, CA., compiled 9 August 1882–25 December 1914. NARA microform publication M1414, 32 Rolls. NAI 4481626. Records of the Immigration and Naturalization Service, 1787–2004, Record Group 85. The National Archives at Washington, D.C.: *United States Obituary Collection; Sixteenth Census of the United States, 1940.* Washington, D.C.: National Archives and Records Administration, 1940. T627, 4,643 rolls; *Passenger and Crew Lists of Airplanes Arriving at Seattle, WA.,* March 1947-November 1954. Micropublication M1386. 3 rolls. NAI 4499524. Records of the Immigration and Naturalization Service, 1787–2004, Record Group 85. The National Archives at Washington, D.C; *Fourth Registration Draft Cards (WWII). Indiana State Headquarters ca. 1942.* NAI: 623285. The National Archives at St. Louis, MO; *Department of State, Division of Passport Control Consular Registration Applications; World War I Selective Service System Draft Registration Cards, 1917–1918.* Washington, D.C.: *National Archives and Records Administration.* M1509, 4,582 rolls; "Illinois, Cook County Marriages, 1871–1920." Index. FamilySearch, Salt Lake City, 2010. Illinois Department of Public Health records. "Marriage Records, 1871–present." Division of Vital Records, Springfield; 1920; Census Place: *Gardner, Johnson, KS;* Roll: T625_535; Page: 5A; Enumeration District: 105; Image: 591.
95. *Find A Grave; The Obituary Daily Times.* http://www.rootsweb.ancestry.com/~obituary; *Minnesota Marriages, 1997–2001.* Minnesota Department of Health, St. Paul. 1940; Census Place: *Foldahl, Marshall, Minnesota;* Roll: T627_1936; Page: 2A; Enumeration District: 45–19. *U.S., School Yearbooks, 1880–2012,* Warren High School, 1942. *Minnesota Statewide Divorce Index, 1970–1995.* St Paul: Minnesota Department of Health. *U.S., Navy Casualties Books, 1776–1941.*

96. *Muster Rolls of U.S. Navy Ship.*
97. *Ibid.*
98. *Ibid.*
99. The National Archives Southeast Region; Atlanta, GA; *Records of the Selective Service System, 1926–1975*; Record Group: *RG 147*; Class: *RG147, North Carolina World War II Draft Registration Cards*; Box Number: 69. *Find A Grave.*
100. *U.S., Social Security Applications and Claims Index, 1936–2007. Muster Rolls of U.S. Navy Ships. 1940*; Census Place: *Mount Savage, Allegany, Maryland*; Roll: *T627_1500*; Page: *16B*; Enumeration District: *1–58*.
101. *Muster Rolls of U.S. Navy Ships.*
102. *Ibid.*
103. *Ibid.*
104. *Ibid.*
105. *U.S. City Directories*, Worcester, MA., 1954. *Find A Grave. United States Obituary Collection, The Telegram News*, Worcester, MA, 27 August 2004. *U.S., School Yearbooks, 1880–2012*, Becker Junior College, 1949. *1930*; Census Place: *Worcester, Worcester, MA*; Roll: *971*; Page: *9A*; Enumeration District: *0102*; Image: 57.0; FHL microfilm: 2340706.
106. *Muster Rolls of U.S. Navy Ships.*
107. *Ibid.*
108. *Find A Grave. Decatur Herald & Review*; Publication Date: *31 03 2010*; Publication Place: *Decatur, IL, USA. U.S., Department of Veterans Affairs BIRLS Death File, 1850–2010. 1930*; Census Place: *Buck, Edgar, IL*; Roll: *513*; Page: *1B*; Enumeration District: *0002*; Image: 19.0; FHL microfilm: 2340248.
109. *Muster Rolls of U.S. Navy Ships.*
110. *Ibid.*
111. *Ibid.*
112. *Ibid.*
113. *Ibid.*
114. *Dallas Morning News*, www.legacy.com/obituaries/.../obituary.aspx?...fred-m-kuehne. *Muster Rolls of U.S. Navy Ships. U.S., School Yearbooks, 1880–2012*, Culver Military Academy. "Illinois. Cook County Birth Registers, 1871–1915" Index. FamilySearch, Salt Lake City. Illinois. Cook County Birth Registers, 1871–1915. Illinois Department of Public Health. Division of Vital Records, Springfield. *Social Security Death Index, Master File.* Social Security Administration.
115. *1930*; Census Place: *McCurtain, Haskell, OK*; Roll: *1906*; Page: *8B*; Enumeration District: *0011*; Image: 186.0; FHL microfilm: 2341640. *California Death Index, 1940–1997.* Sacramento: State of California Department of Health Services, Center for Health Statistics. *U.S., Social Security Applications and Claims Index, 1936–2007. Missouri Marriage Records.* Jefferson City: Missouri State Archives. Microfilm. *1940*; Census Place: *McCurtain, Haskell, OK*; Roll: *T627_3297*; Page: *6A*; Enumeration District: *31–11*. *1907*; Arrival: New York, New York; Microfilm Serial: *T715, 1897–1957*; Microfilm Roll: *Roll 0840*; Line: *8*; Page Number: *66*. *1920*; Census Place: *Diamond, Haskell, Oklahoma*; Roll: *T625_1462*; Page: *10A*; Enumeration District: *30*; Image: *338. Oklahoma, Find A Grave Index, 1800–2012. 1910*; Census Place: *Chant Ward 2, Haskell, OK*. Roll: *T624_1254*; Page: *9A*; Enumeration District: *0088*; FHL microfilm: *1375267. Applications for Headstones for U.S. Military Veterans, 1925–1941.* Microfilm publication M1916, 134 rolls. ARC ID: 596118. Records of the Office of the Quartermaster General, Record Group 92. National Archives.
116. Retired Commissioned and Warrant Officers, Regular and Reserve, of the United States Navy, *United States Military Registers, 1902–1985*. Salem, OR: Oregon State Library.
117. *Muster Rolls of U.S. Navy Ship.*
118. *Ibid.*
119. *Ibid.*
120. Another Andrew J. Coviello lived in Port Chester as well. He was born in 1917 but records indicate he joined the Army during World War II. There is, however, the possibility that the personal information here is incorrect.
121. *Muster Rolls of the U.S. Marine Corps, 1798–1892. Muster Rolls of U.S. Navy Ship.*
122. *U.S., Obituary Collection, 1930–2015, 08/28/2004*: Prichard, AL.
123. *Pennsylvania, Veteran Compensation Application Files, WWII, 1950–1966. 1940*; Census: *Upper Darby, Delaware*; Roll: *T627_3498*; Page: *26A*; Enumeration District: *23–218. U.S., Social Security Applications and Claims Index, 1936–2007. U.S. World War II Navy Muster Rolls, 1938–1949.*
124. *Muster Rolls of U.S. Navy Ship.*
125. *U.S., Department of Veterans Affairs BIRLS Death File, 1850–2010. Muster Rolls of U.S. Navy Ships.*
126. *Muster Rolls of U.S. Navy Ships.*
127. *Pennsylvania, Veteran Compensation Application Files, WWII, 1950–1966. Muster Rolls of U.S. Navy Ships. California Death Index, 1940–1997.* Sacramento. *1940*; Census: *Johnstown, Cambria, Pennsylvania*; Roll: *T627_3455*; Page: *16B*; Enumeration District: *11–106. U.S., Find A Grave.*
128. *Muster Rolls of U.S. Navy Ships.*
129. *Ibid.*
130. *1930*; Census: *Indianapolis, Marion*; Roll: *614*; Page: *10B*; Enumeration District: *0161*; Image: 22.0; FHL microfilm: 2340349. *Marion County, IN., Marriage Index, 1925–2012. U.S. Cemetery and Funeral Home Collection. U.S., Find A Grave Index. Muster Rolls of U.S. Navy Ships.*
131. *Muster Rolls of U.S. Navy Ships.*
132. *Ibid.*
133. *Ibid.*
134. *Ibid.*
135. *Ibid.*
136. *Ibid.*
137. *Ibid.*
138. *Ibid.*
139. *Ibid.*
140. *Muster Rolls of U.S. Navy Ships. U.S., Department of Veterans Affairs BIRLS Death File, 1850–2010. U.S., Find A Grave. MGI Cemeteries:* South Bend Area Genealogical Society. http://www.sbags.org/michgenidx2.htm.
141. *Muster Rolls of U.S. Navy Ships.*
142. *Ibid.*
143. *Ibid.*
144. *Ibid.*
145. *Ibid.*

Bibliography

Books

Bartley, William S. *Iwo Jima: Amphibious Epic.* Washington: Government Printing Office, 1954.
Baumler, Raymond A. *Ten Thousand Men and One Hundred Thirty "Mighty Midget" Ships.* Rockville, MD: PIP, 1992.
Bureau of Ships. *Instructions for LCS (L) (3) I Class.* Boston: George Lawley & Son, 1944.
Burroughs, Geoffrey. *Destiny Answers.* Charleston, SC: CreateSpace, 2011.
Craven, Wesley Frank, and James Lea Cate, eds. *The Army Air Forces in World War II*, Vol. V. Chicago: University of Chicago Press, 1953.
Cunningham, Chet. *The Frogmen of World War II: An Oral History of the U.S. Navy's Underwater Demolition Units.* New York: Pocket, 2005.
Eddy, William Crawford, Archibald Hart Brolly, Eugene Smith Pulliam, Elmer Charles Upton, and George William Thomas. *Wartime Refresher in Fundamental Mathematics.* Upper Saddle River, NJ: Prentice-Hall, 1943.
Estes, Steve. *I Am a Man! Race, Manhood, and the Civil Rights Movement.* Chapel Hill: University of North Carolina Press, 2006.
Frank, Benis M., and Henry I. Shaw Jr. *Victory and Occupation: History of the U.S. Marine Corps Operations in World War II*, Vol. V. Washington, D.C.: Government Printing Office, 1968.
Friedlander, Saul. *The Years of Extermination: Nazi Germany and the Jews, 1939–1945.* New York: HarperCollins, 2007.
Genealogical and Personal History of the Upper Monongahela Valley, West Virginia. Baltimore: Genealogical Publishing, 1978.
Gillespie, Oliver A. *The Official History of New Zealand in the Second World War 1939–1945: The Pacific.* Edited by Howard Karl Kippenberger. Wellington, NZ: Historical Publications Branch, 1952.
Gleichauf, Justin F. *Unsung Sailors: The Naval Armed Guard in World War II.* Annapolis, MD: Naval Institute, 1990.
Goldberg, Harold J. *D-Day in the Pacific: The Battle of Saipan.* Bloomington: Indiana University Press, 2007.
Greenfield, Kent R. "Germany First" in *Command Decisions.* Washington, D.C.: Department of the Army, 1959.
Honey, Michael Keith. *Black Workers Remember: An Oral History of Segregation, Unionism, and the Freedom Struggle.* Los Angeles: University of California Press, 2001.
Hornfischer, James D. *The Last Stand of the Tin Can Sailors.* New York: Bantam Dell, 2005.
Hunt, Ray C., and Bernard Norling. *Behind Japanese Lines: An American Guerrilla in the Philippines.* Lexington: University Press of Kentucky, 1986.
Inoguchi, Rikihei, and Tadashi Nakajima. *The Divine Wind: Japan's Kamikaze Force in World War II.* Annapolis: United States Naval Institute, 1958.
Klein, Maury. *A Call to Arms: Mobilizing America for World War II.* New York: Bloomsbury, 2013.
Kurzman, Dan. *Fatal Voyage: The Sinking of the Indianapolis.* New York: Broadway, 2001.
Leckie, Robert. *Okinawa: The Last Battle of World War II.* New York: Viking Penguin, 1995.
MacArthur, Douglas. *Reports of General MacArthur: Japanese Operations in the Southwest Pacific Area*, Vol. II—Pt. II. Washington, D.C.: U.S. Government Printing Office, 1966.
Manchester, William. *American Caesar: Douglas MacArthur, 1880–1964.* New York: Dell, 1978
Martin, Herbert L. *Not All Were Heroes: A Private in the Corps of Engineers in the Pacific During World War II.* Bennington, VT: Merriam, 2003.

Maurer, Maurer, ed. *Air Force Combat Units of World War II*. Washington, D.C.: Government Printing Office, 1983.

Moomaw, Jimmie Meese. *Southern Fried Child in Home Seeker's Paradise*. Bloomington, IN: AuthorHouse, 2010.

Mooney, James L. ed. *Dictionary of American Naval Fighting Ships*, Vol. III. Washington, D.C.: Government Printing Office, 1969.

Moore, Deborah D. *GI Jews: How World War Two Changed a Generation*. Cambridge, MA: Belknap Press of Harvard University, 2004.

Morgan, Lillian Natsue. *Made in Japan: Lillian Natsue Uehara Morgan's Life Story*. Bloomington, IN: Xlibris, 2011.

Morison, Samuel Eliot. *History of the United States Naval Operations in World War II*, Vol. XIV. Boston: Little, Brown, 1960.

Naito, Hatsuho. *Thunder Gods: The Kamikaze Pilots Tell Their Story*. New York: Kodansha, 1989.

National Association of LCS (L) 1–130 Editorial Staff. *LCS (L): Landing Craft Support (Large)*. Paducah, KY: Turner, 1995.

Newcomb, Richard F., and Harry Schmidt. *Iwo Jima: The Dramatic Account of the Epic Battle That Turned the Tide of World War II*. New York: Henry Holt, 1965.

Ohnuki-Tierney, Emiko. *Kamikaze Diaries: Reflections of Japanese Student Soldiers*. Chicago: University of Chicago Press, 2006.

Rielly, Robin L. *Kamikaze Attacks of World War II: A Complete History of Japanese Suicide Strikes on American Ships, by Aircraft and Other Means*. Jefferson, NC: McFarland, 2010.

_____. *Mighty Midgets at War: The Saga of the LCS(L) Ships from Iwo Jima to Vietnam*. Central Point, OR: Hellgate, 2000.

Roscoe, Theodore. *United States Destroyer Operations in World War II*. Annapolis, MD: United States Naval Institute, 1953.

Ross, Bill D. *Iwo Jima: Legacy of Valor*. New York: Vintage, 1985.

Shaw, Henry I., Jr. *The United States Marines in North China 1945–1949*, 2d ed. Washington, D.C.: Government Printing Office, 1962.

Sheftall, M. G. *Blossoms in the Wind: Human Legacies of the Kamikaze*. New York: NAL Caliber, 2005.

Sloan, Bill. *Ultimate Battle*. New York: Simon & Schuster, 2007.

Smith, Lawrence B. *Aboard LCS 11 in WW II: A Memoir by Lawrence B. Smith*. Bloomington, IN: Xlibris, 2011.

Smith, S.E., ed. *The United States Navy in World War II: The One-Volume History, from Pearl Harbor to Tokyo Bay*. New York: William Morrow, 1966.

Snyder, Timothy. *Bloodlands: Europe Between Hitler and Stalin*. New York: Basic, 2012.

State Historical Society of Wisconsin. *History of Penobscot County, Maine: With Illustrations and Biographical Sketches*. Cleveland, OH: William Chase & Co., 1882.

Stauffer, Alvin P. *US Army in WW 2: The Quartermaster Corps: Operations in the War Against Japan*. Washington, D.C.: Government Printing Office, 2004.

Taylor, A. Hoyt. "The Vocabulary of Radio." In *Radio Reminiscences: A Half Century*. Washington, D.C.: U.S. Naval Research Laboratory, 1948.

Thomas, Evan. *Sea of Thunder: Four Commanders and the Last Great Naval Campaign, 1941–1945*. New York: Simon & Schuster, 2006.

Ugaki, Matome, Gordon William Prange, Donald M. Goldstein, and Catherine Dillon. *Fading Victory: The Diary of Admiral Matome Ugaki, 1941–1945*. Pittsburgh: University of Pittsburgh Press, 1991.

War Department. *TM 9–225, Browning Machine Gun, Caliber .50, M2, Aircraft, Fixed and Flexible*. Washington: Government Printing Office, 1942.

Warner, Dennis, Peggy Warner and Sadao Seno. *The Sacred Warriors: Japan's Suicide Legions*. New York: Van Nostrand Reinhold, 1982.

Wilde, E. Andrew Jr., ed. *The USS Drexler (DD-741) in World War II: Documents, Photographs, Recollections*. Needham, MA: Self-published, 2003.

Wright, Derrick. *The Battle for Iwo Jima 1945*. Gloucestershire, UK: Sutton, 1999.

Periodical Articles, DVDs

"B-29 Armada Lashes Nagoya." *Moorhead Daily News* (Minnesota), 14 May 1945.

Edge, John T. "Fast Food Even Before Fast Food." *New York Times*, 30 September 2009.

"Forgotten Ships Long Time Gone." *The Palm Beach Post-Times*, 10 September 1944.

Harper, John, Larry Cullen and Virgil Thill. "A Short History of LCS(L)(3) 52," www.navsource.gov, n.d.

Hess, Margaret Johnston, ed. "A Real-Life Experience by Virgil Thill." *Moody Monthly* (March 1967): 35–38, 80–82.
Hillson, Franklin J. "Barrage Balloons for Low-Level Air Defense." *Airpower Journal* (Summer 1988).
Hoffman, Nancy. "Oren Tweet Watched the Flag Being Raised on Mount Suribachi." *Daily Astorian,* 12 January 2007.
"Home Wedding Unites Couple." *Reno Evening Gazette,* 14 February 1944.
"Iwo Like a Pork Chop Sizzling on Yank Skillet." *The Brooklyn Daily Eagle* (New York), 19 February 1945.
The Lassen Advocate (Susanville, CA), June 14, 1945.
"Last Letters of Kamikaze Pilots." *Manoa* (Summer 2001): 120–123.
Manny, Janine. "Clatskanie's Oren Tween Served His Town Well." *Longview Daily News,* 16 February 2006.
Martin, Francis. "Delinquency of Adolescent Boys." *The Journal of Education* 106, no. 14 (1927): 357–361.
Martinez, Deborah. "Ward Island Was Hush-Hush Radar School." *Corpus Christi Caller-Times,* 7 March 2000.
Mason, William J., ed. *A Home Away from Home.* San Francisco, 8 July 2014. DVD.
_____. *Journey Home.* San Francisco, 8 July 2014. DVD.
_____. *The Last Mighty Midget.* San Francisco, 8 July 2014. DVD.
_____. *Mission Accomplished.* San Francisco, 8 July 2014. DVD.
_____. *WWII Training Film.* San Francisco, 8 July 2014. DVD.
Ozawa, Hiroshi. "The True Account of the Last Moments of Admiral Ugaki." *Maru Magazine* (March 1999).
Parkyn, Michael. "Operation Beleaguer: The Marine III Amphibious Corps in North China, 1945–49." *Marine Corps Gazette* (July 2001): 32–38.
Rasmen, Fred. "Maryland Survived Pearl Harbor Attack Battleship: A Week Later 'Fighting Mary' Was Able to Sail Away for Repairs and Later Lived Up to Its Nickname as the U.S. Pushed Japan Back in the Pacific." *Baltimore Sun,* 7 December 1997.
"School News Digest." *The Clearing House* 19, no. 6 (1945): 382–400.
"Scout Awards Go to 105 at Honor Court." *Hammond Times,* 17 February 1939.

Correspondence

Bledsoe, Gerald, to John Harper. Unknown date, circa 1997. From collection of Carol Harper Marsh.
Brantly, Jerry, to Virgil Thill. Letter. Unknown date, circa 1994. From the collection of Virgil Thill.
Burns, Laton, to Kathleen Dezarn. Letters. Various dates, July 1944–August 1945. From the collection of Kathleen D. Burns.
Burns, Laton. *Wartime Journal.* Courtesy Diane Burns Brads.
Burroughs, Geoffrey. E-mails to author, various dates, 20 June–19 July 2014.
Cook, Claude, to Caroline Artman. Letters. Various dates, 23 August 1944–30 September 1945. From the collection of Mike Kaloz.
Copeland, Russell, to Virgil Thill. Letter. 9 February 1994. From the collection of Virgil Thill.
Cullen, Charles L. Letters home. Various dates, July–August 1945. From the collection of Norma Cullen Vines.
Harper, John O. *Memoirs.* Courtesy Carol Harper Marsh.
Johnson, Beverly, to author. Letter. 15 April 2014.
Kaloz, Mike. E-mails to author, various dates, January 2013–December 2016.
Linn, Bud, to Virgil Thill. Letter. 20 February 1994. From the collection of Virgil Thill.
Parker, Albert, to Virgil Thill. Letter. 18 March 1998. From the collection of Virgil Thill.
Vines, Norma Cullen. E-mails to author, various dates, December 2012–December 2016.

Government and Official Documents

Bush, George W. *Remarks on the 60th Anniversary of V-J Day in San Diego, California, August 30, 2005.* Washington, D.C.: Government Printing Office, 2005.
Groves, Leslie. *Memorandum for the Secretary of War,* 18 July 1945. Harry S. Truman Library, Papers of Lansing Lamont.
LCS 52. Action Report, 1 May 1945.
_____. Action Report, 28 May 1945.
_____. Muster Roll of Crew & Report of Changes, 23 September 1944–22 May 1946.
_____. Ship's Logs, 23 September 1944–22 June 1945.
_____. War Diaries, Nov. 1–30, Dec. 1–30, 1944, Jan. 1–31, Feb. 1–28, Mar. 1–31, Apr. 1–30, Jun. 1–30, Jul. 1–31, Aug. 1–31, Oct. 1–31, 1945.

LCS 61. Action Report, 1–31 May 1945.
_____. Deck log, 27–28 May 1945.
_____. War Diary, 1–31 May 1945.
Roosevelt, Franklin D. *Development of United States Foreign Policy: Addresses and Messages of Franklin D. Roosevelt.* Washington, D.C.: Government Printing Office, 1942.

Index

USS *Achernar* 104
Achilles, Albrecht 46
Adams, Annette 54, 222
Adrian Daily Telegram 37
USS *Agenor* 230
Albina Engine Works 11–12, 13, 37
Allard, Ernest T. 199
Alma College 45, 221
USS *Alpine* 104
USS *Alshain* 230
USS *Alvin C. Cockrell* 186, 207
Antioch College 195
Antonescu, Mareşal Ion 62
APA 21 *see* USS *Crescent City*
APA 179 179, 203, 209, 212, 246n44; *see also Lauderdale*
APC 21 215
APC 38 178
Araki, Haruo 113–114
Araki, Shigek 113
USS *Arizona* 2–3, 177
Arnold, Gen. Henry H. "Hap" 141
USS *Artigas* 48
ATA 206 235
ATF 76 111
USS *Atlas* 230
atomic bombs: Bockscar (B-29) 147; Enola Gay (B-29) 146–147; Manhattan Project 143–144
Aylward, Commodore T.C. 130

Bagdonas, Paul J. 230
Baker, "Bad" Tom 20
Baker, Taylor 84
Barber, Gladys 224
Barber, Persis A. 224
Barber, William G. 175, 223–224
Barron, John 96
Barron, Lydia M. 96
Barron, Margaret B. 95
Barron, Porter, Jr. 70, 95–97, 134, 199
Barron, Robert 95

Battle of El Alamein 47
Battle of Guadalcanal 10
Bauer, Clarence A. 118, 120–121, 184, 199
Bauer, F.A. 121
Bauer, Frank 120
Bauer, Ida 120
Bauer, Joseph A. 120
Bauer, Joseph G. 120
Bauer, Mary Amberg 199
USS *Beaconhill* 48, 240n10
Beittel, Ben, Jr. 189
Beittel, Benjamin L. 118–121, 189, 200
Beittel, Charles R. 120
Beittel, Elizabeth 243n8
Beittel, Gertrude Albright 118
Beittel, Grace 189
USS *Bennett* 97
Bennett, Ervin 175, 200
Bennett, Kate 200
Bennett, Kenney 200
USS *Bennion* 113
Berea College 20, 239n21
USS *Bering* 48
Bielsk Brothers 62
Bigos, Casimir 110
Bilton, Ardyth 13
Bilton, Gerald P. 13, 123, 175, 200
Bledsoe, Charlotte 75
Bledsoe, Frank 75–76
Bledsoe, Gerald E. 75–76, 184, 189–191
Bledsoe, Joan 189
Blough, Bernice M. 201
Blough, Russell J. 73, 175, 200–201, 214
Booth, John 30
Bradshaw, Robert W. 230
Brantley, Christopher C. 145
Brantley, Ethel Rogers 194
Brantley, Freda Brown 145, 194
Brantley, Jordon L. 58, 144–145, 175, 193–194
Brantley, Mary Clements 145

Brantley, Roger A. 193
Brashers, Albert L. 201
Brashers, Ethel M. 201
Brashers, Florence M. 201
Brashers, Leroy C. 201
Brokaw, Tom 179, 196, 243n1
Bryant Stratton Business School 217
USS *Bunker Hill* 114
Burnette, Frankie P. 201
Burnette, Horace Clinton, Jr. 123, 130, 184, 201
Burnette, Horace, Sr. 201
Burnette, Margurette R. 201
Burns, Ambrose 19, 20–21
Burns, Ambrose, Jr. 108, 245n50
Burns, Dan 187
Burns, Diane Brads 39, 67, 79, 100, 173, 187, 251
Burns, Florida Roberts 19
Burns, James A. 20
Burns, Kathleen Dezarn 21, 22, 23, 50, 187, 251
Burns, Ken 241n2
Burns, Laton 6, 18–23, 35, 50, 57, 65, 72, 73, 78, 79, 82, 83, 84–85, 86, 93, 97, 98, 108, 117, 140, 148–149, 153, 154, 160, 167–169, 171, 173, 175, 187, 194, 244n33, 251
Burns, Milton 20, 187
Burns, Polly 20, 21
Burroughs, Brooke 54
Burroughs, Elaine Baker 53–55, 117, 222
Burroughs, Ephraim S. 52, 53
Burroughs, Geoffrey 240n24, 240n25, 241n28, 241n29, 245n3, 249, 251
Burroughs, Gladys 52, 53, 56
Burroughs, H.D. 52
Burroughs, Olga A. Wemple 52, 53, 56
Burroughs, Ens. Spencer 26, 46, 49, 52–56, 68, 71, 83, 107, 117, 122–123, 125, 128, 129, 131,

135, 180–181, 191, 198, 222–223, 240n22
Bush, George W. 196

USS *Cacapon* 191
USS *California* 177
USS *Calvert* 215
Campbell, George P. 150
Carlisle Indian Industrial School 119
USS *Carpenter* 191
Castle Films 29
Cazee, Beulah R. 202
Cazee, Hanford H. 73, 153, 175, 201–202
Cazee, Lillian M. 202
Cazee, Logan 202
Chaney, Charles Ross 45
"Charge of the Light Brigade" 77
USS *Charger* 205
USS *Charles Carroll* 215
USS *Charles H. Roan* 193
USS *Chaumont* 235
Chavez, Joe F. 69, 70, 175, 202, 213–214
Chiang Kai-shek 170
USS *Chicago* 235
Chicago Defender 32
Chicago Tribune 83
Chico State College 46
China Marines 28
Chinese Communist forces 174
Christensen, Christian S. 46
Christman, Amelia F. 224
Christman, Arlene 224
Christman, Eugene E. 224
Christman, Russell R. 131, 224
Churchill, Winston 47, 109
USS *City of Omaha* 47–48, 49
Civilian Conservation Corps 4–5, 36, 39, 46, 119, 176
Clack, Alvis S. 225
Clack, Annie L. 225
Clack, Harold L. 131, 224–225
USS *Clay* 216
Cockburn, James 183
Cockburn, Janet 183
Colby College 74
USS *Cole* 230
Columbia University 49
USS *Comfort* 108
Commercial-News [Danville] 218
Concordia University 125
Connors State Agricultural College 137
USS *Consolation* 202
Cook, Annie 40
Cook, Ben, Jr. 42
Cook, Benjamin 40
Cook, Caroline Artman 12, 97, 98, 99, 113, 114, 137, 148, 152, 159, 183, 251
Cook, Charles 40

Cook, Claude 2, 12, 13, 40–43, 74, 81, 97, 98, 99, 113, 114, 131, 137, 139, 140, 141, 143, 144, 147, 152, 153, 154, 155, 156, 157, 158–159, 160, 183, 188–189, 202, 251
Cook, Jack 41
Cook, Mary A. 40
Copeland, Betty 125, 203
Copeland, Joseph W. 126
Copeland, Russell S. 69, 122–123, 126, 148, 175, 202–203, 251
Copeland, Verna B. 126
Coviello, Andrew 231
Coviello, Andrew J. 230–231, 248n120
Coviello, Anna M. 231
Coviello, Christina 231
Coviello, John 231
Coward, Noël Peirce 54
Cramer, Stuart, Jr. 152
Crane, Stephen 3
USS *Crescent City* 129, 204, 215, 246n36
Criger, John D.W. 131, 142, 225–226
Crosby, Bing 144
Crossing the Line ceremonies: Order of Golden Shellbacks 174; Order of Mossbacks 174; Order of Northern Domain of the Polar Bear 174; Order of the Golden Dragon 174–175; Order of the Shellback 174; Royal Order of the Blue Nose 174
Crowe, Anna M. 203
Crowe, Jesse 203
Crowe, Wilford C. 203
Crowe, Wilford C., Jr. 203
Crump, Edward "Boss" 34
Cullen, Alma M. 25, 203
Cullen, Bessie French 24, 203
Cullen, Frank 26
Cullen, Harold D. 24, 203
Cullen, Lawrence C. 23–25, 51, 52, 66, 68, 70, 71, 73, 83, 84, 89, 110, 117, 119, 120, 122–123, 126, 127, 133, 151–152, 175, 191, 203, 223, 250, 251
Cullen, Lewis 25
Cullen, Norma Vines 25, 26, 251
Cumberland Evening Times 39
Cummings, Donald J. 145–146
USS *Curtiss* 134–135, 137

Dahlem, Kenneth J. 203
Daily Jeffersonian [Cambridge] 216
USS *Daly* 108
Dandridge, Charlie 231–232
Dandridge, James 231, 232

Dandridge, Joyce 231
Dandridge, Kathleen E. 231
Dandridge, Leonard 231, 232
Dandridge, Marvin M. 231
Dandridge, Nellie 231
Dandridge, Stanley 231
Darnell, Charles C. 131, 144, 145–146, 194, 226
Darnell, Florence Hiser 145
Darnell, Patricia Marchand 194
Darnell, Wilbert 145, 226
USS *Darter* 189, 245n28
Davis, Bessie D. 204
Davis, Gerald 71, 153, 204
Davis, Iva Morgan 204
Davis, Wilson 204
Dear John letter 129
Dearborn Independent 61
Death March 78, 140
USS *Decatur* 96
Del Castillo, Carmen V. 204
Del Castillo, Felix 204
De Maio, Eugene A. 58, 59, 70, 123, 129, 175, 204–205, 241n39
De Maio, Josephine Bertolozzi 204
De Maio, Gloria A. 205
De Maio, Vincent 204
Detroit Bible College 182, 183
Dezarn, Glenn 20
Dezarn, Neil 20
Dezarn, Paul 20
Dickinson College 118
Dillon, Edward J. 97, 242n27
Di Priter, Angelo 205
Di Priter, John 69, 205
Di Priter, Mary 205
Dönitz, Karl 109
Douglas, Stephen A. 132
USS *Douglas H. Fox* 109
Downey, Jessie W. 209–207
Doyle, Patrick 227
USS *Drexler* 116, 128–129, 130
Duvendeck, Anna E 186
Duvendeck, Emma 44
Duvendeck, Isabelle F. Purdy 45
Duvendeck, Ens. Jerry P. 44–45, 67, 69, 91, 106, 122, 130, 131, 133, 162, 186, 221–222
Duvendeck, Marguerite 44, 222
Duvendeck, Ray H. 44, 222
Duvendeck, William 44
Dyment, Ellen 151
Dyment, George 151

SS *E.A. Bryan* 32
Eastern Kentucky University 187
Edwards, Doris Zimmerman 227
Edwards, Vance, Jr. 227
USS *Elizabeth C Stanton* 215
Elvgren, Gil *see* pinup girls
USS *Epping Forest* 235

Index

Escanaba Daily Press 36
USS *Eugene A. Greene* 203
USS *Evans* 112
Evening Independent [Massillon] 146
SS *Exhibitor* 46, 240n7

Fairbanks, Douglas (actor) 144
SS *Fairport* 46–47, 240n7
Fields, Robert R. 175, 205
USS *Finnegan* 94
USS *Foss* 191
Fox, Robert 53
USS *Francis Scott Key* 48, 49
USS *Franklin* 101
Free Speech 34
USS *Fulton* 99
Furuta, Y. (Kamikaze pilot) 164–165, 166–167

Gagne, Linwood 119
Gaham, Jack C. 206, 214, 225
Gaham, Madonna R. Rice 206
Gahan, Imogene Hire 206
Gahan, Ralph J. 206
Gallant G.P. 13
Gardner, Gertrude 207
Gardner, William 50, 58, 98, 184
Gaston, Eva R. 232
Gaston, Valerie 232
Gaston, Victor, Jr. 232
Gaston, Victor, Sr. 232
Gaudette, Alice 228
Gaudette, Harold E. 228–229
Gaudette, Howard B. 228
Gaudette, Lucien C. 228
USS *Gearing* 203
USS *Gen. J.C. Breckinridge* 211
USS *George Clymer* 31, 203, 211
Germany First Policy 3, 9–10
Geronimo, Apache chief 119
Gierke, Leda 35
USS *Gleaves* 46
Gloor, Clarence 111
Gloor, Eunice 111
Gloor, Jack D. 110–111, 129, 186, 207
Gloor, Rex 111
Goldman, Hugh J. 131, 175, 228
Gordon, Blair 39
Gordon, Nepha 39
USS *Gosper* 137
Grant, Ulysses 55, 132
Great Minnesota Execution 120
Green, Robert D. 232
USS *Greer* 30
Griffin, John M. 228
Griffiths, Harold 150
Groves, Leslie R. 143–144, 251

Hailman, Cecile O. 208
Hailman, Charles M. 208
Hailman, Emily Blackstone 208

Hailman, William T. 207–208, 209
Hall, James S. 208
Hall, Lace 208
Hall, Lille White 208
Hall, Vaudna Peck 208
Halsey, Adm. William F. 77, 116, 168–169
Hamlin, L.W. 132
Hancock, Capt. George S. 46
Handy, W.C. 34
Hanning, Erma M. 209
Hanning, Paul A. 123, 208–209
Hanning, Paul H. 209
Hanover College 133, 188
USS *Hansford* 193, 201, 209, 211, 217
Harper, Carol 16, 51, 80, 251, 252, 251, 252
Harper, John H. 14
Harper, Lt. John O. 4, 14–18, 23, 44, 51, 52, 54, 55, 56, 57, 60, 63, 64, 67, 79, 80, 84, 86–87, 88, 90, 91, 92, 93, 94, 97, 98, 99, 103, 105, 107, 108, 109, 110, 116, 117, 121, 122, 124, 125, 126–127, 129, 130, 137, 138, 139, 140, 148, 156, 158, 161, 162, 164, 169, 170, 171, 180–181, 186, 189, 190–191, 195, 209, 221, 222–223, 241n57, 242n4, 250, 251
Harper, Lyda L. 14
Harper, Marjorie Halley 17, 18
USS *Harry F. Bauer* 109
USS *Harry Lee* 215
Hart, Fannie 62
Hart, Harris 62
Hart, William I. 62
Harvard University 89
Hashimoto, Lt. Cmdr. Mochitsura 144, 146
Hastings Law School 54
Hawks, James, Jr. 123, 124, 127, 129, 180, 198, 209
Hawks, James, Sr. 209
Hawks, Rhoda Alberty 209
Hayashi, Ens. Ichizo 130
Hedger, Donald C. 58, 123, 129, 209
Hedger, June C. Cornelius 209
Hedger, Raymond C. 209
USS *Helena* 215
USS *Hendry* 236
Henie, Sonja 44
USS *Henry W. Tucker* 230
USS *Hercules* 7
Hildebrandt, Dorthy 232
Hildebrandt, Eric G. 232–233
Hildebrandt, Evlyian 232
Hildebrandt, George P. 232
Hildebrandt, Mary 232
Hildebrandt, Wallace 232

Hile, Donald 112, 113, 211
Hile, George 112
Hile, Helen 113
Hile, Margaret 113
Hile, Minnie 112
Hile, Richard F. 71, 112–113, 123, 130, 184, 209, 211
Hile, Shirley 211
Hill, Harry, Jr. 211
Hill, Louise Knipp 211
USS *Hinsdale* 102
Hirohito, Emperor 158
Hitler, Adolf 29, 33, 53, 109, 120
Hobson, Ralph E. 131, 225, 228
Holland, Muscoe C. 30–32, 45, 73, 82, 83, 96, 140, 175, 211
Holland, Muscoe, Sr. 30
Holland, Muscoe, III 211
Holland, Theresa Bondurant 30
Holland, Virginia W. 211
Homberoff, Albert L. 233
Hood, George W. 116, 130
Hoover, Herbert 171, 244n37
USS *Hope* 129
Hourigan, Kenneth 163
USS *Hudson* 108
USS *Hugh W. Hadley* 112
Hunt, Grover 119
Hunt, Ray C. 78
Hutton, Betty 144

I-58 (Japanese) 144, 146
USS *Idaho* 235
HMS *Indefatigable* 104
USS *Indianapolis* 143
Inoguchi, Rikihei 100
USS *Intrepid* 231
USS *Israel Putnam* 48
Iwo Jima 10, 59–60, 70, 82, 87, 99, 184–185, 196; battle 58, 65, 73, 8–85, 86, 88, 90–91, 94–95, 97, 98, 143, 178; flag raising 92–93

Jacobson, Dora Hart 62
Jacobson, Edward 61
Jacobson, Jack 61
Jacobson, Morris 60, 61, 62
Jacobson, Philip 60–61, 62–63, 174
Jacobson, Saralee 61
Jakovich, Cecelia A. 233
Jakovich, Elizabeth Kinback 233
Jakovich, Joseph F. 233
Japan Times 168
Japanese military 28, 31, 63, 64, 77, 82, 85, 89–90, 105, 106, 113, 141, 157, 163; *Bimbo Butai* 103; Fifth Air Fleet 166; 51st Shinbu Special Attack Squadron 113; 56th Shinmu Squadron 113; Japan Maritime Self-Defense Force 184;

256 INDEX

kamikazes (suicide) 74, 100–102, 102–103, 104, 105, 106, 108, 109, 112, 117, 121, 124, 126, 128–129, 130, 134, 137, 142, 143, 145, 152, 160, 161, 164–166, 167, 180, 197, 223, 242n2; Q-boats 101–102, 106; 7th Showa Squadron 114; Thunder Gods Corps 105; Tokushima Shiragiku Unit 161
USS *Jared Ingersoll* 96
Jawor, Alfreda H. 212
Jawor, Anthony D. 58, 73, 123, 129, 132, 175, 198, 212
Jim Crow laws 33, 34
Jinsen P.O.W. camp 169
USS *John A. Bole* 230
Johnson, Beverly Holling 212, 251
Johnson, Dewane L. 76, 212
Johnson, Dorothy Shannon 34
Johnson, Florence Henderson 34
Johnson, George O. 76
Johnson, Ida Smith 76
Johnson, Johnny W. 34
Johnson, Ulysses 34–35, 58, 59, 68, 193

Kaiser Shipbuilding 11, 54
Kauffman, Draper 58
USS *Kearny* 29, 46, 47, 211
Keilty, Edward, Jr. 71, 194
Keilty, Edward, Sr. 72
Keilty, John T. 68, 71–72, 184, 194, 212, 213, 219
Keilty, Margaret 72
Keilty, Shirley Stamatis 194
Keith, Evelyn Sparks 84
Keith, J.C. 84
Keith, Lloyd C. 22, 67, 83–84, 86, 117, 140, 153, 154, 187–188, 213, 214
Keith, Mildred 84
Keith, Perlina 83
Keith, Taylor 83–84
Kennedy, John F. 80
Kennon, Harold E. 131, 228–229
King, Admiral Ernest 141
Kinkaid, Thomas C. 77
Kirkpatrick, John D. 186
Kirkpatrick, L. Pearl 186
USS *Kittson* 76
Klein, Victor D. 175, 233
Kochanowicz, Charles J. 96–97, 213
Kubli Khan 100, 242n1
Kuehne, Fred, Jr. 131, 132
Kuehne, Fred, Sr. 132
Kuehne, Fred III 131–132, 229–230
Kuehne, Jayne Patterson 230
Kuehne, Vivian Pratt 131

Kuribayashi, Gen. Tadamichi 88–89, 90, 185
Kuribayashi, Yoshii 185

Lang, Fred 36
Lang, Myrtle 35
USS *Lauderdale* 129
LC (FF) 423 137
LC (FF) 482 215
LC (FF) 484 see LCI 448
LCI 23 31, 32, 211
LCI 24 31
LCI 63 31
LCI 65 31
LCI 423 see LC 423
LCI 454 233
LCI 482 226
LCI 484 130, 131, 215
LCI 627 64, 94
LCI 728 226
LCS 7 197
LCS 8 197
LCS 14 198
LCS 15 197
LCS 18 108
LCS 20 198
LCS 24 237
LCS 25 198
LCS 26 197
LCS 27 197
LCS 31 90, 98, 99, 106, 198
LCS 32 60, 229
LCS 33 197, 198
LCS 36 138, 197
LCS 37 197
LCS 48 11, 197
LCS 49 197
LCS 50 197
LCS 51 94, 198
LCS 53 99, 107, 131
LCS 54 99
LCS 56 99
LCS 57 197, 198
LCS 58 197
LCS 61 127
LCS 78 11
LCS 86 164
LCS 88 109, 110, 111, 113, 114, 197
LCS 92 191
LCS 93 198
LCS 102 7, 191
LCS 109 109, 111, 114
LCS 110 108
LCS 113 244n7
LCS 114 109, 127, 128–129, 114
LCS 116 197
LCS 119 197
LCS 121 131, 198
LCS 123 113
LCSs: Battle of Okinawa 197; sailors killed in action 198; sunk in combat 197

LCSs 28–30 197
LCSs 40–47 197
LCT 1029 97
Leahy, Adm. William 141
Leatherneck magazine 92
Lewis, Sinclair 120
Libby, Galen C. 74, 97–98, 175, 186
Libby, Joy Kirkpatrick 186
Libby, Perley Leroy 74
Libby, Susie Gildden 74
Lincoln, Abraham 120, 132
Lindbergh, Charles 54, 56
Linn, Georgia Small 213
Linn, Glorian Gladhart 213
Linn, James L. 175, 198, 213–214, 252
Linn, Simon P. 213
USS *Livermore* 46
Liversedge, Col. Harry 88
Lizer, Lt. Gilbert D. 160
USS *Los Angeles* 215
Lowery, SSgt. Louis R. 92
USS *Lowry* 116
Loyola University of Chicago Stritch School of Medicine 127
LSM 118 233
LSM 198 108
LSM 262 235
LSM 378 227
LSM 289 192, 221
LSM 437 194, 213
LSM 476 230
LST 15 see USS *Phaon*
LST 224 97
LST 242 213
LST 296 166
LST 353 56
LST 354 178
LST 475 235
LST 480 56
LST 614 227, 229, 232, 234
LST 675 132, 142, 145, 146, 212, 224, 225, 226, 228, 229
LST 738 224
LST 742 224
LST 783 99
LST 850 235
LST 904 226
LST 952 226, 234
LST 980 224
LST 1079 226
LST 1096 226
LST 1119 206
Lynch, John 127
Lynch, Julia F. 127
Lynch, Dr. Phillip C. 127, 131

"Maiden Voyage" 25–26
Manchuria 229; invasion by Japan 28, 44
Mankato Normal School 120

Index

Mare Island 7, 143, 192; Naval Ammunition Depot 32–33, 224, 230, 233, 237
Marshall, Gen. George 141
USS *Maryland* 176, 177, 178
Masahisa, Uemura (Kamikaze pilot) 165
Mason, William J. 164, 244n22, 251
USS *Matagorda* 203
Matome, Adm. Ugaki 166
May, Alice Kunkle 214
May, Elizabeth Miller 214
May, Joseph H. 214–215
May, Viola 214, 215
May, William T. 214
USS *Mayo* 46
McClement, Betty 234
McClement, Donald A. 233–234
McClement, Gladys 234
McClement, Grace 234
McClement, H.H. 234
McClement, William H. 234
McCormick Theological Seminary 188
McDonald, Charles C. 160–162
McVay, Charles III 143, 146, 243n18
Meese, Joe 34
Mefferd, Lt. G.W. 109–110, 111, 242n18
Mercer, Charles 234
Mercer, Roger H. 234
Mercer, Ruby F. 234
Michigan State College 186
Miller, Ann (actress) 141
Miller, Doris "Dorie" 33, 35
USS *Missouri* 152, 168, 205
USS *Mizar* 236
USS *Mobile City* 48, 49
Mochitsura Hashimoto 144
USS *Monssen* 30
Montgomery, Gen. Bernard 47
Montgomery, J.W. 45
Moorhead State Teacher's College 125
Morgan, Lillian Natsue Uehara 156
Morse, John G. 234
Moschner, Ens. Albert 136–137, 192–193
Moschner, Henry 136, 192
Moschner, Mary C. 136
Moschner, Raymond 136
Moschner, Virginia 192
Movietone News 29
MS *Tarn* 46, 47
Munising Journal 41

Nagoya POW camps 163
Nationalist Chinese forces 171–172

Navajo Code Talkers 185
Nelson, Jim 69, 73, 207, 215
USS *Nevada* 92
USS *New York* 225
News-Journal (Dayton Beach) 194
News-Palladium (Benton Harbor) 176
Nicola, Francis J. 234
Nimitz, Adm. Chester 10, 141, 146
USS *North Carolina* 230
Northwestern University of Illinois 132, 230

Oakley, Gerald P. 234
Ogawa, Ens. Kiyoshi 114
Ohio State University 165
Ohnishi, Vice Adm. 100
USS *Oklahoma* 176, 177, 178
Oldfield, Otis (painter) 53
Olenski, Ens. Kazimer 160
Olney, Donald D. 175, 216
Olney, Shelba C. Gregg 216
Olney, Vernon L. 216
Olney, Weltha Welch 216
Olsen, George E. 216
Oneida Baptist Institute 20, 21, 51, 57, 83
Oneida Mountaineer 57
Onishi, Adm. Takijiro 165, 166
Operation Coronet 141
Operation Downfall 141
Operation Iceberg (Okinawa) 76, 168, 178, 197
Operation Olympic 141
Operation Starvation I and II 157
Operation Watchtower 10
Oppenheimer, J. Robert 143–144
Orland Park Herald 233
Otake, Lt. Col. Michiji 163
Our Navy magazine 97
USS *Owen* 76
Owens, Fred L. 234
USS *Ozark* 236

Parham, Elah 216
Parham, L.E., Jr. 73, 153, 216–217
Parham, L.E., Sr. 216
Parham, Zula Lowery 217
Park College 133
Parker, Albert G. 133
Parker, Ens. Albert III 46, 57, 72, 73, 74, 79, 84, 87, 89, 93, 130, 131, 133, 134, 186, 188, 223, 244n33, 251
Parker, Harriet 133
Parker, Jane 133, 188
Parker, Joanne Lindberg 188
Parker, Katherine 133

Parrish, Robert R. 235
Parsons, Capt. William 147
Pasko, John T. 206
Paterson, Capt. James G. 46
Payne, Robert G. 107, 122, 123, 129, 148, 153, 217
PC-564 230
PC-1079 37
USS *Perkins* 195
Perry, Commodore Matthew C. 150
Pfohl, Anita D. Angelica 143
Pfohl, Dorothy Pierson 143
Pfohl, John N. 143, 160, 217
Pfohl, Walter 143
PGM 20 110, 114
USS *Phaon* 65
pinup girls 77–78, 241n11; Betty Grable 78; Elvgren girls 78; Jane Russell 78; Rita Hayworth 78
Pitcher, Molly 118
Plant, Louis 63
Plantation Mentality 33, 34
poems 50; "Charge of the Light Brigade" 77; "Maiden Voyage" 25–26
Poindexter, Howard R. 175, 217
USS *Pollux* 215
Port Chicago explosion and mutiny 32–33
Portsmouth Daily Times 45
Potsdam Declaration 157
Pratt, Josephine 131
Pratt, Richard 119
Prendergast, Margaret Reed 217
Prendergast, Mary 83
Prendergast, Ralph, Jr. 70, 83, 98, 184, 207, 217
Prendergast, Ralph, Sr. 83
Prendergast, Robert 83
SS *President Jackson* 133
Princeton University 133
Puckett, John R. 229
Pueblo Chieftain 234

SS *Quinault Victory* 32

Racine, Eugene B. 235
Radio Tokyo 156
Rainbow (military strategies) 9–10
Ramsey, Clyde B. 235
Ramsey, Henry 235
Ramsey, Hope 235
Ramsey, Lee 235
Ramsey, Martha 235
USS *Rankin* 193
Reed, Carl L. 175, 184, 207, 217–218
Reed, Cathrine Bradford 218
Reed, James E. 218
Reed, Lucy Catlett 218

Reed, Opal 176
USS *Relief* 144, 199, 201
USS *Rhodes* 9
Ring, Wayne D. 177
Rio Grande College 14
Robbins, Glenn J. 229
Rockey, Gen. Keller E. 170
Rommel, Field-Marshal Erwin 47
Roop, Isaac 53
Roosevelt, Franklin D. 4, 9, 29
Roosevelt, Theodore 95, 119
Roseluke, Andy 182, 245n8
Rosenthal, Joseph J. 92–93

Sacramento Junior College 53
Sadow (servant) 53
St. Clare Sentinel 188
USS *St. George* 160
USS *Samaritan* 94
Samons, Sally Music 236
Samons, Richard M. 235–236
Samons, W.L. "Lewis" 236
Sample, Adm. William 160
USS *San Francisco* 226, 235
San Jose State College 46
Sasaki, Mildred 53
Saulpaugh, Thomas 120–121
Schmidt, Paul E. Jr. 236
Schrier, Lt. Harold 92
Schroeder, Harvey W. 52, 60, 218
Schrow, Henry 149–150
Schultz, Amelia 107
Schultz, Donald H. 107, 137, 218
Schultz, Dorothy 217
Schultz, Earl W.H. 131, 229
Schultz, Harry 107
Schultz, Herman 107
USS *Scribner* 234
Scurrah, Abraham A. 148–150, 151, 193, 218
Scurrah, Agnes Kirk 148
Scurrah, Arnold A. 148, 193
Scurrah, Barbara A. 193
Scurrah, Elizabeth 148
Scurrah, Herbert 149, 151, 193
Scurrah, Ruth Dyment 151
Sears, Julia 120
SS *Seatrain Texas* 47
Seisaku (Adachiyama) 169
shadow factories 163
Shantung Christian University 133
Shirley Industrial School 150
USS *Sierra* 201, 226, 144
Skid Row 181–182
Skunk Patrol 105, 106, 140
USS *Sloat* 96, 213
RN *Smith* 113
Smith, Callie L. 152
Smith, Jesse H. 152–153

Smith, Kate (singer) 139
Smith, Lincoln 152, 153–154, 218–219
Smith, Zerma 152
Snyder, Timothy (author) 62
USS *Solace* 94
USS *Spikefish* 189
USS *Spokane* 193
Stewart, Ens. Clifford L. 45, 46, 49, 60, 82, 84, 90, 107, 133, 161, 174, 191, 222
Stewart, Dorothy 191
Stewart, Jeptha L. 46
Stewart, Lola M. 46
USS *Sticknell* 191
Stoia, Helen Codrea 195
Stoia, Nick 3, 12, 60, 68, 69, 71, 72–73, 107, 118, 138, 170, 184, 190, 191, 194–195, 219
Stoia, Ralph 195
Stoia, Sofia 107
Stoia, Solomon 107
Stone, Cmdr. Frank P. 60, 63, 107, 130, 156, 161, 162
Strandquist, Adler W. 123–125, 136, 184, 188, 223
Strandquist, Andrew 124
Strandquist, Bernice Olson 125
Strandquist, Lilly 124
Strandquist, Ruth Barnes 223
Suicide Cliffs (Saipan) 245n14
USS *Suwanee* 160, 208
Swartout, Addie M. Seaton 220
Swartout, Alpha J. 220
Swartout, Donald 219–220
Swartout, Joyce E. Johnson 219
Swartout, Maryaleen R. 219
Swartout, Roger 220
Swartout, Victor 220
Sweeney, Maj. Charles *see* atomic bombs
Sweeny, Grace Akolt 94
Sweeny, Lt. John J. 94
Sweeny, Michael 94
Swisher, Art 196
Swisher, Chester, Jr. 176, 178, 195–196, 236
Swisher, Chester, Sr. 176
Swisher, Cleo Heyer 195
Swisher, James 176
Swisher, Lullia Reed 176
Swisher, Vema 176
Syrian, John A. 38–40, 68, 73, 127, 220
Syrian, Kathleen L. 39
Syrian, Lizzy 38
Syrian, Pete 39, 220
Syrian, Rose 38
Syrian, Salvatore "Sam" 38

T-8031 45
Takao, Furukawa (kamikaze pilot) 165

Tarawa 102, 196; Battle of 10, 58
HMS *Tarn* 46, 47
USS *Tennessee* 177, 178
Tennyson, Alfred *see* poems
Terai, Mitsunori (photographer) 167
USS *Terry* 220
USS *T.H. Fraser* 113
Thiel, Edward J. 236
Thill, David 35
Thill, Ida 35
Thill, Lois 183, 184, 195, 208, 220
Thill, Lyle 35, 37
Thill, Virgil 19, 35–38, 51–52, 57, 64, 67, 68, 70, 71, 72, 89, 93, 95, 97, 107, 108, 109, 110, 117, 124, 126, 127, 133–134, 137, 139, 140–141, 142, 162, 164, 165, 166–167, 169, 171, 172, 173, 175, 181, 182–183, 184, 191, 194, 195, 202, 220, 251
USS *Thomas Hartley* 48
USS *Thomason* 191
Thorpe, Jim 119
Tibbets, Paul *see* atomic bombs
Tokyo Rose 239n5
USS *Torrance* 199, 205, 213, 216, 221
Towne, Capt. Kenneth G. 47
USS *Trinity* 235
USS *Trippe* 203
Truman, Harry 172
Tucker, Harry E. 60, 175, 229
Tucker, Jessie Silver 60
Tucker, Robert L. 60
Tucker, Rosie Lee 60
Turner, Adm. Kelly 11, 58, 85, 239n5
Tweet, Alice 93
Tweet, Ellen Aho 192
Tweet, John 93
Tweet, Olive Hayes 93
Tweet, Oren C. 93–94, 123, 137, 142, 184, 192–193

U-103 (German) 150–151
U-161 (German) 46
Uemura Masahisa 166
U.S. Army: Co. D, 192nd Tank Bn. 163; 1st Cavalry Div. 139; 32nd Inf. Div. 31; 77th Inf. Div. 84, 105, 139; 313th Bombardment Wing 157; 330th Bombardment Grp. 161 (*see also* atomic bombs)
U.S. Marines: 1st Div. 170, 220; 2nd Div. 76, 102, 231; 3rd Div. 59; 3rd Marine Raider Bn. 88; 4th Div. 58, 59; 4th Marine Raider Bn. 31; 4th Mar. Regt. 28; 5th Div. 58, 88; 5th Mar.

Regt. 231; 23rd Mar. Regt 97; 25th Mar. Regt. 96; 28th Mar. Regt. 88, 92; Underwater Demolition Teams 58, 87, 105, 106
U.S. Navy: Coastal Surveillance Force (Vietnam) 191; Columbia River Grp. (19th Fleet) 192, 194, 195, 212, 221, 230, 233, 234, 235, 236; Demonstration Group (512 9) 99, 102, 104; Flotilla One 197; Flotilla Three 197; Flotilla Four 197; Flotilla Five 197; Flotilla Seven 215; Patrol Squadron 205 160; Task Force 58 100, 101; *see also* ships
University of Alabama 25
University of California 54, 88, 222
University of Cincinnati 62
University of Illinois 188
University of Notre Dame 15–16, 17, 18, 54, 79, 107, 115, 116, 128, 155, 223
University of San Francisco 194
Urbana University 195

USS *Vammen* 104
Van Buren, June A. 221
Van Buren, Donald A. 221
Vanderpool, H.J. 131
USS *Van Valkenburgh* 108
Vassar College 133
Veach, W.L. 131
USS *Vega* 226
USS *Vestal* 177
USS *Vicksburg* 94

Walsh Institute of Accounting 183
Walt Disney Productions 29
USS *Warrick* 234
USS *Wasatch* 161
USS *Washington* 235
Washington, George 118
Watson, Lt. George F. 65
Watson, James E. 60
Wedemeyer, Gen. Albert 172
Wells, Ida B. (activist) 34
Wertz, Carl E. 175, 220, 236
West, Charles C. 237
USS *West Virginia* 33, 178
Wheen, Wesley (author) 3
Whitehouse, Robert 206

USS *Wilkes-Barre* 46, 219, 230
Williams, Edwin J. 221
Williams, Howard J. 73, 131, 175, 221
Williams, Johanna M. Cleary 221
Williams, Joseph 237
Williams, Marie Prosch 221
Williams, Robert J. 237
Willis, Bob (singer) 13
USS *Wiltsie* 189, 200
USS *W.L. Steed* 150
Woodrow Wilson College of Law 219
Works Projects Administration 38, 176, 245n51
Wright, Adm. Jerauld 99
USS *Wyoming* 84, 93, 153, 209, 212, 216–217, 220

IJN *Yamato* 102, 105–106
YMS 267 233
YMS 317 233
Yoder, Don L. 237
Yoshitaro, Yonetsu (Kamikaze pilot) 166
USS *Yukon* 236